# Principles and Practice of Maryland Administrative Law

# Principles and Practice of Maryland Administrative Law

**Arnold Rochvarg**
UNIVERSITY OF BALTIMORE SCHOOL OF LAW

CAROLINA ACADEMIC PRESS
Durham, North Carolina

Library of Congress Cataloging-in-Publication Data

Rochvarg, Arnold.
Principles and practice of Maryland administrative law / Arnold Rochvarg.
p. cm.
ISBN 978-1-61163-055-8 (alk. paper)
1. Administrative law--Maryland. 2. Administrative procedure--Maryland. 3. Judicial review of administrative acts--Maryland. 4. Maryland. Office of Administrative Hearings--Rules and practice. I. Title.
KFM1640.R63 2011
342.752'06--dc23

2011019452

Paperback ISBN: 978-1-5310-0487-3

Carolina Academic Press
700 Kent Street
Durham, North Carolina 27701
Telephone (919) 489-7486
Fax (919) 493-5668
www.cap-press.com
2021 Printing

Printed in the United States of America

*To Courtney and Molly*

# Contents

# Preface

Administrative Law has a pervasive role in the practice of law. Lawyers not familiar with the principles of Administrative Law will not be able to fully provide effective representation to their clients. It is not just in those cases that might be labeled "Administrative Law" cases where knowledge of Administrative Law is required. For example, many cases which may be more properly described as criminal, family or personal injury also require knowledge of Administrative Law. This book, therefore, is not just for lawyers who work for government agencies or who represent private clients who have regular dealings with government agencies, but also for those lawyers whose law practices do not regularly handle cases which involve the government.

Administrative Law impacts important individual rights and societal values. Lawyers must understand Administrative Law in order to fully protect the rights of their clients. Lawyers who work for government agencies must understand Administrative Law in order to help further the important economic and social policies which agencies create and enforce. Judges must understand Administrative Law to ensure that important public policy goals can be achieved without violating individual rights.

This book is descriptive, analytical, and prescriptive. Maryland Administrative Law is of relatively recent development and will continue to be a dynamic area of law into the foreseeable future. Although this book is thorough, lawyers must also be prepared to read the actual cases, the statutes, and the regulations which control the decision in the case. The Appendices to the book provide the practicing lawyer with most of the primary sources needed to represent a client before the Office of Administrative Hearings and administrative agencies, as well as in the courts upon judicial review.

I would like to thank J. Bernard McClellan, an administrative law judge at the Office of Administrative Hearings, and Alan Lazerow, a former student, for helpful comments on an earlier draft of the book. I also express my thanks to three students at the University of Baltimore School of Law, Erin Gzrech, Emily Keller and Kerri Smith for their research and production assistance. Above all, I want to thank my assistant, Laurie Schnitzer, for her amazing efforts in preparing the numerous drafts and final manuscript of this book.

I welcome comments and suggestions for updates and future editions. I can be reached at the University of Baltimore School of Law by email at arochvarg@ubalt.edu.

# Principles and Practice of Maryland Administrative Law

# Chapter 1

# Introduction

## § 1.1. What Is Administrative Law?

Administrative Law deals with how administrative agencies create and enforce economic and social policy, and how courts review the decisions made by these agencies. Administrative agencies are governmental bodies which make decisions that impact virtually every aspect of life. Administrative agencies make decisions involving education, health care, transportation, the environment, public safety, prisons, taxes, land use, consumer protection, housing, professional licensing, insurance, gambling, agriculture, elections, government procurement, gas and electric service, employment, worker's compensation, and numerous other areas of society. Administrative agencies exist at the federal, state, and local levels of government. Most of the focus on Administrative Law in law school and in scholarship is on Federal Administrative Law. Most of the actual practice of Administrative Law is at local and state agencies.

Administrative agencies exist because the legislative branch of government does not have, and cannot be expected to acquire, the necessary knowledge and time to properly regulate the numerous areas of society for which the government has taken responsibility. Additionally, the judicial branch, already overburdened by its caseload, is not a viable forum for resolving the numerous disputes that must be resolved in the context of a vast regulatory scheme. In order to carry out the policy and regulatory goals that government seeks to further, broad powers are typically delegated to administrative agencies.

Agency powers fall within two general categories—quasi-legislative powers and quasi-judicial powers. An agency acts like the legislature when it proposes and adopts regulations. Validly adopted agency regulations have the same force of law as a statute adopted by the legislature. An agency acts like the judiciary when it holds trial-type hearings where witnesses testify subject to cross-examination, and the agency decision is based on the evidence introduced at the hearing. Usually, the dispute being litigated at the agency is between the government and an individual person or business, but it could also involve a dispute between two private persons or businesses.

The lawyer representing the government and the lawyer representing the regulated person or business in order to properly represent their clients must understand both the substantive law involved in the case, and the procedures by which this substantive law is presented to the agency. For example, an attorney representing the Board of Physicians in a case where the Board is seeking to revoke a physician's license to practice medicine must of course know the statutory grounds for the revocation of a physician's license.[1] The government attorney must also understand the proper way by which the Board must

1. *See* Maryland Code Annotated, Health Occupation § 14-404.

proceed in order to accomplish its statutory task.[2] Failure to understand and comply with the required procedures could lead to a physician who substantively should be disciplined, not being disciplined; this would clearly be contrary to the public interest. Similarly, the attorney representing a physician subject to discipline must have a complete substantive understanding of physician discipline, and a complete understanding of the administrative process in order to properly represent his/her client. Moreover, the attorney for the client and for the agency must understand the judicial review process which serves as a check on the agency's exercise of its powers.

The law referred to as "Administrative Law" focuses on the procedural aspects of the administrative process as opposed to the substantive areas of regulation. Administrative Law can be analogized to be law of Civil Procedure and Evidence in the civil judicial process. Without knowledge of the procedures that must be followed, a client cannot be adequately represented no matter how much substantive expertise an attorney possesses.

Most attorneys who must know the principles of Administrative Law do not identify themselves as "Administrative Law lawyers." Rather, these lawyers might refer to themselves as criminal defense lawyers who represent clients involved in a drunk driving case; health care lawyers who represent clients who have been denied coverage by their health insurance carrier; or elder law lawyers who represent clients who seek medical assistance. Lawyers tend to focus on the substance of their law practice, not the process that needs to be followed. It cannot be overemphasized that without an understanding of the administrative process, proper representation of a client is impossible.

Unfortunately, the administrative process and Administrative Law are generally not well understood by many attorneys and even judges. This is due, in my opinion, because the "language" of Administrative Law is much different than other areas of law. Administrative Law has created an entire process separate from the more familiar legislative and judicial systems.

Administrative Law is a relatively new area of law. On the federal level, most Administrative Law can be traced to the New Deal legislation of the 1930s and the economic and social legislation of the 1960s and 1970s. On the Maryland state level, Administrative Law is even of a more recent vintage. Although there are some significant Maryland Administrative Law cases prior to 1990, most of what a Maryland attorney needs to know about Administrative Law has been developed in the past twenty years. This is true because of several significant developments in Maryland in the past two decades. These developments include the growing breadth and complexity of state and local government regulation, the increased caseloads in the state court system, and the creation of a centralized hearing office, the Office of Administrative Hearings (OAH). In 2001, in the Forward to an earlier book of mine on Maryland Administrative Law, John W. Hardwicke, Maryland's first Chief Administrative Law Judge, wrote that the "most impressive work in the field [of Administrative Law] is now being performed at the state level through central hearing agencies." This is still true a decade later.

There are more administrative hearings held each year than there are court cases in Maryland. But the significance of Administrative Law in Maryland should not be based solely on the quantity of the cases. The decisions made by Maryland agencies are very significant not only to the parties in the specific matter, but also to the Maryland public.

2. *See* Maryland Code Annotated, Health Occupation § 14-401.

Administrative agency decisions in individual cases often have an important impact on broader issues of public policy.[3] Simply stated, the importance of Administrative Law cannot be overstated.

The purpose of this book is to set forth, discuss, and analyze the principles of Maryland Administrative Law which are essential to the practice of law in Maryland, either as an attorney for the government or a private client. The book focuses on the procedural aspects of the administrative process as well as judicial review as opposed to the substantive areas of regulation. This book does not focus on any particular agency, but discusses principles that generally apply to all agencies. It is essential to understand, however, that statutes and regulations specific to a particular agency or type of case may change the process in a specific case from the general principles that this book discusses.

## § 1.2. Administrative Agencies

Maryland Administrative Law covers agencies at the state, county and city levels. An agency can be called several different names—a Commission, Department, Board, Division, Office, Council, Administration or even Court. For example, the Maryland administrative agency that handles certain tax cases is called the "Tax Court," although as frequently stated in court opinions, the Tax Court is an agency within the Executive Branch of the state government, not a court within the Judicial Branch.

Some agencies are headed by one person, for example, the Secretary of Transportation. Other agencies are composed of several persons at the top of their organizational chart, for example, the Board of Pharmacy. Some agency heads are full-time, salaried, professional public employees, while other agency heads volunteer their service on a part-time basis, perhaps spending only a few days per year in service to the agency. Some agency head positions are highly sought after; some positions go begging to be filled.

Some agencies have substantial budgets, significant staff members, and large office space. Other agencies are significantly smaller in budget, staff and space. Some agencies make thousands of decisions each year. Other agencies make only a handful of decisions, perhaps none, in a particular year.

Most agencies focus on one area of substantive law. For example, there are different agencies for pharmacists, physicians, dentists, veterinarians, social workers, chiropractors, barbers, and insurance companies. Some agencies are regulatory in that their primary task is to enforce certain standards of the regulated industry or profession. Other agencies are "benefactory" in that they decide which persons are entitled to receive certain benefits or privileges from the government.

In some circumstances, the principles of Administrative Law vary depending on the type of agency involved. Usually, however, the principles of Administrative Law apply across all agencies with perhaps only a variation on the theme involved. Attorneys must always be on their guard for the agency that operates differently than what is generally followed.

3. *See* Arnold Rochvarg, *How Administrative Law Halted the Death Penalty in Maryland*, 37 University of Baltimore Law Forum 119 (2007).

## § 1.3. Sources of Administrative Law

Administrative Law is based on several sources of law. Most important are the statutes that create the agency and delegate powers to the agency. These "enabling statutes" and supplemental legislation must be analyzed carefully in representing a client before any administrative agency. Second, agency regulations, also known as rules, must be considered. Regulations have the force of law and are binding on both the agency and the public. The third important source is the Constitution of Maryland and of the United States. Much of Administrative Law involves constitutional issues. Next, caselaw from the Maryland Court of Appeals, and to a lesser degree the Maryland Court of Special Appeals, have also created a common law of judicial review of administrative decisions. Also important to the practice of Administrative Law in Maryland are the Maryland Rules governing judicial review of administrative decisions. These rules are found in Title 7, Chapter 200 and Chapter 400.

## § 1.4. Maryland APA

Of utmost importance is the Maryland Administrative Procedure Act (APA) (note that it is the singular "Procedure" not the plural "Procedures" Act). A full understanding of the Maryland APA is crucial when dealing with those agencies governed by its provisions. The Maryland APA, however, does not apply to all agencies in Maryland. The Maryland APA, in general, only applies to state agencies and agencies that operate in more than one county. Its provisions, therefore, do not apply to local agencies that operate in only one county. Moreover, some state agencies are expressly excluded from certain portions of the Maryland APA. For example, the Injured Workers' Insurance Fund and the Rural Maryland Council are not governed by the rulemaking sections of the Maryland APA. The Public Service Commission, the Tax Court, the State Workers' Compensation Commission, the Parole Commission, the Maryland Automobile Insurance Fund, and most unemployment insurance cases at the Department of Labor, Licensing and Regulation are not covered by the Maryland APA provisions governing contested cases.[4] Even for these exempted agencies, however, principles of Administrative Law developed in cases involving the Maryland APA are often relevant.

The first Maryland APA was enacted in 1957. It was based on the Model State Administrative Procedure Act adopted in 1946 by the National Conference of Commissioners on Uniform State Laws. The Model State Administrative Procedure Act was revised in 1961. Maryland did not adopt any of the 1961 revisions until 1978. In 1984, the Maryland APA was recodified as Title 10 of the State Government Article, but with no substantive changes. In 1991, a commission was formed to study and recommend changes to the APA. Based on this commission's recommendations, legislation was enacted in 1993 that made major changes to the Maryland APA.

Subtitle 1 of the APA governs what is referred to as the quasi-legislative power of an agency—the power of an agency to engage in rulemaking. Subtitle 1 sets forth the procedures an agency must follow to adopt a valid, legally binding regulation. It also contains provisions for judicial review of a regulation.

4. Maryland Code Annotated, State Government § 10-203.

Subtitle 2 of the APA governs what is referred to as the quasi-judicial power of an agency—the power of an agency to hold contested cases, also known as agency adjudications or agency hearings. Subtitle 2 sets forth in various sections the contested case process including such matters as notice, rules of evidence and the conduct of the hearing. It also sets forth the provisions for judicial review of an agency's decision in a contested case.

Subtitle 3 of the APA governs "Declaratory Rulings." A Declaratory Ruling is a mechanism by which an agency, upon request, can inform an interested person about how the agency would apply a regulation, order or statute that the agency enforces.

This book is organized in a manner similar to the Maryland APA. Chapters 2 and 3, discuss the quasi-legislative rulemaking powers of agencies and judicial review of regulations. Chapters 4 through 24 discuss the quasi-judicial, contested case powers of agencies and judicial review of contested cases. Chapters 4 through 24 will also discuss principles of Maryland Administrative Law applicable to agencies both governed by the APA and those that are not. Chapter 25 discusses Declaratory Rulings, which apply only to agencies governed by the APA.

# Chapter 2

# The Rulemaking Process

This chapter discusses the law as it relates to an agency's exercise of its quasi-legislative power, its power to propose and adopt regulations. Chapter 3 discusses judicial review of regulations once they have been adopted by agencies.

## §2.1. Introduction

Validly adopted administrative regulations are laws that are just as binding on the public and agencies as are statutes adopted by the legislature. The Maryland legislature meets for only three months. The number of laws that can be enacted by the legislature is limited by the relatively short duration of the legislative session. Moreover, many laws require a level of expertise that is not available in the legislature. Administrative agencies therefore exist in part to supplement the laws that the legislature does not have the time or expertise to enact. Consistent with democratic theory, there must be limits on the ability of unelected agency officials to make laws. These limits are an important component of what is called "Administrative Law."

## §2.2. What Is a Regulation?

The terms "regulation" and "rule" today are usually used interchangeably.[1] The Maryland APA when first adopted in 1957 used "rule" rather than "regulation." The 1961 revisions to the APA also used "rule." In both the 1957 and 1961 versions of the APA, "rule" was defined essentially as "regulation" is now defined in the APA. Therefore, there is no substantive difference between the terms rule and regulation.

"Regulation" is defined in the Maryland APA as a statement, or an amendment or repeal of a statement, that has "general application," "future effect," and is adopted by the agency to "detail or carry out a law that the agency administers" or which governs the agency's "organization, procedure or practice."[2] The APA further provides that a regulation may take "any form" including a "guideline, rule, standard, statement of interpretation, or a statement of policy."[3] However, an agency statement that concerns only the internal management of the agency and does not affect directly the rights of the public or the procedures available to the public is not a regulation.[4] The APA also provides that an agency

1. *See* Maryland Code Annotated, State Government § 10-101(g)(1)(iv)(regulation includes a rule).
2. Maryland Code Annotated, State Government § 10-101(g)(1).
3. Maryland Code Annotated, State Government § 10-101(g)(1)(iv).
4. Maryland Code Annotated, State Government § 10-101(g)(2)(i).

response to a petition for a regulation or a response to a petition for a Declaratory Ruling is not a regulation.[5]

## § 2.3. Substantive Regulations

The Maryland APA definition of a regulation includes what are usually separately labeled (1) substantive (or legislative) rules, (2) interpretive rules, and (3) procedural rules.[6] Substantive rules are said to make "new law" by supplementing the agency's enabling statute which has delegated rulemaking powers to the agency.[7] For example, in the State Boat Act, the legislature delegated to the Department of Natural Resources (DNR) the power to adopt regulations to govern the operation of vessels in Maryland waters.[8] The DNR adopted a regulation which prohibited the operation of a jet ski in Maryland waters by anyone under the age of fourteen.[9] This regulation is an example of a substantive or legislative regulation.[10]

## § 2.4. Interpretive Regulations

Interpretive rules are regulations that do not supplement existing law, but only clarify or explain existing law.[11] The existing law being clarified or explained is usually a statute, but it could also be a substantive regulation. For example, if the DNR adopted a regulation that stated that the term "vessel" in the State Boat Act included a jet ski, this regulation would properly be labeled an interpretive rule. Whether a particular regulation is substantive or interpretive is often difficult to determine.[12] There are numerous cases from federal courts trying to decide whether a regulation is substantive or interpretive. Under the federal APA, this distinction is critical because interpretive rules are generally exempt from the federal APA procedures required to adopt substantive regulations.[13] This is not true in Maryland. The same procedures that a Maryland agency must follow to adopt a substantive rule must be followed to adopt an interpretive rule.[14] Procedurally, therefore, there is no difference in Maryland between substantive and interpretive rules. The only significant difference between substantive and interpretive rules that I have found in Maryland involves application of the *ex post facto* clauses of the United States[15] and

5. Maryland Code Annotated, State Government § 10-101(g)(2)(ii), (iii).
6. Maryland Code Annotated, State Government § 10-101(g)(1).
7. Dep't of Pub. Safety & Corr. Servs. v. Demby, 390 Md. 580, 606–07, 890 A.2d 310, 325–26 (2006).
8. Maryland Code Annotated, Natural Resources § 8-704(b)-(d)(1).
9. Md. Code Regs. 08.18.02.05(A)(2), COMAR 08.18.02.05(A)(2).
10. *See* Christ v. Md. Dep't of Natural Res., 335 Md. 427, 644 A.2d 34 (1994).
11. Dep't of Pub. Safety & Corr. Servs. v. Demby, 390 Md. 580, 604–05, 890 A.2d 310, 324–25 (2006).
12. Dep't of Pub. Safety & Corr. Servs. v. Demby, 390 Md. 580, 606, 890 A.2d 310, 325 (2006). *See* Chamber of Commerce v. OSHA, 636 F.2d 464 (D.C. Cir. 1980) where Judge Bazelon wrote in his concurring opinion that the distinction between an interpretive rule and a substantive rule have "fuzzy perimeters" and "depend on distinctions enshrouded in considerable smog." 636 F.2d at 471.
13. *See* 5 U.S.C. § 553(b)(3)(A), (B).
14. Maryland Code Annotated, State Government § 10-101(g)(1); *see* Eng'g Mgmt. Servs. v. Md. State Highway Admin., 375 Md. 211, 232–33, 825 A.2d 966, 978 (2003).
15. U.S. Const. art. 1, § 9, cl. 3, § 10, cl. 1.

Maryland Constitutions.[16] In holding that certain Department of Correction (DOC) regulations violated the prohibition against *ex post facto* laws, the Court of Appeals in *Department of Public Safety and Correctional Services v. Demby*,[17] stated that "when an agency promulgates an interpretive rule, the *Ex Post Facto* Clause is inapplicable."[18] The DOC regulations in *Demby*, however, were not interpretive and thus were subject to the *Ex Post Facto* Clause.

## § 2.5. Procedural Regulations

Procedural rules do not create new law nor clarify existing law, but set forth the procedures the public must follow when presenting matters before the agency, and the procedures which the agencies must follow in making their decisions. Procedural rules do not themselves alter the rights or interests of the public, but do alter the manner in which the public presents itself or its views to the agency.[19] The distinction between substantive rules and procedural rules has much greater significance in Federal Administrative Law than in Maryland Administrative Law. Under the federal APA, federal agencies do not need to follow the same procedures to adopt a procedural rule as they must follow to adopt a substantive rule.[20] Under the Maryland APA, both substantive rules and procedural rules are "regulations" that are required to be adopted by the same procedures.[21]

## § 2.6. Code of Maryland Regulations (COMAR)

Regulations which have been adopted by Maryland agencies are published in the Code of Maryland Regulations, abbreviated COMAR. The web page for COMAR is www.dsd.state.md.us/comar. By statute, the Office of Secretary of State, Division of State Documents, is required to make COMAR available online to the public at no cost.[22]

COMAR is first organized by "title." Each title includes the adopted regulations of a different state agency. There are currently thirty-five titles. Although the titles are numbered 1–35, Title 6 is vacant, but there is a Title 13A and 13B. Moreover, there is no Title 19, but there is a Title 19A. Below is a list of the thirty-five COMAR titles.

01 Executive Department

02 Office of the Attorney General

03 Comptroller of the Treasury

04 Department of General Services

05 Department of Housing and Community Development

06 Vacant

16. 17 Md. Const. Decl. Rights art. 17.
17. 390 Md. 580, 890 A.2d 310 (2006).
18. 390 Md. 580, 604–05, 890 A.2d 310, 325 (2006).
19. Jem Broadcasting Co. v. FCC, 22 F.3d 320, 326 (D.C. Cir. 1994).
20. 5 U.S.C. § 553(b)(A) & (B), and 5 U.S.C. § 553(d).
21. Maryland Code Annotated, State Government § 10-101(g)(1).
22. Maryland Code Annotated, State Government § 7-206.2(b)(1).

07 Department of Human Resources
08 Department of Natural Resources
09 Department of Labor, Licensing and Regulation
10 Department of Health and Mental Hygiene
11 Department of Transportation
12 Department of Public Safety and Correctional Services
13A State Board of Education
13B Maryland Higher Education Commission
14 Independent Agencies
15 Department of Agriculture
16 Department of Juvenile Services
17 Department of Budget and Management
18 Department of Assessments and Taxation
19A State Ethics Commission
20 Public Service Commission
21 State Procurement Regulation
22 State Retirement and Pension Systems
23 Board of Public Works
24 Department of Business and Economic Development
25 Office of the State Treasurer
26 Department of the Environment
27 Critical Area Comm. for the Chesapeake and Atlantic Coastal Bays
28 Office of Administrative Hearings
29 Department of State Police
30 Maryland Institute for Emergency Medical Services System
31 Maryland Insurance Administration
32 Department of Aging
33 State Board of Elections
34 Department of Planning
35 Maryland Department of Veterans Affairs

Within the titles are "subtitles." For example, Subtitle 11 of Title 11, Department of Transportation, sets forth regulations of the Motor Vehicle Administration. Title 14, Independent Agencies, includes subtitles for each independent agency. Below is a list of some of the subtitles within Title 14:

01—State Lottery Agency
03—Commission on Human Relations
05—Veterans Commission
06—Office of the Public Defender
07—Maryland Automobile Insurance Fund
09—Worker's Compensation Commission

10—Property Tax Assessment Appeal Boards

11—State Higher Education Labor Relations Board

12—Tax Court

18—State Archives

23—Injured Workers Insurance Fund

24—Office of Planning

25—Maryland Stadium Authority

26—Maryland Energy Administration

Within each subtitle are "chapters." For example, Chapter 03 of Subtitle 11 of Title 11 is titled "Summary Suspensions for Alcohol and Drug Related Offenses." Within a chapter are sections, and often subsections.

The citation to a regulation is based on the title, subtitle, chapter, section, and subsection. For example, COMAR 09.08.03.02(A) means Title 9 (Department of Labor, Licensing and Regulation), Subtitle 08 (Home Improvement Commission), Chapter 03 (Claims Against the Home Improvement Guaranty Fund), Section 02 (Processing of Claims), Subsection A (Filing of Claims).

There are several search options for finding COMAR regulations from the COMAR website. Searches can be by word, phrase or codification number. The codification number includes only the title, chapter, and subtitle, not the section or subsection number. No results will be found if the section or subsection are included in the search request. A word or phrase search can also be limited to a specific title. Alternatively, a search can be performed through the Table of Contents, which will display content by title, subtitle and chapter. Regulations appear only individually, not as part of a full chapter. Therefore, each regulation must be opened individually, and must be cut and pasted into one document if an entire chapter or subtitle is needed. Research assistance for COMAR is available at support@sos.state.md.us. There is also a list of frequently made mistakes in searching COMAR which can be accessed by clicking "Search tips" on the COMAR website.

A search on the COMAR website will obtain not only the actual regulation, but also its Administrative History. This will include all amendments and effective dates. The COMAR website is updated every two weeks.

COMAR is also available in print form in loose leaf binders. The printed version of COMAR is technically the only "official" version of COMAR. Any conflict between the printed and web versions is decided in favor of the print version. Law libraries throughout Maryland, including the law libraries at both law schools, have the printed COMAR in their reference section. Also, LexisNexis publishes in print version "Michie's Index to the Code of Maryland Regulations." This index is organized by topic and by descriptive words. Topical indexes follow the organization of COMAR titles. The descriptive word indexes include non legal terms and popular names.

## § 2.7. Maryland Register

The Maryland Register is the official publication of the State of Maryland. It is published every two weeks. The Maryland Register publishes various types of information regarding Maryland government. For example, Governor's Executive Orders, Governor's Appointments to State Offices, Attorney General's Opinions, Open Meeting Compliance Board Opinions,

State Ethics Commission Opinions, and Court of Appeal Hearing Calendars are published in the Maryland Register. Significant to Administrative Law practitioners, the Maryland Register publishes notices of agency hearings and meetings, and synopses of decisions by Administrative Law Judges (ALJ) at the Office of Administrative Hearings (OAH) which are considered to be of public interest. Crucial to the rulemaking process is that the Maryland Register publishes regulations that are proposed for adoption. Moreover, the Maryland Register serves as the temporary supplement to COMAR for regulations which have been adopted, but which do not yet appear in COMAR.

The Maryland Register is available in several formats. A paper copy is available by subscription and is delivered by first class mail. Paper copies are also available at law libraries in Maryland. There is also an "e-subscription" where the Register is emailed the Friday morning of the publication date. Moreover, there is online access to the Register, but online access is limited to the eight most current issues. For issues over two months old, archived issues can be ordered in PDF format or in a hard copy. Additionally, a CD can be ordered which contains a single year of the Maryland Register. Fees are charged for archived issues.

## §2.8. The APA Rulemaking Process

Subtitle 1 of the Maryland APA sets forth the rulemaking process for Maryland agencies. Subtitle 1 is set forth in Appendix I. Its sections include (1) the procedures that Maryland agencies must follow to adopt a valid regulation; (2) exceptions when these procedures need not be followed; and (3) provisions for judicial review of an adopted regulation. Local agencies that operate in one county are not subject to Subtitle 1 of the APA.[23] Attorneys involved in rulemaking matters before local agencies need to review statutes other than the APA to determine what process needs to be followed by that local agency. Additionally, Subtitle 1 does not apply to the Injured Worker's Insurance Fund or the Rural Maryland Council.[24] Nor is the Governor subject to the rulemaking provisions of the APA because the Governor is not considered an "agency." This point was made in *Maryland v. Maryland State Family Child Care Association*[25] where an executive order of Governor O'Malley was challenged because it had been adopted without following the APA. The Court of Special Appeals held that the "legislative history of the APA gives no indication that the rulemaking sections of the APA were intended to apply to the Governor, as opposed to agencies under his or her control." Also, based on other sections of the APA, "it becomes clear that subtitle 1 of the APA does not apply to the Governor."[26]

## §2.9. The Proposed Rule

The rulemaking process begins with an idea for a new regulation.[27] Usually, this idea comes from within the agency or from the Governor's Office. The APA also provides that

23. Maryland Code Annotated, State Government §10-102(a)(2)(ii).
24. Maryland Code Annotated, State Government §10-102(b)(3), (5).
25. 184 Md. App. 424, 966 A.2d 939 (2009).
26. 184 Md. App. 424, 440, 966 A.2d 939, 948 (2009).
27. *See* Maryland Code Annotated, State Government §10-102.

any "interested person" may submit to the agency a petition for adoption of a regulation.[28] There is no statutory definition of "interested person," and no case has involved its meaning. It would seem that to be eligible to petition an agency to initiate a rulemaking proceeding, no special injury need be alleged comparable to what is required for standing to obtain judicial review of an adopted regulation.[29] If someone has made the effort to submit a petition for rulemaking, they would appear to be "interested" in the proposed rule, and have the right to file a petition requesting the agency to propose that rule.

Once a petition for rulemaking is filed, the agency must give consideration to the request. Within sixty days, the agency must in writing deny the petition and state reasons for the denial, or initiate the procedures for adoption of a regulation.[30] Although there are no Maryland cases on point, under Federal Administrative Law, an agency decision to deny a petition for rulemaking is judicially reviewable under the arbitrary or capricious standard.[31]

Whether based on a petition from a member of the public or on its own initiative, if the agency decides to propose a new regulation for adoption, the agency must then submit the proposed regulation to the Office of Attorney General for its approval. Any proposed regulation not receiving the Attorney General's approval may not be adopted, and if adopted, is not effective.[32]

The next step is a preliminary review of the proposed regulation by the Joint Committee on Administrative, Executive and Legislative Review (AELR Committee). This is a joint House and Senate committee. The agency must submit the proposed regulation to the AELR Committee at least fifteen days before the date a proposed regulation is submitted to the Maryland Register for publication as a proposed regulation.[33] During this preliminary review period, the AELR Committee can approve or disapprove the proposed regulation.[34] The AELR Committee, however, is not required to take any action during this preliminary review. Failure by the AELR Committee to approve or disapprove the regulation during the preliminary review period does not mean that the AELR Committee approves or disapproves it.[35] Prior to having submitted the proposed regulation to the AELR Committee for preliminary review, the agency "is encouraged" to consult with the AELR Committee concerning the form and content of the regulation.[36]

The process continues with the agency submitting to the Administrator of the Division of State Documents two certified copies of the proposed regulation and a notice of the proposed adoption for publication in the Maryland Register.[37] The notice of proposed adoption must contain several things. First, the notice must state the estimated economic impact of the proposed regulation on the revenues and expenditures of agencies of the state and local governments, and on consumer, industry, taxpayer, and trade groups.[38]

28. Maryland Code Annotated, State Government § 10-123(a).

29. Maryland Code Annotated, State Government § 10-222(a).

30. *See* Maryland Code Annotated, State Government § 10-123(b).

31. American Horse Protection Association v. Lyng, 812 F.2d 1 (D.C. Cir. 1987).

32. Maryland Code Annotated, State Government § 10-107(b). For certain agencies, the proposed rule is submitted to the counsel's office for that agency, e.g., the Public Service Commission, State Ethics Commission, and Human Relations Commission. *See* State Government § 10-107(d).

33. Maryland Code Annotated, State Government § 10-110(b).

34. Maryland Code Annotated, State Government § 10-110(c). The proposed regulation is also submitted to the Department of Legislative Services.

35. Maryland Code Annotated, State Government § 10-110(d).

36. Maryland Code Annotated, State Government § 10-110(d).

37. Maryland Code Annotated, State Government § 10-112(a)(2).

38. Maryland Code Annotated, State Government § 10-112(a)(3)(i).

The estimated economic impact statement must state whether the proposed regulation imposes any mandate on a local government unit.[39] A mandate is defined as a directive that requires a local government unit[40] to perform a task or assume a responsibility that has a discernible fiscal impact on the local government unit.[41] If a proposed regulation imposes a mandate, the fiscal impact statement must include whether the regulation is required to comply with a federal statutory or regulatory mandate, and must include the estimated effect on local property tax rates.[42] The notice of proposed adoption must also set a date, time, and place for a public hearing at which oral or written views and information can be submitted. A telephone number that a person may call to comment, and an address to which comments can be sent must also be included in the published notice.[43]

Once the Administrator of the Division of State Documents (Administrator) receives the proposed regulation and the notice of proposed adoption from the promulgating agency, the Administrator prepares one copy for publication and sends one copy to the printer.[44] If the proposed regulation amends or repeals an already adopted regulation, the text of the proposed regulation published in the Maryland Register must show the changes.[45]

After publication in the Maryland Register, two processes take place—the public comment process and review by the AELR Committee. No proposed regulation can be adopted for at least 45 days after its first publication in the Maryland Register.[46] During at least 30 of the 45 days, the agency must accept comments from the public as set forth in the notice of proposed adoption.[47]

## §2.10. AELR Review

During the 45 days after publication of the proposed regulation in the Maryland Register, the AELR Committee performs its full review of the proposed regulation. If the AELR committee determines that an appropriate review cannot reasonably be conducted within 45 days and that an additional period of review is required, it may delay the adoption of the regulation by notifying the promulgating agency and the Division of State Documents in writing prior to the expiration of the 45-day period.[48] In the event the AELR Committee has notified the promulgating agency of the need for more time, the promulgating agency may not adopt the regulation until it notifies the AELR Committee in writing of its intention to adopt the regulation and provides the AELR Committee with a further period of review.[49] This further period of review terminates not earlier than the later of the

39. Maryland Code Annotated, State Government § 10-112(a)(4).
40. "Unit" is defined in State Government § 10-101(i) as "an officer or unit authorized by law to adopt regulations."
41. Maryland Code Annotated, State Government § 10-101(e).
42. Maryland Code Annotated, State Government § 10-112(a)(4)(ii).
43. Maryland Code Annotated, State Government § 10-112(a)(3)(v).
44. Maryland Code Annotated, State Government § 10-112(d).
45. Maryland Code Annotated, State Government § 10-112(c).
46. Maryland Code Annotated, State Government § 10-111(a)(1)(ii).
47. Maryland Code Annotated, State Government § 10-111(a)(3).
48. Maryland Code Annotated, State Government § 10-111(a)(2)(i).
49. Maryland Code Annotated, State Government § 10-111(a)(2)(ii).

thirtieth day following the notice that more time was needed or the seventy-fifth day following the initial publication of the regulation in the Maryland Register, whichever is later.[50]

The AELR Committee decides whether it should oppose adoption of the proposed regulation. The AELR Committee decision is based on whether the regulation is in conformity with the statutory authority of the promulgating authority, and whether the proposed regulation reasonably complies with the legislative intent of the statute under which the regulation is being promulgated.[51] A vote of the AELR Committee to oppose the adoption of the proposed regulation is by majority vote.[52] If the AELR Committee votes to oppose the proposed regulation, it must notify the promulgating agency and the Governor of its action.[53] Upon notification by the AELR Committee of opposition to its proposed regulation, the promulgating agency may withdraw the regulation, modify it, or submit it to the Governor with a statement justifying why it has refused to withdraw or modify it.[54] If the agency refuses to withdraw or modify the proposed regulation, and the Governor has been notified, the Governor may consult with the AELR Committee and the agency to resolve the conflict.[55] Thereafter, the Governor may instruct the agency to withdraw the regulation, instruct the agency to modify the regulation, or approve the adoption of the regulation.[56] A proposed regulation opposed by the AELR Committee can only be adopted if it is approved by the Governor.[57]

## § 2.11. Withdrawal of Proposed Regulation

An agency may withdraw a proposed regulation at anytime before its adoption.[58] Withdrawal can be based on the agency's own initiative or based on action by the AELR Committee or the Governor.[59] Notice of withdrawal of a proposed regulation is published in the Maryland Register.[60] Additionally, the failure of the agency to adopt the proposed regulation within one year after its publication in the Maryland Register constitutes withdrawal.[61] Once a proposed regulation has been withdrawn, it cannot be adopted unless the agency proposes it again and restarts the rulemaking process.[62]

---

50. Maryland Code Annotated, State Government § 10-111(a)(2)(ii).
51. Maryland Code Annotated, State Government § 10-111.1(b).
52. Maryland Code Annotated, State Government § 10-111.1(a)(1). In Medstar Health v. Maryland Health Care Commission, 376 Md. 1, 27–48, 827 A.2d 83, 99–111 (2003), the dissenting opinion discussed that although individual members of the AELR Committee had written letters to the Governor, legislators and the Commission expressing concern or opposition to the proposed regulation, they never took a formal vote and therefore had never formally opposed its adoption.
53. Maryland Code Annotated, State Government § 10-111.1(c)(1).
54. Maryland Code Annotated, State Government § 10-111.1(c)(2).
55. Maryland Code Annotated, State Government § 10-111.1(c)(3).
56. Maryland Code Annotated, State Government § 10-111.1(c)(3).
57. Maryland Code Annotated, State Government § 10-111.1(d).
58. Maryland Code Annotated, State Government § 10-116(a)(1).
59. Maryland Code Annotated, State Government § 10-116(a)(2).
60. Maryland Code Annotated, State Government § 10-116(b)(2).
61. Maryland Code Annotated, State Government § 10-116(b)(1).
62. Maryland Code Annotated, State Government § 10-116(a)(2).

## § 2.12. Economic Impact Statement

Prior to its decision to adopt the proposed rule, the agency must prepare an economic impact statement which must include the impact on "business" of the proposed regulation.[63] Business is defined in the APA as "a trade, professional activity, or other business that is conducted for profit."[64] In evaluating the proposed regulation's impact on business, the agency must consider the costs and difficulty of compliance of the proposed regulation on different size businesses.[65] Based on this evaluation, the agency may adopt one or more regulations that apply differently to classes of business.[66]

## § 2.13. Notice of Adoption

After giving consideration to all relevant matters, if the agency decides that the proposed regulation should be adopted, the agency submits for publication in the Maryland Register a "Notice of Adoption" to the Administrator of the Division of State Documents.[67] The Notice of Adoption must contain the full text of the regulation, unless with approval from the AELR Committee, the agency decides to publish only a synopsis of the regulation.[68] If only a synopsis is published, the full text must be published in the permanent supplement to COMAR within 90 days.[69] If the text of the adopted regulation is the same or substantially similar to the proposed regulation, the Notice of Adoption shall state that the texts are the same or substantially similar, and cite the date of the Maryland Register where the proposed regulation was originally published.[70] Any changes in the adopted regulation from the proposed regulation must be identified in the published Notice of Adoption.[71]

If the text of the regulation that the agency intends to adopt substantially differs from the text of the proposed regulation, the Administrator of the Division of State Documents must refuse to publish the Notice of Adoption.[72] An exception to this is if the Notice is accompanied by a certification from the Attorney General that the changes were not substantially different from the proposed regulation.[73] This certification must contain a description of each change, and why the Attorney General has concluded that the change was not substantially different from the proposed regulation. The certification is also published in the Maryland Register as part of the Notice of Adoption.[74]

The effective date of an adopted regulation is the tenth calendar day after the Notice of Adoption is published in the Maryland Register or a later date if that later date is set forth in the Notice of Adoption.[75]

---

63. Maryland Code Annotated, State Government § 10-124(b).
64. Maryland Code Annotated, State Government § 10-124(a).
65. Maryland Code Annotated, State Government § 10-124(b)(2).
66. Maryland Code Annotated, State Government § 10-124(c).
67. Maryland Code Annotated, State Government § 10-114(a).
68. Maryland Code Annotated, State Government § 10-114(b)(1), (3).
69. Maryland Code Annotated, State Government § 10-114(b)(3).
70. Maryland Code Annotated, State Government § 10-114(b)(2).
71. Maryland Code Annotated, State Government § 10-114(b)(2).
72. Maryland Code Annotated, State Government § 10-113(c)(1).
73. Maryland Code Annotated, State Government § 10-113(c)(1).
74. Maryland Code Annotated, State Government § 10-113(c)(2).
75. Maryland Code Annotated, State Government § 10-117.

## §2.14. Modification and Reproposal

The APA public comment requirement is intended to educate the agency and to assure fair and mature consideration by the agency of all relevant concerns. The agency, prior to issuing the proposed rule, cannot be expected to have all the information relevant to deciding whether the regulation should be adopted. It is especially important for the agency to learn any unintended consequences of the proposed rule. The rulemaking process works best when the public informs the agency of its concerns before the regulation is adopted.

The agency, after considering public comments, has three options: (1) adopt the regulation as proposed; (2) reject the adoption of any regulation; or (3) adopt a regulation which is based on the proposed regulation but which has changes in response to the public comments.[76] The problem with the third option is that when a regulation is adopted which differs from the proposal, it can be (and has been) argued that the public was denied its right to notice and opportunity to comment. The federal courts have adopted a "logical outgrowth" test to determine when a second round of notice and comment procedures under the Federal APA will be required. Under this approach, if an adopted regulation is a logical outgrowth of the proposed rule, the adopted regulation is valid. If the adopted rule is not a logical outgrowth of the proposed rule, the adopted rule is held invalid, and the rulemaking process must start anew. This analysis has been applied in many federal cases.[77]

In Maryland, this issue is expressly addressed by the Maryland APA in a manner differently from the federal approach. State Government §10-113(a) provides that if an agency wants "to change" the text of a proposed regulation so that any part of the text "differs substantively" from the text previously published in the Maryland Register, the agency may not adopt the proposed regulation unless it is proposed anew and adopted in accordance with the requirements of the rulemaking procedures of the APA.[78] The issue in Maryland, therefore, is not whether the final rule is a logical outgrowth of the proposed rule, but whether the rule "differs substantively." What does this mean?

The first place to look is the definition section of the Maryland APA. State Government §10-101(h) defines "substantively" to mean "in a manner substantially affecting the rights, duties, or obligations of a member of a regulated group or profession, or a member of the public." This broad definition does not seem that useful in answering the question when a second round of rulemaking procedures is required in Maryland. Moreover, there are no cases applying this APA provision or discussing when an agency needs to "start from square one" in its rulemaking process. The only authorities that address this issue are two Opinions from the Office of the Attorney General, one of which was written before the adoption of the present section of the Maryland APA. These two Attorney

76. Maryland Code Annotated, State Government §§10-123, 10-111.1, 10-113.

77. *See* Chocolate Manufacturers Ass'n v. Block, 755 F.2d 1098 (4th Cir. 1985) (notice is adequate if the changes in the original plan "are in character with the original scheme," and the final rule is a "logical outgrowth" of the notice and comments already given); BASF Wyandotte Corp. v. Costle, 598 F.2d 637, 642 (1st Cir. 1979), *cert. denied*, 444 U.S. 1096 (1980); Sierra Club v. Costle, 657 F.2d 298 (D.C. Cir. 1981); Taylor Diving & Salvage Co. v. Dep't of Labor, 599 F.2d 622 (5th Cir. 1979); Rowell v. Andrus, 631 F.2d 699 (10th Cir. 1980); Arnold Rochvarg, *Adequacy of Notice of Rulemaking*, 31 Am. U. L. Rev. 1 (1981).

78. Maryland Code Annotated, State Government §10-113(a).

General Opinions are of course non-binding, and, in my opinion, not accurate, although somewhat useful in shedding light on the issue.

In 1976, the Attorney General was asked "to clarify the requirements of notice where the final text of a proposed agency rule contains provisions that are substantially different from the text as originally proposed."[79] The Attorney General's opinion was that "whenever the affected class reasonably could not have anticipated from the published notice the substance of a regulation finally proposed for adoption, the agency should treat its revised version as a newly proposed rule and once again apply the rulemaking procedures."[80] The Attorney General's Opinion then suggested that if the agency were to include in its notice (1) the purpose of its intended action, (2) that revision of the rule is not foreclosed, and (3) that the nature of any revision would depend upon public reaction to the proposed rule and other relevant considerations, the agency would then have far greater latitude for change without having to repeat the rulemaking procedures for fear of having given inadequate notice.[81]

Subsequent to the 1976 Attorney General Opinion, the rulemaking provisions of the APA were changed to their present form. In 1990, the Attorney General was asked, in light of the new APA provisions, to provide "guidance in determining the circumstances under which an agency need not republish a regulation that is changed from the text originally published for comment."[82] The Attorney General's Opinion was that an agency need not re-propose a portion of a regulation that is changed from the text originally published for comment if: (1) the changed regulation does not include material that goes beyond the scope of the issues raised by the proposed rule—provisions that could not reasonably have been anticipated by participants in the rulemaking must be republished; and (2) the groups affected by the regulation, including the general public, are not disadvantaged in any significant way by the changes compared to their situation if the proposed regulation had been adopted without change. Under this second test, if any group's benefits are reduced or its burdens increased appreciably by the change, or if the agency is uncertain about the significance of the change, the agency must republish the changed part. The Attorney General's Opinion noted that "stylistic and clarifying changes need not be re-proposed."

In its 1990 Opinion, the Attorney General presented two examples. The first example was that an agency, as part of a regulation intended to limit a form of pollution, proposes to require that an industry use a particular type of filter. During the comment period, someone points out to the agency that another type of filter, less costly to install, would be just as effective. If that comment convinces the agency that use of the new filter would have substantially the same environmental effect as would use of the proposed filter, the agency may incorporate permission to use the new filter in the final regulation without republishing a proposed Rule. In this example, the Attorney General opined, no one will have been substantially affected by the difference between the proposed and final regulation. Likewise, no one can reasonably claim surprise, given that the agency included a provision on filtration in its proposed regulation. The Attorney General continued, however, that if the agency was not convinced by the comments that the filter different from the one proposed was as effective as the proposed filter, the rulemaking process would need to be repeated with a new proposal.

79. 61 Op. Att'y Gen. 6 (1976).
80. 61 Op. Att'y Gen. 6 (1976).
81. 61 Op. Att'y Gen. 6 (1976).
82. 75 Op. Att'y Gen. 27 (1990).

I disagree with both Opinions of the Attorney General. My disagreement is based both on the adopted standards and the application of those standards. I disagree with the Attorney General's position in the 1976 Opinion that a re-proposal is not required if the agency includes a statement in the original proposal that it is reserving the right to revise the regulation based on comments received. This should not be sufficient. Merely reserving such a right does not provide the notice of the substance of the new regulation which is required to be given prior to adoption. Although this position was not expressly abandoned by the Attorney General in the 1990 Opinion, the standard applied in the 1990 Opinion would not seem to be satisfied by the mere reservation of the agency's right to revise. The two part test set forth in the 1990 Opinion is more useful; however, I disagree with its application to the hypothetical fact patterns set forth in the Opinion. Under the standard announced in the 1990 Opinion, a new rulemaking process would appear to have been necessary in both examples.

An issue that deserves some thought is whether federal cases which apply the logical outgrowth test may be useful in deciding Maryland cases in which Maryland courts must apply the statutorily imposed "differs substantively" test.[83] Review of cases from other states might also be helpful in trying to understand when a Maryland agency, which adopts a regulation different than the proposed regulation, will be required to start a new rulemaking process.

The dilemma which this section of the Maryland APA presents to Maryland agencies is illustrated by *Suburban Hospital, Inc. v. Maryland Health Resources Planning Commission.*[84] The Commission had proposed regulations involving the establishment of new open heart surgery programs. All the procedures required by the APA were followed. Many public comments were received, and seriously considered by the Commission. When the Commission met to vote on final approval to the adoption of the proposed regulations, an amendment was offered by one member to the proposed regulations to take into account information learned during the public comment process. A commissioner by commissioner vote on the amendment then followed. Six commissioners voted in favor of the amendment. Before the other three commissioners recorded their votes, the vote was interrupted by counsel to the Commission. Counsel advised the commissioners that if the amendment passed, the agency would need to restart the rulemaking process. The vote was then reopened. The previous votes were changed, and the commissioners voted to reject the amendment. The original proposed regulation was then adopted without modification. The scenario presented in *Suburban Hospital, Inc. v. Maryland Health Resources Planning Commission* is unfortunate. The commissioners initially wanted to adopt amended regulations that reflected concerns that were identified by the public rulemaking process. To do this, however, would have led to delay and expense. The end result was the public's and the commissioners' own concerns about the proposed regulations were ignored.

## §2.15. APA Exceptions to Required Procedures

The Maryland APA recognizes only two exceptions when an agency can adopt a regulation without following the full rulemaking process discussed in the previous sections.

83. Maryland Code Annotated, State Government §10-113(a).

84. 125 Md. App. 579, 726 A.2d 807 (1999), *vacated as moot*, 364 Md. 353, 772 A.2d 1239 (2001).

These two exceptions are (1) emergency regulations, and (2) if the regulation concerns only the internal management of the agency and does not affect directly the rights of the public or the procedures available to the public.[85] Before discussing these two exceptions, it is important to note that the Maryland APA provides for far fewer exceptions to the rulemaking process than are recognized by the Federal APA.[86] Federal agency regulations dealing with a military or foreign affairs function, a matter relating to agency management or personnel, or a matter relating to property, loans, grants, benefits or contracts are all exempt from the Federal APA rulemaking procedures.[87] Moreover, except when notice or a hearing is required by the federal agency's enabling statute, notice and comment procedures under the Federal APA do not apply to interpretive rules, general statements of policy, rules of agency organization, procedure or practice, or if the agency finds that good cause exists that notice and public procedures are impracticable, unnecessary, or contrary to the public interest.[88] There are numerous cases from the federal courts interpreting these exceptions.

Although a military and foreign affairs exception has no relevance to a Maryland agency, the other federal APA exceptions could have been adopted in Maryland, but were not. Most significantly, in Maryland, an agency's procedural rules, interpretive rules, and statements of policy are not exempt from the rulemaking process. Nor does Maryland recognize a good cause exception absent an emergency. Even when emergency adoption is appropriate, various procedures must still be followed. Moreover, the emergency regulation is only valid temporarily. It seems clear, therefore, that Maryland agencies are under an obligation in more circumstances to follow full-blown rulemaking procedures than are federal agencies.

## § 2.16. Emergency Adoption of Regulations

The Maryland APA provides that under certain circumstances a proposed regulation may be adopted "immediately."[89] As discussed below, the word "immediately" is not accurate because the emergency adoption process is not immediate.

Under the heading "Emergency adoptions" in the Maryland APA, it is provided that an agency may adopt a proposed regulation "immediately" if the following steps are complied with:

1. The agency declares that emergency adoption is necessary;
2. The agency prepares a fiscal impact statement;
3. The agency submits the proposed regulation and the fiscal impact statement to the AELR Committee and the Department of Legislative Services which must include:
    (i) an estimate of the impact of the emergency regulation on the revenues and expenditures of the State;

85. Maryland Code Annotated, State Government § 10-101(g)(2)(i).
86. *See* 5 U.S.C. § 553.
87. 5 U.S.C. § 553(a).
88. 5 U.S.C. § 553(b)(3)(A), (B).
89. Maryland Code Annotated, State Government § 10-111(b)(1).

(ii) whether the State budget for the fiscal year in which the regulation will become effective contains an appropriation of the funds necessary for the implementation of the emergency regulation;

(iii) if an appropriation is not contained in the State budget, the source of the funds necessary for the implementation of the emergency regulation; and

(iv) whether the emergency regulation imposes a mandate on a local government unit. If the emergency regulation imposes a mandate on a local government unit, the fiscal impact statement shall indicate whether the regulation is required to comply with a federal statutory or regulatory mandate. Also, if the information may be practicably obtained given the emergency circumstances of the regulations, the agency must include an estimate of the impact of the emergency regulation on the revenues and expenditures of local government units. Also, if applicable, and if the required data is available, the agency must include the estimated effect on local property tax rates.

4. Emergency adoption is valid only if approved by the AELR Committee. AELR Committee adoption may be by a majority of its members who are present and voting at a public hearing, or by AELR staff if necessary to protect the public health or safety. If a member of the AELR Committee requests a public hearing on the emergency adoption of a regulation, a public hearing must be held.[90]

Obviously, these procedures take time, and thus a regulation even under an emergency procedure cannot be adopted "immediately." Moreover, the Maryland APA provides that unless the "Governor declares that immediate adoption is necessary to protect the public health or safety, the [AELR] Committee may not approve the emergency adoption of a regulation earlier than 10 business days after receipt of the regulation."[91] Perhaps most significant about emergency regulations is that once adopted, they are not valid for more than 180 days.[92] During this 180 day period, the agency must adopt the regulation pursuant to the full procedures required to adopt all final regulations. A regulation under the emergency adoption process therefore is just a temporary regulation.[93]

There is no requirement in the Maryland APA that the agency actually justify or explain the emergency upon which emergency adoption is based. This should be compared to the Federal APA which requires the agency to publish in the Federal Register a "brief statement of reasons" why "notice and public procedure ... are impracticable, unnecessary, or contrary to the public interest."[94] There are numerous cases in federal courts challenging both the substantive component of the agency's decision, arguing that the circumstances do not establish good cause, and the procedural component, i.e., the agency's explanation, was inadequate.[95]

The emergency regulation process in Maryland has not received much judicial analysis. There appears to be no case where the issue of whether an emergency actually existed was litigated. Only a few cases mention emergency regulations, and in none of the cases is there a significant discussion of the emergency regulation process. For example, in *Massey*

90. Maryland Code Annotated, State Government § 10-111(b), (c).

91. Maryland Code Annotated, State Government § 10-111(b)(2)(iv).

92. Maryland Code Annotated, State Government § 10-111(b)(4)(ii).

93. Maryland Code Annotated, State Government § 10-111(b)(4)(iii).

94. 5 U.S.C. § 553(b)(3)(B).

95. *See, e.g.*, Hawaii Helicopter Operators Ass'n v. FAA, 51 F.3d 212 (9th Cir. 1995); Tennessee Gas Pipeline Co. v. FERC, 969 F.2d 1141 (D.C. Cir. 1992); San Diego Air Sports Center, Inc. v. FAA, 887 F.2d 966 (9th Cir. 1989); Reeves v. Simon, 507 F.2d 455 (Temp. Emer. Ct. App., 1974).

*v. Department of Public Safety and Correctional Services*,[96] the Court of Appeals held invalid "Directives" of the Department of Correction regarding inmate discipline because the agency had failed to follow the procedures required by the APA to adopt regulations. Because the directives had been "put into place in order to comply with Federal due process requirements," in a footnote the court wrote: "It is not our function to advise the Secretary how to proceed. We do call her attention, however, to State Gov't § 10-111(b) [the emergency adoption section of the Maryland APA]." In *Department of Public Safety and Correctional Services v. Beard*,[97] the Court of Special Appeals mentioned in a footnote that a regulation involving discipline of state employees which had been properly adopted via full rulemaking procedures had been originally adopted as an emergency provision. There is no mention of the existence of any emergency at the time of emergency adoption, nor is there any mention of the fact that the emergency provision was effective February 2, 1997 and the permanent regulation became effective more than 180 days later on September 8, 1997.

*Oyarzo v. Maryland Department of Health and Mental Hygiene*[98] involved a regulation which prohibited the sale of fractional ownership interests in cows when such fractional arrangements had been used to circumvent the statutory prohibition on the sale of raw milk for human consumption. This regulation had originally been adopted as an emergency measure. In this case, the agency in support of its motion for summary judgment filed an affidavit which discussed the health risks of raw milk. Although the Court of Special Appeals discussed at length the dangers of consuming raw milk, there is no discussion of whether any emergency actually existed to justify the emergency adoption.

Although the temporary adoption of emergency regulations is a useful tool for effective regulation in appropriate circumstances, my view is that emergency adoptions should be limited to "emergency" situations. Emergency regulations should not be an escape mechanism for agencies who prefer to proceed without providing the full set of rulemaking procedures.

## § 2.17. Internal Management Exception

The Maryland APA definition of "regulation" excludes an agency "statement that concerns only the internal management of the [agency], and does not affect directly the rights of the public or the procedures available to the public."[99] Although technically the internal management exception is not truly an "exception" to the rulemaking procedure requirements because an internal management statement is not considered a regulation, the practical result is the same. An agency can adopt an internal management statement which is valid and binding on the public and the agency without following the APA procedures. There is one Attorney General's Opinion and several cases discussing this APA provision.

In 1990, the Department of Health and Mental Hygiene (DHMH) asked the Attorney General to opine on whether a letter, referred to as Transmittal No. 91, which had been sent by DHMH to physicians relating to contract administration of the Medicaid Program,

---

96. 389 Md. 496, 886 A.2d 585 (2005).

97. 142 Md. App. 283, 790 A.2d 57, *cert. denied*, 369 Md. 180, 798 A.2d 552 (2002).

98. 187 Md. App. 264, 978 A.2d 804, *cert. denied*, 411 Md. 601, 984 A. 2d 245 (2009).

99. Maryland Code Annotated, State Government § 10-101(g)(2).

needed to have been adopted according to the APA rulemaking provisions. DHMH had sent the letter without any AELR review or opportunity for public comment. In its request, DHMH wrote that it did not believe it needed to follow the rulemaking procedures because the letter was "merely an interpretation of an existing regulation."

In response to this request, the Attorney General first stated that DHMH's rationale for not following the APA rulemaking procedures was wrong.[100] The Maryland APA does not exempt interpretive rules from the rulemaking procedural requirements. The Attorney General, however, then opined on the internal management exception. The Attorney General wrote:

> A statement does not "concern only internal management" if it is addressed to persons outside the agency.... Whether a staff directive or other similar statement is exempt from rulemaking by virtue of the "internal management" exception depends on the practical consequences for members of the public. The exception applies only if the internal guidance does not significantly affect either the procedural steps that interested persons must take in their dealings with an agency or the allocation of substantive benefits or burdens. Thus we have distinguished between management directives that have little direct effect on the public, and those that have a direct, substantial effect. Examples of the former include instructions that merely spell out operational details like what forms to fill out, what approvals to obtain, or what evidence to look at to determine whether an applicant meets a statutory standard. Instructions that have a greater effect on the public include those that impose application procedures, establish eligibility criteria not set forth in statute, restrict access to a statutory benefit, or impose fees. The "public" are those outside the agency whose situation is changed as a result of the agency's internal management statement.

Despite the fact that this letter impacted physicians involved in the Medicaid program, the Attorney General's Opinion concluded that the letter fell within the internal management exception.

The most elaborate discussion of the internal management exception by the Court of Appeals is found in *Massey v. Department of Public Safety and Correctional Services.*[101] *Massey* involved "Directives" that created and defined administrative offenses for which prisoners were subject to discipline. The directives also prescribed the kinds of discipline imposed for these offenses, set forth procedures for charging prisoners with these offenses, and established procedures for receiving, considering and adjudicating complaints made by inmates regarding policies, procedures, and conditions in prison. The Court of Appeals unanimously rejected the State's position that the internal management exception applied. Its opinion invalidating the directives made the following points:

1. If a regulation affects fundamental rights, it is not one that can be characterized as pertaining only to routine internal management.
2. Agencies could too easily subvert public rulemaking requirements if they could avoid procedures for anything they called an internal directive to staff. The public's rights can as easily be defined by statements addressed only to staff.
3. The internal management exception is very narrow. It applies only to matters purely of concern to the agency and its staff.

---

100. 75 Op. Att'y Gen. 37 (1990).
101. 389 Md. 496, 886 A.2d 585 (2005).

4. The internal management exception does not apply if the agency statement substantially affects rights of the public that are enforceable against the agency or parties.
5. The internal management exception does apply to purely internal personnel practices and directions that "face inwards" and do not substantially affect any legal rights of the public or any segment of the public.

The court then held that because prison inmates are part of the public, the directives at issue in *Massey* were not exempt from the APA rulemaking procedural requirements.

Although the *Massey* holding is clearly correct, one point in the majority's opinion deserves comment. The majority wrote that "rules governing the details of prison life—what inmates may wear, what they may or may not keep in their cells or on their persons, the rules governing security, sanitation, hygiene, phone calls, mail, and visits" may be covered by the internal management exception.[102] Without knowing what these hypothetical rules might be, I would be careful in concluding they were exempt from the rulemaking procedures required by the APA. For example, a directive imposing a general prohibition on mail from a prisoner to a family member would clearly in my opinion not come under the internal management exception. On the other hand, a directive providing the time for mail delivery to an inmate would, in my opinion, come under the internal management exception, and could be adopted by the agency without complying with the APA rulemaking process.

The next significant Maryland case involving the internal management exception is *Evans v. Maryland*,[103] which halted the death penalty in Maryland. Evans had been sentenced to capital punishment by lethal injection following his conviction of two counts of first degree murder. Lethal injection had been adopted by the Maryland legislature as the method of administering capital punishment in 1994. The 1994 legislation provided that "the manner of inflicting the punishment of death shall be the continuous intravenous administration of a lethal quantity of an ultra short-acting barbiturate or other similar drug in combination with a chemical paralytic agent until a licensed physician pronounces death according to accepted standards of medical practice."[104] In response to this legislation, the Department of Corrections (DOC) adopted an "Execution Operations Manual" ("EOM") which set forth the details of how the execution should be implemented. The EOM included topics such as the responsibilities of DOC personnel, pre-execution procedures, security for inmates awaiting executions, and a "Lethal Injection Checklist" which set forth the contents of the lethal injection and the method of injecting it.

A few weeks after *Massey* had been decided, Evans filed a request for administrative relief based on the argument that the lethal injection execution protocol set forth in the EOM constituted regulations that were invalid because they had been adopted without following the Maryland APA procedures for a regulation. After several administrative hearings were held, the DOC denied relief because the EOM "is not a regulation requiring adoption pursuant to the APA rulemaking provisions." When Evans' case reached the Court of Appeals, the Court unanimously rejected the agency's position. In response to the argument that the EOM concerned only the internal management of DOC and did

102. Massey v. Department of Public Safety and Correctional Services, 389 Md. 496, 524, 886 A.2d 585, 602 (2005).

103. 396 Md. 256, 914 A.2d 25 (2006).

104. 1994 Md. Laws ch. 5.

not directly affect the rights of the public, the Court responded that the EOM affected "not only the inmates and the correctional personnel, but the witnesses allowed to observe the execution and the public generally, through its perception of the process." Because the EOM had not been adopted pursuant to the APA procedures, the lethal injection protocols were "ineffective and may not be used until such time as they are properly adopted." The death penalty in Maryland was halted "until such time as the contents of [the lethal injection] checklist ... are adopted as regulations in accordance with the requirements of the Administrative Procedure Act or the General Assembly exempts the checklist from the requirements of the Act."[105]

## §2.18. Judicial Challenges to What Is a Regulation

There are several cases involving the APA definition of "regulation" and the agency's failure to follow rulemaking procedures. This section will discuss these cases.

In *Department of Health & Mental Hygiene v. Chimes, Inc.*,[106] the issue was whether a cost containment measure for reimbursement to providers of services to persons with developmental disabilities was a regulation. The Developmental Disabilities Administration (DDA), a state agency in charge of programs that provide services to persons with developmental disabilities, had adopted in 1987 a payment system for the reimbursement of private providers. This payment system, known as "PPS," had been adopted after DDA had followed the rulemaking procedures required by the APA. Under the PPS, payments to providers were based on two general categories: (1) cost of providing routine services to clients and (2) cost of administration, and general, capital, special and transportation costs. To be included in the PPS program, a provider had to agree to operate under a contract with DDA for two years. The contract gave DDA the right to review the provider's costs. During the years 1990–1993, DDA instituted numerous cost containment measures.[107] None of these measures were considered a regulation by DDA, and there were no challenges to DDA's failure to follow the procedures set forth in the APA for adopting a regulation. In August 1993, DDA imposed a growth cap for costs in the second category, i.e., administration, general, capital, special and transportation costs. Chimes, a provider whose reimbursement rate was cut, challenged the growth cap. Chimes argued that the growth cap was a regulation that was invalid because it had not been adopted following the rulemaking procedures required by the APA. The circuit court held that the growth cap was a regulation and thus invalid. Before argument in the Court of Special Appeals, the Court of Appeals granted certiorari.[108]

The Court of Appeals reversed the circuit court, and held that "the 'growth cap' was not a 'regulation' in the sense contemplated by the APA and need not have been promulgated according to APA rulemaking procedures."[109] The majority opinion was based on four

105. Evans was followed by the Kentucky Supreme Court in Bowling v. Kentucky Dep't of Corrections, 301 S.W.3d 478 (Ky. 2010) which halted executions in Kentucky.

106. 343 Md. 336, 681 A.2d 484 (1996).

107. These included setting a ceiling for certain costs at one standard deviation above the average costs for all providers, cutting the annual inflation rate, and freezing hourly rates.

108. This is not an infrequent occurrence with administrative law cases. See discussion of "Bypass Jurisdiction" in Chapter 13.

109. 343 Md. 336, 348, 681 A.2d 484, 489 (1996).

factors. First, the growth cap did not have "widespread application" because it applied only to a limited number of providers in a particular program in a particular year in response to a particular budget crisis. Second, the growth cap did not change existing law because the statute and regulations already in effect limited DDA's expenditures to budget appropriations, and the contract between DDA and the providers provided for cost containment. The third factor was that the growth cap did not apply retroactively. The fourth factor was that "DDA had a strong interest in adopting a cost containment policy as quickly as possible."[110]

In my opinion, the majority opinion in *Chimes* provided an inaccurate analysis of the issue presented for several reasons. First, the majority's discussion of the APA definition of regulation is incorrect. "Regulation" is defined in the APA as an agency statement that has general application and future effect, and is adopted to detail or carry out a law that the agency administers. In *Chimes*, there was no dispute that the growth cap had future effect and detailed a law that DDA administered. The only relevant issue therefore was whether the growth cap had "general application." The majority never addressed this issue. Instead, the majority discussed whether the growth cap had "widespread application." "Widespread" is more encompassing than "general." Something can have general application but not widespread application. A second problem with the majority's opinion is its position that because the growth cap did not apply retroactively, it was not a regulation. But regulations never have retroactive application. The fact that the growth cap did not apply retroactively is irrelevant to the issue of whether the growth cap was a regulation.

Another error in the majority opinion is that it relied on a line of cases concerning whether an agency decision in a contested case can be invalidated on the ground that the agency was required to use rulemaking procedures. While this is a possible argument to invalidate an agency decision in a contested case, as discussed elsewhere in this book,[111] it had no relevance to *Chimes*. DDA had not adopted the PPS via a contested case.

Chief Judge Bell in dissent had a much better handle on this case. Judge Bell correctly analyzed whether the growth cap had "general application." He wrote that although policies aimed at those in contractual relations with an agency are "ordinarily" not of general application, this is not always the case, and that "even though an action applies to persons within a small class, the action is of general application if that class is described in general terms and new members can be added to the class." This was true regarding DDA providers. Moreover, the "number of program beneficiaries to be impacted by the 1994 cost containment policy is potentially enormous." Judge Bell also wrote that any doubt as to whether a new agency policy has general application should be resolved in favor that it does. He believed that the term "regulation" should be "broadly construed." He also properly expressed the concern that the need for an agency to move quickly does not relieve the agency of its obligation to follow the APA.

Although Judge Bell's dissent is clearly the better opinion in *Chimes*, there is one argument he presented which I do not believe is fully accurate. In discussing whether the growth cap was a regulation, the dissent disagreed with the majority's position that the growth cap was not a new statement of policy. While I agree that in *Chimes*, DDA created new policy with its growth cap, I do not believe this is relevant to whether the growth cap

110. 343 Md. 336, 348, 681 A.2d 484, 489 (1996).

111. See discussion in Chapter 21.

was a regulation requiring adoption by APA procedures. Under the APA definition of regulation, an agency action can be a regulation even if it does not change agency policy.[112]

Another case is *Maryland Association of Health Maintenance Organizations v. Health Services Cost Review Commission.*[113] One issue here was whether an "inflation adjustment system" (IAS) adopted by the Health Services Cost Review Commission pursuant to its authority to regulate costs and rates of hospitals and other health care institutions was invalid because the Commission had not followed the APA procedures for the adoption of a regulation. The health providers, relying on the APA definition of regulation, argued that "the IAS, as a statement, standard, and Rule of Commission policy, with general application and future effect is indisputably a regulation under the APA." The Court of Appeals response to this was that "this court's opinions have made clear [that] whether an agency policy technically fits the APA definition of regulation is not the test for determining if the agency is required to proceed by formal rulemaking." The opinion cited *Chimes* and cases which held that "the choice made between proceeding by general rule or by individual, ad hoc litigation is one that lies primarily in the informed discretion of the administrative agency."

In my view, both *Chimes* and *Maryland Association of Health Maintenance Organizations* present an incorrect analysis. Fortunately, in *Delmarva Power & Light Co. v. Public Service Commission,*[114] the Court of Appeals without expressly repudiating its earlier cases, properly analyzed the issue of whether the Public Service Commission (PSC) had improperly failed to follow APA rulemaking procedures. *Delmarva* involved the PSC's attempt to deal with regulatory issues arising from the diversification and expansion of business activities by regulated entities into areas of non-regulated business activities. For example, Baltimore Gas & Electric (BG&E), which was regulated by the PSC in its supply of gas and electric service, had formed subsidiaries to sell home appliances and perform home improvement services. The PSC was concerned with whether, and to what extent, it could regulate BG&E's non-core utility services. In 1993, issues relating to BG&E's diversification had been addressed in a rate case specific to BG&E, particularly whether BG&E was using revenue from its regulated utility operations to subsidize its appliance and kitchen remodeling business. The PSC's conclusion was that it had the authority to assure that rates charged for regulated gas and electric service were not adversely affected by BG&E's unregulated business ventures. As part of its decision in this rate case, the PSC adopted four standards to prevent unfair cross-subsidization. Subsequent to this rate case, the PSC adopted other standards that would apply to all electric and gas utilities, not just BG&E, in transactions with their affiliates. Although these standards were not adopted pursuant to the APA procedures required for the adoption of regulations, no challenge to these standards was brought. In 1999, the PSC in response to renewed concern over this issue, revisited it, and eventually adopted more standards. These standards were challenged in *Delmarva.* The argument was made that the standards were invalid because the PSC had failed to follow the procedures required to adopt regulations. The PSC responded that the standards it had adopted were not regulations, and therefore need not be adopted pursuant to the APA procedures required to adopt a regulation.

112. In Chimes, the agency had argued initially that its "growth cap" fell within the internal management exception. This issue was not addressed by the Court of Appeals in its opinion.

113. 356 Md. 581, 741 A.2d 483 (1999).

114. 370 Md. 1, 803 A.2d 460 (2002).

Applying the definition of a regulation set forth in the APA, the Court of Appeals unanimously rejected the PSC position. The court wrote that "with limited exception, [the PSC standards] have general application to all electric and gas utilities and their various affiliates; they have future effect; they were adopted by a "unit"—the PSC—to carry out laws that the PSC administers; they were in the form of statements of policy; and they fall within none of the exceptions stated in [State Government] § 10-101(g)(2)."[115] The court rejected the PSC's position that the standards did not have "general application" because they addressed "one narrow subject matter, utility-affiliate transaction."[116] The court's response was that the standards applied to the entire gas and electric industry that was regulated by the PSC, and thus had "general applicability."

General response to *Delmarva* was that it was inconsistent with *Chimes*, and would require agencies to change how they had been operating for years. That is why *Delmarva* is so significant. For years, agencies had been adopting policies and procedures without bothering to follow the APA procedures. Not until *Delmarva* was an agency told by a court that this was illegal. The extent of this agency conduct was, and still is, unclear, but several cases brought subsequent to *Delmarva* indicate that the problem may be widespread.

*Massey v. Secretary, Department of Public Safety & Correctional Services*[117] involved "Directives" adopted by the State Department of Public Safety and Correctional Services (DPSCS) which created and defined administrative offenses for which inmates were subject to administrative discipline. The directives also prescribed the types of discipline which could be imposed upon a finding of guilt, set forth procedures for charging inmates with offenses and imposing discipline, and established procedures for inmate complaints. These directives were adopted without compliance with the APA. In *Massey*, the Court of Appeals cited the APA definition of regulation, and wrote that the directives were "clearly" regulations:

> They constitute statements that have general application throughout all of the correctional institutions in DOC and apply to all inmates in those institutions; they have future effect; they are adopted by a "unit" to carry out law that the unit administers; and they are in the form of rules, standards, statements of interpretation, and statements of policy.[118]

In a footnote, the court "caution[ed] the Secretary and the Commissioner to review very carefully all of the directives that they have issued … and determine, at least from their perspective, whether, in light of this Opinion, they need to be adopted in the form of regulations.[119]

The most significant case on this issue resulted in the death penalty being halted in Maryland because the Department of Corrections (DOC) had adopted an Execution Operations Manual (EOM) without following the APA rulemaking process. In *Evans v. Maryland*,[120] the Court of Appeals rejected the agency's position that the EOM was not a regulation. After citing the APA definition of regulation, the court wrote that "there can be no legitimate doubt that the portions of the EOM that govern the method of and procedure for administering the lethal injection have general application and future effect,

115. 370 Md. 1, 26, 803 A.2d 460, 474 (2002).
116. 370 Md. 1, 26, 803 A.2d 460, 474 (2002).
117. 389 Md. 496, 886 A.2d 585 (2005).
118. 389 Md. 496, 508, 886 A.2d 585, 592 (2005).
119. 389 Md. 496, 508 n.3, 886 A.2d 585, 592 n.3 (2005).
120. 396 Md. 256, 914 A.2d 25 (2006).

and were adopted to detail or carry out a law that DOC administers, and govern the procedure of DOC."

In *Watkins v. Secretary, Department of Public Safety and Correctional Services*[121] the sole issue was whether DOC directives establishing policies on work release and family leave for prisoners violated the *ex post facto* clauses of the Maryland and United States Constitutions. For example, one directive prohibited life sentence inmates from participating in a work release program. It was argued that the directives imposed greater punishment for previously committed crimes. The Court of Appeals rejected the *ex post facto* challenge on the basis that the directives were not "Laws" within the "ambit of the *ex post facto* clauses." The court stated "whether an administrative provision qualifies as a 'Law' for *ex post facto* purposes depends in large part on the manner and extent that it limits an agency's discretion. If the provision ... simply announces how an agency is likely to execute its discretion, the *ex post facto* clause does not apply." The court continued that "if the rules are 'merely guides' that may be discarded where circumstances require, they are not subject to the *ex post facto* prohibitions." Interestingly, however, the court wrote the following in a footnote:

> As we indicated, the sole issue raised in this appeal is whether the [directives] at issue constitute *ex post facto* laws and, for that reason, are invalid under Article I of the United States Constitution and Article 17 of the Maryland Declaration of Rights. No argument was made that the [directives] constitute regulations under the Administrative Procedure Act, that they were adopted without compliance with the requirements of that Act, and for that reason they are unenforceable. See *Delmarva Power v. PSC.* Nothing in this Opinion is intended to address that issue.

In my opinion, if the argument had been presented that the directives were regulations under the APA, the directives would have been held invalid.

*Delmarva* has also been applied to purely procedural rules. As discussed elsewhere in this book, an agency can delegate to the Office of Administrative Hearings (OAH) the authority to hold a contested case hearing and to make a proposed decision.[122] After OAH makes the proposed decision, exceptions can be filed with the agency before it makes the final decision. *Davis v. Maryland Board of Physicians*[123] involved the exception process at the Board of Physicians. Although the Board had a few regulations published in COMAR relating to the exception process, these regulations were far from complete. In response to a request from the attorney for Davis, a Board official advised by letter that it was the "policy of the Board to limit the length of the exceptions and the response to the exceptions to no more than fifteen (15) pages, double-spaced, in at least 12 point type, that number of pages to include all appendices and addenda ... Any further replies or answers to the exceptions and responses are limited to no more than five (5) pages, double-spaced, in at least 12 point type." When Davis filed exceptions greater in length than fifteen pages, the assistant attorney general who was prosecuting the case moved to strike the exceptions. Davis filed a petition in Circuit Court for Harford County seeking an order declaring the page and type size limitations invalid and unenforceable. The circuit court judge in a written Memorandum Opinion easily found, based on the APA definition of regulation, that the page limitations were invalid regulations which the Board could not enforce.

121. 377 Md. 34, 831 A.2d 1079 (2003).

122. See discussion in Chapter 9.

123. Harford County Circuit Court Case No. 12-C-07-2362, Memorandum Opinion, September 14, 2007.

# § 2.19. Granting an Appropriate Remedy

The case law makes clear that in the aftermath of *Delmarva*, agencies will not be allowed to adopt regulations without following the APA procedures. When determining whether the agency action is a regulation, it is the definition of a regulation in the APA that controls. An agency cannot avoid rulemaking procedures by labeling its action a directive, manual, guideline, bulletin, policy or anything else. Nor can the agency avoid rulemaking by announcing its policy in a letter or internal memorandum.

The full extent of the invalid regulation problem in Maryland is not clear. Only the agencies themselves are able to ascertain how many regulations exist within their agencies that have not been properly adopted. Agencies must be more cognizant of this issue, and should act to either get rid of unadopted regulations which are no longer useful or initiate rulemaking proceedings.

One problem is that the remedy ordered in past cases has at times not been broad enough to create a sufficient incentive for agencies to follow rulemaking procedures. For example, in *Massey*,[124] after holding that the DOC directives were invalid because the "legislature has made clear that regulations are not effective unless and until there has been compliance with the [APA] requirements, and we have enforced that legislative determination,"[125] the court directed the clerk to withhold the mandate for 120 days to permit the agency to adopt the regulations properly. Because "the directives at issue were put into place in order to comport with Federal due process requirements, ... simply declaring them immediately ineffective and leaving nothing in their place is not an option. That would bring prison disciplinary proceedings to a halt." Although the unique circumstances of the *Massey* case seem to justify the delayed mandate, the litigant, Massey, was denied any specific relief. As Chief Judge Bell wrote in his separate opinion, Massey should have received the relief he requested. Judge Bell wrote that "because the regulations were invalidly promulgated and thus are a nullity, the effect of that holding necessarily is that the actions taken pursuant thereto are nullities, as well. The appellant's additional punishment therefore is of no effect and this Court should clearly and unhesitatingly say so."[126] Likewise in *Davis v. Maryland Board of Physicians*,[127] although the court invalidated the page limitation regulation, it refused Davis' request to enjoin the exception process at the Board until the Board validly adopted regulations concerning the entire exceptions process.

Courts should be more willing to grant appropriate relief beyond the mere invalidation of the improperly adopted regulation. Despite *Delmarva* and its progeny, it does not appear that agencies have responded adequately to the invalidly adopted regulations problem. One possible remedy is to access attorney fees against a state agency when a litigant is successful in invalidating a regulation for failure to follow required procedures. This approach has been adopted in Florida.[128] Incentives need to be created to force Maryland agencies to comply with the APA rulemaking requirements.

---

124. 389 Md. 496, 886 A.2d 585 (2005).

125. 389 Md. 496, 525, 886 A.2d 585, 602 (2005).

126. 389 Md. 496, 530, 886 A.2d 585, 605 (2005).

127. Harford County Circuit Court Case No. 12-C-07-2362, Memorandum Opinion, September 14, 2007.

128. Florida Statutes Annotated § 120.595.

# Chapter 3

# Judicial Review of a Regulation

This chapter will discuss the procedural and substantive issues relating to judicial review of a regulation.

## §3.1. How to File a Challenge to a Regulation in Court

The APA provides that "any person whose legal right or privilege is impaired or is threatened to be impaired by a regulation" may challenge the validity of the regulation in court.[1] There are no cases in Maryland discussing the degree of impairment required in order to have standing to challenge a regulation.

The pleading that is filed to judicially challenge a regulation is a "Petition for Declaratory Judgment."[2] This is a special pleading created in the APA which should not be confused with a request for a Declaratory Judgment under the Courts and Judicial Proceedings Article, Section 3-409. The Petition for Declaratory Judgment to challenge a regulation is filed in the Circuit Court for the county where the petitioner resides or has a principal place of business.[3]

The exhaustion doctrine, discussed elsewhere in this book[4] in regards to judicial review of a final decision in a contested case, has no application to Petitions for Declaratory Judgment and judicial review of regulations. The APA expressly provides that there is no need for the petitioning party to have "ever asked the agency to consider the validity of the regulation."[5] In *Delmarva Power & Light Co. v. Public Service Commission*,[6] a regulation was successfully challenged for failure to follow the APA procedures even though that issue had never been raised at the agency. Additionally, a party is not required to wait until a regulation is enforced against it to seek a declaratory judgment that the regulation is invalid. For example, in *Oyarzo v. Maryland Department of Health and Mental Hygiene*,[7] the court reviewed a challenge to a regulation despite the fact that petitioners had not violated the regulation.

Provisions in a regulation are considered severable unless the regulation expressly states otherwise.[8] If a court finds that a provision of a regulation is invalid, only that provision

1. Maryland Code Annotated, State Government § 10-125(b).
2. Maryland Code Annotated, State Government § 10-125.
3. Maryland Code Annotated, State Government § 10-125(a)(2).
4. See discussion of Exhaustion in Chapter 14.
5. Maryland Code Annotated, State Government § 10-125(a)(1).
6. 370 Md. 1, 803 A.2d 460 (2002).
7. 187 Md. App. 264, 978 A.2d 804, *cert. denied*, 411 Md. 601, 984 A. 2d 245 (2009).
8. Maryland Code Annotated, State Government § 10-128(a).

is invalid unless the court finds that any other provision of the regulation is now "so incomplete that it cannot be carried out in accordance with the purpose of the regulation."[9] If a court has declared all or part of a regulation invalid, notice must be published in the Maryland Register and in COMAR.[10]

## § 3.2. APA Grounds to Invalidate a Regulation

The APA provides three grounds upon which a regulation will be held invalid. The three grounds are: (1) the regulation is unconstitutional; (2) the regulation exceeds the statutory authority of the agency; and (3) the regulation was adopted without compliance with the statutory requirements for adoption of a regulation.[11] As discussed below, there are also other arguments to challenge a regulation beyond these three grounds.

## § 3.3. Challenges to the Constitutionality of a Regulation

A regulation which is unconstitutional is invalid.[12] Constitutional attacks on regulations have been made on various constitutional arguments.

## § 3.4. Separation of Powers

Article 8 of the Maryland Declaration of Rights provides:

> That the Legislative, Executive, and Judicial powers of Government ought to be forever separate and distinct from each other; and no person exercising the functions of one of said Departments shall assume or discharge the duties of any other.[13]

All Maryland administrative agencies are part of the Executive Branch. In a few cases, a regulation has been challenged based on the argument that it violated the separation of powers doctrine under Article 8 for an executive branch agency to "make law" via its quasi-legislative rulemaking power.

*Christ v. Maryland Department of Natural Resources*[14] involved a regulation adopted by the Department of Natural Resources (DNR) prohibiting the operation of certain watercraft in Maryland waters by any person under fourteen years old. One argument

9. Maryland Code Annotated, State Government § 10-128(b).
10. Maryland Code Annotated, State Government § 10-129.
11. Maryland Code Annotated, State Government § 10-125(d).
12. Maryland Code Annotated, State Government § 10-125(d)(1).
13. *See also* Article II, section 1 of the Maryland Constitution providing that the executive power is vested in a governor; Article III, section 1 of the Maryland Constitution providing that the legislature shall consist of a Senate and House of Delegates; and Article IV, section 1 of the Maryland Constitution vesting judicial power in the courts.
14. 335 Md. 427, 644 A.2d 34 (1994).

was that the State Boat Act unconstitutionally delegated legislative power to DNR, an agency in the executive branch, in violation of Article 8 of the Maryland Declaration of Rights. The Court of Appeals rejected the challenge. The court stated Article 8 does not impose a complete separation between the branches of government. Separation of powers may constitutionally "encompass a sensible degree of elasticity."[15] The doctrine of separation of powers "does not forbid the exercise by one department of powers that could appropriately be exercised by another department."[16] The court noted that the delegation of legislative power to an executive branch agency "ordinarily does not violate the constitutional separation of powers requirement as long as guidelines or safeguards" are provided by the legislature.[17] The court then added that,

> [T]he requirement of guidelines is not an absolute one; it has been relaxed in many circumstances in light of the complexity of modern conditions with which government must deal.... [W]here the discretion to be exercised relates to regulations for the protection of pubic morals, health, safety, or general welfare, and it is impracticable to fix standards without destroying the flexibility necessary to enable the administrative officials to carry out the legislative will, legislation delegating such discretion without such restrictions may be valid.[18]

The court also noted that the "modern tendency of the courts is toward greater liberality in permitting grants of discretion to administrative officials in order to facilitate the administration of the laws as the complexity of governmental and economic conditions increases."[19]

The *Christ* court also responded to the argument, based on cases from California, that "fundamental policy making" decisions cannot constitutionally be delegated by the legislature to an executive branch agency.[20] The court held that although the legislature cannot delegate a function that is "expressly and unqualifiedly" vested by the Constitution in the legislature, i.e., the powers to impeach, to propose constitutional amendments, and enact statutes, the "constitutionality of administrative regulations reflecting policy determinations which have been just as 'fundamental' as the age restriction" in this case has been "repeatedly upheld." Executive branch agencies may be delegated "broad power to promulgate legislative-type rules or regulations in order to implement the statute."[21] In fact, "when the General Assembly enacts a statute, embodying its policy decision or decisions, the Legislature often must delegate significant authority to the executive branch which is vested with the constitutional responsibility of administering the statute."[22] The court thus concluded that the delegation of legislative authority to DNR, pursuant to which DNR had adopted the minimum age regulation, did not constitute a violation of the separation of powers doctrine as expressed in Article 8 of the Maryland Declaration of Rights.

Another separation of power challenge was raised in *Benson v. Maryland*.[23] *Benson* involved the collection by the Department of Budget and Management (DBM) of a commission fee on collect calls placed by prison inmates. The Court of Appeals reiterated that

15. 335 Md. 427, 441, 644 A.2d 34, 41 (1994).
16. 335 Md. 427, 441, 644 A.2d 34, 41 (1994).
17. 335 Md. 427, 441, 644 A.2d 34, 40 (1994).
18. 335 Md. 427, 441–42, 644 A.2d 34, 40–41 (1994).
19. 335 Md. 427, 442, 644 A.2d 34, 41 (1994).
20. 335 Md. 427, 444, 644 A.2d 34, 42 (1994).
21. 335 Md. 427, 445, 644 A.2d 34, 42 (1994).
22. 335 Md. 427, 445, 644 A.2d 34, 42 (1994).
23. 389 Md. 615, 887 A.2d 525 (2005).

the power to enact legislation is a non-delegable duty which the legislature cannot delegate to an agency. This is true because "the people of Maryland, having delegated to the Legislature of Maryland the power of making its laws, that body could not legally or validly redelegate the power and the authority thus conferred upon it to the people themselves."[24] The power to set the amount of a government charge, however, is not a non-delegable function of the legislature. The legislature "may choose to delegate the discreet power of setting the amount of government charges ... to an Executive Branch agency ... without violating the separation of powers."[25] The court also wrote in *Benson* that

> "[the] delegation by the legislature of legislative powers to Executive Branch agencies does not by itself usually violate Article 8 if guidelines or safeguards, sufficient under the circumstances, are contained in the pertinent statute or statutes.... Guidelines, however, are not required uniformly by the Constitution in all cases. The court has 'relaxed' the necessity for the same many times in light of the complexity of modern conditions with which government must deal."[26]

## § 3.5. Other Constitutional Challenges to Regulations

*Fogle v. H & G Restaurant, Inc.*[27] involved numerous challenges, some of which involved constitutional issues, to regulations adopted by the Division of Labor and Industries which prohibited the use of tobacco products in enclosed workplaces. The petitioners in *Fogle* first argued that the due process guarantees in Article 24 of the Maryland Declaration of Rights and the Fourteenth Amendment of the U.S. Constitution had been violated because petitioners were deprived of their right to be heard on the issue of the regulation's compliance with federal law. The court held that no such right existed, and thus no due process rights were violated. The second constitutional attack was that the regulation was unconstitutionally vague. This argument was also rejected. The court said that "[j]ust because [the regulation] is broad does not necessarily make it vague. We believe that persons of ordinary intelligence will be perfectly capable, without having to guess, of understanding this regulation's meaning and application, i.e., what conduct on their part is affected by the regulation."[28] Another constitutional argument was that the regulation amounted to a denial of the right not to be deprived of property without due process of law in violation of Article 24 of the Maryland Declaration of Rights and the Fourteenth Amendment of the U.S Constitution. This claim was rejected by the court without much discussion. The next challenge was that the regulation was invalid because it violated the state and federal right to privacy found in the penumbra of Articles 2, 8, 19, 24, 40, and 45 of the Maryland Declaration of Rights, and the First, Fourth, Ninth, and Fourteenth Amendments of the U.S. Constitution to the extent the regulation prohibited smoking in private homes and private vehicles. The court rejected the privacy claim because the regulation did not apply to these private areas. Finally, the court rejected the argument that the regulation was unconstitutional in violation of the state and federal right to

24. 389 Md. 615, 641, 887 A.2d 525, 540 (2005).
25. 389 Md. 615, 641, 887 A.2d 525, 540 (2005).
26. 389 Md. 615, 644–45, 887 A.2d 525, 542 (2005).
27. 337 Md. 441, 654 A.2d 449 (1995).
28. 337 Md. 441, 467, 654 A.2d 449, 462 (1995).

freedom of speech as protected by Article 40 of the Maryland Declaration of Rights and the First Amendment of the U.S Constitution because it required posting of "no smoking" signs at the entrance of every enclosed workplace.

A successful challenge to the constitutionality of regulations was made in *Department of Public Safety & Correctional Services v. Demby.*[29] Regulations had been adopted which prohibited some inmates from receiving special housing credits for double-celling. These regulations were held invalid under the *ex post facto* clause in the United States Constitution and Article 17 of the Maryland Declaration of Rights. The regulations imposed a more severe punishment on the prisoners than what was annexed to their actions at the time they had committed their crimes.

## § 3.6. In Excess of Statutory Authority

The Maryland APA also provides that a regulation which is in excess of the agency's statutory authority is invalid.[30] An agency only has the powers granted to it by the legislature. Therefore, if a regulation is beyond the statutory powers delegated to the agency, the regulation is invalid. This issue has been presented in a few cases.

*Christ v. Maryland Department of Natural Resources*[31] involved the agency's adoption of a regulation which prohibited persons under the age of fourteen from operating a jet ski on Maryland waterways. The State Boat Act gave the DNR the power to promulgate regulations "governing the operation of any vessels" on Maryland waterways. It was argued that because the Act did not provide that the DNR had the power "to promulgate regulations which prohibit the use of vessels by an entire class of citizens of the State," the regulation was invalid. The court rejected this argument. The court wrote that, "the broad authority to promulgate regulations governing the ... operation of any vessels plainly encompasses a regulation prohibiting the operation of certain motor vessels by persons under [fourteen]." The court in *Christ* added that specificity of delegated powers is not required, and whether "there should be a broad general delegation of regulatory authority to administrators, or a more specific delegation, is a choice for the General Assembly," especially "where it is impracticable for the legislature to set specific guidelines to govern the day-to-day exercise of the rule-making power."

*Lussier v. Maryland Racing Commission*[32] involved a challenge to regulations adopted by the Racing Commission which gave it the power to impose a fine up to $5,000 for violation of other Racing Commission regulations. There was no express statutory delegation to the Racing Commission to impose any fines. The majority upheld the regulation, writing that "We have repeatedly rejected the argument ... the Legislature was required expressly or explicitly to authorize the particular regulatory action." Chief Judge Bell dissented in *Lussier*. Judge Bell's position was that "delegations to the administrative agency should be reasonably specific and provide some guidelines for the agency to follow."

"Excess of statutory authority" arguments were also presented, and rejected, in *Fogle v. H & G Restaurant, Inc.*[33] involving workplace-smoking regulations adopted by the

29. 390 Md. 580, 890 A.2d 310 (2006).
30. Maryland Code Annotated, State Government § 10-125(d)(2).
31. 335 Md. 427, 644 A.2d 34 (1994).
32. 343 Md. 681, 684 A.2d 804 (1996).
33. 337 Md. 441, 654 A.2d 449 (1995).

Division of Labor and Industries. It was argued that the regulation of smoking had been preempted by the General Assembly, and therefore any agency smoking regulation exceeded the powers granted to the agency by the legislature. The court's response was that the General Assembly had "not regulated smoking in so all-encompassing a fashion as to suggest that it meant to reserve to itself for direct legislative action all regulation of smoking." The agency's regulation, therefore, was not in excess of its statutory authority.

On the other hand, in *Fields v. Department of Human Resources Howard County Department of Social Services*,[34] a regulation of the Howard County Department of Social Services which set forth the steps required to appeal a finding of "responsible for indicated child abuse" was held invalid. The regulation imposed procedures more burdensome than those prescribed in the governing statute. Because the regulation's procedures were not allowed by the statute, the regulation went "beyond the statutory authority" of the agency.

## § 3.7. Improper Procedure

The third ground provided in the APA for invalidating a regulation is the agency's failure to comply with the statutory requirements for adoption of a regulation.[35] Most of the cases involving this issue have been discussed in Chapter 2's discussion of an agency's failure to follow any procedures because the agency's position was that it had not adopted a regulation. In addition to these cases, the improper procedure argument could arise when the agency recognizes that it is adopting a regulation, and the agency follows some procedures, but it is argued that the procedures followed were inadequate. An example of this is *Fogle v. H & G Restaurant, Inc.*[36] involving regulations adopted by the Division of Labor and Industries which prohibited the smoking of tobacco products in enclosed workplaces. Among the many challenges to this regulation was that although the agency had performed the statutorily required economic impact and feasibility assessment, the assessment was inadequate. The court reviewed the agency's "Estimate of Economic Impact" which had been published in the Maryland Register, as well as a separate economic impact report that the agency had prepared, and concluded that the agency had complied with the APA procedures.

## § 3.8. Bias Challenges to Regulations

An adopted regulation can also be challenged based on the bias of the agency. Because due process requires an impartial decision maker in administrative rulemaking, this argument could be included under constitutional challenges to a regulation. There are generally three types of disqualifying bias in administrative law—personal, financial and prejudgment bias. There are no Maryland cases discussing personal or financial bias in rulemaking. The law is most likely identical for personal and financial bias in rulemaking

34. 176 Md. App. 152, 932 A.2d 824 (2007).
35. Maryland Code Annotated, State Government § 10-125(d)(3).
36. 337 Md. 441, 654 A.2d 449 (1995).

as in contested cases which is discussed in Chapter 16. If an agency official deciding whether the agency should adopt a regulation has a financial interest impacted by the regulation, the official must be disqualified from participating in the consideration of the regulation's adoption. Likewise, if an agency official has a personal interest in the proposed regulation, that official must be disqualified. Any regulation adopted with the involvement of a personally or financially biased official must be invalidated.

More significant to rulemaking is prejudgment bias. Maryland has followed the approach of Federal Administrative Law that treats rulemaking prejudgment bias differently from contested case prejudgment bias. In order to disqualify a decision-maker in a rulemaking, it must be shown that the decision-maker had an "unalterably closed mind on matters critical" to the adoption of the regulation.[37] Less than an unalterably closed mind can lead to disqualification in a contested case.[38] Prejudgment bias was discussed in *Fogle v. H & G Restaurant, Inc.*[39] in a challenge to regulations of the Division of Labor and Industries that prohibited tobacco smoking in enclosed workplace areas. It was argued that the Commissioner had an unalterably closed mind concerning the need for the workplace smoking ban prior to the initiation of the rulemaking process. The impacted businesses argued that they had been deprived of their meaningful opportunity for public comment on the proposed regulation. The challengers contended that the "decision to impose the workplace smoking ban [had been made] before the time for public comment had even ended and before any meaningful evaluation of the evidence submitted."[40] The Court of Appeals held that disqualifying prejudgment bias had not been established. The rulemaking process was "comprehensive," including several public hearings with live testimony. Moreover, the Commissioner's explanation for adopting the regulation was set forth in COMAR. The court added that the fact that "the Commissioner did not change his position regarding [the regulation] in light of contrary evidence in the rulemaking record does not mean that there was not a meaningful opportunity for comment."

## § 3.9. Substantial Evidence Review of Regulations

Substantial evidence review is not applied in judicial review of a regulation. As discussed in Chapter 17, substantial evidence review in judicial review of contested cases involves the review of a formal, closed record created at an agency hearing to determine if the agency decision was based exclusively on the information properly introduced into the record, and whether the agency decision was reasonable. No formal agency record is created by a rulemaking proceeding. In rulemaking, the agency, although required to consider the comments received from the public, is not bound by them. The agency is permitted to rely on information which was not formally presented to the agency. Because no formal record is created in a rulemaking proceeding, there can be no substantial evidence review of a regulation. This point was made in *Fogle v. H & G Restaurant, Inc.*[41] and is consistent with the plain language of the Maryland APA.

37. Fogle v. H & G Rest., Inc., 337 Md. 441, 426, 654 A.2d 449, 459 (1995).
38. *See* Chapter 16.
39. 337 Md. 441, 654 A.2d 449 (1995).
40. 337 Md. 441, 462, 654 A.2d 449, 459 (1995).
41. 337 Md. 441, 654 A.2d 449 (1995).

## § 3.10. Arbitrary or Capricious Review of Regulations

The Maryland APA does not provide for judicial review of a regulation under the arbitrary or capricious standard. Under the Maryland APA, arbitrary or capricious review only applies to judicial review of a contested case.[42] In Federal Administrative Law, the arbitrary or capricious standard is applicable to rulemaking as well as adjudications.[43] It seems appropriate to apply arbitrary or capricious review to rulemaking in Maryland for a few reasons. First, unlike substantial evidence review that requires a formal agency record and exclusiveness of the record, and thus can be applied only to a contested case proceeding, arbitrary or capricious review is not based on any formal agency record. As discussed in Chapter 20, arbitrary or capricious review is an overall reasonableness review of the agency decision based on all facts and circumstances. A regulation adopted following the proper procedures which is not unconstitutional and is not in excess of the agency's statutory authority nevertheless is invalid if the regulation is an unreasonable exercise of the agency's power. The legal term for such unreasonable exercise of power is arbitrary or capricious.

Maryland courts when reviewing a challenge to a regulation have considered "arbitrary or capricious" arguments, and have applied arbitrary or capricious analysis. For example, in *Fogle v. H & G Restaurant, Inc.*,[44] it was argued that the no-smoking regulation was invalid because it was contrary to the enabling statute's requirement that an occupational and health standard not place an undue burden on interstate commerce. An argument that an agency action is contrary to its enabling statute is usually treated as an argument that the agency has acted in an arbitrary or capricious manner. Likewise, in *Christ v. Maryland Department of Natural Resources*,[45] one argument made to invalidate the regulation prohibiting the use of personal watercraft on Maryland waters by persons under the age of fourteen was that "the age restriction conflicts with the overall spirit of the State Boat Act, in which ... the Legislature indicated its preference for educating young boaters rather than prohibiting their operation of certain vessels." This argument also falls within the umbrella of "arbitrary or capricious." In *Paek v. Prince George's County Board of License Commissioners*,[46] the Court of Appeals stated that regulations adopted by an administrative agency must be reasonable and consistent with the letter and spirit of the statute under which the agency acts. This is classic arbitrary or capricious review.[47]

The "consistent with the letter and spirit of the law" standard was also applied in *Fields v. Department of Human Resources Howard County Department of Social Services*[48] to invalidate a regulation which imposed steps to appeal a finding of "responsible for indicated child abuse" beyond those in the relevant statute. The court held that "the requirement

---

42. *Compare* Maryland Code Annotated, State Government § 10-125 *with* Maryland Code Annotated, State Government § 10-222(h).

43. *See* Citizens to Preserve Overton Park, Inc. v. Volpe, 401 U.S. 402 (1971).

44. 337 Md. 441, 654 A.2d 449 (1995).

45. 335 Md. 427, 644 A.2d 34 (1994).

46. 381 Md. 583, 851 A.2d 540 (2004).

47. *See also* Bd. of Educ. of Talbot County v. Heister, 392 Md. 140, 896 A.2d 342 (2006); and Medstar Health v. Md. Health Care Comm'n, 391 Md. 427, 459, 893 A.2d 1099, 1118 (2006) (dissenting opinion) ("the question whether a particular regulation is arbitrary or unreasonable, or not fairly within the scope of the delegate power, is subject to judicial review").

48. 176 Md. App. 152, 932 A.2d 824 (2007).

of a second mailing to initiate an appeal is not consistent with the letter or spirit of the law under which the agency acts."

Additionally, as discussed in Chapter 13, even absent statutory authorization, Maryland courts have the inherent power to review and correct any agency action that is "arbitrary, capricious or unreasonable." For example, *Fritszche v. Maryland State Board of Elections*[49] involved a COMAR provision of the Board of Elections which established a deadline for the postmark of absentee ballots. In response to a challenge to the application of the regulation, the Court of Appeals wrote: "In order to succeed on the merits, the petitioner must show that the election regulation establishing the deadline for the postmark of absentee ballots, as executed and applied, is 'arbitrary, capricious or unreasonable'." Therefore, although the Maryland APA does not provide for judicial review of agency regulations under the arbitrary or capricious standard, regulations should be, and have been, reviewed under this standard.

## § 3.11. Judicial Deference in Judicial Review of Regulations

How much deference should a court give to the agency when deciding whether a regulation is valid? In my opinion, the amount of deference given to the agency by the reviewing court depends on the type of challenge presented. If the challenge is that the regulation is unconstitutional, no deference should be given to the agency. Courts are clearly more expert on constitutional issues, and it is always the function of the judicial branch to rule on the constitutionality of a government action. Because bias claims are constitutionally based, no judicial deference should be given to the agency's claim of lack of bias.

Nor should any deference be given to the agency when the challenge is based on failure to follow the proper procedures. An agency's characterization of its action as not constituting a "regulation" has never been given any deference by a court. Nor has any court deferred to the agency's position that whatever procedures the agency decided to follow were sufficient.

Challenges to a regulation as being in excess of the agency's statutory authority should also be judicially reviewed without any deference to the agency's position. This type of challenge involves statutory interpretation of the agency's enabling statute. Courts have greater expertise in statutory interpretation than do agency officials. Pure issues of law are the province of the courts, not agencies. As discussed in Chapter 18, although there are cases that give some deference to an agency's interpretation of its own powers when reviewing a contested case decision, no case seems to have afforded such deference when reviewing a regulation. In fact, *Oyarzo v. Maryland Department of Health and Mental Hygiene*[50] noted that there is "a limit to judicial deference to an agency's rulemaking authority," when the argument is made that the agency acted outside the scope of its statutory authority.

Judicial deference is appropriate when the argument is presented that the regulation is arbitrary or capricious. As discussed in Chapter 20, arbitrary or capricious review is a

49. 397 Md. 331, 916 A.2d 1015 (2007).

50. 187 Md. App. 264, 978 A.2d 804, *cert. denied*, 411 Md. 601, 984 A. 2d 245 (2009).

reasonableness review. Whenever the agency decision can be reversed only if it is unreasonable, the presumption is that the agency acted properly. Under any reasonableness review, the court cannot substitute its own judgment for what the court believes is a better decision. This is especially true when some substantive expertise of the agency is involved. This is illustrated by *Fogle v. H & G Restaurant, Inc.*[51] involving regulations prohibiting the smoking of tobacco products in enclosed workplaces. On the issue of whether there was a "significant risk" of exposure to second hand smoke, the reviewing court gave "great deference" to the agency's conclusion. On the issue whether the agency had based its decision on the "best available evidence," the court wrote that it was a well-established administrative law principle that the existence in the record of evidence contrary to the agency's conclusion does not prevent the court from upholding the agency action. The court wrote that "We do not second guess the judgmental basis upon which the agency chose to weigh the conflicting evidence."

When engaging in judicial review of a regulation, it is not the court's role to decide whether the court would have adopted the same regulation if the judge was working at the agency. Nor is it the court's role to determine if the agency could have adopted a "better" regulation. The court's role in its substantive review of a regulation is limited to whether the agency's regulation is reasonable. In making this determination, the court should give deference to the agency's decision.

## § 3.12. Judicial Review of a Regulation as Part of Judicial Review of a Contested Case

Although the APA provides that a regulation can be challenged by the filing of a Petition for a Declaratory Judgment,[52] judicial review of a regulation can also be obtained as part of judicial review of a contested case. If the agency decision in a contested case is based on a violation of a regulation, a party aggrieved by the contested case order may challenge the regulation as part of its challenge to the order. This is what occurred in *Lussier v. Maryland Racing Commission.*[53] *Lussier* involved a fine on a racehorse owner. The fine was based on a regulation of the Maryland Racing Commission that authorized the agency to impose a fine not exceeding $5,000. The challenge was that the agency regulation was in excess of the agency's statutory authority in that the enabling statute did not expressly authorize the agency to impose a fine upon racehorse owners. Although the Court of Appeals rejected this argument, the court did review the validity of the regulation as part of its review of the contested case.

It is a matter of strategy whether to challenge a regulation by filing a Petition for Declaratory Judgment before the regulation has been applied against a regulated person by the agency or whether it is better to wait to challenge the regulation after it has been applied by the agency in a contested case. If the regulation will certainly be applied against the client, it is probably advisable to file a challenge to the regulation as soon as it is adopted. On the other hand, if it is not clear that the regulation will be applied against a client, it probably makes more sense to wait to see if the regulation is actually applied. If there is uncertainty whether the regulation will be applied directly against a client, but

51. 337 Md. 441, 654 A.2d 449 (1995).
52. Maryland Code Annotated, State Government § 10-125.
53. 343 Md. 681, 684 A.2d 804 (1996).

the client's business or personal conduct will be impacted by the possible application of the regulation, it is probably advisable to challenge the regulation immediately through a Petition for Declaratory Judgment.

# Chapter 4

# Contested Cases: Right to a Contested Case Hearing

In exercising the quasi-judicial powers delegated to them, administrative agencies hold contested case hearings, also known as adjudications. This chapter will discuss when an agency must decide a matter through the contested case process.

## §4.1. Quasi-Judicial and Quasi-Legislative Proceedings

In determining whether an agency must hold a contested case hearing to decide a matter, the first step is to determine whether the agency is acting in its quasi-judicial capacity. An agency is acting in a quasi-judicial capacity when it considers "facts about the parties and their activities, business and properties ... [that] answer the questions of who did what, where, when, how, why, with what motive or intent."[1] When exercising quasi-judicial powers, the agency is making a decision on individual, as opposed to general, grounds. The agency engages in a deliberative fact-finding process based on the weighing of evidence presented at a hearing.[2] On the other hand, when an agency is exercising its quasi-legislative powers, its decision is based on facts that do not usually concern the immediate parties, but on facts that generally apply to the public. When exercising its quasi-legislative powers, the agency is deciding questions of policy and discretion.[3]

When distinguishing whether the agency is acting quasi-judicially or quasi-legislatively, the distinctions between fact and policy, and individual and general are helpful. A decision that is based on individual facts is quasi-judicial. A decision that is based on general policy is quasi-legislative. A few cases are helpful here.

*Bethel World Outreach Church v. Montgomery County*[4] involved the denial of a request by a church to change the water and sewer category designation of its property so that the church could build a new church building and related facilities. Because the county agency's denial was based on general policy grounds, not on the particular characteristics of the church's property, the decision was deemed to be quasi-legislative. The significance of this holding in *Bethel World* concerned the proper method of obtaining judicial review.

1. Armstrong v. Mayor of Baltimore, 169 Md. App. 655, 668, 906 A.2d 415, 423 (2006); Bethel World Outreach Church v. Montgomery County, 184 Md. App. 572, 588, 967 A.2d 232, 242 (2009).
2. Md. Overpak Corp. v. Mayor of Baltimore, 395 Md. 16, 909 A.2d 235 (2006).
3. Bethel World Outreach Church v. Montgomery County, 184 Md. App. 572, 967 A.2d 232 (2009).
4. 184 Md. App. 572, 967 A.2d 232 (2009).

*Mayor & Council of Rockville v. Woodmont Country Club*[5] involved whether a contested case hearing was required in a proceeding to determine a special property assessment to pay for the construction of a road and water transmission main. The Mayor and Council of Rockville (Rockville), a municipal corporation, is authorized to assess the costs of public improvement projects against private property owners who will be specially benefitted by the projects. In order to determine the amount of the special assessment, a public hearing was held where appraisals completed by appraisers hired by Rockville were introduced. The appraisers did not attend the hearing and were not available for cross examination. Woodmont Country Club, one of the property owners being assessed, presented live testimony from three witnesses disputing the reports of Rockville's appraisers. After the hearing, Rockville's appraisers reaffirmed their earlier appraisals in an additional report. Woodmont was then given an opportunity to respond in writing to this additional report. After Woodmont Country Club was assessed an amount it believed was too high, it sought judicial review. The Court of Appeals held that the hearing provided was not adequate.

The court held that the special assessment on Woodmont involved the quasi-judicial powers of Rockville. The court stated that "the particular amount of the special assessment to be levied based on the amount of the benefit to a specific piece of property ... is classically the type of adjudicatory determination to which the right of cross-examination attaches."[6] The court discussed the difference between adjudicative facts and legislative facts. Adjudicative facts concern the parties and their activities, businesses, and properties. Legislative facts do not usually concern the immediate parties, but are general facts that help decide questions of law, policy, and discretion. The decision whether to impose *any* special assessment is quasi-legislative; the decision as to *how much* to assess a particular property is quasi-judicial. The court also relied on the fact that a statute provided for judicial review of the special assessment. Only quasi-judicial decisions are subject to full judicial review, not quasi-legislative decisions.

*Woodmont Country Club* was relied upon in two zoning cases, *Maryland Overpak Corporation v. Mayor and City Council of Baltimore*,[7] and *Bucktail, LLC v. County Council of Talbot County*.[8] In *Maryland Overpak*, the Court of Appeals held that the Baltimore City Council's approval of an amendment to the previously approved planned urban development (PUD) constituted quasi-judicial action, and was a judicially reviewable zoning action. The court stated that the "principal characteristic of a quasi-judicial proceeding is that of fact-finding" even if the facts are undisputed. In the zoning context, the proceeding is quasi-judicial where at a minimum, there is "a fact-finding process that entails the holding of a hearing, the receipt of factual and opinion testimony and/or forms of documentary evidence, and a particularized conclusion, based upon delineated standards, for the unique development proposal for the specific parcel or assemblage of land in question."[9] In *Bucktail*, the Court of Appeals, after citing *Woodmont Country Club*, stated that in the context of a zoning decision, "the granting or denying a map amendment utilizing a growth allocation is legislative in nature, [but] the process of applying the Zoning ordinance standards to the particular facts of Bucktail's property" was quasi-judicial.[10]

---

5. 348 Md. 572, 705 A.2d 301 (1998).
6. 348 Md. 572, 583, 705 A.2d 301, 306 (1998).
7. 395 Md. 16, 909 A.2d 235 (2006).
8. 352 Md. 530, 723 A.2d 440 (1999).
9. 395 Md. 16, 37–53, 909 A.2d 235, 247–256 (2006).
10. 352 Md. 530, 548, 723 A.2d 440, 448 (1999).

*Carriage Hill Cabin-John, Inc. v. Maryland Health Resources Planning Commission*[11] involved an application for a Certificate of Need (CON) for development of nursing home beds. The Court of Special Appeals drew a distinction between the "State Health Plan" that creates an integrated system of care to assure geographic and financial access to a range of quality health care services at a reasonable cost for all citizens, and a CON that provides approval for a person or entity to develop or operate a health care project consistent with the State Health Plan. The development of the State Health Plan is quasi-legislative; the CON process is quasi-judicial because individual rights, duties, entitlements, or privileges are at issue. The CON process, therefore, required contested case procedures.

*1000 Friends of Maryland v. Ehrlich*[12] involved the decision by the Board of Public Works to approve funding for the expansion of Route 32 in Howard County. "Smart Growth" legislation mandates that no state funding can be approved for a project not located within a priority funding area unless the Board "determines that extraordinary circumstances exist." The Board heard statements from the State Highway Administration, legislators, representatives of interest groups, and concerned citizens before it approved the funding. One challenge to the decision was that the Board failed to articulate factual findings on what extraordinary circumstances existed. The Court of Special Appeals rejected this challenge because "[i]n approving funding of a growth-related project, the Board is not adjudicating a contested case involving the fundamental rights of life, liberty, or property. Rather, it is performing a 'quasi-legislative' function, such as promulgation of a regulation or approving a budget.... [W]here ... the action is quasi-legislative in nature, the concepts applicable to an adversary proceeding have no relevance." Because findings are only required in contested cases,[13] the Board's decision was not invalid because it had not issued findings.

## §4.2. Right to Contested Case Hearing Under the APA

The starting point for deciding whether an agency that is governed by the APA is required to hold a contested case hearing is the definition of contested case in the APA. State Government §10-202(d)(1) defines contested case as

> A proceeding before an agency to determine (i) a right, duty, statutory entitlement or privilege of a person that is required by statute or constitution to be determined only after an opportunity for an agency hearing; or (ii) the grant, denial, renewal, revocation, suspension, or amendment of a license[14] that is required by statute or constitution to be determined only after an opportunity for an agency hearing.

State Government §10-202(d)(2) then provides that a contested case "does not include a proceeding before an agency involving an agency hearing required only by regulation

11. 125 Md. App. 183, 724 A.2d 745 (1999).
12. 170 Md. App. 538, 907 A.2d 865, *cert. denied*, 396 Md. 12, 912 A.2d 648 (2006).
13. *See* Chapter 7.
14. License is defined in Maryland Code Annotated, State Government §10-202(e) to mean "all or any part of the permission that ... is required by law to be obtained from an agency [and] that is not required only for revenue purposes."

unless that regulation expressly, or by clear implication, requires the hearing to be held in accordance with" the contested case provisions of Subtitle 2 of the Maryland APA.

It is important to recognize that the APA itself does not grant a right to a contested case hearing. That right must be based on a requirement imposed by a statute, due process, or a regulation. There are several leading Maryland cases discussing the right to a contested case hearing and these APA sections.

## §4.3. No Contested Case Hearing Required

*Sugarloaf Citizens Association v. Northeast Maryland Waste Disposal Authority*[15] involved the issue whether the Maryland Air Management Administration of the Maryland Department of the Environment was required to hold a contested case hearing before ruling on an application for a Prevention of Significant Deterioration (PSD) permit,[16] the first step in a three step process to build a solid waste disposal facility. The PSD permit would be followed by an application for a construction permit and then an operations permit. A citizen's group had requested that the agency hold a contested case hearing with the right to cross-examine witnesses. This request was denied by the agency. The agency convened only an informational, non-trial type public hearing limited to submission of written and oral comments. Upon judicial review, the Court of Appeals considered the three situations when a contested case hearing is required. First, the relevant statutes only required a contested case hearing at the construction permit stage. Although a statute required a "public hearing" for a PSD, the "public hearing" language was "simply mandating ... that the hearing be open to the public. The Legislature is not determining, by use or omission of the word 'public,' whether the hearing is a contested case hearing."[17] Nor did the relevant COMAR provisions require a contested case hearing. COMAR permitted the agency to follow the same non-contested case type hearings that the federal Environmental Protection Agency followed. Finally, there was no contention that there was any due process right to a contested case hearing at the PSD application stage.

A motion for reconsideration was filed with the court. In its opinion denying this motion, the Court of Appeals first emphasized that the definition of contested case in the APA is determinative of whether the hearing required is a contested case hearing. Second, the opinion recognized that in deciding whether a statute requires a contested case hearing, express judicial review provisions indicate legislative intent that a contested case hearing is required. This is true because informational-type hearings are not subject to judicial review, except to determine if the agency acted unconstitutionally or in excess of its jurisdiction.[18]

Another leading case on contested cases is *Weiner v. Maryland Insurance Administration*[19] which involved the Insurance Administration's approval of a contract between BlueCross BlueShield of Maryland (BCBS) and participating pharmacists. The contract set forth a

15. 323 Md. 641, 594 A.2d 1115 (1991).

16. The purpose of the PSD permit process is to prevent degradation of the ambient air quality in areas where air quality is already superior to that required by National Ambient Air Quality Standards. PSD approval is required before any potential source of air pollution can be located in a PSD area.

17. 323 Md. 641, 657 n.12, 594 A.2d 1115, 1123 n.12 (1991).

18. 323 Md. 641, 672–673, 594 A.2d 1115, 1130 (1991).

19. 337 Md. 181, 652 A.2d 125 (1995).

formula for the reimbursement to pharmacies for filling prescriptions for members of BCBS's drug plans. The agency approved the contract without holding any hearing. The Maryland Pharmacists Association (MPA) requested a hearing to challenge the new formula. The agency agreed to hold an "informational hearing" where all sides could present their positions. One issue that made its way to the Court of Appeals was whether the MPA was entitled to a contested case hearing on the BCBS contract. The court ruled no. The court first stated that it "is well settled that a party is entitled to a quasi-judicial hearing before an administrative agency only if that type of hearing is required by statute or regulation or mandated by constitutional due process concerns."[20] The relevant statutes and regulations here did not require a contested case hearing. The court also reiterated that the "mere fact that a statute calls for a hearing is not in and of itself sufficient to make the subject of that hearing a 'contested case.'"[21] The role of the Insurance Administration in this case was to obtain information in a quasi-legislative manner. The proceeding did not satisfy the definition of contested case under the APA because the proceeding did not involve a right, duty, statutory entitlement, privilege, or license. Finally, the court rejected the MPA's due process argument. The court held that a contested case hearing "is not a requirement of procedural due process where an administrative agency does not act in a quasi-judicial capacity and the facts to be determined are 'legislative' rather than adjudicative in nature."[22]

A contested case hearing was also deemed not required in *Harvey v. Marshall*.[23] In that case, Harvey challenged the Child Support Enforcement Administration's (CSEA) refusal to forgive child support arrearages. The Court of Appeals ruled that the agency's decision not to exercise its discretion to forgive Harvey's arrearages did not "implicate a right, duty, statutory entitlement, or privilege" that was required by statute or constitution to be determined only after a contested case hearing. It should be noted that legislation has since changed this, and a contested case hearing is now granted when the CSEA does not accept in full settlement an arrearage that is less than the total amount owed.

## §4.4. Contested Case Hearing Required

*C.S. v. Prince George's County Department of Social Services*[24] involved whether a contested case hearing was required before a person accused of child neglect or child abuse was placed on a central registry. The Prince George's County Department of Social Services (PGDSS) conducted an investigation regarding an incident of child abuse involving C.S. The PGDSS decided to place C.S.'s name on a central registry. Pursuant to regulations of the Social Services Administration of the State Department of Human Resources, C.S. requested a hearing with PGDSS. In response, PGDSS merely reviewed some records, and based on this review declined to modify its decision. At that point, pursuant to another regulation, the case was delegated to the Office of Administrative Hearings (OAH). The Administrative Law Judge (ALJ) at OAH conducted an in-camera review of the documents, permitted C.S. to submit additional written information, and heard oral argument, but did not hold a contested case hearing. The ALJ upheld the PGDSS's decision. The Court

20. 337 Md. 181, 186, 652 A.2d 125, 127 (1995).
21. 337 Md. 181, 192, 652 A.2d 125, 130 (1995).
22. 337 Md. 181, 193, 652 A.2d 125, 131 (1995).
23. 389 Md. 243, 884 A.2d 1171 (2005).
24. 343 Md. 14, 680 A.2d 470 (1996).

of Appeals held that the procedures employed were inadequate; a contested case hearing was required. The court wrote that "[o]ne of the key elements of a contested case hearing is whether the entity conducting the hearing acts in an adjudicatory capacity, i.e., by determining the facts of a case and applying those facts to some legal standard in order to reach a conclusion."[25] It cited *Sugarloaf* for the proposition that where a hearing is merely preliminary, it is not a contested case. In the case of the child abuse registry, "the ALJ must sift between potentially conflicting information presented by the [State] and the alleged abuser to determine whether there are sufficient facts to meet the definitions" of abuse or neglect.[26] Therefore, the court concluded that a contested case hearing with the right to cross examination of witnesses was required.

*Charles County Department of Social Services v. Vann*[27] also involved the entry on the central registry of an "indicated child abuser." Vann had hit his son with a belt that caused some injuries. On the issue as to whether a contested case hearing was required, the court wrote that it was "well established" that a challenge to the entry of one's name to the central registry required a contested case hearing under the APA.

## §4.5. Special Statutory Provisions Limiting a Contested Case Hearing

A statute or regulation which grants the right to a contested case hearing can also negate that right in certain situations. Such a statutory provision was implicated in *Howard County Department of Social Services v. Linda J.*[28] which involved the State's attempt to place Linda J. on the central registry of suspected child abusers. Although as just discussed by *C.S.* and *Vann*, a contested case hearing is generally required for such a determination, a special statutory provision eliminates that requirement if "the individual requesting the hearing is found guilty of any criminal charge arising out of the alleged abuse or neglect."[29] In *Linda J.*, a mother had pleaded guilty to second degree assault and had received probation before judgment (PBJ). There was no dispute that the attempt to place Linda J. on the central registry arose from the criminal charge to which she had pleaded guilty. It was argued, however, that because Linda J. had received a PBJ, she had not been "found guilty" under the statute, and thus she was entitled to a contested case hearing to challenge her placement on the central registry. The Court of Special Appeals rejected Linda J.'s argument. Linda J.'s guilty plea satisfied the "found guilty" language of the statute, and thus no contested case hearing was required.

The same statute was involved in *Tabassi v. Carroll County Department of Social Services.*[30] Tabassi was convicted at a criminal trial of reckless endangerment and providing access of a firearm to a child. In response to the Carroll County Department of Social Service (DSS) "notice of action" stating that it found Tabassi responsible for "indicated child

---

25. 343 Md. 14, 32, 680 A.2d 470, 479 (1996).
26. 343 Md. 14, 33, 680 A.2d 470, 479 (1996).
27. 382 Md. 286, 855 A.2d 313 (2004).
28. 161 Md. App. 402, 869 A.2d 404 (2005).
29. 161 Md. App. 402, 409, 869 A.2d 404, 408 (2005).
30. 182 Md. App. 80, 957 A.2d 620 (2008).

neglect," Tabassi filed a request for a contested case hearing at OAH. DSS filed a Motion to Dismiss Tabassi's request because he had been "found guilty of reckless endangerment and firearms—access by minors, criminal charges arising out of the alleged neglect." The OAH ALJ granted the Motion to Dismiss based on a statute that reads: "If after final disposition of the criminal charge, the individual requesting the hearing is found guilty of any criminal charge arising out of the alleged abuse or neglect, the Office of Administrative Hearings shall dismiss the administrative appeal."[31] The Court of Special Appeals held that the statutory limitation on Tabassi's right to a contested case hearing did not apply because the criminal charges did not arise out of the alleged abuse or neglect. In particular, the criminal charges did not require proof that Tabassi was a person who had permanent or temporary care or custody or responsibility for supervision of the child, which was a necessary element of the neglect that the State must prove prior to someone being listed on the central registry. The case was remanded to OAH for a contested case hearing on the statutory requirements for placement on the central registry.

A comparable statute limiting the right to a contested case hearing was discussed in *Rudman v. Maryland State Board of Physicians*.[32] A physician threatened with the revocation of his license to practice medicine is generally entitled to a contested case hearing on the charges of misconduct. A statute provides, however, that if the licensee is convicted of or pleads guilty or nolo contendere with respect to a crime involving moral turpitude, no contested case hearing is required to revoke the physician's license. Dr. Rudman was accused of several instances of improper sexual contact with female patients. As part of a plea agreement, he entered an *Alford* plea to one count of second-degree assault with respect to one patient. All other charges were nolle prossed. Rudman was granted probation before judgment (PBJ), and placed on three year's supervised probation. The Court of Appeals held that the statutory provision denying him a contested case hearing did not apply. Although the *Alford* plea and the PBJ satisfied the guilty plea component, the Court held that second-degree assault was not a crime of moral turpitude.

It is beyond the scope of this book to discuss every statute that grants the right to a contested case hearing and every statute which limits such a right. It is important to understand that the statutes for each agency and for each type of proceeding must be carefully reviewed and analyzed if the issue of whether there is a statutory right to a hearing arises.

## §4.6. Due Process Right to a Hearing

A contested case hearing can also be required by constitutional due process. Even if no applicable statute or regulation requires one, a person may be entitled to a contested case hearing based on the person's right to due process. In general, there is a due process right to a contested case hearing if three things are true: (1) the agency decision will be based on disputed, material adjudicative (not legislative) facts; (2) the agency action will adversely impact the person's liberty or property interests; and (3) there is no emergency that requires the agency decision to be made without a hearing.

31. 182 Md. App. 80, 87, 957 A.2d 620, 624 (2008); Maryland Code Annotated, Family Law §5-706.1(b)(3).

32. 414 Md. 243, 994 A.2d 985 (2010).

The United States Supreme Court has analyzed the due process right to a hearing in various contexts. It is beyond the scope of this book to discuss these cases in any detail. A sampling of these cases illustrates the wide range of interests that implicate the due process right to a contested case hearing. For example, a due process right to a contested case hearing has been recognized when the state seeks to revoke a driver's license;[33] revoke parole;[34] suspend a student from public school;[35] terminate Social Security disability payments;[36] cut off of utility services by a public utility;[37] admit a person involuntarily to a mental institution;[38] and fire a public employee for cause.[39]

In Maryland, in the majority of cases, the right to a contested case hearing is based on a statute. But due process analysis has also been employed in determining whether a contested case hearing was required. One such case is *Reese v. Department of Health and Mental Hygiene.*[40] Reese was the guardian of Virginia Mossa who was mentally retarded. Reese sought to have Mossa admitted to a state residential center (SRC). The agency with the authority to make this decision, DHMH, denied the admission on the basis that Mossa's placement in a community based program was an appropriate, less restrictive setting. Reese then requested a hearing at OAH on this denial. DHMH responded that there was no right to a hearing at OAH on the denial of a request for admission to a SRC. The relevant statute provided for a hearing only if admission had been ordered and the person wanted to challenge his admission. At a hearing challenging an admission order to a SRC, the agency has the burden by clear and convincing evidence to prove that (1) the individual has mental retardation; (2) the individual needs residential services for the individual's adequate habilitation; and (3) there is no less restrictive setting in which the needed services can be provided that is available to the individual or will be available to the individual within a reasonable time after the hearing.[41] By statute, a person challenging admission to a SRC has the right to a contested case hearing on these three issues. The statute, however, does not provide for a hearing if the person is placed in a community based setting and is denied admission to a SRC. It should be noted that in most cases, a community based setting is preferable to a SRC, but as this case indicates, this is not always true.

Because no statute or regulation granted the right to a contested case hearing when a SRC admission was denied, Reese argued that there was a constitutional due process right to such a hearing. DHMH's response was that due process requires a hearing only when the state seeks to deprive an individual of a liberty or property interest, and Mossa had neither interest in admission to a SRC. The case made its way to the Court of Special Appeals which agreed with Reese's position. After discussing numerous authorities, the Court of Special Appeals wrote, "to prevail in an action alleging a denial of procedural due process, a plaintiff must demonstrate that he had a protected property interest, that he was deprived of that interest by the State, and that he was afforded less procedure than

33. *See* Bell v. Burson, 402 U.S. 535 (1971).
34. *See* Morrissey v. Brewer, 408 U.S. 471 (1972).
35. *See* Goss v. Lopez, 419 U.S. 565 (1975).
36. *See* Mathews v. Eldridge, 424 U.S. 319 (1976).
37. *See* Memphis Light, Gas & Water Div. v. Craft, 436 U.S. 1 (1978).
38. *See* Vitek v. Jones, 445 U.S. 480 (1980).
39. *See* Cleveland Bd. of Educ. v. Loudermill, 470 U.S. 532 (1985).
40. 177 Md. App. 102, 934 A.2d 1009 (2007).
41. 177 Md. App. 102, 141 n.20, 934 A.2d 1009, 1032 n.20 (2007); Maryland Code Annotated, Health-General § 7-503.

was due."[42] The court concluded that Mossa satisfied this test, and that she was entitled to a contested case hearing on the denial of her admission to a SRC.[43]

## § 4.7. Flexible Due Process

If it is determined that due process requires a contested case hearing, it must still be determined what procedures will satisfy due process. The basic procedures to satisfy due process include the right to adequate notice of the basis of the agency action, the right to counsel, the right to present evidence, the right to challenge opposing evidence, the right to an impartial decisionmaker, the right to have the decision based on the record created at the hearing, and the right to be given reasons for the decision. But not every contested case hearing required by due process needs to provide the identical procedural rights. The United States Supreme Court and Maryland courts have recognized that due process can be satisfied in different ways depending on the individual situation. This is known as "flexible due process."

The genesis of the concept of flexible due process is *Mathews v. Eldridge*,[44] a 1976 decision by the U.S. Supreme Court. *Mathews* involved the termination of social security disability benefits. The initial termination decision was made after the recipient received notice of the proposed termination and was given the opportunity to comment in writing. It was only after the actual termination of benefits that a trial-type contested case hearing was provided. If the recipient prevailed at this post-termination hearing, retroactive benefits would be paid from the date of initial termination. In deciding whether a post-termination hearing procedure satisfied due process, the Supreme Court developed a three-part balancing test that has become well established as the test for evaluating due process issues in the context of administrative procedures.

In *Mathews*, the Supreme Court stated that "due process is flexible and calls for such procedural protections as the particular situation demands."[45] Flexible due process analysis involves a cost-benefit test balancing three factors:

(1) The private interest that will be affected by the official action;

(2) The risk of an erroneous determination through the process accorded and the probable value of added procedural safeguards; and

(3) The public interest and administrative burdens, including costs, that the additional or substitute procedures would entail.[46]

The first factor involves a consideration of the importance of the right involved. Matters dealing with survival, for example, welfare payments, are considered more weighty than an interest such as a driver's license. The second factor involves an evaluation of whether

42. 177 Md. App. 102, 152, 934 A.2d 1009, 1038 (2007).

43. *See also* Towson University v. Conte, 384 Md. 68, 862 A.2d 941 (2004), where Judge Eldridge in dissent writing on an issue not essential to his dissent stated that "[a]n employee in the Executive Branch of the State Government, who can only be disciplined or terminated for cause, is, as a matter of constitutional due process, entitled to a hearing at which the employee is given the opportunity to refute the charge against him or present defenses."

44. 424 U.S. 319 (1976).

45. 424 U.S. 319, 334 (1976).

46. 424 U.S. 319, 335 (1976).

the agency's existing procedures are likely to lead to an accurate result to a reasonable degree. Perfect accuracy is not required. The third factor involves consideration of the cost, financially and administratively, to the agency if more procedures are required.

Maryland courts have relied upon *Mathews v. Eldridge* in deciding due process issues relating to procedures required by Maryland agencies. For example, in *Maryland Racing Commission v. Castrenze,*[47] one issue was whether the Due Process Clause of the Fourteenth Amendment to the U.S. Constitution or of Article 24 of the Maryland Declaration of Rights required that horse trainers be given notice and a contested case hearing prior to the effective date of a suspension when the suspension was based on a reciprocal proceeding from another state. Citing *Mathews*, the Court of Appeals wrote that "[d]ue process does not require adherence to any particular procedure. On the contrary, due process is flexible and calls only for such procedural protections as the particular situation demands."[48] The court then applied the *Mathews* balancing test. Although the "magnitude of the trainer's interest in being notified that the Maryland racing authorities intend to recognize an out-of-state suspension ... is substantial, [b]alanced against that interest ... is the State's own interest in ensuring the integrity of racing." The court concluded that "[b]y granting a hearing promptly after the reciprocal actions went into effect, and considering the limited scope of the issues at the hearing,[49] the Maryland Racing Commission gave [the suspended] trainers the process that was due."[50]

*Mathews v. Eldridge's* flexible due process analysis was also employed by the Court of Appeals in *Maryland Department of Human Resources v. Bo Peep Day Nursery*[51] which involved the revocation of a child care center's license. One issue was whether the agency's reliance on statements by children regarding abuse at the center when those children did not testify at the hearing and were not subject to cross examination violated the child care center's owner's due process rights. Relying on *Mathews*, the court held there was no due process violation in relying on the children's statements because (1) the revocation of a day care center license did not place any liberty interest at stake; (2) there had been two hearings on the issue of abuse; (3) the agency decision was based only partly on the children's testimony; (4) additional procedures would have only minimal value; (5) adult witnesses were subject to cross examination; and (6) the state had an interest in protecting the children from further anxiety.[52]

The Court of Appeals also applied flexible due process in *Motor Vehicle Administration v. Lytle.*[53] In *Lytle*, it was argued that the MVA's failure to take into account a 0.01 margin of error of the instrument used to test blood alcohol concentration violated due process. The Court of Appeals applied *Mathews v. Eldridge* in rejecting the due process claim. Requiring consideration of the margin of error would result in a burden on the state disproportionate to the benefit to the individual. The Court of Appeals also applied *Mathews*

47. 335 Md. 284, 643 A.2d 412 (1994).

48. 335 Md. 284, 292, 643 A.2d 412, 419 (1994).

49. The only relevant issues were whether the trainer was the same person who was the subject of the action in the other state, and whether the other state had jurisdiction.

50. 335 Md. 284, 300, 643 A.2d 412, 420 (1994). *See also* Md. Racing Comm'n v. Belotti, 130 Md. App. 23, 55–56, 744 A.2d 558, 576 (1999) (due process does not require a hearing at the initial stage or at any particular point or at more than one point in an administrative proceeding so long as the requisite hearing is held before the final order becomes effective).

51. 317 Md. 573, 565 A.2d 1015 (1989), *cert denied sub nom.* Cassilly v. Md. Dep't of Human Res., 494 U.S. 1067 (1990).

52. 317 Md. 573, 595–602, 565 A.2d 1015, 1025–1029 (1989).

53. 374 Md. 37, 821 A.2d 62 (2003).

*v. Eldridge* in *Coleman v. Anne Arundel County Police Department*[54] in reaching its conclusion that a county police department could terminate a police officer's employment based on the preponderance of the evidence standard. The court rejected the argument that due process required use of the clear and convincing standard.

## § 4.8. Summary Suspension

Due process analysis recognizes that in certain emergency type situations, an agency can act without providing a contested case hearing. An early case from the U.S. Supreme Court, *North American Cold Storage Co. v. Chicago*,[55] upheld the destruction of diseased poultry to protect the public health without any hearing. Additionally, mislabeled drugs have been seized,[56] and unsafe mines shut down without a hearing.[57] This principle is also recognized in Maryland. For example, a driver's license can be confiscated immediately by a police officer in certain situations involving drunk driving under Maryland's Implied Consent Law, § 16-205.1 of the Transportation Article.[58]

54. 369 Md. 108, 797 A.2d 770 (2002).
55. 211 U.S. 306 (1908).
56. *See* Ewing v. Mytinger & Casselberry, Inc., 339 U.S. 594 (1950).
57. *See* Hodel v. Va. Surface Mining & Reclamation Ass'n, 452 U.S. 264 (1981).
58. See Chapter 12.

# Chapter 5

# Contested Cases: General Procedural Matters

There are various general procedural principles that apply to contested cases. Of course, these procedural principles can be changed for a particular agency or for a particular type of contested case by statute or regulation. Whenever an attorney is representing a client or the agency, the attorney must thoroughly understand the specific statutes and regulations that apply to that individual case. This chapter will discuss procedural matters that are generally followed in contested cases based on the Maryland APA and common law principles of Administrative Law.

## § 5.1. Notice of Agency Action

The initial pleading in a contested case is the Notice of Agency Action ("Notice").[1] For agencies not covered by the APA, the particular agency's enabling statute or regulation will set forth the requirements for the Notice. For agencies covered by the APA, the requirements for the Notice are found in State Government § 10-207 of the Maryland Code. This statute provides that the Notice must include the facts or issues involved stated in a concise and simple manner; the pertinent statutory and regulatory sections under which the agency is acting; and the proposed or potential sanctions or penalty. Additionally, unless a hearing will be automatically scheduled, the Notice must inform the recipient of its right to request a hearing. The Notice must also disclose any relevant time requirements, and the consequences, sanctions or potential penalty if no request for a hearing is made or if the recipient fails to appear for the scheduled hearing.[2] Delivery by regular mail is sufficient, unless a statute provides for service other than by regular mail. Publication in the Maryland Register does not constitute reasonable notice to a party.[3]

The principal purpose of the Notice is to enable the recipient to prepare a suitable defense.[4] However, if the party has actual notice of the facts and charges prior to the hearing to allow a defense to be prepared, the failure of the agency to comply with the statutory requirements is not prejudicial, and the agency action will not be vacated. In *Brown v. Handgun Permit Review Board*,[5] an applicant for a handgun license received notice from the agency that the license had been denied due to his "propensity for instability"—one of the statutory grounds to deny a handgun license. Brown requested a

1. Maryland Code Annotated, State Government § 10-207.
2. Maryland Code Annotated, State Government § 10-207(b).
3. Maryland Code Annotated, State Government § 10-207(d).
4. Bragunier Masonry Contractors v. Maryland Commissioner of Labor & Industry, 111 Md. App. 698, 684 A.2d 6 (1996), *cert. denied*, 344 Md. 566, 688 A.2d 445 (1997).
5. 188 Md. App. 455, 982 A.2d 830 (2009), *cert. denied*, 412 Md. 495, 988 A.2d 1008 (2010).

hearing to challenge the denial of the license. Four months before the hearing, the Board informed Brown that the "real reason" for the license denial was not his propensity for instability, but his conviction of a "disqualifying crime," another statutory ground to deny a handgun license. The Court of Special Appeals held that because Brown had sufficient notice of the basis of the denial of his license application prior to the hearing, this "negate[d] any prejudice."[6] The license denial by the Board was affirmed by the court.

In *Carven v. State Retirement and Pension System of Maryland*,[7] a letter that contained the information required by State Government § 10-207(b) was held to constitute proper notice of the agency action so that the 180-day time limitation to request a hearing ran from the date of the letter.

## § 5.2. Notice of Hearing

The next step is the Notice of Hearing. The Notice of Hearing is generally sent by the agency that is holding the hearing—usually either OAH or the agency itself if it has not delegated any authority to OAH. An agency could, however, retain the power to send the Notice of Hearing even if the hearing authority has been delegated to OAH.

The Notice of Hearing must be sent in a timely fashion to give all parties "reasonable written notice of the hearing."[8] The APA requirements for the Notice of Hearing are set forth in State Government § 10-208(b) of the Maryland Code. The following must be included:

1. the date, time, place, and nature of the hearing;
2. the right to call witnesses and submit documents or other evidence;
3. any applicable right to request subpoenas for witnesses and evidence, and the cost, if any, associated with such a request;
4. that a copy of the hearing procedure is available on request, and any cost of such request;
5. any right or restriction pertaining to representation;
6. that failure to appear for the scheduled hearing may result in an adverse action against the party; and
7. that, unless otherwise prohibited by law, the parties may agree to the evidence, and waive their right to appear at the hearing.

The Notice of Hearing is sent by regular mail. Publication in the *Maryland Register* does not constitute reasonable notice to a party.[9]

## § 5.3. Representation: Maryland Attorneys

The practice of law is within the original, exclusive jurisdiction of the Court of Appeals. Administrative agencies, which are part of the Executive Branch, cannot grant the right

6. 188 Md. App. 455, 470, 982 A.2d 830, 839 (2009).
7. 416 Md. 389, 7 A.3d 38 (2010).
8. Maryland Code Annotated, State Government § 10-208(a).
9. Maryland Code Annotated, State Government § 10-208(d).

to practice law to an individual who is not authorized to practice law, interfere with the right of a lawyer to practice before an agency, or prohibit any party from being advised or represented at the party's own expense by an attorney, or if permitted by law, other representative.[10] Absent a special statute, there is no right to have the State provide an attorney to represent a person at an administrative contested case if the person cannot afford an attorney.

There are four categories of persons who may represent a party at an administrative contested case: (1) an attorney licensed to practice law in Maryland; (2) an attorney admitted in a state other than Maryland if the special rule for the admission of out-of-state attorneys is satisfied; (3) a non-attorney if permitted by a special statute; and (4) the party as a pro se litigant.

An attorney who is admitted to practice law in Maryland by the Court of Appeals can represent a party in a contested case before any agency. No special examination or knowledge is required. Attorneys should enter their appearance with the agency before or at the contested case hearing.[11] Once an appearance has been entered, the attorney of record must be copied on all notices, pleadings, and other correspondence.[12]

## § 5.4. Representation: Out-of-State Attorneys

An attorney admitted in a state other than Maryland cannot represent a party in a contested case unless specially admitted. In *Attorney Grievance Commission v. Brown*,[13] it was held to constitute the improper unauthorized practice of law for an attorney admitted only in Virginia to represent a client at a hearing at the Maryland Department of Economic and Employment Development. For an out-of-state attorney to represent a client at a Maryland agency contested case, the attorney must be specially admitted by satisfying Rule 14 of the Rules Governing Admission to the Bar of Maryland. In relevant part, Rule 14 requires an out-of-state attorney to file a motion in the circuit court for the county in which the principal office of the agency is located or in any other circuit to which the action can be "appealed."[14] The motion must include the moving attorney's signed certification that copies of the motion have been furnished to the agency and to all parties. In the motion, the out-of-state attorney must certify the number of times the attorney has been specially admitted during the twelve months immediately preceding the filing of the motion. This certification may be filed as a separate paper or included in the motion under a separate heading. The certification must include court cases and administrative contested cases. Although in Maryland, there is no set numerical limit on the number of times an out-of-state attorney can be specially admitted, the certification is aimed at prohibiting extensive or systematic practice by attorneys not licensed in Maryland. Rule 14 also requires that the out-of-state attorney who is specially admitted act only as co-counsel with a Maryland attorney. The Maryland attorney is required to accompany the specially admitted attorney at the administrative hearing unless the Maryland attorney's

10. Maryland Code Annotated, State Government § 10-206.1(a). *See also* Md. Code Regs. 28.02.01.08 (A)-(B), COMAR 28.02.01.08(A)-(B).

11. *See* OAH Rule 08D, Md. Code Regs. 28.02.01.08D, COMAR 28.02.01.08D.

12. *See* OAH Rule 08E, Md. Code Regs. 28.02.01.08E, COMAR 28.02.01.08E.

13. 353 Md. 271, 725 A.2d 1069 (1999).

14. As discussed in Chapter 13, the word "appealed" is improper. The Rule should read: "In a circuit court in which a petition for review can be filed."

presence is waived. It is unclear if an agency, including OAH, has the power to waive the presence of a Maryland attorney at the hearing. The prudent course is for the specially admitted attorney to ask the circuit judge to include in the Order granting special admission a waiver of the Maryland attorney's presence or a statement that the agency has the discretion to waive the presence of a Maryland attorney.

## § 5.5. Non-Attorney Representation

In certain situations, a party to a contested case can be represented by a non-attorney. First, there are provisions for non-attorney representation for certain business entities. For example, in a matter involving a motor vehicle liability insurance policy under a section of the Insurance Article, a corporation can designate an employee who is not a lawyer to represent it.[15] Additionally, a corporation or a partnership can designate a non-attorney employee, officer, or partner as its representative in certain matters before the Home Improvement Commission, the Occupational Health and Safety Commission, and in a proceeding to decertify a minority business enterprise.[16] The non-attorney designated as the representative for the business entity in these special situations must provide the agency with a power of attorney sworn by the employer that certifies that the designated employee is an authorized agent of the business entity on matters pending before the agency.[17]

The designated employee may not be a disbarred or suspended lawyer in any state.[18] Moreover, the business entity may not contract, hire, or employ another business entity, other than an attorney, to provide representation services.[19] An employee designated by a business entity in the home improvement, occupational safety and health, and minority business decertification cases may not be assigned on a full time basis to appear before an agency on behalf of the entity.[20] In addition to these designated non-attorney employees of business entities, insurers can also designate non-attorney employees as their representatives in certain Insurance Administration cases as long as the employee is employed by the insurer in claims or underwriting.[21] In addition to the exceptions just discussed, there are various special statutory provisions that permit individuals who are not attorneys to represent persons at certain agency proceedings. For example, non-attorney representation is permitted in cases involving certain entitlement programs funded by the federal government where benefits are based on income and resources.[22] As always, the existence of any statutes specific to the case must be researched and analyzed.

An interesting issue is whether an out-of-state attorney may represent a party at an administrative contested case hearing without being specially admitted under Rule 14 in those cases where non-attorney representation is permitted. Two situations should be considered. If the out-of-state attorney has undertaken representation for compensation

15. Maryland Code Annotated, Insurance § 27-605.
16. Maryland Code Annotated, State Government § 9-1607.1(a)(4).
17. Maryland Code Annotated, State Government § 9-1607.1(b).
18. Maryland Code Annotated, State Government § 9-1607.1(b)(1).
19. Maryland Code Annotated, State Government § 9-1607.1(b)(2).
20. Maryland Code Annotated, State Government § 9-1607.1(b)(3).
21. Maryland Code Annotated, State Government § 9-1607.1(a)(5).
22. *See* Maryland Code Annotated, State Government § 9-1607.1(a)(2).

in a case that does not require attorney representation, it is generally agreed that the out-of-state attorney must be specially admitted by a circuit court. On the other hand, in a case that does not require attorney representation, if the out-of-state attorney is a friend or relative of a party and will appear without compensation and is truly appearing as a "friend" or "relative," the out-of-state attorney might not be required by the agency to be specially admitted by a Maryland circuit court.

## § 5.6. Pro Se Representation

A party may also represent himself or herself.[23] Parties proceeding pro se are required to follow all the procedural rules in the same manner as those represented by counsel. In *Department of Labor, Licensing & Regulation v. Woodie*,[24] an applicant for unemployment compensation (Woodie) represented himself unsuccessfully at the agency. Woodie then hired an attorney who sought to offer new evidence to the circuit court after filing a Petition for Judicial Review. Woodie's attorney argued that his client did not present the proper evidence to the hearing examiner, because "he did not know how to go about doing it." The circuit court judge "sympathized" with the argument, saying that "a layman is always sort of at a disadvantage understanding the procedures and understanding the law."[25] The circuit court ordered a remand to the agency to allow the evidence to be presented. The Court of Special Appeals reversed. It held that the circuit court erred in giving Woodie a "second bite at the apple simply because he was not represented by counsel during the administrative hearings." The court reiterated the "well-established principle of Maryland law that pro se parties must adhere to procedural rules in the same manner as those represented by counsel."[26]

Although the above-stated "well-established principle" is true, it would not be entirely accurate to state that pro se litigants are never treated differently from parties represented by counsel. This can be illustrated by *Wisniewski v. Department of Labor, Licensing & Regulation*[27] where a pro se litigant at an unemployment insurance hearing who had been unsuccessful at the agency, argued to the court upon judicial review that the hearing examiner "had a duty to inquire about all the facts and circumstances surrounding the disputed events, but did not adequately inquire of the witnesses." Because there was no Maryland case directly on point regarding the precise scope of a hearing examiner's duty to develop the facts on behalf of a pro se party, cases from other jurisdictions were cited. A North Carolina case had held that a presiding officer at an administrative hearing had a duty to ask pro se claimants the right questions necessary to produce evidence relevant to the claim.[28] A Vermont case had held that a presiding officer owed the pro se claimant "every assistance in presenting his case consistent with the referee's duty to impartially decide the issues."[29] An Oregon case involving unemployment insurance had held that

23. Maryland Code Annotated, State Government § 9-1607.1(c); OAH Rule 08A, Md. Code Regs. 28.02.01.08A, COMAR 28.02.01.08A.
24. 128 Md. App. 398, 738 A.2d 334 (1999).
25. 128 Md. App. 398, 405, 738 A.2d 334, 338 (1999).
26. 128 Md. App. 398, 411, 738 A.2d 334, 341 (1999).
27. 117 Md. App. 506, 700 A.2d 860 (1997).
28. Johnson v. U.S. Textiles Corp., 414 S.E.2d 374 (N.C. Ct. App. 1992).
29. Langlois v. Dep't of Employment & Training, 546 A.2d 1365, 1367 (Vt. 1988).

the presiding officer "must seek out all the relevant facts."[30] The Court of Special Appeals in *Wisniewski* did not resolve the issue of the proper role of the presiding officer in such pro se cases. The court stated, "assuming, *arguendo*, that the Hearing Examiner had an affirmative duty to query the parties in order to elicit all possible relevant evidence, we are satisfied ... that the Hearing Examiner fulfilled that duty, so that the parties were offered a fair hearing."[31]

In *Wisniewski*, the court stated in a footnote that "[o]ur comments with respect to the issue of the Hearing Examiner's duty are limited to hearings in regard to unemployment insurance benefits. Our comments should not be construed to apply to hearings conducted by the Office of Administrative Hearings." I do not agree the treatment of pro se litigants should be different for contested cases involving unemployment insurance and contested cases involving other areas of administrative law held at OAH or any other agency.

OAH has a regulation which provides that the ALJ shall "examine witnesses and call witnesses as necessary to insure a full and complete record."[32] A presiding officer at OAH or any agency is interested in creating a full record in order to make the proper decision. The ALJ or other presiding official may at times "assist" the pro se litigant in order to create a proper record. The extent to which the ALJ involves himself/herself will vary based on the type of case involved and the sophistication of the pro se litigant, but it seems clear that the ALJ or presiding officer will not let a pro se litigant be totally disadvantaged. Of course, this does not mean that a competent attorney may not make a difference.[33]

## § 5.7. Agency Subpoenas

Although it is generally recognized that courts and legislatures have inherent power to compel appearance of witnesses and production of documents, administrative agencies in Maryland have the power to subpoena only if there is an express statutory grant of the subpoena power by the legislature to the agency.[34] Most Maryland agencies, including OAH, have been delegated such power. In ruling on whether an agency subpoena should be enforced, Maryland courts have applied the three part test established by the U.S. Supreme Court in *Oklahoma Press Publishing Co. v. Walling*.[35] Under this analysis, the court will consider whether (1) the inquiry is authorized by statute; (2) the information sought is relevant to the inquiry; and (3) the demand is not too indefinite or overbroad.

*Miller v. Baltimore County Police Department*[36] involved a subpoena for cell phone records of a police officer accused of "fraternizing" with a female in a car while the officer was on duty. The subpoena was issued to Verizon Wireless during the initial internal investigation. After Verizon complied with the subpoena and produced the officer's cell phone records, the officer filed a complaint in circuit court alleging that the Police

30. Dennis v. Employment Div., 728 P.2d 12, 16 (Or. 1986).

31. 117 Md. App. 506, 522, 700 A.2d 860,868 (1997).

32. OAH Rule 11B(5), Md. Code Regs. 28.02.01.11B(5), COMAR 28.02.01.11B(5).

33. *See* Wisniewski v. Dep't of Labor, Licensing & Regulation, 117 Md. App. 506, 524, 700 A.2d 860, 869 (1997) ("To be sure, if appellant had been represented by counsel at the hearing, who could have gathered evidence and better presented appellant's case, the outcome may have been different.").

34. *See* Miller v. Baltimore County Police Dep't, 179 Md. App. 370, 946 A.2d 1, *cert. denied*, 405 Md. 349, 952 A.2d 225 (2008).

35. 327 U.S. 186 (1946).

36. 179 Md. App. 370, 946 A.2d 1, *cert. denied*, 405 Md. 349, 952 A.2d 225 (2008).

Department had violated his rights under the Law Enforcement Officer Bill of Rights (LEOBR) because the Department did not have the statutory authority to issue subpoenas during its internal investigation. The officer requested that any information obtained in response to the subpoena request be stricken. Pending resolution of the subpoena issue, the administrative proceedings were stayed, and no contested case hearing was held. The Court of Special Appeals agreed with the police officer that the governing statute, the LEOBR, did not grant subpoena power to the agency for purposes of a pre-charge investigation. The statutory subpoena powers under the LEOBR only exist after a disciplinary violation charge has been filed. Because the inquiry was not authorized by statute, the subpoena was not valid.

*Lubin v. Agora, Inc.*[37] involved an investigation by the Maryland Securities Commissioner of a company that published books and newsletters on several topics involving investments. The investigation followed an offer by the publisher to disclose the name of a corporation about which the publisher claimed it had inside information. The publisher agreed to disclose the corporation's name for a fee of $1,000. The Commissioner was investigating whether the publisher had violated several provisions of Maryland securities law. Two subpoenas duces tecum were served on the publisher seeking the subscriber lists and other documents containing information identifying the publisher's subscribers. The Commissioner argued that the subpoena was valid because the Commissioner's inquiry was authorized by statute; the information sought was relevant to its inquiry; and the request was not too indefinite or overbroad. The publisher's response was that the subpoena infringed upon its constitutional right of speech under the United States Constitution and Maryland Declaration of Rights, and thus could only be enforced if there was a compelling need for the information and there was no other available means of obtaining such information. The Court of Appeals agreed with the publisher. The argument presented by the Commissioner that the subscriber list "would be useful" fell short of establishing a compelling need. Enforcement of the subpoena was denied.

*Doe v. Maryland Board of Social Work Examiners*[38] involved a subpoena duces tecum served on a licensed social worker for the treatment records of two of her clients as part of an investigation by the Board of the social worker for her alleged failure to report suspected child abuse. The social worker moved to quash the subpoena based on the statutory social worker-client privilege and her client's right to privacy. The Court of Appeals upheld the subpoena. The court held that "where the Legislature has specifically provided a health agency such as the Board with the power to issue subpoenas for the purposes of investigating allegations that one of its licensees committed serious violations of her professional duties, the social worker-client privilege ... must yield to such an investigation." The court also held that the "interest of the public in having the conduct of a licensed social worker, accused of having violated her statutory duties, thoroughly investigated and, if appropriate, properly disciplined, outweighs the individual privacy interests."[39]

In *Solomon v. State Board of Physician Quality Assurance*,[40] a doctor (Solomon) refused to comply with a subpoena duces tecum for the medical records of nineteen of her patients. There were three reasons for Solomon's refusal to turn over the patient records—she was

37. 389 Md. 1, 882 A.2d 833 (2005).

38. 384 Md. 161, 862 A.2d 996 (2004).

39. 384 Md. 161, 168, 862 A.2d 996, 1000 (2004). *See also* Dr. K. v. State Bd. of Physician Quality Assurance, 98 Md. App. 103, 632 A.2d 453 (1993), *cert. denied*, 334 Md. 18, 637 A.2d 1191, *cert. denied*, 513 U.S. 817 (1994).

40. 155 Md. App. 687, 845 A.2d 47 (2003).

not under investigation by the Board for misconduct; the subpoena was overbroad; and compliance with the subpoena would violate her patients' right of privacy. The Court of Special Appeals rejected each argument. The fact that the Board had closed the case on a previous complaint filed against Solomon by a patient did not terminate the Board's authority to perform a follow-up investigation. Nor was the subpoena overbroad. Review of the requested records would "undoubtedly yield information regarding the quality of medical care Dr. Solomon provided," and elicit information about her coding and billing practices. The privacy argument was rejected because "a patient's constitutional right to privacy in her medical records is outweighed by the State's compelling interest in obtaining those records for the purpose of investigating possible disciplinary action against a physician."

## § 5.8. Refusal to Issue a Subpoena

If the agency refuses to issue a subpoena upon proper request, the agency must explain the basis of its refusal. This is based on two cases involving the Motor Vehicle Administration. In *Forman v. Motor Vehicle Administration*,[41] the court wrote that when the agency is requested to issue a subpoena, it has three options: (1) accept the proponent's proffer and issue the subpoena; (2) reach no conclusion regarding the truth of the proffer, but issue the subpoena anyway; or (3) reject the proffer and subpoena request, and provide an explanation for the rejection. This third option is to dispose of frivolous or otherwise improper subpoena requests. The court emphasized that the agency may deny a subpoena request only if a reason is given for the rejection.

*Forman* was applied in *Fowler v. Motor Vehicle Administration*[42] where the ALJ had denied a request to subpoena a police officer who had signed a written certification that Fowler had been advised that if he refused to take a chemical breath test, his license would be suspended. Fowler sought to subpoena the officer to support Fowler's position that he had not been fully advised of the consequences of refusing to take the test. After Fowler's proffer of why the subpoena for the officer should be granted, the ALJ denied the subpoena stating that "the licensee was fully advised.... I don't see the need to call the officer to cross-examine him.... I don't see the need to call the officer to clarify anything." The Court of Appeals ruled that the ALJ had acted improperly because "the ALJ did not state clearly his decision or enunciate fully his rationale."[43]

## § 5.9. Enforcement of Subpoenas

If the agency issues the subpoena, but it is ignored, the agency cannot hold the person served with the subpoena in contempt. Under the separation of powers doctrine, the power of contempt belongs exclusively with the judicial branch. Therefore, if the agency wants to enforce its subpoena, the agency must go to circuit court to have the court order

41. 332 Md. 201, 630 A.2d 753 (1993).
42. 394 Md. 331, 906 A.2d 347 (2006).
43. 394 Md. 331, 348, 906 A.2d 347, 357 (2006).

compliance with the subpoena.[44] The agency, however, is not under a mandatory obligation to seek enforcement in circuit court of every subpoena that it has issued but which has been ignored. It is within the agency's discretion whether to seek enforcement of its subpoena in circuit court. This point is illustrated in *Board of License Commissioners for Prince George's County v. Global Express Money Orders, Inc.*[45]

In *Global Express*, a liquor licensee in a license renewal proceeding requested the issuance of subpoenas for three persons it intended to call to testify. Although the subpoenas were issued for all three, none testified. One refused to appear at the hearing. The second appeared at the hearing, but left after a brief stay without testifying. The third also appeared, but refused to testify, stating that as a member of the police department, it would violate police department policy for him to testify. Counsel for the licensee requested the Board to seek an order from the circuit court ordering all three witnesses to testify. The Board refused to pursue the matter in circuit court. Although the relevant statute read: "If any witness summoned refuses or neglects to attend, or if attending, refuses to testify, the official issuing the summons shall report the facts to the circuit court," the Court of Special Appeals held that the statute "does not automatically require a board to report to circuit court a failure of a witness to testify, but a board is empowered to do so." The Court of Special Appeals interpreted "shall" in the statute to be directory, not mandatory. The court then ruled that the Board's decision not to seek enforcement of its subpoenas from the circuit court was "not arbitrary or capricious" for several reasons: The board explained its actions; the request to issue the subpoena came one day before the hearing without an acceptable explanation why it has not been made earlier; there was no proffer that the witnesses had been properly served; there was no proffer of the expected testimony; and there was considerable contrary evidence.

*Maryland State Board of Physicians v. Eist*[46] involved the discipline of a psychiatrist for failing to cooperate with an investigation of the Board. The Board had received a complaint from the estranged husband of a patient of Dr. Eist alleging that Eist had overmedicated his wife and sons. In response to this complaint, the Board issued a subpoena duces tecum for the medical records of the wife and sons. Eist responded that he would not release the records without the consent of his patients. Neither the wife nor the sons consented. Although the records were eventually provided to the Board, the Board disciplined Eist for failure to cooperate. Interestingly, review of the medical records led to the Board's decision not to charge Eist with any disciplinary violations based on the allegations in the original estranged husband's complaint. A hearing was held at OAH on the Board's charge of failure to cooperate. The ALJ's recommended decision was in favor of Eist. The ALJ indicated that the Board had the obligation to seek judicial enforcement of the subpoenas in order to sustain the failure to cooperate charge. The Board rejected the ALJ's recommended decision, and issued a final order reprimanding Eist and imposing a $5,000 fine. Both the circuit court and the Court of Special Appeals held that the Board's order was improper. The Court of Appeals, however, upheld the Board's sanction. The Court of Appeals held that it was Eist's obligation to file in court a motion to quash or a motion for a protective order. Moreover, a health care provider is required to provide medical records to the Board regardless of patient authorization. Three judges dissented on the ground that because Eist had relied upon advice of counsel in not providing the medical records, he could not be disciplined for failing to cooperate with a Board investigation.

44. *See* OAH Rule 14F, Md. Code Regs. 28.02.01.14F, COMAR 28.02.01.14F.
45. 168 Md. App. 339, 896 A.2d 432 (2006).
46. 417 Md. 545, 11 A.3d 786 (2011).

## § 5.10. Discovery

In general, discovery does not play as large a role in administrative contested case litigation as it does in civil cases in circuit court. There is no provision in the Maryland APA on discovery. Individual agency regulations, however, often provide for some discovery, although discovery tends to be limited. Individual agency regulations should be consulted when representing a client in an upcoming contested case. OAH has its own discovery rules, discussed in Chapter 10, which OAH applies to supplement any discovery regulation of an agency that has delegated its hearing authority to OAH. OAH discovery rules are discussed in Chapter 10.

In *Salerian v. Maryland State Board of Physicians*,[47] a disciplinary case against a psychiatrist accused of improperly divulging confidential information, the psychiatrist sought to take a deposition of the person whose confidential information was allegedly disclosed. This request was denied, and the Court of Special Appeals found no error in this denial. The Board of Physicians does have its own discovery regulation, COMAR 10.32.02.03(E), but this regulation only permits limited discovery of witness lists and statements of expert opinions, not depositions.

In *Hammen v. Baltimore County Police Department*,[48] a police officer filed a request under the Maryland Public Information Act (MPIA) to gain access to a videotape in the police department's custody. The officer wanted to use the tape at an administrative hearing in support of his claim for disability retirement benefits. Although the actual controversy had become moot by the time the Court of Appeals decided this case, the court did write that a "party to an administrative proceeding might, pursuant to a proper MPIA request, be able to access information not normally available to that party under the prevailing administrative [discovery] rules or if that party were a party to a court action and making such a request subject to the discovery rules."[49]

## § 5.11. Statute of Limitations

The general rule is that statutes of limitations do not apply to administrative hearings. A motion seeking dismissal of a contested case based on Maryland's statutes of limitation will be unsuccessful. For example, Maryland Code Annotated, Courts & Judicial Proceedings § 5-107 provides that a "prosecution or suit for a fine, penalty or forfeiture shall be instituted within one year after the offense was committed." In *Nelson v. Real Estate Commission*,[50] a real estate broker sought to avoid suspension of his broker's license based on the fact that his alleged misconduct had occurred more than one year before the administrative complaint was filed. The Court of Special Appeals rejected the broker's argument because a hearing before an administrative agency is not a "prosecution" or "suit" within the meaning of the statute of limitations. Likewise, in *Maryland Securities Commissioner v. U.S. Securities Corporation*,[51] a registered securities broker-dealer challenged a fine based

47. 176 Md. App. 231, 932 A.2d 1225 (2007).
48. 373 Md. 440, 818 A.2d 1125 (2003).
49. 373 Md. 440, 457, 818 A.2d 1125, 1135 (2003).
50. 35 Md. App. 334, 370 A.2d 608, *cert. denied*, 280 Md. 733 (1977).
51. 122 Md. App. 574, 716 A.2d 290 (1998).

on conduct that occurred over one year before the administrative proceeding was initiated. The Court of Special Appeals, relying on *Nelson*, held that proceedings before the Securities Commission were neither prosecutions nor suits under the statute of limitations.

## § 5.12. Intervention

In some cases, a person or organization may want to intervene and become a party to the contested case. The Maryland APA has no provision for intervention. Agencies, however, may have their own regulations that provide for intervention. For example, regulations governing intervention at the Department of Health and Mental Hygiene can be found at COMAR 10.01.03.24. OAH has a regulation permitting intervention, which is discussed in Chapter 10. In general, to be granted intervention, a person must demonstrate an interest relating to the contested case which is not adequately represented by the existing parties.[52] Intervention may be denied if it would cause delay.[53] It seems that case law involving intervention in civil cases in circuit court would be useful in analyzing intervention requests in contested cases at agencies.

## § 5.13. Open Hearings

The APA provision on open hearings applies only to hearings at OAH. State Government § 10-212(a) of the Maryland Code provides that except as otherwise provided by law, a contested case hearing conducted at OAH shall be open to the public. There are several laws that provide for closed hearings or partially closed hearings at OAH. Other statutes and regulations of individual agencies must be evaluated to determine whether the contested case hearings at these agencies are open to the public.

*Venter v. Board of Education of Howard County*[54] discussed whether a party can waive his right to a closed hearing and request the presiding official to open the hearing to the public. *Venter* involved the termination of the chief business officer of the Howard County public school system. Venter wanted the hearing on his termination to be open to the public. The Board took the position that this was a "closed personnel matter." The Board argued that because it had no subpoena power, it relied on the voluntary agreement of witnesses to testify. The Board argued that a closed hearing was necessary because testimony often reveals private matters, and cross-examination can impugn or question the reputation of witnesses. Venter's response was that he had a "common law right to an open judicial proceeding," and that if he wanted to waive his right to confidentiality, the hearing must be open. The Court of Special Appeals held that the common law right to an open, public hearing applied only to criminal cases, not administrative hearings. The court cited an Opinion of the Attorney General which stated:

> if the employee waives confidentiality and requests an open hearing, the County Board should consider whether any other interests would justify a closed hearing. If it identifies such an interest relating to its own processes or other individuals, ...

52. *See* OAH Rule 15A(2), Md. Code Regs. 28.02.01.15A(2), COMAR 28.02.01.15A(2).
53. *See* OAH Rule 15C(1), Md. Code Regs. 28.02.01.15C(1), COMAR 28.02.01.15C(1).
54. 185 Md. App. 648, 972 A.2d 328, *cert. denied*, 410 Md. 561, 979 A.2d 709 (2009).

> it may close the hearing. If it can identify none, it should open the hearing to avoid a later claim of error.[55]

Based on these standards, the Board's decision to close the hearing to the public was upheld.

## § 5.14. Ashbacker Doctrine/Comparative Hearings

In 1945, the U.S. Supreme Court decided *Ashbacker Radio Corporation v. Federal Communications Commission*[56] in which the Court held that when two or more persons apply for a license from the government, and the license applications are mutually exclusive in that only one license can be granted, the agency must hold one comparative hearing where each applicant participates and argues why it deserves the license. The concept of a comparative hearing for mutually exclusive licenses has become known as the *Ashbacker* doctrine.

The *Ashbacker* doctrine is widely accepted among the states, including Maryland. For example, *Carriage Hill-Cabin John, Inc. v. Maryland Health Resources Planning Commission*[57] involved applications for a certificate of need for new nursing home beds. Because cumulatively the several applicants were seeking to develop more nursing home beds than were projected as needed by the State Health Plan, the Commission was required to conduct a comparative review of the competing applications "to determine not simply whether a particular applicant satisfied the basic criteria for a CON [certificate of need], but which of the applicants best satisfied the criteria." Similarly, a comparative hearing was held in *Adventist Health Care, Inc. v. Maryland Health Care Commission*[58] where the Commission was deciding whether to grant approval of an open heart surgery center.

## § 5.15. Mental Competency

In *Coleman v. Anne Arundel County Police Department*,[59] the issue of a police officer's mental competency at an administrative disciplinary hearing was raised. In its discussion of this issue, the Court of Special Appeals equated competency to defend oneself at an administrative hearing with competency to stand trial in a criminal case, i.e., the ability to consult with counsel and the ability to understand the proceedings.[60] A word of warning is needed here. *Coleman* should not be read to require that parties to administrative hearings be competent to stand trial at a criminal trial. Clearly, persons who are not competent to stand trial are subject to administrative orders. Mental incompetency is not a defense to an administrative charge. For example, many persons who are involuntarily

55. 185 Md. App. 648, 683, 972 A.2d 328, 348 (2009).
56. 326 U.S. 327 (1945).
57. 125 Md. App. 183, 724 A.2d 745 (1999).
58. 392 Md. 103, 896 A.2d 320 (2006).
59. 136 Md. App. 419, 766 A.2d 169 (2001), *aff'd*, 369 Md. 108, 797 A.2d 770 (2002).
60. 136 Md. App. 419, 436, 766 A.2d 169, 178 (2001).

admitted to a psychiatric hospital by administrative order are incompetent to stand trial in a criminal case. The Court of Appeals in its opinion in *Coleman* made no mention of the competency issue.

## §5.16. Right to Jury Trial

There is no right to a trial by jury in an administrative contested case proceeding. This issue has been discussed in several cases. *Maryland Aggregates Association v. Maryland*[61] involved a statutory compensation scheme for property owners whose land was damaged by surface mining. Under the statute, compensation was determined by the Department of Natural Resources. An association that represented the interests of the surface mining industry argued that because actions for damages to land have historically been actions at law with a right to a jury trial under Article 23 of the Maryland Declaration of Rights, the administrative compensation scheme violated the right to trial by jury. The Court of Appeals rejected this argument, and wrote that where the:

> General Assembly has provided that a matter shall not be resolved in a judicial proceeding, by legislatively abrogating or modifying a cause of action, no question concerning the right of a jury trial arises. Since, under such circumstances, the matter shall not be resolved in a judicial proceeding, the question as to whether a judge or jury shall resolve the matter simply does not arise.[62]

Further, the court held that the right to a jury trial was "inapplicable where the legislature has committed to an administrative agency the initial decisionmaking function with respect to a particular class of disputes."

*Consumer Protection Division v. Morgan*[63] involved the alleged unfair and deceptive trade practices by a property investor, a mortgage lender, and two real estate appraisers. One argument raised by Morgan was that the "administrative adjudication violated his state and federal constitutional right to a jury trial under Article 23 of the Maryland Declaration of Rights and the Seventh Amendment to the United States Constitution." Morgan conceded that "were the [CPD] seeking a pure restitution remedy, then a jury trial would be less likely," but since the CPD "seeks monetary damages," this triggered his right to a jury trial. Citing *Maryland Aggregates*, the Court of Appeals rejected this argument, reiterating its position that there is no right to a jury trial when the legislature has committed the initial decisionmaking to an administrative agency. Moreover, the right to a jury trial does not apply to statutory administrative actions unknown at common law.

*Bergmann v. Board of Regents of the University System of Maryland*[64] involved the administrative agency's determination of whether a student attending a state university was domiciled in Maryland so that the student qualified for in-state resident tuition. The Court of Special Appeals rejected the claim that the student was entitled to a jury trial on this issue.

---

61. 337 Md. 658, 655 A.2d 886, *cert. denied sub nom.*, Genstar Stone Prods. Co. v. Maryland, 514 U.S. 1111 (1995).
62. 337 Md. 658, 680, 655 A.2d 886, 897 (1995).
63. 387 Md. 125, 874 A.2d 919 (2005).
64. 167 Md. App. 237, 892 A.2d 604 (2006).

# § 5.17. Interpreters

Under the Maryland APA, in any contested case, a party or witness may request the appointment of a qualified interpreter to assist that person if the party or witness is deaf or because of a hearing impediment cannot readily understand or communicate the spoken English language.[65] In such a circumstance, the agency "shall appoint a qualified interpreter." An interpreter appointed under this statute is entitled to reasonable compensation paid by the agency. If the agency has the authority to tax for services and expenses as a part of the cost of a case, the agency may tax the amount paid to an interpreter in accordance with the federal Americans with Disabilities Act.

This APA provision for an interpreter only applies to those who need an interpreter because of a hearing defect. It does not cover persons who need the assistance of an interpreter because they do not speak or understand English. Individual agencies often have regulations providing for interpreters of languages other than English. For example, the Department of Labor, Licensing and Regulation[66] and the Department of Mental Health and Hygiene[67] have regulations for a witness that cannot readily understand or communicate the English language. The OAH regulations for interpreters are discussed in Chapter 10.

# § 5.18. Electronic Hearings

The Maryland APA authorizes contested case hearings by telephone, video conferencing or other electronic means.[68] A party may object "for good cause" to the agency decision to hold an electronic hearing.[69] There are no cases discussing what constitutes good cause in this context. A general objection based on the desire to have all participants together at the same location in person in order to permit "better" confrontation of adverse witnesses or to permit "better" evaluation of witness credibility have usually been unsuccessful. My view is that agencies should be more sensitive to claims of inability to effectively cross-examine a witness at an electronic hearing, especially a hearing held by telephone. OAH has its own regulations dealing with electronic hearings which are discussed in Chapter 10. Electronic hearings at other agencies may also be governed by regulations adopted by that agency.

An interesting case that involved telephone testimony is *Salerian v. Maryland State Board of Physicians*.[70] Salerian was a psychiatrist licensed in Maryland who had been hired by a criminal defense lawyer to evaluate the lawyer's client who was a defendant in a federal criminal espionage case. It was alleged that Salerian improperly disclosed confidential information he had learned during his forensic psychiatric evaluation of the criminal defendant—referred to as the "Evaluee" in the court's opinion. The Board of Physicians ordered that Salerian be placed on probation for engaging in "unprofessional conduct in the practice of medicine." One issue presented on judicial review was the ALJ's and Board's

65. Maryland Code Annotated, State Government § 10-212.1.
66. Md. Code Regs. 09.01.02.15, COMAR 09.01.02.15.
67. Md. Code Regs. 10.01.03.19, COMAR 10.01.03.19.
68. Maryland Code Annotated, State Government § 10-211(a).
69. Maryland Code Annotated, State Government § 10-211(b)(1).
70. 176 Md. App. 231, 932 A.2d 1225 (2007).

reliance on telephone testimony of the Evaluee at the administrative hearing. At the time of the administrative hearing at OAH, the Evaluee was in federal prison in Colorado. Because of security restrictions, the telephone testimony could be sustained only for fifteen minutes at a time, at which point the connection was dropped and had to be reconnected. Also, because of technical problems, there were times when Evaluee could not be heard clearly. Salerian argued that the telephone testimony was "so fraught with problems" that it denied him a fair hearing. Initially, the ALJ had ruled that she would not consider the telephone testimony because she did have "the confidence that the record would be clear and complete." But upon reconsideration, she reversed herself because after reviewing her notes and the transcript of the testimony, she concluded that there had been "every fair opportunity to request that the Evaluee repeat his responses to the satisfaction" of Salerian's counsel. The Court of Special Appeals held that the ALJ acted "quite properly" when she held that "she would consider the telephonic testimony."[71]

## § 5.19. Substitution of Presiding Officer and the Institutional Decision

Another issue involves the situation where an ALJ or an agency head who has participated in the contested case hearing is not available to complete the hearing or to render a decision. This may be the result of illness, retirement, or resignation. The cases indicate that there is no need for the entire contested case to begin anew.

In *Citizens for Rewastico Creek v. Commissioners of Hebron*,[72] a citizens' group requested an adjudicatory hearing to challenge a sewage discharge permit. The Department of Health and Mental Hygiene (DHMH) appointed William Jensen as the hearing examiner.[73] A five-day hearing was held during which extensive evidence was presented. After the hearing, but before any decision was rendered, Jensen resigned. The citizens' group requested a totally new hearing before a new hearing examiner. This request was denied, but DHMH did order a substitute hearing examiner to personally hear the testimony of specific witnesses whose credibility was at issue. Both sides proposed which witnesses should testify before the substitute hearing examiner. After the substitute hearing examiner was appointed, she decided not to personally hear any witnesses. The substitute hearing examiner, based on her reading of the record, issued proposed findings of fact and conclusions of law, and a recommendation. Upon judicial review, the citizens' group argued that the refusal to hold a *de novo* hearing for all the witnesses, and the decision by the substitute hearing examiner to not hear any witnesses denied the group its right to a "live adjudicatory hearing." The Court of Special Appeals held that it was not error to deny a *de novo* hearing. It cited federal cases for the proposition that a *de novo* hearing before a substitute hearing examiner was required only if credibility evaluations based on hearing and seeing the witnesses testify were necessary.[74] In this case, the credibility of the witnesses was not a material factor. The "fact that there is conflicting testimony does

71. 176 Md. App. 231, 256, 932 A.2d 1225, 1240 (2007).

72. 67 Md. App. 466, 508 A.2d 493, *cert. denied*, 307 Md. 260, 513 A.2d 314 (1986).

73. This case was before the creation of OAH.

74. The court listed the elements of credibility: the behavior of the witness upon the stand; the manner of testifying; the reasonableness and probability of the testimony; the opportunity the witness had to see, hear, and know the things about which the witness is testifying; the witness's memory, candor, intelligence, interest, bias; any relationship of the witness to the case; and the extent to which

not automatically require a determination of credibility."[75] Although under current law, DHMH could not hire its own hearing examiner, the reasoning of *Citizens for Rewastico Creek* would still apply to non-APA agencies which are not required to either use OAH or have the agency heads preside at their hearings. OAH has its own regulation on the substitution of an ALJ which is discussed in Chapter 10.

The substitution of one presiding officer by another before the conclusion of the hearing, or the substitution of one agency head by another after the beginning of the hearing but before the final decision, involves what is known in Administrative Law as the "institutional decision." Administrative agency decisions are made by an institution —the agency—not by persons. It is said that "OAH decided," not that "ALJ Roberts decided." It is said that the "Board of Pharmacy" decided, not that "Board Members Smith and Jones" decided. Change of persons that work for the agency, therefore, is not seen as significant. An illustrative case is *People's Counsel for Baltimore County v. Country Ridge Shopping Center, Inc.*[76] In this case, there was a change in membership of two members of a three member board between the time of the Board's initial decision and its subsequent decision following a court order vacating and remanding the initial decision. The Court of Special Appeals "conceptualized" the board as an "ongoing governmental entity.... with an institutional life that transcends the tenure of any of its members."[77] The court rejected the argument that a *de novo* hearing was required before the new members, even if there was a need to resolve on remand the credibility of witnesses.

## § 5.20. Decisionmaking In Cases Not Delegated by APA Agencies to OAH

The Maryland APA in State Government § 10-216 sets forth some rules for agencies governed by the APA which have not delegated their cases to OAH. This APA provision recognizes that some agency decisions are made by one person, and some agency decisions are made by more than one person, i.e., the entire board or commission.

If no part of the case has been delegated to OAH, and the final decisionmaker is a single individual who has not personally presided at the contested case hearing, the final decision may not be made until each party is given notice of the proposed decision, given the opportunity to file exceptions with the agency to the proposed decision, and given an opportunity to present argument to the final decisionmaker on whether the proposed decision should be affirmed, reversed or remanded.[78] If no part of the case has been delegated to OAH, and the final agency decision is to be made by more than one person, i.e., a multi-member board or commission, if a majority of the board members or commissioners did not personally preside at the contested case hearing, a final decision cannot be made until each party has been given notice of the proposed decision, the opportunity to file exceptions to the proposed decision, and the opportunity to present argument to a majority of the officials who are to make the final decision.[79]

---

the witness is supported or contradicted by other evidence. 67 Md. App. 466, 482, 508 A.2d 493, 501 (1986).

75. 67 Md. App. 466, 484, 508 A.2d 493, 502 (1986).
76. 144 Md. App. 580, 799 A.2d 425 (2002).
77. 144 Md. App. 580, 603, 799 A.2d 425, 438 (2002).
78. Maryland Code Annotated, State Government § 10-216(a)(1).
79. Maryland Code Annotated, State Government § 10-216(a)(2).

When exceptions have been filed or arguments presented, the official or officials who are to make the final decision must personally consider each part of the record that a party cites in its exceptions or argument.[80] If the final decision differs from the proposed decision, any changes, modifications or amendments must be identified along with an explanation of the reasons for the changes.[81] The final decision and order in a contested case can be either stated on the record or in writing.[82] A statement of appeal rights must be included with the decision.[83] A copy of the final decision or order must be delivered or mailed to each party or each party's attorney of record.[84] The decisionmaking process when OAH has been delegated the authority to make a proposed or final decision is discussed in Chapter 11.

## § 5.21. Reconsideration

After the agency has made its final decision, a Motion for Reconsideration may be appropriate. A request for reconsideration usually does not stay the decision, and does not toll the time for filing a petition for judicial review. Additionally, the ruling on reconsideration is interlocutory in nature and not directly appealable.

In *Calvert County Planning Commission v. Howlin Realty Management, Inc.*,[85] it was argued that a county planning commission had no authority to reconsider its approval of a subdivision plan because no statute or regulation authorized reconsideration by the commission of its earlier decisions. The Court of Appeals rejected this argument. It held that it was

> clear that a statute (or rule) expressly permitting a reconsideration or setting the standard for reconsideration is not necessary.... An Agency ... may reconsider an action previously taken and come to a different conclusion upon a showing that the original action was the product of fraud, surprise, mistake, or inadvertence, or that some new or different factual situation exists that justifies the different conclusion.[86]

*Cinque v. Montgomery County Planning Board*[87] involved the Planning Board's reconsideration of a subdivision request which had been originally denied, but approved on reconsideration. The Court of Special Appeals first noted that "Maryland, along with the federal courts and the majority of state courts that have addressed the issue, recognizes the inherent authority of agencies to reconsider their own quasi-judicial decisions" regardless of whether a statute or regulation expressly authorizes reconsideration. An agency cannot reconsider its decision, however, based on a "mere change of mind."[88] Proper grounds for reconsideration are fraud, surprise, mistake or inadvertence. *Cinque* explained that the reconsideration in *Howlin* had been proper because the commission in *Howlin* had been misled into a mistaken belief that all existing property owners in the

80. Maryland Code Annotated, State Government § 10-216(a)(3).
81. Maryland Code Annotated, State Government § 10-216(b).
82. Maryland Code Annotated, State Government § 10-221(a).
83. Maryland Code Annotated, State Government § 10-221(b)(2).
84. Maryland Code Annotated, State Government § 10-221(c).
85. 364 Md. 301, 772 A.2d 1209 (2001).
86. 364 Md. 301, 325, 772 A.2d 1209, 1223 (2001).
87. 173 Md. App. 349, 918 A.2d 1254 (2007).
88. 173 Md. App. 349, 361, 918 A.2d 1254, 1261–62 (2007).

subdivision had given written consent to the re-subdivision. A twist in *Cinque* was that the Montgomery County Planning Board had a special rule governing reconsideration, and as the court wrote "where a statue or rule exists, it governs as to the circumstances under which the agency may grant reconsideration."[89] Reconsideration was held proper under the Planning Board's own rule.

89. 173 Md. App. 349, 361, 918 A.2d 1254, 1261 (2007).

# Chapter 6

# Contested Cases: Evidentiary Principles

The rules of evidence that apply in circuit court do not apply at administrative agency contested case hearings. This does not mean that everything is admissible. Maryland courts have repeatedly stated that "although administrative agencies are not bound by the technical common law rules of evidence, they must observe the basic rules of fairness as to the parties appearing before them."[1] This chapter will discuss the various issues involving the admissibility of evidence in contested cases in Maryland.

## § 6.1. Privilege

The rules of privilege that apply in civil cases apply in administrative hearings.[2] The statutory testimonial privileges are set forth in Title 9, Subtitle 1 of the Courts and Judicial Proceedings Article. Therefore, evidence that would violate the attorney-client privilege, clergy-penitent privilege, husband-wife privilege, journalist-source privilege, accountant-client privilege, social worker-client privilege, or patient-psychiatrist/psychologist privilege is not admissible at an administrative hearing, and cannot be considered by OAH or any agency in making its decision. Interestingly, there is no physician-patient privilege in Maryland.[3]

The journalist privilege as codified in Maryland's Shield Law was discussed in *Prince George's County v. Hartley*.[4] The court held that at a police department disciplinary hearing, a newspaper reporter was entitled to a determination of whether he could refuse to answer a question on the ground that the answer would result in the disclosure of privileged information. The social worker-client privilege was discussed in *Doe v. Maryland Board of Social Work Examiners*[5] where the Court of Appeals held that the privilege did not prohibit an agency from subpoenaing the patient records of a social worker being investigated for failure to report child abuse.

1. *See* Cecil County Dep't of Social Servs. v. Russell, 159 Md. App. 594, 612, 861 A.2d 92, 103 (2004).
2. Maryland Code Annotated, State Government § 10-213(e).
3. *See* Solomon v. State Bd. of Physician Quality Assurance, 155 Md. App. 687, 845 A.2d 47 (2003).
4. 150 Md. App. 581, 822 A.2d 537 (2003).
5. 384 Md. 161, 862 A.2d 996 (2004).

## § 6.2. Irrelevant

Evidence that is irrelevant should not be admitted into the agency record.[6] Maryland Rule 5-401 defines evidence to be relevant if it has any tendency to make the existence of any fact that is of consequence to the determination of the action more probable or less probable than it would be without the evidence. In a false advertising case involving the effectiveness of certain products that claimed to cure cancer and AIDS, *T-Up, Inc. v. Consumer Protection Division*,[7] the ALJ refused to admit affidavits from customers who wrote that they were satisfied with the products. The ALJ decision not to admit the affidavits was held not reversible error because the "fact that eighty consumers were satisfied with the products does not necessarily mean that the products were effective."[8]

In *Solomon v. State Board of Physician Quality Assurance*,[9] a physician challenged the revocation of her medical license because of her failure to cooperate with the Board's investigation. One of the issues presented on judicial review was the ALJ's denial of Dr. Solomon's request to call as witnesses at the hearing nineteen patients whose medical records had been subpoenaed but which Solomon had refused to provide to the Board. Each patient planned to testify that they did not want their confidential records be given to the Board. The Court of Appeals held that the ALJ had not abused her discretion in excluding this testimony because the "proffered testimony of these witnesses simply was not relevant to the issues before the ALJ—whether Dr. Solomon failed to cooperate with an investigation by the Board."[10] Prior cases had made clear that patients have no veto power over subpoenas issued by the Board in the course of investigating a physician.

Another issue in *Solomon* involved the exclusion of testimony from a dentist who sought to testify that he had not been disciplined for failing to comply with a subpoena which the Board of Dental Examiners had issued during an investigation of him. The court ruled that the dentist's "testimony was properly excluded because the proceedings conducted by the Board of Dental Examiners against him have absolutely no bearing on" Solomon's case.[11] The proferred testimony of a retired administrative law judge was also held irrelevant in *Solomon*. The retired ALJ sought to testify that the law did not require Solomon to comply with the Board's subpoena request because it was overbroad. The Court of Special Appeals upheld the exclusion of this testimony because "it is the general rule that an expert witness may not opine on questions of law, except for those concerning the law of another jurisdiction."[12]

## § 6.3. Immaterial

Evidence that is immaterial should not be admitted into the agency record.[13] Material evidence is evidence that relates to one of the substantive issues in the case. If evidence is

6. Maryland Code Annotated, State Government § 10-213(d)(2).
7. 145 Md. App. 27, 801 A.2d 173, *cert. denied*, 369 Md. 661, 802 A.2d 439 (2002).
8. 145 Md. App. 27, 67, 801 A.2d 173, 196 (2002).
9. 155 Md. App. 687, 845 A.2d 47 (2003).
10. 155 Md. App. 687, 706, 845 A.2d 47, 58 (2003).
11. 155 Md. App. 687, 706, 845 A.2d 47, 58 (2003).
12. 155 Md. App. 687, 706, 845 A.2d 47, 58 (2003).
13. Maryland Code Annotated, State Government § 10-213(d)(3).

offered to prove a proposition that is not a relevant issue in the case, the evidence is immaterial and excludable.

## § 6.4. Incompetent

Evidence that is incompetent should not be admitted into the agency record.[14] Evidence may be relevant and material, but excludable on the basis of incompetency. Incompetency covers several bases. For example, proffered testimony from an attorney which would violate the attorney-client privilege is incompetent. A proffered expert opinion from someone not qualified to render an expert opinion would also be incompetent. For example, *T-Up, Inc. v. Consumer Protection Division*[15] involved a false advertising case against the marketer of two products claimed by the marketer as cures for cancer and AIDS. The marketer sought to call as an expert a person who claimed expertise in the human body and chemistry. Although the proferred expert had formal education and professional training in inorganic chemistry, and "an interest in matters of organic chemistry and biochemistry in the human body," he had no professionally supported or supervised training in these areas, and had no professionally competent research in these areas.[16] Nor was his opinion based on any systematic or formal study. The Court of Special Appeals upheld the exclusion of this proferred expert testimony because the witness' credentials and experience did not establish him as an expert.

An agency regulation can also be the basis of evidence being incompetent. For example, COMAR 07.02.26.12 provides that children younger than fourteen years old may not be called to testify in a child abuse and neglect hearing unless the child's testimony is essential, and there is no likelihood of emotional harm to the child. Also, COMAR 28.02.01.18 D(4) provides that an Administrative Law Judge or other individual who conducts an alternative dispute resolution proceeding at the Office of Administrative Hearings may not be called to testify or otherwise provide information in any subsequent proceeding related to the alternative dispute resolution proceeding.

An issue that Maryland has decided differently than most other jurisdictions is the competency of an attorney to testify at a contested case hearing in which the attorney is representing a party. Rule 3.7 of the Maryland Rules of Professional Conduct prohibit a lawyer from serving as an advocate at a "trial" in which the lawyer is likely to be a necessary witness. In *Heard v. Foxshire Associates, LLC*,[17] the Court of Special Appeals, although recognizing that courts in other jurisdictions "have reached disparate results" on the issue, held that the prohibition in Rule 3.7 did not apply to administrative hearings. The court drew a "distinction between counsel's conduct in trials before courts of record and hearings conducted by legislative or adjudicatory bodies."[18] Citing Black's Law Dictionary, the court wrote that a "trial is a judicial examination," which is different from a "hearing before administrative agencies." An attorney serving as advocate, therefore, may offer evidence at an administrative hearing "by way of statement or narrative as an advocate."[19] When offering testimony, the attorney must be under oath.

---

14. Maryland Code Annotated, State Government § 10-213(d)(1).
15. 145 Md. App. 27, 801 A.2d 173, *cert. denied*, 369 Md. 661, 802 A.2d 439 (2002).
16. 145 Md. App. 27, 51, 801 A.2d 173, 187 (2003).
17. 145 Md. App. 695, 806 A.2d 348 (2002).
18. 145 Md. App. 695, 706, 806 A.2d 348, 355 (2002).
19. 145 Md. App. 695, 707, 806 A.2d 348, 355 (2002).

Subsequent to the opinion in *Heard*, the Maryland Court of Appeals amended the Comment to Rule 3.7. The new Comment uses the word "Tribunal" which is defined to include both a court and an administrative agency. The text of Rule 3.7, however, was not changed; it still speaks only of testifying at "trials." The issue of the application of the rule prohibiting an attorney from serving as advocate and witness in administrative adjudications is discussed in an article I wrote, *The Attorney as Advocate and Witness: Does the Prohibition of an Attorney Acting as Advocate and Witness at a Judicial Trial Also Apply in Administrative Adjudications?*, 26 J. NAT'L ASSOC. ADMIN. LAW. JUDGES 1 (2006).

## § 6.5. Unduly Repetitious

At a certain point at a contested case hearing, evidence which is unduly repetitious should be excluded.[20] There is no bright line when evidence becomes unduly repetitious, and it is within the presiding official's discretion to determine when to stop the testimony.[21] It is doubtful that any agency decision would be subject to reversal because unduly repetitious evidence had been admitted, but attorneys should understand that this is a ground upon which an objection to admissibility is proper. In *T-Up, Inc. v. Consumer Protection Division*,[22] the marketer of a cure for cancer and AIDS sought to introduce affidavits from eighty of its satisfied customers to dispute charges of false advertising. Prior to the offer of these affidavits, about a dozen witnesses had testified about their satisfaction with the products purchased, and the marketer had placed into evidence a "Success Stories" exhibit. The Court of Special Appeals upheld the ALJ's refusal to admit the eighty affidavits. The court wrote that "[i]n view of the amount of evidence that already had been received concerning customer's opinions, the ALJ was entitled to cut off anecdotal evidence from eighty more consumers."[23]

## § 6.6. Probativity

The APA provides that in a contested case the "presiding officer may admit probative evidence that reasonable and prudent individuals commonly accept in the conduct of their affairs and give probative effect to that evidence."[24]

*Department of Public Safety & Correctional Services v. Scruggs*[25] involved a disciplinary hearing of a correctional officer. Polygraph evidence obtained from three female prison inmates who alleged that the correctional officer, Scruggs, had engaged in sexual relations with them had been admitted at the hearing. The Court of Special Appeals held that the admission of the polygraph evidence required the reversal of the agency's decision to remove Scruggs from state employment. The court responded to the argument that the polygraph evidence was admissible because administrative agencies are not bound by the

20. Maryland Code Annotated, State Government § 10-213(d)(4).

21. *See* Md. Code Regs. 28.02.01.11 B (6), COMAR 28.02.01.11 B (6).

22. 145 Md. App. 27, 801 A.2d 173, *cert. denied*, 369 Md. 661, 802 A.2d 439 (2002).

23. 145 Md. App. 27, 68, 801 A.2d 173, 197 (2002).

24. Maryland Code Annotated, State Government § 10-213(b); *see also* OAH Rule 21B, Md. Code Regs. 28.02.01.21B, COMAR 28.02.01.21B.

25. 79 Md. App. 312, 556 A.2d 736 (1989).

technical common law rules of evidence by saying that although "administrative proceedings do allow more 'flexible' evidentiary guidelines," there are "boundaries to this flexibility."[26] The court identified the critical question to be whether polygraph evidence was "so unreliable as to deem it incompetent."[27] The court held that the distrust of polygraph evidence was "well documented," and that, therefore, it was improper to admit such evidence at the disciplinary hearing.[28]

## § 6.7. Authentication

Although the rules of evidence do not apply at administrative agency contested case hearings, in order for documentary evidence to be admitted into the agency record, the authenticity of the documents should be established.

*Department of Public Safety & Correctional Services v. Cole*[29] involved a decision by an ALJ to admit a videotape at a disciplinary hearing for a correctional officer accused of using excessive force against a prison inmate. The prison guard, Cole, objected to the admission of the tape because "there was nobody there to authenticate the tape and nobody to say, in fact, if the tape reflected what had happened was accurate." After an adverse administrative decision, Cole sought judicial review. He was successful in both the circuit court and the Court of Special Appeals. Both courts held that the tape was not admissible because it was admitted without proper foundation. The Court of Appeals, however, held that the videotape was admissible under the "silent witness" theory of admissibility. Significant to the instant discussion, the Court of Appeals did not hold that proper authentication was not required because the videotape was being introduced at an administrative hearing. The court applied the same authentication standards to the administrative hearing as applied in a court proceeding.

## § 6.8. Expunged Records

The admissibility at a contested case of expunged records is not clear. *Gigeous v. Eastern Correctional Institution*[30] involved the issue of whether expunged records from a criminal investigation were admissible at a subsequent administrative disciplinary hearing. Gigeous, a correctional officer at a state prison, was charged with possession of a controlled dangerous substance. The charges, however, were *nol prossed* by the State's Attorney Office, and an order of expungement of his arrest and prosecution was issued. An administrative hearing then was held to determine whether Gigeous should be terminated from state employment. Gigeous moved to exclude any evidence from police and court documents relating to his arrest and prosecution, and to exclude testimony relating to his arrest and prosecution because the arrest and prosecution had been expunged. The ALJ, however, admitted into evidence records that were covered by the expungement order. At the conclusion of the

26. 79 Md. App. 312, 321, 556 A.2d 736, 740 (1989).
27. 79 Md. App. 323, 321, 556 A.2d 736, 741 (1989).
28. The court also rejected the argument that admission of the polygraph evidence was harmless. See Chapter 24.
29. 342 Md. 12, 672 A.2d 1115 (1996).
30. 132 Md. App. 487, 752 A.2d 1238 (2000), *aff'd*, 363 Md. 481, 769 A.2d 912 (2001).

administrative hearing, the ALJ issued a proposed decision adverse to Gigeous. This was affirmed by the Secretary of Personnel. Among other issues, the Court of Special Appeals addressed the admissibility of the expunged records. The court held that the statute involving expungement of records prohibited the use of expunged records for any reason except police investigative purposes. Because the administrative hearing was not related to a police investigation, any evidence that stemmed from the expunged file was inadmissible at the administrative hearing. The case was reviewed by the Court of Appeals, but it decided not to address the issues raised by the expungement statute. It decided to "neither bless nor curse the positions taken in the Court of Special Appeals's opinion directed to interpretation or application" of the expungement statute.[31]

## § 6.9. Illegally Seized Evidence

Absent a special statute or regulation, illegally seized evidence is admissible at a contested case. *Sheetz v. Mayor and City Council of Baltimore*[32] involved the termination from employment of a correctional officer. Police had seized cocaine, marijuana and related drug paraphernalia without probable cause and without a warrant. Criminal charges were dropped when the district court judge ruled that all the evidence was unconstitutionally seized and was inadmissible at a criminal trial. Administrative disciplinary charges were then filed to remove Sheetz from public employment. The issue presented was whether the illegally seized evidence could be used to prove that Sheetz had conducted himself in a manner "unbecoming of an employee of the city" to support his removal. The Court of Appeals held that the exclusionary rule applicable to illegally seized evidence did not "generally apply" to administrative public employee discharge cases. The deterrent benefits of applying the exclusionary rule in discharge proceedings were "minimal." "Administrative discharge proceedings are typically designed to evaluate employees' actions as they relate to future job performance, rather than to punish employees for past wrongs."[33] Because the police are "responsible for punishing criminals by enforcing criminal laws, ... their primary interest is not typically in discharge proceedings. The police are not especially tempted to violate the fourth amendment in order to obtain evidence for such proceedings." The court in *Sheetz* continued, however, that "as a matter of Maryland Administrative Law," illegally seized evidence "is inadmissible in civil administrative discharge proceedings where the defendant establishes that the police were improperly motivated to illegally seize evidence to benefit civil proceedings."[34] The court then listed five non-exclusive factors which might prove a finding of bad faith which would lead to exclusion of the illegally seized evidence. These five factors are: (1) whether at the time of the illegal search, the police were aware of the potential effect of using such evidence in civil proceedings; (2) whether the severity of the consequences of civil proceedings roughly paralleled or exceeded that of the criminal proceedings; (3) whether a reasonable officer would have believed the search to be a proper one; (4) whether there was an agreement between the police and another party to pursue the investigation which led to the improperly obtained

31. 363 Md. 481, 498–99, 769 A.2d 912, 923 (2001).
32. 315 Md. 208, 553 A.2d 1281 (1989).
33. 315 Md. 208, 214, 553 A.2d 1281, 1284 (1989).
34. 315 Md. 208, 215–16, 553 A.2d 1281, 1285 (1989).

evidence; and (5) whether the police had a special interest in the case.[35] The court ordered a remand for a new hearing to consider this bad faith exception.

*Motor Vehicle Administration v. Richards*[36] involved whether the exclusionary rule applied in a Motor Vehicle Administration (MVA) hearing to suspend a driver's license. To determine this issue, the Court of Appeals applied the U.S. Supreme Court decision of *United States v. Janis*.[37] The *Richards* court balanced the benefits against the costs of applying the exclusionary rule to administrative license suspension hearings. In evaluating the benefits, the court did "not view any possible deterrent effect to be sufficiently significant." First,

> there would likely be only scant marginal deterrence because the police already suffer the exclusion of unlawfully seized evidence from criminal proceedings.... Furthermore, because the MVA is a separate and independent agency from the police department and has no control over the actions of police officers, imposing the exclusionary rule in license suspension proceedings would add little force to the deterrence of unlawful police action.... There is scarce reason to believe that police would be motivated to seize evidence illegally simply to use it in license suspension proceedings.[38]

The costs, however, of applying the exclusionary rule were great according to the court. The protection of the public would be "undermined." Moreover, "[r]equiring hearing examiners to apply the exclusionary rule would unnecessarily complicate and burden an administrative proceeding." The Court of Appeals in *Richards* therefore held that the exclusionary rule did not apply to MVA license suspension cases.[39]

Even though the Fourth Amendment exclusionary rule does not apply to MVA license suspension cases, MVA has a regulation that excludes evidence if the police officer in obtaining or seizing the evidence "acted in bad faith and not as a reasonable officer should act in similar circumstances."[40] In *Richards*, the court held that the initial police stop was made in good faith.

## § 6.10. Prior Criminal Cases

Often, a criminal trial precedes an administrative contested case hearing. The issue can arise as to the admissibility at the agency hearing of evidence, pleas, and verdicts from the criminal case. A few cases deal with this issue.

*Eichberg v. Maryland Board of Pharmacy*[41] involved a pharmacist who was indicted for criminal violations of various drug abuse statutes. A jury trial began and several witnesses testified. Before conclusion of the trial, a mistrial was ordered because a newspaper article about the trial was found in the jury room. Eichberg subsequently entered an *Alford* plea of guilty on a lesser charge to avoid prosecution on the more serious charges. After the criminal proceedings were concluded, the Board of Pharmacy filed disciplinary charges.

---

35. 315 Md. 208, 216, 553 A.2d 1281, 1285 (1989).
36. 356 Md. 356, 739 A.2d 58 (1999).
37. 428 U.S. 433 (1976).
38. 356 Md. 356, 374–75, 739 A.2d 58, 69 (1999).
39. *See also* Motor Vehicle Administration v. Shea, 415 Md. 1, 997 A.2d 768 (2010).
40. Md. Code Regs. 11.11.02.10H(1), COMAR 11.11.02.10H(1).
41. 50 Md. App. 189, 436 A.2d 525 (1981).

At the administrative hearing, a certified copy of the testimony of one of the prosecution's witnesses at the aborted criminal trial was introduced. The Court of Special Appeals held that the transcribed testimony was admissible because it was under oath, the witness had been cross-examined by Eichberg's counsel, and the witness was unavailable to testify in person. In response to the argument that the testimony was inadmissible because it was "biased and self-serving," the court emphasized that "the test of admissibility under the Maryland APA is the probative value of the evidence, not its credibility."[42]

*Powell v. Maryland Aviation Administration*[43] involved an employee of the Maryland Aviation Administration who made harassing telephone calls to a co-worker. The co-worker filed a criminal complaint against Powell who was then charged with criminal telephone misuse. At a bench trial, Powell was found guilty, and later given probation before judgment (PBJ). Between the time of the verdict and the disposition of PBJ, administrative charges were filed to remove Powell from state employment. Powell requested that the administrative charges be dismissed. His argument was that disciplinary charges would not have been brought against him had there been no criminal conviction. Because he had subsequently been given a PBJ, there was no conviction, and thus no basis for discipline. The ALJ reserved judgment on Powell's motion to dismiss and held the hearing. Powell testified and denied making the harassing calls. Three witnesses testified contrary to Powell. The ALJ then ruled against Powell. In making his decision, the ALJ refused to "ignore the guilty finding of the court and retry" Powell, and refused to "substitute his judgment as to the guilt" of Powell from that of the judge in the criminal proceeding. The ALJ then held that "[f]or purposes of this administrative hearing, the Circuit Court judge's finding of guilty ... is sufficient to support" the disciplinary charges.[44] The ALJ's recommended decision was adopted by the Secretary of Personnel. Upon judicial review in circuit court, Powell argued that "the whole decision here is premised solely on the guilty finding and not on what the witnesses had to say." The circuit court agreed with Powell that the "factual finding of guilt can be given no weight by the ALJ," and ordered a new hearing.[45] The Court of Special Appeals disagreed and upheld Powell's removal. It held that "Powell's probation before judgment disposition rendered the fact of his misconduct beyond dispute" and that Powell had no right "to relitigate the issue of his guilt."

The Court of Appeals disagreed with the ALJ, the circuit court, and the Court of Special Appeals. The Court of Appeals held that the ALJ "erred in giving conclusive effect to the guilty finding."[46] The Court of Appeals stated that the ALJ could "second guess" the circuit court judge in the criminal case, and could decide for himself whether Powell had engaged in the misconduct. The ALJ's decision should be based on the evidence introduced at the OAH hearing, not the criminal trial. The court next addressed whether the guilty finding was admissible at all. The court's first response was that under Maryland evidence law, evidence of a criminal conviction is not admissible in a subsequent civil case to prove the underlying facts.[47] But, the court continued, this was an administrative proceeding and "that which is inadmissible in a judicial proceeding is not per se inadmissible in an administrative proceeding."[48] If the evidence has sufficient reliability and probative value to

42. 50 Md. App. 189, 193–94, 436 A.2d 525, 529 (1981).
43. 336 Md. 210, 647 A.2d 437 (1994).
44. 336 Md. 210, 216, 647 A.2d 437, 440 (1994).
45. 336 Md. 210, 216, 647 A.2d 437, 440 (1994).
46. 336 Md. 210, 219, 647 A.2d 437, 441 (1994).
47. This is contrary to Fed. R. Evid. 803(22).
48. 336 Md. 210, 220, 647 A.2d 437, 442 (1994).

satisfy procedural due process, it is admissible. The court then held that there was probative value to the fact of guilt underlying the probation before judgment. According to the Court of Appeals, the guilty verdict was admissible, but not conclusive.

I do not agree with the court's holding in *Powell*. If the guilty verdict is not conclusive, it should not be admissible. In determining whether substantial evidence supports the finding that Powell made the harassing telephone call, only the factual record before the ALJ should be considered. The guilty verdict is a legal conclusion, not a fact, and thus should not be considered. On the other hand, giving conclusive effect to the guilty verdict would make more sense. *Powell* should be compared with *Howard County Department of Social Services v. Linda J.*,[49] where a special statue provided that no contested case hearing was required before a person was placed on a central registry of suspected child abusers if the person had been found guilty of any criminal charges arising out of the alleged abuse. The application of this statute to Linda J., who had received a PBJ in an earlier criminal case, made the guilty verdict in the criminal case conclusive on the administrative determination.

## §6.11. Hearsay

Probably the most important evidentiary issue in administrative contested cases is the treatment of hearsay. Evidence is hearsay if it was made by the declarant outside of the administrative hearing, and is offered for the purpose of proving the truth of the matter asserted in it.[50] It is clear that in administrative contested cases "evidence may not be excluded solely on the basis that it is hearsay."[51] Objecting to the admission of evidence at an administrative contested case hearing on the basis of hearsay is the most common mistake made by lawyers unfamiliar with contested case litigation. In *Eichberg v. Maryland Board of Pharmacy*,[52] an argument was made that a pharmacist license revocation proceeding based on a violation of criminal drug laws is "quasi-criminal," and thus hearsay evidence should be excluded. The Court of Special Appeals responded that it knows of "no such mutation in Maryland law" as a "quasi-criminal" case and therefore, hearsay was properly admitted.[53]

Not only is hearsay admissible in Maryland, but if reliable, credible, and sufficiently probative, hearsay may be the sole basis of the decision.[54] In this respect, Maryland is consistent with the federal court's approach to hearsay and administrative adjudication.[55] Some states, however, refuse to permit an agency decision to be based solely on hearsay.[56]

49. 161 Md. App. 402, 869 A.2d 404 (2005).

50. Maryland Rule 5-801(c).

51. Maryland Code Annotated, State Government § 10-213(c); *see also* Md. Code Regs. 28.02.01.21C, COMAR 28.02.01.21C.

52. 50 Md. App. 189, 436 A.2d 525 (1981).

53. 50 Md. App. 189, 195, 436 A.2d 525, 529 (1981).

54. Hammen v. Baltimore County Police Dep't, 373 Md. 440, 818 A.2d 1125 (2003).

55. *See* Richardson v. Perales, 402 U.S. 389 (1971).

56. *See* Beehive Tel. Co. v. PSC of Utah, 89 P.3d 131 (Utah 2004) (evidence that is entirely hearsay is admissible during agency hearings; however, a finding of fact cannot be based solely on hearsay evidence, but must be supported by a residuum of legal evidence competent in a court of law); Mollette v. Kentucky Personnel Bd., 997 S.W.2d 492 (Ky. 1999) (hearsay evidence is admissible in an administrative hearing if it is the type of evidence that reasonable and prudent persons would rely on in their daily

Even though in Maryland hearsay is admissible and can be the sole basis of an agency decision, reliance on hearsay by an agency to reach its final decision raises various concerns. All agency adjudicatory decisions must be supported by substantial evidence and must comport with due process. The substantial evidence requirement and due process create special problems when an agency decision is based on hearsay. As discussed in Chapter 17, in order to satisfy the substantial evidence test, there must be reliable evidence in the agency record to reasonably support the agency's findings of fact. Cross-examination is considered the most effective tool for testing the reliability of evidence, yet when hearsay is admitted, there is no opportunity for cross-examination. Moreover, cross-examination is part of the due process required in administrative hearings. There is a tension, therefore, between the substantial evidence requirement and the right of cross-examination on the one hand, and an agency's obligation to admit hearsay evidence on the other. Because of this tension, agency decisions based on hearsay are subjected to special scrutiny. Although an agency decision based on hearsay will not be reversed because of the admission of hearsay, a decision based on hearsay will be closely scrutinized to determine if the decision is supported by substantial evidence.

In 1991, I wrote a law review article that discussed the Maryland courts' treatment of the use of hearsay in administrative adjudications.[57] As discussed in that article, from an early period, Maryland adopted the rule that hearsay by itself could support an agency decision as long as the reviewing court was assured of the hearsay's reliability. The Maryland courts, however, had not employed a coherent, consistent reliability analysis for evaluating the hearsay. My article proposed a framework for evaluating the reliability of hearsay in order to determine whether an agency decision based solely on hearsay could constitute substantial evidence. Among the factors I suggested should be considered were the nature of the claim or issue; the nature of the evidence including whether the evidence was conclusory, ambiguous, under oath, made close to the time of the event, and whether it was corroborated; the identity of the out-of-hearing declarant including factors such as whether the declarant was identified, traditionally reliable (e.g., a doctor), disinterested or biased; the availability of non-hearsay evidence; the reason for the declarant's unavailability; the value of cross examination; the right to subpoena the out-of-hearing declarant; the nature and caseload of the agency's hearings; and the relevant standard of proof.

The most useful Maryland case on hearsay and administrative adjudications is *Travers v. Baltimore Police Department*,[58] written by Judge Harrell when he was on the Court of Special Appeals. *Travers* involved a disciplinary proceeding against a police officer. Travers was accused of assaulting his girlfriend and then refusing to leave her apartment contrary to orders of a police lieutenant, both in violation of police department regulations. The alleged victim, Nelson, did not testify at the administrative hearing. Her version of what happened was introduced through the testimony of two police officers who responded to the scene. Nelson's version of the events was contradicted by live testimony by Travers. One issue on judicial review of the agency's decision to terminate Travers as a police officer was the agency's reliance on the hearsay evidence from Nelson. The Court of Special Appeals wrote that although hearsay may form the sole basis for the agency's decision,

---

affairs, but hearsay evidence alone is not sufficient in itself to support an agency's findings of fact unless it would be admissible over objections in civil actions).

57. Arnold Rochvarg, *Hearsay in State Administrative Hearings: The Maryland Experience and Suggestions for Change*, 21 U. Balt. L. Rev. 1 (1991).

58. 115 Md. App. 395, 693 A.2d 378 (1997).

"hearsay evidence must demonstrate sufficient reliability and probative value to satisfy the requirement of procedural due process." The court continued:

> It is improper for an agency to consider hearsay evidence without first carefully considering its reliability and probative value. One important consideration for a hearing body is the nature of the hearsay evidence. For instance, statements that are sworn under oath, ... or made close in time to the incident, ... or corroborated ... ordinarily [are] presumed to possess a greater caliber of reliability.[59]

In this case, although Nelson's statements were not sworn, their reliability was indicated by several factors. Her comments to the police officers if made knowingly false with the intent to deceive the officers could have subjected her to criminal penalties. Her statements to the police officers were made a "relatively short period" after the time of the alleged incident. Nelson's testimony was corroborated by in-person testimony from police officers that Nelson had red marks on both sides of her neck and that her face was red and puffy. Additionally, although Nelson as the victim was not a "neutral and detached" witness, the court believed this was "less weighty in cases when hearsay statements come into evidence through a disinterested witness."[60]

The court in *Travers* distinguished two Maryland cases that had reversed agency decisions based on hearsay. *Kade v. Charles H. Hickey School*[61] involved the suspension of a school supervisor for alleged misconduct involving some students at a state-operated detention facility. At the administrative hearing, the school's superintendent, who was not present during the alleged incident, testified as to statements made by students who had allegedly witnessed the supervisor's misconduct. The agency's decision to suspend the supervisor was based solely on this hearsay. The agency decision was reversed by the Court of Special Appeals. The court found significant that the hearsay statements were not sworn, dated, or verified; the statements did not indicate the students' age or any information about them; there was no explanation as to why the hearsay declarants did not testify; and the hearsay had been contradicted by live testimony. The court in *Travers* distinguished *Kade*. In *Kade*, only one live witness testified, the circumstances under which the statements were prepared were not disclosed, the statements were not dated, the declarants ages were not indicated, and there was no corroboration by any live witness. The hearsay in *Travers* "possessed a greater quantum of reliability" then the hearsay in *Kade*.[62]

The court in *Travers* also discussed *Tron v. Prince George's County*.[63] *Tron* involved a disability claim by a county employee allegedly arising from a work related injury. The claimant (Tron) presented live testimony from a doctor who testified that the injury was work related. The county offered no witnesses, but introduced a booklet containing written reports of three doctors who had examined Tron, and a written opinion by another doctor who had read the other reports but never examined Tron. Although the examining doctors' reports did not address the issue of whether Tron's condition was work related, the written report by the non-examining doctor concluded that the disability was not work related. On this evidence, the agency denied the disability claim. The Court of Special Appeals reversed. Critical to the court's decision was that the local agency had no subpoena power, and therefore Tron had no opportunity to subpoena the out-of-hearing declarants. The

59. 115 Md. App. 395, 413, 693 A.2d 378, 386–87 (1997).
60. 115 Md. App. 395, 417, 693 A.2d 378, 388 (1997).
61. 80 Md. App. 721, 566 A.2d 148 (1989).
62. 115 Md. App. 395, 416, 693 A.2d 378, 388 (1997).
63. 69 Md. App. 256, 517 A.2d 113 (1986).

court emphasized Tron's lack of ability to cross-examine any live witnesses. In *Travers*, however, Travers had been informed of his right to subpoena witnesses, but failed to exercise his right to subpoena Nelson. Therefore, he had waived his right to complain about a denial of the opportunity to cross-examine Nelson. For all these reasons, the Court of Special Appeals concluded in *Travers* that the agency's reliance on the hearsay statements to terminate Travers as a police officer "did not vitiate [his] right to a fair administrative hearing."[64]

The significance of the right to subpoena the hearsay declarant was also discussed in *Rosov v. Maryland State Board of Dental Examiners*.[65] This dentist discipline case involved complaints about improper sanitary practices. A six day hearing was held at OAH. One issue on judicial review involved the ALJ's reliance on a report by a Board investigator who did not testify at the hearing. The Court of Special Appeals noted that the failure of the investigator to testify in person was not the fault of "the State or the ALJ, but by [the dentist's] own failure to subpoena the witness."[66] The license revocation was upheld.

Maryland courts do appear to give special attention to agency decisions based on hearsay. This is illustrated by *Parham v. Department of Labor, Licensing & Regulation*.[67] In this case, Parham filed for unemployment benefits. The agency denied her claim based on its finding that she left her employment voluntarily. The issue as to whether Parham had quit voluntarily was based on a conversation Parham had with Wolferman, the manager on duty at the time. Wolferman did not testify at the administrative hearing. However, Kaufman, a department head, and Stokes, a human resources coordinator for the employer, did testify at the hearing about what Wolferman had told them. Parham's live testimony contradicted the hearsay testimony from Kaufman and Stokes. The Court of Special Appeals reversed the agency's decision. The court discussed that the hearsay had been directly contradicted by more reliable evidence, and there was no explanation for Wolferman's failure to testify. The finding based on hearsay that Parham had quit her job voluntarily was not supported by substantial evidence.

*Parham* reminds us that even though Maryland law is clear that hearsay is admissible and can constitute substantial evidence even when there is no non-hearsay supporting the agency decision, there is some uneasiness with reliance on hearsay. Most ALJ's and agency officials prefer to base their decisions on non-hearsay testimony. It is therefore better to present the case without relying on hearsay. However, requiring all witnesses to appear in person adds a cost to the process. Should you ask a supporting witness to take time off from work, incur travel expenses or child-care expenses to appear personally when an affidavit might be sufficient? There is no easy answer to this question. The decision whether to rely on hearsay is a professional judgment that must be made on a case-by-case basis.

## §6.12. Missing Witness Rule

Under the "missing witness rule," if a party has it peculiarly within its power to produce a witness whose testimony would be material to the case, the fact that the party does not

64. 115 Md. App. 395, 419, 693 A.2d 378, 389 (1997).
65. 163 Md. App. 98, 877 A.2d 1111 (2005).
66. 163 Md. App. 98, 117, 877 A.2d 1111, 1122 (2005).
67. 189 Md. App. 604, 985 A.2d 147 (2009).

call that witness creates a presumption that the testimony from that witness would be unfavorable to that party. In *Bereano v. State Ethics Commission*,[68] this rule of evidence was held to have been incorrectly applied by the State Ethics Commission in its order suspending a lobbyist from engaging in lobbying for ten months. The primary opinion—no opinion obtained a majority of the judges—held that the missing witness rule was misapplied because the "missing witness" was not "peculiarly" available to the accused lobbyist prior to the hearing. The "missing witness" had made himself available for an interview at the Commission's office, had responded to all document requests, and had invited staff counsel to call him if further assistance was desired. The opinion stated that the Commission's staff counsel could not "have its cake and also eat it."[69]

Although one of the issues on which the Court of Appeals granted certiorari in *Bereano* was "[w]hether the missing witness rule should be applicable to administrative agency proceedings in Maryland," this issue was never directly decided. The primary opinion, however, casts some doubt on whether the rule would ever be applicable at an administrative hearing. After reviewing the relaxed rules of evidence in agency contested cases and the lack of a jury, the primary opinion wrote in response to the dissenting opinion's position that the missing witness rule had been proven in this case:

> While many other jurisdictions are curtailing the use of the missing witness inference in civil and criminal cases, the dissent here would expand its scope in the less protected environment of an administrative hearing where the inference is relied on without warning to the charged party appearing before it.[70]

Other statements in the primary opinion suggest that even if the elements of the missing witness rule had been established in the *Bereano* case, the court would have held that the missing witness rule was not applicable in administrative contested cases. Considering the unusual composition of the court that decided *Bereano*—of the seven active judges of the Court of Appeals, only two, Judges Harrell and Greene, sat; the other five judges were all retired and specially assigned—it is unclear what the full Court of Appeals would decide on the application of the missing witness rule in administrative contested cases.

## § 6.13. Official or Administrative Notice

In creating the evidentiary record, the agency, including OAH, may take official or administrative notice of certain facts.[71] Official notice operates in a similar manner as judicial notice in the court system, but official notice is broader. First, an agency may take official notice of a fact that is proper under judicial notice. Judicial notice covers facts that are generally known and commonly accepted. Judicial notice also covers facts capable of accurate and ready determination by resort to sources whose accuracy cannot reasonably be questioned. Second, an agency may take official notice of facts within the general, technical, or scientific specialized knowledge and expertise of the agency.[72] This is broader

68. 403 Md. 716, 944 A.2d 538 (2008).
69. 403 Md. 716, 752, 944 A.2d 538, 559 (2008).
70. 403 Md. 716, 754–55, 944 A.2d 538, 560 (2008).
71. Maryland Code Annotated, State Government § 10-213(h); OAH Rule 21F, Md. Code Regs. 28.02.01.21F, COMAR 28.02.01.21F.
72. Maryland Code Annotated, State Government § 10-213(h)(1)(ii); OAH Rule 21F(1)(b), Md. Code Regs. 28.02.01.21F(1)(b), COMAR 28.02.01.21F(1)(b).

than judicial notice. For example, if a circuit court judge is an expert in a particular area, that judge cannot take judicial notice of facts within that individual judge's expertise. An agency, on the other hand, is allowed to take official notice of facts within its specialized knowledge.

It is not entirely clear how far official notice extends. In *Eastern Services Centers, Inc. v. Cloverland Farms Dairy, Inc.*,[73] a gasoline station filed a zoning request to include a convenience food mart. One issue was whether there was substantial evidence in the record that a convenience store was an accessory use to a gasoline station. Although apparently no evidence was presented on this issue at the administrative hearing, the Court of Special Appeals noted that "it is generally known that the sale of some products at gasoline stations, or the sale of gasoline in connection with convenience store operations, is becoming commonplace in this country."[74] The Court of Special Appeals approved of the circuit judge's comment that a "court and an administrative body can take almost judicial notice of what's happening."[75]

Because of the dearth of cases in Maryland discussing the scope of official notice, it may be helpful to consider cases from other states. For example, in *Kyu Son Yi v. State Board of Veterinary Medicine*,[76] the Commonwealth Court of Pennsylvania reviewed a decision of the Pennsylvania Veterinary Board revoking the license of a veterinarian based on his treatment of a Pomeranian who had multiple fractures to his left hind leg which eventually required amputation. One argument presented on judicial review was that "some of the Board's findings and discussion rely upon information and veterinary precepts that are nowhere in evidence." The Board's response to this argument was that since "the Board includes members with expertise in veterinary medicine, the Board may draw the proper conclusions without expert testimony." The court's response was that although an agency "may use its expertise to filter evidence," it may not "use its expertise as a substitute for evidence."[77] The court also held that it was improper for the Board to "use the internet or a treatise on small animal pain management to make findings of fact."[78] Because the information gathered from these sources was not offered into evidence by either party, such information could not be used to support the Board's findings. The revocation ordered was reversed.

Although it is clear that an ALJ at OAH may take official notice of certain facts, the scope of official notice at OAH is not clear. OAH has no specialized knowledge or expertise, other than in the process of conducting contested cases. Therefore, the scope of official notice at OAH is most likely limited to those facts which are proper under judicial notice. Any special knowledge of the agency that has delegated its authority to OAH would need to be presented at the hearing by the agency and made part of the record at OAH. If the agency has retained the final decisionmaking power and has delegated to OAH only the power to make a proposed decision, it would appear the agency could take full official notice of additional facts as part of its final decisionmaking process.

There are several important procedural safeguards against the improper use of official notice. Before a fact can be officially noticed, each party must be notified of the fact that

73. 130 Md. App. 1, 744 A.2d 63 (2000).
74. 130 Md. App. 1, 11, 744 A.2d 63, 68 (2000).
75. 130 Md. App. 1, 11, 744 A.2d 63, 68 (2000).
76. 960 A.2d 864 (Pa. Commw. Ct. 2008).
77. 960 A.2d 864, 871–72 (Pa. Commw. Ct. 2008).
78. 960 A.2d 864, 873 (Pa. Commw. Ct. 2008).

is being officially noticed, and given the opportunity to contest that fact.[79] Facts that are officially noticed without prior notification and an opportunity to rebut cannot properly be considered by OAH or the agency. Objection to official notice could be based on the argument that the fact does not fall within the parameters of what can be properly officially noticed, or that the fact itself is not accurate.

Official notice can be taken at any stage of the proceeding. Official notice may even be taken for the first time in the proposed decision as long as the opportunity for objection is provided.[80]

## § 6.14. Reopening the Hearing for Additional Evidence

*Maryland State Police v. Zeigler*[81] involved a hearing board's decision to reopen the hearing for additional evidence after both sides had completed presentation of their cases and the board members had begun their deliberations. Zeigler was a state trooper who was charged with violating several state police regulations. One charge involved giving false information during an investigation. A two-day hearing was held before a three-member board during which the board heard from fourteen witnesses, received eighteen exhibits, and heard opening and closing arguments from each party. After closing argument, the board began its deliberations. After three and one-half hours, the board reconvened the hearing, and announced to the parties that it was

> the opinion of this board, of each member of this board, that there are additional witnesses who have not been called to this hearing who have evidence or testimony to give which is pertinent to this matter. We feel that it is in the best interest of the defendant and the agency, and in the best interest of fairness for the board to call additional witnesses to this hearing.[82]

The board then identified four persons it intended to call. Zeigler's attorney objected, stating that it was the board's duty to decide the case based on the evidence presented by the parties. The board overruled the objection, and reopened the hearing. Only one witness was called by the board, which conducted the examination. This new witness was then cross-examined by both parties. Both parties then made final statements, and the board adjourned the hearing. After further deliberations, Zeigler was cleared of three charges, but was found to have violated one charge of submitting a false report.

Upon review in circuit court, the judge held that the "board acted inappropriately by taking additional testimony after retiring to deliberate." The Court of Special Appeals agreed. The Court of Special Appeals held it was a "denial of due process to seek further evidence when [the State Police] failed to meet its burden of proof," and that the board had abused its discretion in reopening the case. The board was also criticized for giving "almost no explanation" for why it wanted additional testimony. The Court of Special Appeals also stated that "since the evidence, prior to reopening, was not deemed sufficient

79. Maryland Code Annotated, State Government § 10-213(h)(2); OAH Rule 21F(2), Md. Code Regs. 28.02.01.21F(2), COMAR 28.02.01.21F(2).

80. *See* Maryland Code Annotated, State Government § 10-213(h)(2).

81. 330 Md. 540, 625 A.2d 914 (1993).

82. 330 Md. 540, 547, 625 A.2d 914, 917 (1993).

by the board to convince it of Zeigler's guilt on all charges, fundamental fairness demanded that they find him not guilty, and that it was unfair to seek further evidence."[83]

The Court of Appeals disagreed with both the circuit court and Court of Special Appeals, and upheld the board's action. The Court of Appeals wrote that it "is an established principle that an administrative agency has broad discretion to consider evidence submitted after the close of an evidentiary hearing as long as there is compliance with procedural due process."[84] Such discretion is broader than that accorded to trial judges to reopen the record since agencies are not bound by the common law rules of evidence. There was no abuse of discretion by the board in this case because both sides cross-examined the new witness, offered rebuttal, and made additional closing arguments. The Court of Appeals also stated that its conclusion did "not depend upon which side the additional evidence supports or upon the weight of the additional evidence compared with the evidence at the initial hearing."[85]

*Zeigler* is an interesting case because it illustrates a certain tension in Administrative Law. On the one hand, administrative adjudication accepts the adversary system. Each party, including the agency, presents its own witnesses, cross-examines opposing witnesses, and argues for the decision it desires. No party is expected to present a neutral case with all the facts on both sides. This adversarial system was developed for a judicial system with neutral judges and juries who theoretically have no policy making functions. An administrative agency, on the other hand, exists to further certain policy goals set forth by the legislature. Achievement of the agency's policy goals may at times be thwarted unless the agency steps in and plays a more active role in the contested case process than a judge would play in a court trial. In *Zeigler*, it seems to me that the Board members wanted to make the correct decision based on as complete a factual record as possible.[86] The litigating parties had not made a factual record which the Board members felt was adequate for it to perform its statutory role. The Board members, therefore, did what they thought was necessary to create a proper record. This once again demonstrates the difference between administrative litigation and courtroom litigation. No judicial trial would permit a jury or judge after closing arguments and after a few hours of deliberation to call more witnesses to testify.

## § 6.15. Exclusiveness of the Record

In a contested case, findings of fact must be based exclusively on the evidence introduced into the record at the hearing.[87] This requirement is known as "exclusiveness of the record." In making its decision, OAH or the decision-making agency can consider only matters that were either admitted at the hearing, the subject of a stipulation,[88] or that were officially

83. 330 Md. 540, 552, 625 A.2d 914, 920 (1993).

84. 330 Md. 540, 557, 625 A.2d 914, 922 (1993).

85. 330 Md. 540, 561, 625 A.2d 914, 924 (1993).

86. *See* OAH Rule 11B(5), Md. Code Regs. 28.02.01.11B(5), COMAR 28.02.01.11B(5) (ALJ has power to call witnesses as necessary to ensure a full and complete record). *See also* B & S Mktg. Enters., LLC v. Consumer Prot. Div., 153 Md. App. 130, 835 A.2d 215 (2003), *cert. denied*, 380 Md. 231, 844 A.2d 427 (2004).

87. Maryland Code Annotated, State Government § 10-214(a).

88. *See* OAH Rule 21G, Md. Code Regs. 28.02.01.21G, COMAR 28.02.01.21G. A stipulation may be filed in writing or entered on the record at the hearing. An ALJ may require additional development of stipulated matters.

noticed. Consideration of any other material would be a violation of the parties' right to a hearing.

## §6.16. Ex parte Communications

Because of the exclusiveness of the record requirement in contested cases, ex parte communications are prohibited. The APA provides that "a presiding officer may not communicate ex parte directly or indirectly regarding the merits of any issue in the case, while the case is pending, with any party to the case or the party's representative or attorney; or any person who presided at the previous stage of the case."[89] An individual who is involved in the decision-making process and who is personally aware of an ex parte communication must give notice to all parties; must include in the record each written communication received, a memorandum that states the substance of each oral communication received, each written response to a communication, and a memorandum that states the substance of each oral response to the communication; and must send to each party a copy of each communication, memorandum, and response.[90] A party may be given the opportunity to rebut an ex parte communication. If an ex parte communication has been made, the agency official who was the recipient of the improper communication may withdraw from the proceeding, or the proceeding may be terminated without prejudice. If the proceeding is terminated without prejudice, the order of termination must state the last date by which a party may reinstate the case.[91]

Related to the exclusiveness of the record requirement and the prohibition on ex parte communications is that an agency decision-maker cannot seek out information on his own to get a better or more complete understanding of the facts.[92] A classic case from Federal Administrative Law is *Banegas v. Heckler*[93] where after hearing evidence on whether a claimant was eligible for social security disability benefits, the administrative law judge followed the claimant and his lawyer to the parking lot where the ALJ observed the claimant walking freely without any visible problems. Based on his own observation, the ALJ denied the disability claim. This denial was reversed by the reviewing federal court.

There is an exception to the ex parte communication rule that applies to agency heads and advisory staff and legal counsel. An agency head, commissioner, or board member who is presiding over a contested case is permitted to communicate with members of an advisory staff or legal counsel who did not participate in the contested case.[94] This exception was discussed in *Blaker v. State Board of Chiropractic Examiners*[95] which involved a disciplinary proceeding against a chiropractor, Blaker. Blaker argued that the Board's counsel had engaged in improper communications with the Board members. The Board admitted that its counsel had attended the evidentiary hearing,[96] had discussed with the Board members possible sanctions and penalties, and had prepared the findings of fact,

89. Maryland Code Annotated, State Government § 10-219(a)(1).
90. Maryland Code Annotated, State Government § 10-219(c).
91. Maryland Code Annotated, State Government § 10-219(e).
92. Maryland Code Annotated, State Government § 10-219(a)(1).
93. 587 F. Supp. 549 (W.D. Tex. 1984).
94. Maryland Code Annotated, State Government § 10-219(a)(2).
95. 123 Md. App. 243, 717 A.2d 964, *cert. denied*, 351 Md. 662, 719 A.2d 1261 (1998).
96. The hearing was held by the Board of Chiropractic Examiners because it had not delegated any authority to OAH.

conclusions of law, and final order. The issue for the Court of Special Appeals was whether the Board's counsel had "participated" in the contested case or whether the statutory exception exempting counsel who did not participate applied. The Court of Special Appeals held that the word "participate" as used in the statute means to assume the role of advocate or decisionmaker at the time of the communication. The statue should not be construed to prohibit the Board from consulting its counsel on any matter with which counsel was once involved. The court further held because counsel did not participate in the case, she was able to provide legal advice and other assistance to the Board without violating the ex parte communication prohibition.

# Chapter 7

# Contested Cases: Standard of Proof and Findings

## § 7.1. Standard of Proof

The general rule is that in an administrative contested case, the agency has the burden to prove its case by a preponderance of the evidence.[1] The agency therefore must prove that it is more likely than not (a greater than 50 percent chance) that a fact is true.

"Beyond a reasonable doubt," the standard of proof used in criminal trials, is never applied in Administrative Law.[2] However, the higher civil case standard of "clear and convincing" is the required standard of proof in certain contested cases. The "clear and convincing" standard has been explained by the Court of Appeals to mean that "the witness to a fact must be found to be credible, and that the facts to which they have testified are distinctly remembered and the details thereof narrated exactly and in due order, so as to enable the trier of the facts to come to a clear conviction, without hesitancy, of the truth of the precise facts in issue."[3]

The "clear and convincing" standard of proof is required if imposed by regulation, statute or constitutional due process.[4] For example, the Department of Human Resources has a regulation, COMAR 07.01.04.12 that requires the party with the burden of persuasion to prove an intentional program violation by clear and convincing evidence. Maryland Code Health General Article § 7-503(e) is a statute that requires the Department of Health and Mental Hygiene to prove certain factors by clear and convincing evidence before someone is involuntarily admitted to a state mental residential center.[5]

Constitutional due process may also require a clear and convincing standard of proof. In *Addington v. Texas*,[6] the U.S. Supreme Court when faced with the issue of the required standard of proof in order for the state to involuntarily commit someone for an indefinite period to a state mental hospital wrote:

---

1. Bereano v. State Ethics Comm'n, 403 Md. 716, 944 A.2d 538 (2008); Maryland Code Annotated, State Government § 10-217.

2. Addington v. Texas, 441 U.S. 418 (1979), stating "beyond reasonable doubt" is a "unique" standard of proof, historically reserved for criminal cases.

3. Attorney Grievance Comm'n v. Mooney, 359 Md. 56, 79, 753 A.2d 17, 29 (2000); Attorney Grievance Comm'n v. Bear, 362 Md. 123, 763 A.2d 175 (2000).

4. Maryland Code Annotated, State Government § 10-217.

5. *See* Reese v. Department of Health & Mental Hygiene, 177 Md. App. 102, 934 A.2d 1009 (2007). The factors are: the individual has an intellectual disability; the individual needs residential services for the individual's adequate habilitation; and there is no less restrictive setting in which the needed services can be provided that is available to the individual or will be available to the individual within a reasonable time after the hearing.

6. 441 U.S. 418 (1979).

> The function of a standard of proof, as that concept is embodied in the Due Process Clause and in the realm of fact finding, is to instruct the factfinder concerning the degree of confidence our society thinks he should have in the correctness of factual conclusions for a particular type of adjudication.[7]

In *Addington*, the Supreme Court applied *Mathews v. Eldridge*[8] flexible due process analysis in holding that the Texas statutory requirements to involuntarily admit someone to a state mental institution needed to be established by clear and convincing evidence.

An interesting situation exists in the area of physician discipline. For many years, the statute required the Board of Physicians in a physician discipline case based on a doctor's failure to meet the appropriate standard of medical care to prove the case by clear and convincing evidence. But Health Occupation Article § 14-405(b)(3) was amended effective January 11, 2005 to require proof only by a preponderance of the evidence. Cases in some other jurisdictions have held that it violates the due process right of a physician to have his license revoked based on a preponderance of evidence standard. A full discussion of this issue can be found by the Washington Supreme Court in *Nguyen v. State Department of Health, Medical Quality Assurance Commission*[9] which held that the Due Process Clause of the United States Constitution requires proof by clear and convincing evidence in a medical disciplinary proceeding. The Washington Supreme Court recognized that several state courts had disagreed on whether the preponderance standard was sufficient to satisfy due process in medical discipline cases, but stated that "the more recent decisions trend toward requiring the higher standard of proof."[10] Its conclusion was that due process required the state to apply the clear and convincing standard in medical disciplinary proceedings.

In Maryland, the due process right of a physician not to be disciplined by the Board of Physicians based on a preponderance of the evidence standard has not been decided. Cases involving other agencies do exist challenging an agency's use of the preponderance of evidence standard. In *Everett v. Baltimore Gas & Electric Co.*,[11] the Court of Appeals held that in a contested case hearing at the Public Service Commission to determine whether BGE had legally terminated residential utility service to a customer who allegedly fraudulently obtained utility service, the clear and convincing standard was required. The Court's reason in *Everett* was that at common law, allegations of fraud must be proven by clear and convincing evidence. Moreover, because unauthorized use of utility services could support a criminal charge, the clear and convincing standard was required. *Everett* explained that "certain cases require a more exacting standard because of the seriousness of the allegations."[12]

*Everett* was relied upon by the petitioner in *Coleman v. Anne Arundel County Police Department*.[13] *Coleman* involved a disciplinary action against a police officer for stealing $76 in cash. One argument made upon judicial review was that "in administrative cases arising out of theft or fraud related activity, the burden of proof is clear and convincing."[14] The Court of Appeals in *Coleman* overruled *Everett*, and held that the preponderance of

7. 441 U.S. 418, 423 (1979).
8. 424 U.S. 319 (1976).
9. 29 P.3d 689 (Wash. 2001).
10. 29 P.3d 689, 691 (Wash. 2001).
11. 307 Md. 286, 513 A.2d 882 (1986).
12. 307 Md. 286, 301, 513 A.2d 882, 890 (1986).
13. 369 Md. 108, 797 A.2d 770 (2002).
14. Coleman v. Anne Arundel County Police Dep't, 136 Md. App. 419, 766 A.2d 169, 182–83 (2001).

the evidence standard was sufficient. *Coleman*'s holding was based on a few factors. In *Coleman*, the Court of Appeals found "instructive" that seven years after *Everett*, the legislature added to the APA for the first time that preponderance of the evidence was the "generally applicable standard of proof to be used by covered state administrative agencies in contested case hearings, including, of particular relevance here, disciplinary actions by the Maryland State Police" under the Law Enforcement Officer Bill of Rights.[15] Additionally, the *Coleman* court's application of *Mathews v. Eldridge* led it to conclude the clear and convincing standard was not required in this police disciplinary case. Although recognizing that "in certain limited circumstances, the heightened burden of clear and convincing evidence is required when the government seeks to take unusual coercive action—action more dramatic than entering an award of money damages or other conventional relief—against an individual,"[16] the preponderance standard was sufficient here. The "implementation of the heightened standard of proof sought by Petitioner would [not] so significantly reduce the risk of error that it should be implemented regardless of any additional administrative or financial burdens it would entail."[17] Moreover, the government interest in the internal discipline of corrupt police officers "weigh[ed] heavily" in favor of the preponderance standard. An additional reason supporting the preponderance standard in *Coleman* was that the preponderance standard was the established standard in cases involving State police, and to require a different standard for local police officers "would create an inexplicable disparate impact between officers within the overall law enforcement community itself."[18]

Another case discussing the clear and convincing standard is *Calvert County Planning Commission v. Howlin Realty Management, Inc.*[19] *Howlin* involved a request by opponents of a planned residential subdivision that the Planning Commission rescind its earlier approval of a subdivision. It was argued by the supporters of the subdivision approval that the clear and convincing standard should be applied to overcome the earlier decision. This higher standard was appropriate because of the presumption that the agency had acted properly. The Court of Appeals wrote that while "[i]t is true that there are some factual issues that impinge so directly and significantly on fundamental rights as to require more than mere preponderance of the evidence," in this case, the standard of proof "normally applicable" in administrative proceedings, preponderance of the evidence, was the proper standard.[20]

## § 7.2. The Findings Requirement

Both the APA and Maryland caselaw require that the final decision in a contested case be accompanied by findings of fact and conclusions of law.[21] It is not sufficient for the findings of fact to be stated in statutory language; the final decision must state concisely and explicitly the facts that support the findings.[22] Additionally, if a party submitted

15. 369 Md. 108, 136, 797 A.2d 770, 787 (2002).
16. 369 Md. 108, 143, 797 A.2d 770, 791 (2002).
17. 369 Md. 108, 147, 797 A.2d 770, 794 (2002).
18. 369 Md. 108, 149, 797 A.2d 770, 795 (2002).
19. 364 Md. 301, 772 A.2d 1209 (2001).
20. 364 Md. 301, 327, 772 A.2d 1209, 1224 (2001).
21. Maryland Code Annotated, State Government § 10-221(b)(1).
22. Maryland Code Annotated, State Government § 10-221(b)(3).

proposed findings of fact, the final decision must state a ruling on each proposed finding.[23]

The requirement that the agency provide findings of fact on all material issues and present a clear statement of the rationale for its decision by explaining how the agency applied the relevant facts to the applicable law is often referred to as the "Findings Requirement." As the Court of Appeals wrote in *Fowler v. Motor Vehicle Administration*,[24] "the importance of clear, explicit administrative agency decisions cannot be overemphasized."

There are various reasons why adequate findings which provide an explanation for the agency decision are required:

1. By requiring an agency to explain its decision, the agency decision will be a better, more accurate decision. The quality of agency decision-making is improved by requiring an explanation.
2. By requiring an agency to explain its decision, effective legislative oversight is facilitated. This improves the likelihood that legislative policy goals are being accurately furthered by the agency.
3. As a matter of fundamental fairness, losing parties should know why they lost.
4. By requiring an agency to explain its decision, other persons are given guidance as to how the agency will handle future cases. This permits better compliance by regulated parties who are given a clearer understanding of what is expected from them, and the consequences of non-compliance.
5. In a democratic society, government should not operate in secret. The findings requirement furthers open government. Open government fosters public understanding, respect and acceptance of administrative decision-making.
6. Discriminatory treatment of persons is better avoided when an agency must explain it decision.
7. Responsible judicial review requires an agency to explain its decision.

The last reason—to facilitate judicial review—is the reason most often emphasized by the courts. The Court of Appeals has repeatedly emphasized that "for a reviewing court to perform properly its [judicial review] function, an administrative decision must contain factual findings on all the material issues of a case and a clear, explicit statement of the agency's rationale."[25] Also, as the Court of Special Appeals wrote, "[w]e must know what a decision means before the duty becomes ours to say whether it is right or wrong."[26]

The findings requirement also supports the principle that a court can only uphold the agency decision on the grounds relied upon by the agency.[27] This differs from appellate review of a lower court decision where the lower court decision will be affirmed if it can be upheld for any reason found in the record. Findings are so essential to judicial review that they are required even if there is no express statutory requirement for findings.[28]

---

23. Maryland Code Annotated, State Government § 10-221(b)(4).

24. 394 Md. 331, 906 A.2d 347 (2006).

25. Fowler v. Motor Vehicle Administration, 394 Md. 331, 342, 906 A.2d 347, 353 (2006).

26. Maryland Racing Comm'n v. Belotti, 130 Md. App. 23, 52, 744 A.2d 558, 574 (1999).

27. *See* United Steelworkers v. Bethlehem Steel Corp., 298 Md. 665, 472 A.2d 62 (1984). *See also* Annapolis Market Place, LLC v. Parker, 369 Md. 689, 802 A.2d 1029 (2002).

28. Blackburn v. Bd. of Liquor License Comm'rs for Baltimore City, 130 Md. App. 614, 747 A.2d 725 (2000).

Various statements have been made by the Maryland courts as to what constitutes adequate findings. The following points have been made by the Maryland courts:

1. "At a minimum, one must be able to discern from the record the facts found, the law applied, and the relationship between the two."[29]
2. The findings of fact must resolve all significant conflicts in the evidence. They should set forth which facts have been found to be true, and which evidence has been rejected.[30]
3. Findings of fact must be meaningful, and cannot simply repeat statutory criteria, make broad conclusory statements, or rest on boilerplate resolutions.[31]

If the agency's findings are inadequate, the proper remedy is to remand the case to the final agency decisionmaker so that adequate findings can be made.[32]

## § 7.3. Findings Requirement and the Sanction

Agencies are often granted flexibility in the sanction that they can impose. In order to ensure accurate, fair, and non-discriminatory agency decisions regarding the sanction, the findings requirement should apply to the sanction as well as the underlying facts which led to the sanction. Indeed, all the reasons for the findings requirement just set forth apply equally to requiring findings on the sanction as well as for the basic facts. Moreover, because the major, if not sole, issue in many cases on judicial review is the sanction imposed, a findings requirement for sanctions is essential. Nevertheless, there is controversy in Maryland over whether the findings requirement applies to the sanction. This controversy is discussed in Chapter 23, Judicial Review of the Sanction.

29. Forman v. Motor Vehicle Administration, 332 Md. 201, 221, 630 A.2d 753, 764 (1993).

30. Sweeney v. Montgomery County, Md., 107 Md. App. 187, 198, 667 A.2d 922, 927 (1995).

31. Bucktail, LLC v. County Council of Talbot County, 352 Md. 530, 553, 723 A.2d 440, 451 (1991).

32. Sweeney v. Montgomery County, Md., 107 Md. App. 187, 667 A.2d 922 (1995). *See also* Lewis v. Department of Natural Res., 377 Md. 382, 833 A.2d 563 (2003); Mehrling v. Nationwide Insurance Co., 371 Md. 40, 806 A.2d 662 (2002).

# Chapter 8

# Contested Cases: Res Judicata, Collateral Estoppel and Double Jeopardy

There are several reported cases in Maryland discussing the relationship of contested cases, res judicata, collateral estoppel and double jeopardy. This chapter will discuss these doctrines and their application in the context of Maryland Administrative Law.

## § 8.1. Res Judicata and Collateral Estoppel

Res judicata and collateral estoppel are related but distinct doctrines. Res judicata is the relevant doctrine when there is a second proceeding between identical parties which involves the same cause of action as an earlier proceeding between these parties. Under res judicata, all matters actually litigated or that could have been litigated are deemed to have been conclusively decided by the decision in the first proceeding. Collateral estoppel, also known as issue preclusion, bars a party from re-litigating an issue that he or she has already litigated unsuccessfully in another action. Under collateral estoppel, only those issues or facts actually litigated in the first proceeding are conclusive in the subsequent proceeding.[1] Collateral estoppel can be mutual or non-mutual. Mutual collateral estoppel is when the same parties are involved in both of the relevant proceedings. Non-mutual collateral estoppel is the relevant doctrine when the parties in the two proceedings are not identical. There are two types of non-mutual collateral estoppel—offensive and defensive. Offensive use of non-mutual collateral estoppel occurs when a plaintiff seeks to foreclose a defendant from relitigating an issue the defendant has previously litigated unsuccessfully in another action against a different party. Defensive use of non-mutual collateral estoppel occurs when a defendant seeks to prevent a plaintiff from relitigating an issue the plaintiff has previously litigated unsuccessfully in another action against a different party.[2]

The cases involving contested cases, res judicata, and collateral estoppel involve: (1) cases where both proceedings were administrative proceedings; (2) cases where the first proceeding was judicial and the second proceeding was administrative; (3) cases where the first proceeding was administrative and the second was judicial; and (4) cases where both proceedings were within one agency. The principles of law relevant to determining whether res judicata or collateral estoppel apply do not vary based on the types of

1. *See* Mackall v. Zayre Corp., 293 Md. 221, 443 A.2d 98 (1982); Spencer v. Md. State Board of Pharmacy, 380 Md. 515, 846 A.2d 341 (2004).

2. *See* Rourke v. Amchem Prods., Inc., 384 Md. 329, 863 A.2d 926 (2004).

proceedings involved, but I think it is helpful to consider the reported cases based on these scenarios.

## § 8.2. Two Administrative Proceedings

*Cicala v. Disability Review Board for Prince George's County*[3] involved a proceeding at the Maryland Worker's Compensation Commission followed by a hearing before the Prince George's County Disability Review Board. Cicala was a police officer who became disabled from injuries he claimed were service connected. He first sought to recover Worker's Compensation. The Worker's Compensation Commission, after a contested case hearing, held that Cicala's injury arose "out of and in the course of his employment," and Cicala was entitled to recovery under worker's compensation. Thereafter, Cicala filed for a pension from Prince George's County. If Cicala's disability was "caused by an injury or sickness suffered as a result of his performance of his duties as an Employee" of the Prince George's County police department, Cicala would be entitled to an enhanced pension. At the hearing before the Disability Review Board, Cicala offered the finding of the Worker's Compensation Commission as conclusive proof that he was entitled to the enhanced pension. The Board refused to even consider the Worker's Compensation Commission decision. After being denied the higher pension, Cicala petitioned for judicial review arguing that res judicata applied. The case eventually made its way to the Court of Appeals.

In its opinion in *Cicala*, the Court of Appeals wrote that res judicata applies if three things are true: (1) the issue determined in the first proceeding is identical to the issue in the subsequent proceeding; (2) the parties in both proceedings are the same; and (3) there is a final judgment on the merits in the first proceeding.[4] In this case, the court held that res judicata did not apply because the "identical" issue was not involved in both contested cases. The issue before the Worker's Compensation Commission was whether Cicala's injury "arose out of and [was] in the course of employment." The issue before the Disability Review Board was whether Cicala's disability was "caused by an injury or sickness suffered as a result of his performance of his duties as an Employee." The court cited cases from other jurisdictions that held that "a quasi-judicial determination by one administrative agency is not binding on another administrative agency which is seeking to determine an apparently identical issue under a different statute."[5] Although the issues before the two agencies appeared to be identical, they were not because "different statutes have different legislative histories, purposes, scopes of coverage, language, standards, procedures, and policies which may dictate opposite results."[6] In this case, there were "substantial differences" between the worker's compensation and the disability proceedings.[7] The court further held that the findings from the Worker's Compensation Committee were not even admissible

3. 288 Md. 254, 418 A.2d 205 (1980).
4. 288 Md. 254, 263, 418 A.2d 205, 211 (1980).
5. 288 Md. 254, 264, 418 A.2d 205, 211 (1980).
6. 288 Md. 254, 265, 418 A.2d 205, 211 (1980).
7. For example, the Workers' Compensation Commission had subpoena power, while the Disability Review Board did not. Moreover, the standard for each agency was different: "arising out of and in the course of employment" was different than "caused by an injury or sickness suffered as a result of his performance of his duties as an Employee."

at the hearing before the Disability Review Board. Because the issues in the two cases were so different, the findings from the worker's compensation case were not probative in the case before the Disability Review Board.

The argument that a remand to the agency would create a res judicata issue was deemed "without merit and frivolous" in *Spencer v. Maryland State Board of Pharmacy*.[8] In *Spencer*, a decision by the Board of Pharmacy disciplining Spencer was vacated because of bias among members of the Board. The case was remanded to the Board for a new hearing. Res judicata was not applicable because there was no final judgment in the case; the case was still on appellate review. Moreover, because res judicata (and collateral estoppel) "require a subsequent cause of action in which those doctrines may take effect; [the] appeal is not a subsequent cause of action but all part of the same case."[9]

## § 8.3. Administrative Contested Case Followed by Judicial Proceeding

*Batson v. Shiflett*[10] involved an unfair labor practice hearing before the National Labor Relations Board (NLRB) followed by a subsequent civil lawsuit for defamation in a Maryland circuit court. One of the issues at the defamation trial was whether the NLRB decision at the unfair labor practice hearing precluded certain findings by the jury in the defamation action. The NLRB case involved an attempt by the national union of the Shipbuilding Workers of America to repudiate a collective bargaining agreement reached between Bethlehem Steel Corporation and Local Union 33 of the Shipbuilding Workers of America. Shiflett was the president of the local union; Batson was the president of the national union. The local union and Bethlehem Steel filed an unfair labor practice with the NLRB against the national union alleging that the national union's repudiation of the new agreement constituted an unfair labor practice of a "refusal to bargain." The crucial factual issue at the NLRB hearing was whether Batson and the national union had authorized Shiflett and the local union to negotiate and execute the new collective bargaining agreement. After an adjudicatory hearing, the NLRB dismissed the charges, and held the local union agreement to be null and void.

Following the NLRB ruling, both Shiflett and Batson began distributing handbills to members of the local union. In his handbill, Batson accused Shiflett of conspiracy, perjury, and misuse of union funds. One flyer called Shiflett "a crook." Thereafter, Shiflett filed a civil suit in circuit court alleging defamation, intentional infliction of emotional distress and conspiracy. A ten-day jury trial was held. Batson requested that the jury be instructed that it was bound by the NLRB decision that the local union agreement had been unlawfully executed by Shiflett. The circuit court judge refused such an instruction, and instead instructed the jury that it was not bound by the NLRB decision. The jury returned a verdict in favor of Shiflett. The basic argument presented on appeal was that "if the NLRB's factfindings are credited, each of [the] statements is true," and therefore the defamation action could not succeed.

8. 380 Md. 515, 846 A.2d 341 (2004).
9. 380 Md. 515, 535, 846 A.2d 341, 353 (2004).
10. 325 Md. 684, 602 A.2d 1191 (1992).

The Court of Appeals first wrote that because the initial case was an unfair labor practice charge at the NLRB and the second case was a common law tort action in circuit court, the two cases involved different causes of action, and therefore the relevant doctrine was collateral estoppel, not res judicata. The Court of Special Appeals, in the first level of appellate review, had applied a three part test employed by federal courts:

> Whether an administrative agency's declaration should be given preclusive effect hinges on three factors: '(1) whether the [agency] was acting in a judicial capacity; (2) whether the issue presented to the district court was actually litigated before the [agency]; and (3) whether its resolution was necessary to the [agency's] decision.

The Court of Appeals then held that the "rule in Maryland does not differ in any material respect from that adopted by the federal courts."[11]

The Court of Appeals in *Batson* court then applied this three-part test for collateral estoppel. The first prong was satisfied because by conducting a hearing where the NLRB allowed the parties to present evidence and the NLRB had ruled on a legal dispute, the NLRB had acted in a judicial capacity. The second and third requirements, however, were not satisfied. The NLRB finding of illegal contract ratification was not identical to whether Shiflett had committed any criminal acts. The elements, proof, and nature of any illegal union contract ratification were not identical to the crimes of conspiracy and perjury. The relevant issue actually litigated before the NLRB was whether the local union had the authority to negotiate and reach a binding agreement with Bethlehem Shipbuilding Corporation. The statements in the flyers which were distributed after termination of the NLRB proceeding were obviously not at issue before the NLRB, and therefore were not litigated at the NLRB. As to the third factor, the court wrote that a factual issue is necessary to the resolution to the decision only if its resolution is required to support the judgment entered in the prior proceeding. In this case, the NLRB never explicitly found Shiflett guilty of any wrongdoing. The NLRB decision that the national union had not authorized the local union to enter into the agreement with Bethlehem did not establish the truth of the allegedly libelous statements in the flyer. Therefore, collateral estoppel did not apply to the determination of the falsity of the statements in the flyers.

The collateral estoppel analysis of *Batson* was applied in *Reid v. Maryland*[12] which involved Reid's refusal to take a alcohol concentration breathalyzer test. At the first proceeding held at OAH, the ALJ made two significant factual findings: (1) Reid had not been properly advised of the consequences of refusing to take the test, and (2) Reid had not consumed alcohol on the day he was stopped and asked to take the test. Based on these two findings, the ALJ denied the Motor Vehicle Administration's request to suspend Reid's commercial driver's license. After his success at OAH, Reid moved to dismiss criminal charges pending in circuit court for driving while intoxicated and/or under the influence of alcohol. These charges had been filed against him prior to the administrative hearing. The basis of Reid's motion to dismiss was that the State was collaterally estopped by the OAH decision. The circuit judge refused to dismiss the criminal charges. The Court of Special Appeals affirmed the circuit court. The Court of Special Appeals held that collateral estoppel did not apply in Reid's criminal case because the ALJ's resolution of the issue of

11. 325 Md. 684, 703, 602 A.2d 1191, 1201 (1992).
12. 119 Md. App. 129, 704 A.2d 473 (1998).

whether Reid had been drinking was not necessary to the ALJ' s decision. Under the relevant statute, the failure of the police officer to warn the driver of the consequences of refusing to take the breathalyzer test is a "perfect defense."[13] Once Reid established this perfect defense, "it simply did not matter whether [Reid] had, in fact, consumed alcohol on the night of his arrest."[14] The finding by the ALJ that Reid had not been drinking alcohol, therefore, was not necessary to the administrative decision, and thus collateral estoppel was inapplicable in the criminal case.

A few months after *Reid* was decided, the Court of Appeals decided *Janes v. Maryland*[15] where the issue was whether the State was precluded from criminally prosecuting Janes for driving while intoxicated. In an earlier administrative proceeding to suspend Janes's drivers's license for refusing to take a breathalyzer test, the ALJ had found that Janes was not driving the vehicle at the time central to both the administrative license suspension case and the criminal case. In *Janes*, the Court of Appeals did not employ the three-part collateral estoppel test from *Batson*. The court held that the legislature had overridden common law collateral estoppel in cases involving the refusal to take a chemical test for alcohol. The legislature had enacted a statute that provides that "the determination of any facts by the [MVA] is independent of the determination of the same or similar facts in the adjudication of any criminal charges arising out of the same occurrence."[16] This statute, which is part of a very elaborate statutory scheme relating to chemical tests for alcohol, made it unnecessary to consider the collateral estoppel issue.

*Neifert v. Department of the Environment*[17] also involved collateral estoppel and a judicial proceeding that followed an administrative contested case. The initial proceeding involved an application by several lot owners in Worcester County for sewer system connection and wetland fill permits. These requests were denied by the relevant agencies, including hearings at OAH, based on the finding that the lots were not eligible for sewer service because of their wetland status. Subsequent to the administrative determination, the lot owners filed in circuit court an action under 43 U.S.C.§ 1983 alleging denial of equal protection and other constitutional protections. One issue relevant to the § 1983 case was whether the lot owners were precluded from relitigating the issue of whether their lots were similarly situated to other wetland lots that had obtained sewer service. The Court of Appeals held that the lot owners were not collaterally stopped to argue that their lots were similarly situated. The court applied the three-part test from *Batson*. First, the court held the prior administrative proceeding was a contested case, and thus the agency was acting in a quasi-judicial capacity. Secondly, the similarly situated issue had been addressed in the briefs filed with the agency. The third factor, however, was not established. Resolution of the similarly situated issue was not necessary to the agency's decision in the first proceeding. The ALJ and the Department of the Environment "could have" addressed the lot owner's claim without addressing the similarly situated issue. Moreover, the ALJ's written recommended decision indicated that the contested case at OAH had focused primarily on whether the lots were eligible for sewer service, not whether the lots were similarly situated to others.

13. *See* Maryland Code Annotated, Transportation § 16-205.1(f)(8)(ii)(4).
14. 119 Md. App. 129, 139, 704 A.2d 473, 477 (1998).
15. 350 Md. 284, 711 A.2d 1319 (1998).
16. *See* Maryland Code Annotated, Transportation § 16-205.1(l)(1).
17. 395 Md. 486, 910 A.2d 1100 (2006).

# § 8.4. Judicial Proceeding Followed by Contested Case

*Powell v. Maryland Aviation Administration*[18] involved a claim of res judicata by the State. The first proceeding was a criminal trial in circuit court. Powell, a state employee, had been found guilty of making harassing telephone calls to a co-worker. This was followed by an administrative hearing to remove Powell from state employment. At the administrative hearing, Powell denied making the calls. The ALJ ruled that the circuit court judge's finding of guilt was "sufficient to support" Powell's firing. The Court of Appeals disagreed that the decision in the criminal case had conclusive impact on the administrative state employment termination proceeding. The agency decision needed to be based on the evidence presented at the agency hearing, not the court proceeding.

*Powell* was discussed in Chapter 6 in connection with issues involving admissibility of evidence. In that discussion, I questioned the court's holding. It also seems that application of the three-part res judicata test could lead to a result contrary to the court's holding: the identical issue was determined in both proceedings (whether Powell made the harassing telephone calls); the same parties were involved (the State and Powell); and there was a final judgment on the merits (Powell was found guilty). The fact that Powell received a PBJ, however, could mean that there was no final judgment. This is what the Court of Special Appeals held in *Culver v. Maryland Insurance Commissioner.*[19]

*Culver* involved the revocation of an insurance producer's license. Culver was an attorney who had been disbarred, but who also had an insurance license from the Maryland Insurance Administration (MIA). In May 2004, Culver had been disbarred by the Court of Appeals for several ethical violations including sexual intercourse with a client in a divorce case, advice to a client to obtain credit card loans in order to pay legal fees with the intent to have the debt discharged in bankruptcy, and charging an unreasonable fee. In December 2004, the MIA revoked Culver's insurance producer's license. Culver then requested that a contested case hearing be held at OAH to challenge this MIA revocation. MIA moved for summary disposition. MIA argued that the decision of the Court of Appeals disbarring Culver indicated that he was "untrustworthy, and therefore, did not meet the statutory requirements for a licensed insurance producer." Culver responded that he wanted to contest the findings of fact made by the Court of Appeals in his disbarment case. The ALJ agreed with the MIA that a hearing was not necessary because "there are no material facts needing to be developed at a hearing on the merits."[20] The ALJ ruled that MIA was entitled to revoke Culver's license "as a matter of law." Under the authority delegated to OAH, the ALJ's decision was only a proposed decision. Culver filed exceptions with MIA. The MIA held an exceptions hearing, but did not allow Culver to present any evidence. The MIA then issued a final order of revocation.

The Court of Special Appeals recognized that this case involved offensive use of non-mutual collateral estoppel — it involved a plaintiff (MIA) seeking to foreclose a defendant (Culver) from relitigating an issue the defendant had previously litigated unsuccessfully. The Court of Special Appeals first noted that the "Court of Appeals has recognized defensive non-mutual collateral estoppel but has yet to formally embrace offensive non-mutual collateral estoppel." It added that the Court of Appeals had recognized that the United

18. 336 Md. 210, 647 A.2d 437 (1994).

19. 175 Md. App. 645, 931 A.2d 537 (2007).

20. 175 Md. App. 645, 650, 931 A.2d 537, 540 (2007).

States Supreme Court as an aspect of federal law had expressed some concerns about the "broad application of offensive non-mutuality."[21] There were two reasons for these concerns: first, offensive use of collateral estoppel does not promote judicial economy in the same manner as defensive use does. Defensive collateral estoppel gives plaintiff a strong incentive to join all potential defendants in the first action, while offensive collateral estoppel creates a contrary incentive. Secondly, offensive non-mutual collateral estoppel may be unfair to the defendant for three reasons: (1) defendant in the first action may have little incentive to defend vigorously if small or nominal damages are involved; (2) the judgment relied upon may be inconsistent with another judgment in favor of the defendant; and (3) the second action may afford defendant more procedural rights than those available in the first action.

The Court of Special Appeals then held that none of these concerns applied to Culver. Most importantly, Culver had "every incentive to defend vigorously in the action that resulted in his disbarment."[22] Moreover, the procedural protections in the attorney discipline case were not inferior to those at the MIA. Having decided that offensive use of non-mutual collateral estoppel may be available in this case, the Court of Special Appeals then addressed whether its use was appropriate in this case. The court applied a four-part test:

1. Was the issue decided in the prior adjudication identical with the one presented in the action in question?
2. Was there a final judgment on the merits?
3. Was the party against whom the plea is asserted a party or in privity with a party to the prior adjudication?
4. Was the party against whom the plea is asserted given a fair opportunity to be heard on the issue?[23]

The court held that all four tests had been met, and that Culver was properly barred from relitigating matters before the MIA that had been already decided by the Court of Appeals.

The Court of Special Appeals then addressed Culver's argument that *Powell* required the ALJ to make his own independent findings of fact. The court distinguished *Powell* on the ground that Powell had been granted probation before judgment. Because there was no judgment, res judicata could not apply. Here, in *Culver*, there was a judgment. The court in *Culver* also rejected the argument that its holding denied Culver his right under the Maryland APA to present evidence at the contested case hearing. Because the evidence that Culver "desired to put forth would have constituted nothing more than an attempt to relitigate the findings made in the disbarment action, … there were no material facts at issue."[24] No petition for certiorari to the Court of Appeals was filed in *Culver*.

In *Tamara A. v. Montgomery County Department of Health and Human Services*,[25] the first proceeding was in the circuit court sitting as a juvenile court on a petition filed by the Montgomery County Department of Health and Human Services (DHHS), regarding whether a child of Tamara A., Shirah, should be found a "child in need of assistance" (CINA). Two other children of Tamara A., Nathaniel and Madeline, had previously been found to be children in need of assistance. At the judicial hearing on the CINA petition

21. 175 Md. App. 645, 655, 931 A.2d 537, 543 (2007).
22. 175 Md. App. 645, 656, 931 A.2d 537, 544 (2007).
23. 175 Md. App. 645, 657, 931 A.2d 537, 544 (2007).
24. 175 Md. App. 645, 659, 931 A.2d 537, 545 (2007).
25. 407 Md. 180, 963 A.2d 773 (2009).

regarding Shirah, the circuit court judge took judicial notice of the record in the proceeding involving Nathaniel and Madeline. No other evidence was introduced, and Tamara A. chose not to present any evidence. From this evidentiary record, the circuit court judge ruled that because of Tamara A.'s "psychiatric or psychological or personality disorder," there was substantial risk of harm to Shirah, and that Tamara A. was "unable and unwilling to provide for the need of this child."[26]

About one month after the CINA finding by the circuit court, DHHS informed Tamara that its investigation found that she had been found responsible for "Indicated Child Neglect" with respect to Shirah. The consequence of this finding, if not withdrawn or modified, was that Tarmara A.'s name would go into a central registry of persons found to have abused or neglected a child. Tamara A. was informed of her right to appeal this finding by requesting a hearing at OAH, which Tamara A. did. DHHS then filed a motion to dismiss the appeal at OAH. DHHS argued that the parties before OAH were the same parties at the CINA proceeding, and that the issue of neglect had been litigated and determined by a valid final judgment. The ALJ denied DHHS's motion. The ALJ ruled that although the parties were the same in both proceedings, and that there had been a final judgment in the CINA case, the facts litigated in the CINA case were not the same as the factual issues to be determined in the administrative contested case involving the central registry. The CINA case had been decided on the *potential* of harm to Shirah because of conduct pertaining to two other children of Tamara A. The present central registry case required proof of actual abuse or neglect, not just potential harm. DHHS filed an immediate petition for review with the circuit court. The circuit court affirmed the ALJ ruling. The Court of Special Appeals, however, disagreed, and held that the ALJ erred in not granting the motion to dismiss. The case then went to the Court of Appeals. The Court of Appeals remanded the case to OAH for a hearing on the merits because the denial of the motion to dismiss was not an appealable order. This is discussed in Chapter 11.

Although the Court of Appeals in *Tamara A.* did not base its remand order to OAH on res judicata or collateral estoppel, its opinion does suggest that neither would apply. The court wrote:

> Indeed, although the correctness of the ALJ's decision is not presently before us, the statutory construct itself suggests that an appeal of a finding of indicated child abuse or neglect is not necessarily precluded by a CINA determination. FL § 5-706.1(a) requires DHHS to notify the individual alleged to have abused or neglected a child of its finding and of the opportunity to appeal the finding. FL §§ 5-706.1(b)(3) and (4) require OAH to stay a hearing in such an appeal if either criminal charges based on the alleged abuse or neglect or a CINA proceeding is pending, until any such proceeding is concluded. If the individual is found guilty of criminal charges arising out of the alleged abuse or neglect, OAH must dismiss the administrative appeal. FL § 5-706.1(b)(3)(ii). Conviction, in other words, *does* act as an absolute statutory bar to further prosecution of the administrative appeal. That is not the case with respect to a CINA proceeding, however. In sharp contrast, § 5-706.1(b)(4)(ii) provides that "[a]fter the conclusion of the CINA case, the [OAH] shall vacate the stay and schedule further proceedings in accordance with this section."[27]

26. 407 Md. 180, 184, 963 A.2d 773, 775 (2009).
27. 407 Md. 180, 194, 963 A.2d 773, 781 (2009).

## § 8.5. Intra-Agency Decisions

The Court of Special Appeals held that res judicata was improperly applied by the circuit court in *Maryland State Department of Education v. Shoop*.[28] Shoop was a state employee who worked as an automobile mechanics instructor at the Maryland Correctional Training Center. Initially, Shoop received a one-day suspension for allowing inmate students to have unsupervised access to tools in the auto mechanic shop where he taught. After further investigation, it was found that his violations of regulatory policy were multiple and more egregious than previously thought. He was eventually terminated from state employment. Upon judicial review, the circuit court held that res judicata barred Shoop's termination because initially he had received a one-day suspension for his violations, and "finality is needed in every case." The Court of Special Appeals reversed this ruling. The initial one-day suspension was the result of an internal agency proceeding that was "very informal." In order for res judicata or collateral estoppel to apply, the first proceeding must be "the essential equivalent of a judicial proceeding."[29] Shoop's suspension was not the result of a quasi-judicial proceeding. Moreover, the court viewed the initial suspension as an executive decision, not a judicial or quasi-judicial one. It was proper for Shoop to be terminated when additional information about his violation became known to the agency.

## § 8.6. Law of the Case

*Reier v. State Department of Assessments and Taxation*[30] involved several hearings at OAH on the issue of Reier's termination as a property assessor. In one of the later OAH hearings, the ALJ revised her previous findings of fact. It was argued by the agency, which did not like the revisions, that the revised findings violated the "law of the case" doctrine. The Court of Appeals rejected the application of this doctrine to the situation in *Reier*. The court wrote that:

> The law of the case doctrine is one of appellate procedure. Under the doctrine, once an appellate court rules upon a question presented on appeal, litigants and lower courts become bound by the ruling, which is considered to be the law of the case.[31]

Moreover, the law of the case doctrine applies only to questions of law, not pure questions of fact. Because *Reier* involved the ALJ's findings of fact, the law of the case doctrine was not applicable.

The law of the case doctrine was deemed applicable in *Stavely v. State Farm Mutual Automobile Insurance Co.*[32] In *Stavely*, an ALJ had ruled that State Farm's proposed non-renewal of an automobile liability policy was not justified and thus violated Maryland law. This decision was upheld by the Court of Special Appeals, and certiorari was denied by the Court of Appeals. In a subsequent hearing on the same policy between the same

28. 119 Md. App. 181, 704 A.2d 499, *cert. denied*, 349 Md. 495, 709 A.2d 140 (1998).
29. 119 Md. App. 181, 198, 704 A.2d 499, 507 (1998).
30. 397 Md. 2, 915 A.2d 970 (2007).
31. 397 Md. 2, 20–21, 915 A.2d 970, 981 (2007).
32. 376 Md. 108, 829 A.2d 265 (2003).

parties to determine the issue of attorney's fees, the ALJ ruled that State Farm was justified in not renewing the policy, and thus denied attorney's fees. In *Stavely*, the Court of Appeals held that the second ALJ's ruling that non-renewal was justified was improper based on the doctrine of the law of the case. Unlike *Reier*, *Stavely* involved an appellate decision on an issue of law.

## § 8.7. Double Jeopardy

There are several Maryland cases discussing whether a decision in a contested case violated the Double Jeopardy Clause of the Fifth Amendment to the United States Constitution as applied to the states through the Fourteenth Amendment.[33] One problem with these Maryland cases is that they apply an analysis based on the United States Supreme Court case *United States v. Halper*[34] which has been abandoned and replaced by a different analysis by the Supreme Court in *Hudson v. United States*.[35] This section will discuss the Maryland cases and their application of *Halper* and then discuss *Hudson*.

The Double Jeopardy Clause provides that no person shall "be subject for the same offense to be twice put in jeopardy of life or limb."[36] This Clause has been interpreted to protect not only against multiple prosecutions for the same offense, but also against multiple punishments.

*Ward v. Department of Public Safety & Correctional Services*[37] involved the discipline of a correctional officer who had violated several public employment regulations. Ward's first infraction was not reporting to his superior officer that he had been served with a criminal summons. For this infraction, Ward was suspended for five days. About six months later, Ward failed to report for work and failed to report his absence in a timely fashion. For these infractions, he was reprimanded. A few months later, Ward again failed to report for duty. He received a five day suspension for this. A few months later, he again failed to report for duty, and was again suspended for five days. After these four disciplinary actions, Ward was informed that charges for removal would be filed with the Secretary of Personnel. The basis of his removal were the four infractions. After completing the administrative process, including a hearing at OAH, Ward was removed from state employment. One issue on judicial review was whether his removal violated the Double Jeopardy Clause. Ward argued that he could not be suspended on several occasions and then removed based on the same misconduct. The Court of Appeals applied *United States v. Halper*[38] to this claim. *Halper* held that, for purposes of the multiple punishment aspect of double jeopardy, the labels "criminal" and "civil" were not of paramount importance. The determination of whether a sanction constituted punishment under the Double Jeopardy Clause depended on whether the purpose of the sanction was "retribution or deterrence," in which case it was punishment, or whether the purpose was "remedial," in which case it was not punishment. Applying this test, the Court of Appeals concluded

33. *See* Benton v. Maryland, 395 U.S. 784 (1969).
34. 490 U.S. 435 (1989).
35. 522 U.S. 93 (1997).
36. U.S. Const. Amend. V.
37. 339 Md. 343, 663 A.2d 66 (1995).
38. 490 U.S. 435 (1989).

that the system of progressive discipline that led to Ward's removal was remedial in nature, not punitive, and thus the "principles of double jeopardy simply do not apply."[39]

*State v. Jones*[40] involved a driver of an automobile who was arrested on the charge of driving while intoxicated. A breath test taken with Jones' consent indicated that his blood alcohol content was 0.27, well over the legal limit. About four months after the arrest, an administrative hearing was held, and the ALJ suspended Jones' driver's license for thirty days. About six months later, Jones faced a criminal trial in district court where he was found guilty of driving while intoxicated. Jones raised the argument that it violated the Double Jeopardy Clause to prosecute him for driving while intoxicated after his driver's license had already been suspended for the same conduct. The Court of Appeals rejected this argument. Citing *Halper*, the court identified the issue as whether the administrative suspension of Jones' license constituted a "punishment." The court recognized that prior to *Halper*, the test was whether "the proceeding was criminal or civil in nature," and that under this "mode of analysis," the administrative license suspension would not constitute punishment within the meaning of the Double Jeopardy Clause.[41] But *Halper* had revised Double Jeopardy analysis, and required the court to consider whether the sanction served the "twin aims of retribution and deterrence" as opposed to being remedial. After an extensive analysis, the court in *Jones* held that the license suspension served a remedial purpose of removing potentially dangerous drivers from the highway, and therefore, it did not violate the Double Jeopardy Clause for a driver with a blood alcohol content in excess of the legal limit to be found guilty of driving while intoxicated in a criminal case and to lose his license in the administrative contested case proceeding.

*Maryland State Department of Education v. Shoop*[42] involved several suspensions of a state employee which eventually led to his termination from state employment. It was argued that although the suspensions were remedial, the termination was punishment because the necessary remedial effects were supplied by the original suspensions. The Double Jeopardy claim failed. Since Shoop admitted the first suspension was remedial, it did not matter whether the subsequent termination amounted to punishment.

In *Spencer v. Maryland State Board of Pharmacy*,[43] the court found that the argument that a remand for a new hearing created a double jeopardy issue was "without merit and frivolous." The court wrote that the "Board's enforcement of its licensing and disciplinary requirements serve purposes essential to the protection of the public, which are deemed remedial, rather than punitive, and therefore are not subject to double jeopardy principles."[44] It also cited *McDonnell v. Commission on Medical Discipline*[45] for the principle that the "purpose of disciplinary proceedings against licensed professionals is not to punish the offender but rather as a catharsis for the profession and a prophylactic for the public."[46]

Two other cases have focused on whether a sanction was punishment or remedial in contexts other than the Double Jeopardy Clause. In *Landsman v. Maryland Home Improvement Commission*,[47] the issue was whether an amendment to Home Improvement

39. 339 Md. 343, 351, 663 A.2d 66, 69 (1995).
40. 340 Md. 235, 666 A.2d 128 (1995), *cert. denied*, 516 U.S. 1173 (1996).
41. 340 Md. 235, 242–43, 666 A.2d 128, 131 (1995).
42. 119 Md. App. 181, 704 A.2d 499, *cert. denied*, 349 Md. 495, 709 A.2d 140 (1998).
43. 380 Md. 515, 846 A.2d 341 (2004).
44. 380 Md. 515, 534, 846 A.2d 341, 352 (2004).
45. 301 Md. 426, 483 A.2d 76 (1984).
46. 380 Md. 515, 535, 846 A.2d 341, 352 (2004).
47. 154 Md. App. 241, 839 A.2d 743 (2003).

Guaranty Fund which increased the maximum amount a homeowner could recover for actual loss applied retroactively to contracts entered before the effective date of the amendment. As part of its analysis of this issue, the court discussed whether the possibility of a license suspension of a home improvement contractor was a penalty. The court repeated that professional license suspensions and revocations generally serve remedial, not punitive purposes. In *Young v. Maryland*,[48] the issue was whether the requirement that certain convicted criminal defendants register as sex offenders constituted "punishment" for purposes of *Apprendi v. New Jersey*.[49] *Apprendi* requires that any fact other than a prior conviction that increases the penalty for a crime beyond the statutory maximum must be submitted to a jury and proven beyond a reasonable doubt. In *Young*, the Court of Appeals held that registration under the sex offender statute was not punishment. The intent of the sex offender statute was not to stigmatize or shame offenders, but to protect the public by requiring registrants to supply information to apprise law enforcement officials about an offender residing or working in the area.

The Maryland cases demonstrate that double jeopardy claims have been unsuccessful based on the reasoning that various administrative sanctions are remedial in nature and do not constitute punishment. The holdings of these cases are based on the United States Supreme Court's 1989 opinion in *United States v. Halper*[50] which held that the court's focus in double jeopardy cases should be on whether the multiple sanctions could be viewed as "punitive" as opposed to "remedial." In 1997, however, the Supreme Court decided *Hudson v. United States*.[51] In *Hudson*, the Supreme Court abandoned *Halper*, and established that the test in deciding whether the Double Jeopardy Clause had been violated should focus on whether the sanctions at issue are "criminal" as opposed to "civil," not whether they are punitive as opposed to remedial. This in fact was the test that had been applied prior to *Halper*.

In *Hudson*, the Supreme Court wrote that whether a particular punishment is criminal or civil is initially a matter of statutory construction. Has the legislature expressly or impliedly labeled the sanction civil or criminal? The fact that the sanction is imposed by an administrative agency is prima facie evidence that the legislature intended the sanction to be civil. But even if the legislature intended to create only civil liability, the sanction may still be "criminal" for purposes of double jeopardy analysis if the "statutory scheme was so punitive either in purpose or effect" to convert the intended civil penalty into a criminal one. In determining this issue, the United States Supreme Court in *Kennedy v. Mendoza-Martinez*[52] had developed a seven-factor analysis. The seven factors are (1) whether the sanction involves an affirmative disability or restraint; (2) whether the sanction has historically been regarded as punishment; (3) whether the sanction comes into play only on a finding of scienter; (4) whether the sanction will promote the traditional aims of punishment of retribution and deterrence; (5) whether the behavior to which it applies is already a crime; (6) whether an alternative purpose may be rationally assigned to the sanction; and (7) whether the sanction appears excessive in relation to the alternative purpose assigned. Application of these seven factors can override the legislature label of "civil" based on "only the clearest proof."[53]

48. 370 Md. 686, 806 A.2d 233 (2002).

49. 530 U.S. 466 (2000).

50. 490 U.S. 435 (1989).

51. 522 U.S. 93 (1997).

52. 372 U.S. 144 (1963).

53. 372 U.S. 144, 204 (1963). *See also* LaCrosse v. Commodity Futures Trading Commission, 137 F.3d 925 (7th Cir. 1998).

Maryland courts have not engaged in a detailed *Hudson* analysis to a double jeopardy claim arising from an administrative sanction. Considering that it is generally agreed that *Hudson* limits the application of the Double Jeopardy Clause when compared to *Halper*, and the fact that no double jeopardy argument was successful in Maryland under *Halper* analysis, it is not likely that double jeopardy claims will be successful under *Hudson*. Indeed, in *State v. Jones*,[54] decided after *Halper* but before *Hudson*, the court recognized that if pre-*Halper* analysis which focused on whether the proceeding is criminal or civil in nature was in effect, the double jeopardy claim would fail. The court then applied *Halper* analysis and reached the same conclusion.

54. 340 Md. 235, 666 A.2d 128 (1995), *cert. denied*, 516 U.S. 1173 (1996).

# Chapter 9

# Contested Cases: Office of Administrative Hearings

## §9.1. History

Prior to 1990, each administrative agency in Maryland held its own contested case hearings. These hearings were presided over by either (1) the agency heads, i.e., the commissioners or board members, (2) hearing examiners, sometimes called hearing officers, who were employees of the agency, or (3) persons who contracted with the agency to hear a particular case. The major criticism of this system was the potential lack of impartiality in that the presiding officer either was a member of the agency, was an employee of the agency, or was being paid by the agency. The quality of the decision making was also questioned. There were no uniform minimum qualifications for hearing officers. Many were not attorneys or had no training in the administrative process.

In 1987, Governor William Donald Schaefer appointed a task force to study the administrative hearing process. In 1989, legislation was enacted[1] that created the Office of Administrative Hearings (OAH) as an independent agency within the Executive Branch to serve as the centralized, consolidated hearing office for other agencies. One of the main objectives of this legislation was to provide an impartial presiding official in administrative hearings. Instead of having an agency adjudicate its own cases, the cases would be heard by trained administrative law judges (ALJ) employed by OAH.

Maryland's OAH is part of a trend in state administrative law to move the hearing process out of the various regulating agencies and into a central office of administrative law judges. About one-half of the states have created central administrative hearing offices. Maryland's OAH is considered to be among the best in the nation. Its jurisdiction is among the broadest, and its caseload among the largest in the nation. In drafting its "Model State Central Panel Statute," the American Bar Association relied on Maryland's statute.

## §9.2. Organization of OAH

OAH is headed by a chief administrative law judge (ALJ). The chief ALJ is appointed by the Governor, with the consent of the Senate, for a six-year term. Reappointment is permitted, and there are no term limits. The chief ALJ must be an attorney admitted in Maryland. The chief ALJ has the power to serve as an ALJ at a contested case, although it

1. 1989 Md. Laws Chapter 788.

is not expected that the chief ALJ will hear a full caseload because of the chief ALJ's administrative and supervisory responsibilities. The chief ALJ is responsible for establishing training programs and continuing education programs for the ALJs, and for monitoring the quality of state administrative hearings.[2] The chief ALJ is also responsible for the hiring of ALJs. At the time of the establishment of OAH, there were approximately 92 hearing officers among various agencies. Of these 92, about 74 were offered ALJ positions at OAH. Over the years, the number of ALJs at OAH has decreased. Currently, there are 62 ALJs at OAH.

ALJs are part of the State Personnel Management System, meaning that unlike the chief ALJ, ALJs are not political appointees. ALJs are hired by the chief ALJ as permanent state employees. Removal, suspension, and demotion can only be for cause as determined by the chief ALJ.[3] Unlike a hearing officer under the pre-OAH system, an OAH ALJ "may not perform duties inconsistent with the duties and responsibilities" of an ALJ,[4] and may not be "subject to the supervision or direction of an officer, employee, or agent engaged in the performance of investigative, prosecuting, or advisory functions for an agency."[5] In other words, an OAH ALJ cannot be an employee or agent of any state agency other than OAH. Additionally, an ALJ is not permitted to practice law before any tribunal, court, or administrative agency.[6]

OAH ALJs are bound by the Code of Judicial Conduct for Administrative Law Judges. This Code, based on the Model Code for Federal Administrative Law Judges, consists of five rules. These rules require an ALJ to:

1. uphold the integrity and independence of the administrative judiciary;
2. avoid impropriety and the appearance of impropriety in all activities;
3. perform the duties of office impartially and diligently;
4. regulate his or her extra-judicial activities to minimize the risk of conflict with judicial duties; and
5. refrain from political activity inappropriate to the judicial office.

## §9.3. OAH Rules of Procedure

Unlike other executive branch agencies, OAH has no policy-making responsibility or authority. OAH applies the policy created by the agency for which OAH is holding the hearing. Maryland Code Annotated, State Government §10-214(b) provides that in a contested case, OAH is bound by any agency regulation, declaratory ruling, prior adjudication, or other settled, pre-existing policy, to the same extent as the agency is or would have been bound if it were hearing the case. OAH has no power to promulgate substantive or interpretive rules.

2. Maryland Code Annotated, State Government §9-1604(a).
3. Maryland Code Annotated, State Government §9-1605(a)(2); Md. Code Regs. 28.01.03, COMAR 28.01.03.
4. Maryland Code Annotated, State Government §9-1605(a)(4).
5. Maryland Code Annotated, State Government §9-1605(b).
6. Rule 3(g) of Code of Judicial Conduct for Administrative Law Judges at the Office of Administrative Hearings.

OAH does have the power to promulgate procedural rules which govern the contested case process at OAH. The OAH Rules of Procedure appear in COMAR Title 28, Subtitle 2, Chapter 1. The current rules are set forth in Appendix V. The current rules took effect in 2010. A prior set of rules were in effect from January 2001 until the effective date of the new rules. The OAH Rules of Procedure are intended to supplement the procedures required by other statutes. Unless federal or state law requires that a federal or state procedure be observed, the OAH Rules of Procedure are to take precedence in the event of any conflict.[7]

## § 9.4. OAH Power to Hold Contested Case Hearings

OAH exists as a central hearing agency to hold contested case hearings for other agencies. But not all agencies fall within OAH's hearing authority to hold their hearings, and even for most agencies that do fall within OAH's hearing authority, the agency can decide not to use OAH.[8]

First, agencies not governed by Subtitle 2 of the Maryland APA are not covered by the statutes that set forth OAH powers. Therefore, local agencies that operate in only one county do not have their hearings heard at OAH.[9] For example, zoning board cases are not heard at OAH. Additionally, State Government § 10-203(a) excludes from the application of Subtitle 2 several agencies including the Department of Assessments and Taxation, the Public Service Commission, the State Workers' Compensation Commission, the Parole Commission, the Patuxent Institution Board of Review, the Maryland Tax Court, and the Department of Labor, Licensing and Regulation (DLLR) when deciding unemployment insurance cases. These agencies employ their own hearing officers and operate in manner similar to the pre-1990 process. These agencies, however, can, and do, use OAH on a contractual basis for certain cases.[10] For example, unemployment insurance cases from DLLR have been heard at OAH when an employee of DLLR has applied for unemployment insurance. Additionally, DLLR has contracted with OAH to help with DLLR's backlog of cases. It is important to understand that some Maryland agencies still follow the pre-OAH approach to contested case hearings. Because the procedures employed by these agencies differ from the procedures at OAH, attorneys representing clients before these agencies must give careful attention to that specific agency's procedures.

For those agencies governed by Subtitle 2 of the Maryland APA, absent a special statute, it is still discretionary with the agency whether to have their contested case hearings heard at OAH.[11] Agencies can choose whether to use or not use OAH. However, if an agency is eligible to use OAH to hear its contested case hearings, but chooses not to use OAH, only the agency heads themselves, i.e., the board members, commissioners or the head of a single-member agency, can conduct the hearing and make the final decision.[12] An agency that has the discretion to use OAH, but does not use OAH, cannot employ on a full time, part time, or contractual basis any person to preside at the hearing or make the final

7. OAH Rule 01D, Md. Code Regs. 28.02.01.01D, COMAR 28.02.01.01D.
8. Maryland Code Annotated, State Government § 10-205.
9. Maryland Code Annotated, State Government § 10-202(b).
10. Maryland Code Annotated, State Government § 9-1604(b)(1)(ii).
11. Maryland Code Annotated, State Government § 10-205(a).
12. Maryland Code Annotated, State Government § 10-202(g).

agency decision. Agencies such as the Board of Pharmacy and the Board of Chiropractic Examiners have exercised their discretion not to use OAH, and thus the board members of these agencies must hear and decide the contested cases themselves.[13]

If the agency decides to use OAH, it has two general options. First, the agency can delegate to OAH not only the power to hold the contested case hearing, but also the power to make the final agency decision.[14] In this situation, OAH's decision is not reviewed by the delegating agency.[15] The OAH decision is the decision that is judicially reviewable. For example, the Motor Vehicle Administration (MVA) has delegated to OAH the power to make final decisions in matters involving driver license suspensions. Also, the Department of Health and Mental Hygiene (DHMH) has delegated its final decisionmaking authority to OAH on matters involving involuntary admissions to mental health care facilities.

Another option for the agency is for the agency to delegate to OAH the power to hold the hearing, but to issue only proposed findings of fact, proposed conclusions of law and a proposed sanction.[16] In this situation, OAH issues a proposed decision that is sent to the agency, which then has the power to make the final decision. This has been the choice of an agency such as the Board of Social Work Examiners. An agency can further limit its delegation to OAH. For example, the State Board of Dental Examiners and the Department of Agriculture have delegated to OAH the power to hold their hearings and make proposed findings of fact and proposed conclusions, but they have not delegated to OAH the authority to propose a sanction along with the proposed decision. Whenever an attorney is involved in a contested case, the attorney should determine what, if any, authority has been delegated to OAH. This information is available from both OAH and the agency.

## §9.5. Statutory Delegation to OAH

There are situations where OAH has been delegated the power to hold hearings for a particular agency by the legislature. In these situations, the agency has no discretion as to whether to delegate its hearing authority to OAH. OAH must hold the hearing. Such statutes include matters involving:

- inmate grievances,[17]
- retirement contributions to local school systems,[18]
- admission to the schools for the deaf and blind,[19]
- special education,[20]
- foster care out-of-home placements,[21]

13. *See* Spencer v. Md. State Board of Pharmacy, 380 Md. 515, 846 A.2d 341 (2004).
14. Maryland Code Annotated, State Government § 10-205(b).
15. Maryland Code Annotated, State Government § 10-221(b).
16. Maryland Code Annotated, State Government § 10-205(b). *See also* Maryland Code Annotated, State Government § 10-220(a).
17. Maryland Code Annotated, Correctional Services § 10-207(c)(2).
18. Maryland Code Annotated, Education § 5-203(c)(3).
19. Maryland Code Annotated, Education § 8-307(a).
20. Maryland Code Annotated, Education § 8-413(d).
21. Maryland Code Annotated, Family Law § 5-525(b).

- child abuse and neglect,[22]
- suspension of occupational licenses for child support arrearages,[23]
- state employee whistle blower cases,[24]
- grievances from State executive branch employees,[25] and
- mediation of foreclosures of owner-occupied residential properties.[26]

## §9.6. Workload of OAH

OAH handles approximately 55,000 hearings per year involving over 300 different programs from about thirty different state agencies. About 40 percent of the hearings are held at OAH offices in Hunt Valley. The other hearings are heard at various locations throughout the state, including prisons, Motor Vehicle Administration (MVA) offices, hospitals, and nursing homes. In terms of number of cases, over one-half are from the MVA. Other agencies that provide a significant number of cases for OAH are the Department of Human Resources, Department of Health and Mental Hygiene, Department of Personnel, Insurance Administration, Inmate Grievance Office, Department of Labor, Licensing and Regulation, and Department of the Environment.

The complexity of the cases heard by OAH varies. Some cases, especially MVA cases, can be completed in less than one-half hour. Other cases may involve weeks of hearings.[27] In terms of actual workload, as compared to caseload, MVA represents about 20 percent of OAH's total workload. Listed below are some of the types of cases OAH hears:

- Motor Vehicle Administration: Cases involving driving with an alcohol concentration in excess of the statutory limit; refusal to submit to a chemical test for alcohol; violation of a license restriction; medical advisory board cases involving the ability of someone with a medical condition to drive; license suspension cases for accumulation of points; dealership and inspection facility cases.
- Department of Health and Mental Hygiene: Cases involving admission to a mental health care facility; eligibility for medical assistance; physician discipline cases from the State Board of Physicians; other professional disciplinary cases from boards such as the Board of Social Work Examiners, Board of Dental Examiners, and Board of Nursing Home Administrators; cases involving whether a person is not criminally responsible where OAH makes a recommendation to the circuit court and district court; and cases involving involuntary discharge from nursing homes.
- Department of Human Resources: Cases involving child support enforcement; food stamps; and child abuse and neglect.

---

22. Maryland Code Annotated, Family Law §5-706.1(b).
23. Maryland Code Annotated, Family Law §10-119.3(f).
24. Maryland Code Annotated, State Personnel & Pensions §5-310(b).
25. Maryland Code Annotated, State Personnel & Pensions §12-401. *See* Dep't of Public Safety & Corr. Servs. v. Myers, 392 Md. 589, 898 A.2d 465 (2006).
26. Maryland Code Annotated, Real Property §7-105.1.
27. *See, e.g.*, T-Up, Inc. v. Consumer Protection Division, 145 Md. App. 27, 801 A.2d 173, *cert. denied*, 369 Md. 661, 802 A.2d 439 (2002) (hearing encompassed twenty-seven days between October 1998 and April 1999); *see also* Consumer Protection Division v. Morgan, 387 Md. 125, 874 A.2d 919 (2005) (eighteen days of administrative hearings).

- Department of Labor, Licensing and Regulation: Cases involving the licensing of various trades and professions such as barbers, plumbers, and bay pilots; Home Improvement Commission regulation of contractors, and claims by homeowners against the Home Improvement Guaranty Fund; Real Estate Commission; and Maryland Occupational Safety and Health Commission.
- Department of Budget and Management: Cases involving suspensions and removal of certain state employees; state employee grievances; and whistle blowers.
- Department of Natural Resources: Cases involving boat excise tax assessments; tidal fish license revocations; hunting guide licenses; tree expert licenses; and oyster bottom leasing.
- Commission on Human Relations: Cases involving discrimination in public accommodations, employment, and housing.
- Department of the Environment: Cases involving hazardous and solid waste management; water management; sediment and stormwater management; and air and radiation management.
- Inmate Grievance Office: Cases involving inmate grievances; and disciplinary actions for inmate violation of institutional rules.
- Department of Education: Cases involving student expulsions; teacher dismissals; school redistricting; child care licensing; collective bargaining disputes; special education disputes; and rehabilitation services.
- Maryland Insurance Administration: Cases involving cancellation of automobile and homeowner policies; denial of health care; and discipline of insurance companies and agents.
- Consumer Protection Division of the Office of the Attorney General: Cases involving health clubs; automobile repair facilities; and alleged violations of the consumer protection laws.
- Securities Division of the Office of the Attorney General: Cases involving violations of the Maryland Securities Act.
- Board of Public Works: Cases involving suspensions or debarments of contractors from state contracts.
- Office of the Secretary of State: Cases involving charitable organizations; and condominium and timeshare registration.
- Public Information Act: Cases involving the denial of a request for state documents.
- Mediation of foreclosures of owner-occupied residential properties.
- State Higher Education Labor Relations Board: Cases involving public employee collective bargaining in higher education.

As evidenced by this list, OAH ALJs hear a wide variety of cases involving many different areas of law. Unlike federal ALJs who hear cases from only one agency, and unlike hearing examiners at agencies that do not utilize OAH such as the Public Service Commission, OAH ALJs are generalists and hear cases from every agency that has delegated its hearing authority to OAH. There are no ALJs who hear only a certain agency's cases even if that ALJ had prior experience with that agency or area of law. Nor are there classes of cases to which only certain ALJs are assigned. Although the statute permits the chief ALJ to establish classifications for case assignments on the basis of subject matter, expertise, and case complexity,[28] this authority has not been exercised.

The fact that OAH ALJs have no special substantive expertise is a topic of some controversy. Administrative decisionmaking has traditionally been justified on the basis of expertise. The central panel movement as exemplified by Maryland's OAH places the emphasis on procedural expertise, not substantive expertise. OAH is the expert agency in holding contested case hearings, an expertise which many believe is more important in achieving fairness than substantive expertise. OAH ALJs engage in training programs before being allowed to hear cases. OAH also has an extensive training program for their ALJs where experts in different substantive areas present workshops on recent developments in the law. Nevertheless, it cannot be expected that all ALJs at OAH have the substantive knowledge of all areas of law equal to the knowledge of an ALJ who hears cases in only one area of law. Litigants and their attorneys, both governmental and private, have at times expressed frustration and annoyance at what they perceived in particular cases to be the lack of understanding of the substantive area of law. Some attorneys have complained that cases take longer at OAH because of the need to explain and put into the record basic concepts of law and policy which would be easily understood by substantive expert hearing officials.

It must be understood that Maryland's OAH, like all central panels, represents a tradeoff, a compromise, between the values of substantive expertise and procedural fairness. In general, Maryland's OAH receives high grades for its role in Maryland's administrative process. Early skepticism which turned into early criticism has been generally replaced with confidence in the OAH process. The central panel model employed in Maryland by its OAH is now generally recognized as the best approach to the administrative contested case process.

28. Maryland Code Annotated, State Government § 9-1604(a).

# Chapter 10

# Contested Cases: The OAH Hearing Process

This chapter will discuss the procedures that are followed at an OAH contested case hearing when OAH has been delegated the power to hold the contested case hearing for another agency. This chapter must be read in conjunction with the other chapters that discuss the general principles that apply at contested case hearings. The OAH Rules of Procedure are set forth in Appendix V.

## § 10.1. Initial OAH Involvement

If OAH is the agency that will hold the contested case hearing, OAH acquires jurisdiction over the matter when the "initial pleading" is filed with OAH.[1] The initial pleading could be either the Notice of Agency Action filed by the agency bringing the case, or the appeal of an agency action or request for a hearing filed by the subject of the agency action. In some cases, the appeal or request for a hearing must be transmitted to OAH on a special form provided by OAH or the agency whose action is being challenged.[2] When representing a client, it is important to understand that in some cases, the hearing is based on the agency's request, and in other cases, the hearing is based on the impacted person's request. Failure to request a hearing in a timely fashion will mean that the right to a contested case hearing at OAH has been waived.

The initial pleading requesting a hearing, regardless of the form of the request, must include the following information: the name and mailing address of the person requesting the hearing; the Notice of Agency Action or the name of the person or agency against whom the hearing request has been filed; and any fees, documents, or other information required by law.[3] If the initial pleading is received without the required information, the case may be dismissed,[4] although OAH Rule 03D also provides that instead of dismissing the case, OAH may return the initial pleading for resubmission with all the required items. Return of the initial pleading does not extend the time within which the initial pleading is required to be filed.[5]

A statute or regulation will usually set forth the time period by which the initial pleading must be filed.[6] For example, § 16.205.1 of the Transportation Article of the Maryland

1. OAH Rule 04, Md. Code Regs. 28.02.01.04, COMAR 28.02.01.04.
2. OAH Rule 03A, Md. Code Regs. 28.02.01.03A, COMAR 28.02.01.03A.
3. OAH Rule 03B, Md. Code Regs. 28.02.01.03B, COMAR 28.02.01.03B.
4. OAH Rule 03C, Md. Code Regs. 28.02.01.03C, COMAR 28.02.01.03C.
5. OAH Rule 03D, Md. Code Regs. 28.02.01.03D, COMAR 28.02.01.03D.
6. OAH Rule 04B(1), Md. Code Regs. 28.02.01.04B(1), COMAR 28.02.01.04B(1).

Code requires that a person who refuses to take a chemical breath test for alcohol, or who takes the test and the test indicates an alcohol concentration of .08 or more, must request within ten days a hearing why his/her driver's license should not be suspended. If no time period is specified in the statute or regulation, the initial pleading must be filed within thirty days of the date of the notice of the contested action.[7] The hearing request is considered filed on the earlier of the date the request is postmarked or received by OAH or the moving agency, depending on which agency is designated to receive the request.[8]

## § 10.2. Notice of Hearing

The next step is that OAH will send a Notice of the Hearing. The notice must be in writing.[9] Notice may be sent by U.S. mail or other method of personal or courier delivery.[10] If notice is given by U.S. mail, notice is effective at the end of the fifth day after its deposit in the mail.[11]

The notice of hearing must contain the following information:

1. The date, time, place and nature of the hearing;
2. A statement of the right to present witnesses and documents, or other evidence, and the right to cross-examine any witness another party calls;
3. A statement of the right to request subpoenas for witnesses and evidence, and the cost associated with the request;
4. A statement that a copy of the hearing procedures is available on request;
5. A statement of any rights, restrictions or requirements pertaining to representation;
6. A statement that failure to appear for the scheduled hearing may result in an adverse action against that party; and
7. A statement that the parties may agree to the evidence and may waive their right to appear at the hearing.[12]

## § 10.3. Assignment of ALJs

An ALJ will be assigned to hear the case. Assignments are made on a monthly basis. As discussed earlier, assignments are not based on expertise or experience in the type of case being assigned. By statute, the chief ALJ is authorized to make the case assignments.[13] In practice, this authority has been delegated to the OAH Office of Operations.

7. OAH Rule 04B(2), Md. Code Regs. 28.02.01.04B(2), COMAR 28.02.01.04B(2).
8. OAH Rule 04D, Md. Code Regs. 28.02.01.04D, COMAR 28.02.01.04D.
9. OAH Rule 05A, Md. Code Regs. 28.02.01.05A, COMAR 28.02.01.05A.
10. OAH Rule 05C(1), Md. Code Regs. 28.02.01.05C(1), COMAR 28.02.01.05C(1).
11. OAH Rule 05C(2), Md. Code Regs. 28.02.01.05C(2), COMAR 28.02.01.05C(2).
12. OAH Rule 05B, Md. Code Regs. 28.02.01.05B, COMAR 28.02.01.05B.
13. Maryland Code Annotated, State Government § 9-1604(a)(4).

No party, including the agency that has delegated its contested case hearing authority to OAH, can request that a particular ALJ hear or not hear the case. One of the reasons for the creation of OAH was to avoid the perception of unfairness that existed under the pre-OAH approach when the agency selected the hearing examiner. Moreover, an agency's delegation and transmittal of all or part of a contested case to OAH is final.[14] If this were not the rule, the agency after learning of the identity of the ALJ assigned to hear the case could rescind the delegation if the agency was not pleased with that ALJ.[15]

Nor does a court have the power to interfere with the chief ALJ's power to assign ALJs. In *Powell v. Maryland Aviation Administration*,[16] the agency requested that the remand order to OAH from the court include the requirement that the already existing record be reviewed by the same ALJ who saw and heard the witnesses at the original hearing. The court's response was that "it is at best inappropriate, and at worst unconstitutional, for us to direct that a certain ALJ either be, or not be, assigned to a particular matter ... The Chief Administrative Law Judge must determine which ALJ to assign to this matter on remand."[17]

## § 10.4. Entry of Appearance

An attorney, or other representative permitted by law, should enter his/her appearance with OAH.[18] Once an appearance has been entered, all notices, pleadings and other correspondence must be served on the person whose appearance was entered.[19] An appearance can also be entered orally at the hearing.

## § 10.5. Service

Pleadings, motions, responses, correspondence and any other paper filed with OAH shall be served promptly on all other parties.[20] Unless otherwise required by law, service may be by U.S. mail, personal delivery, or any other form of personal or courier delivery.[21] Proof of service is required. Every paper that is filed with OAH must contain or be accompanied by a certificate of service. The certificate of service must be signed, and contain the date of service, manner of service, name of each person served, and address at which each person was served.[22]

---

14. Maryland Code Annotated, State Government § 10-205(d)(1).

15. There is a narrow exception to this rule. If an agency has adopted regulations specifying the criteria and procedures for the revocation of a delegation of a contested case to OAH, delegation may be revoked in accordance with these regulations as long as the revocation is prior to the issuance of any ruling on a substantive issue or the taking of oral testimony from the first witness. Maryland Code Annotated, State Government § 10-205(d)(2).

16. 336 Md. 210, 647 A.2d 437 (1994).

17. 336 Md. 210, 222, 647 A.2d 437, 443 (1994).

18. OAH Rule 08D, Md. Code Regs. 28.02.01.08D, COMAR 28.02.01.08D.

19. OAH Rule 08E, Md. Code Regs. 28.02.01.08E, COMAR 28.02.01.08E.

20. OAH Rule 10A, Md. Code Regs. 28.02.01.10A, COMAR 28.02.01.10A.

21. OAH Rule 10B, Md. Code Regs. 28.02.01.10B, COMAR 28.02.01.10B.

22. OAH Rule 10C, Md. Code Regs. 28.02.01.10C, COMAR 28.02.01.10C.

## § 10.6. Computing Time

OAH has a regulation that sets forth how time is computed for any matter that has a designated time period.[23] First, the day from which the designated time period begins to run is not counted.[24] Second, the last day of the computed time period is included unless this day is a Sunday or legal holiday. If the last day is a Sunday or legal holiday, the time period runs until the end of the next day which is not a Sunday or holiday.[25] Third, if the last day of the period is a day when OAH is closed for the full day or part of the day, and the filing is to be done at OAH, the time period runs until the end of the next day which is not a Saturday, Sunday, legal holiday, or a day when OAH is not open the entire day.[26] Fourth, when the time period is more than seven days, intermediate Sundays and holidays are counted, but when the time period is seven days or less, intermediate Sundays and holidays are not counted in computing the period of time.[27]

Another regulation of OAH provides that an ALJ may "modify or waive, reasonably and for good cause, any time periods" established by OAH.[28] Time periods set by statute are not subject to waiver by OAH.

## § 10.7. Pre-Hearing Motions

Motions may be filed pre-hearing, during the hearing, and after the hearing.[29] All motions must be in writing, must state the relief or order sought, and must state the grounds in support of the motion.[30] Documents can be attached to the motion as exhibits. If an answer is filed in response to a motion, the answer must be filed within fifteen days after the date the motion was filed or the date of the hearing, whichever date is earlier.[31] "Filed" is defined as the earlier of when the document is postmarked or received at OAH, and when required, served on the other parties or the ALJ.[32] An ALJ may schedule a hearing to consider the motion. Notice of the hearing must be given to all parties.[33] The notice and the hearing may be by telephone.

The ALJ's ruling on the motion may be in writing, stated on the record, or included in the proposed or final decision.[34] The filing or pendency of a motion does not alter or extend any time limits.

Generally, any pre-trial motion that would be appropriate in a civil trial in circuit court can be filed with OAH. For example, a motion in limine, a motion for a more definite statement, and a motion for a protective order all may be filed when appropriate. Two

---

23. OAH Rule 04C, Md. Code Regs. 28.02.01.04C, COMAR 28.02.01.04C.
24. OAH Rule 04C(1), Md. Code Regs. 28.02.01.04C(1), COMAR 28.02.01.04C(1).
25. OAH Rule 04C(2)(a), Md. Code Regs. 28.02.01.04C(2)(a), COMAR 28.02.01.04C(2)(a).
26. OAH Rule 04C(2)(b), Md. Code Regs. 28.02.01.04C(2)(b), COMAR 28.02.01.04C(2)(b).
27. OAH Rule 04C(3),(4), Md. Code Regs. 28.02.01.04C(3),(4), COMAR 28.02.01.04.C(3),(4).
28. OAH Rule 11B(8), Md. Code Regs. 28.02.01.11B(8), COMAR 28.02.01.11B(8).
29. OAH Rule 12B, Md. Code Regs. 28.02.01.12B, COMAR 28.02.01.12B.
30. OAH Rule 12B(1),(2), Md. Code Regs. 28.02.01.12B(1),(2), COMAR 28.02.01.12B(1),(2).
31. OAH Rule 12B(3), Md. Code Regs. 28.02.01.12B(3), COMAR 28.02.01.12B(3).
32. OAH Rule 02B(5), Md. Code Regs. 28.02.01.02B(5), COMAR 28.02.01.02B(5).
33. OAH Rule 12B(4), Md. Code Regs. 28.02.01.12B(4), COMAR 28.02.01.12B(4).
34. OAH Rule 12B(5),(6), Md. Code Regs. 28.02.01.12B(5),(6), COMAR 28.02.01.12B(5),(6).

pre-hearing motions are expressly discussed in the OAH Rules of Procedure. The Motion to Dismiss is appropriate when the initial pleading fails to state a claim for which relief can be granted.[35] The Motion for Summary Decision may be filed at any time during the proceeding, although it is typically filed prior to the hearing. This motion can relate to the entire case or part of the case. This motion argues that there is no genuine dispute as to any material fact and that the moving party is entitled to judgment as a matter of law. A Motion for Summary Decision must be supported by affidavits.[36] The affidavits must be made upon personal knowledge, must set forth the facts that would be admissible in evidence, and must show affirmatively that the affiant is competent to testify to the matters stated in the affidavit.[37] A Response to the Motion for Summary Decision may be filed which identifies the material facts that are disputed. The response may be accompanied by affidavits.[38] If the ALJ finds that there is no genuine dispute as to any material fact, and that the moving party is entitled to judgment as a matter of law, the ALJ may issue the proposed or final decision in the case.[39]

Other preliminary motions relating to disqualification of an ALJ, intervention, discovery, expedited hearings, and postponement are discussed in other sections of this chapter.

## § 10.8. Expedited Hearings

Any party can file a motion for an expedited hearing. The motion must provide reasons for the request.[40] Any response to the motion must be filed within ten days of the date the motion was filed.[41] Usually, the docket specialist at OAH will contact the parties, and attempt to schedule the hearing at a date agreeable to everyone.[42] If the parties cannot agree, a pre-hearing conference may be held, usually by telephone, to consider the motion and any responses. Among the factors usually considered in deciding whether to grant the expedited hearing are any requirements by law, the availability of witnesses and counsel, the nature of the issue to be resolved, and the potential consequences of a delayed hearing. If the motion for an expedited hearing is granted, the regulation provides that the hearing shall be scheduled "as soon as practicable," and that unless agreed otherwise by the parties or there is a statutory requirement to the contrary, the ALJ shall render a decision, whether it is proposed or final, within thirty days after the close of the record.[43]

## § 10.9. Postponements

Except in an emergency, a request for a postponement must be made in writing not less than five days before the scheduled hearing.[44] If an emergency exists, the request can

35. OAH Rule 12C, Md. Code Regs. 28.02.01.12C, COMAR 28.02.01.12C.
36. OAH Rule 12D(1), Md. Code Regs. 28.02.01.12D(1), COMAR 28.02.01.12D(1).
37. OAH Rule 12D(3), Md. Code Regs. 28.02.01.12D(3), COMAR 28.02.01.12D(3).
38. OAH Rule 12D(2), Md. Code Regs. 28.02.01.12D(2), COMAR 28.02.01.12D(2).
39. OAH Rule 12D(4), Md. Code Regs. 28.02.01.12D(4), COMAR 28.02.01.12D(4).
40. OAH Rule 06A, Md. Code Regs. 28.02.01.06A, COMAR 28.02.01.06A.
41. OAH Rule 06B, Md. Code Regs. 28.02.01.06B, COMAR 28.02.01.06B.
42. OAH Rule 06C, Md. Code Regs. 28.02.01.06C, COMAR 28.02.01.06C.
43. OAH Rule 06D, Md. Code Regs. 28.02.01.06D, COMAR 28.02.01.06D.
44. OAH Rule 16A, Md. Code Regs. 28.02.01.16A, COMAR 28.02.01.16A.

be made less than five days before the hearing and can be made by telephone.[45] The OAH regulation defines "emergency" as a sudden, unforeseen occurrence requiring immediate attention, which arises within five days of the hearing.[46] The request for a postponement will only be granted if good cause is established.[47] "Good cause" is not defined in the regulation, and is considered to be a matter within the discretion of the ALJ. Among the factors usually considered are the reason for the request, the proximity of the request to the scheduled hearing date, any requirement by statute or regulation for holding the hearing or issuing the decision by a certain time, the interest at stake, and the history of postponements in the case. Usually, the first postponement is easier to get than a subsequent postponement. Reasons that are generally viewed as stating good cause for a postponement include a documented court conflict of an attorney, and an illness of a necessary hearing participant. Hearings are not postponed because a party is not fully prepared or because a settlement may be forthcoming. Documentation of the reasons for the postponements are required.[48] For example, OAH will require airplane tickets if postponement is sought because counsel plans to be out-of-town.

Postponements are not automatic at OAH. Cases are usually scheduled only after OAH has checked the availability of the attorneys, and therefore OAH's position is that once the attorney has agreed to a hearing at a scheduled date, the attorney should be able to participate.

In the event of inclement weather, OAH's policy is to follow the decision for Maryland state employees. If the state announces "liberal leave" for state employees, all OAH hearings are automatically cancelled. This policy is not part of formally adopted OAH regulations.

## § 10.10. Disqualification of ALJ

As discussed in Chapter 16, an unbiased decisionmaker is one of the requirements of due process.[49] OAH has adopted its own regulations dealing with disqualification of an ALJ because of bias. An OAH ALJ "shall withdraw from participation in any proceeding in which personal bias or other reasons render the [ALJ] unable to provide an impartial hearing and decision, or when an appearance of impropriety may reasonably be inferred from the facts."[50] "Appearance of impropriety" has been described as "whether the conduct would create, in reasonable minds, a perception that the judge's ability to carry out adjudicatory responsibilities with integrity, impartiality and competence is impaired."[51] Bias is presumed in the following situations:[52]

1. The judge has a personal bias or prejudice concerning the proceeding, or a party or a party's lawyer to the proceeding.
2. The judge served as a lawyer in the matter in controversy, or a lawyer with whom the judge previously practiced law served during such association as a lawyer

45. OAH Rule 16D, Md. Code Regs. 28.02.01.16D, COMAR 28.02.01.16D.
46. OAH Rule 16D(1), Md. Code Regs. 28.02.01.16D(1), COMAR 28.02.01.16D(1).
47. OAH Rule 16C, Md. Code Regs. 28.02.01.16C, COMAR 28.02.01.16C.
48. OAH Rule 16B, Md. Code Regs. 28.02.01.16B, COMAR 28.02.01.16B.
49. *See* Schweiker v. McClure, 456 U.S. 188 (1982).
50. OAH Rule 11C(1)(a), Md. Code Regs. 28.02.01.11C(1)(a), COMAR 28.02.01.11C(1)(a).
51. *See* Commentary to Rule 2A of the Code of Judicial Conduct for Administrative Law Judges at OAH.
52. *See* Rule 3D of the Code of Judicial Conduct for Administrative Law Judges at OAH.

concerning the matter, or the judge has been a material witness concerning it. Although a lawyer in a government agency does not necessarily have an "association" with other lawyers employed by that agency, an ALJ formerly employed by an agency should be disqualified in a proceeding where the judge's impartiality might reasonably be questioned.

3. The judge has served in governmental employment and in such capacity participated as counsel, adviser or material witness concerning the proceeding or expressed an opinion concerning the merits of the particular case in controversy.
4. The judge knows that he or she, individually or as a fiduciary, or his or her spouse, parent or child or other family member, has an economic interest in the subject matter in controversy or is a party to the proceeding, or has another interest of more than a *de minimis* nature that could be substantially affected by the proceeding. "Fiduciary" includes being a personal representative, trustee or guardian. "Economic interest" denotes ownership of a more than *de minimis* legal or equitable interest, or a relationship as officer, director, advisor, or other active participant in the business affairs of a party. "*De minimis*" means an insignificant interest that could not raise a reasonable question as to a judge's impartiality.
5. The judge knows that he or she, individually, or his or her spouse, or a person within the third degree of relationship to either of them, or the spouse of such a person is a party to the proceeding, or an officer, director, or trustee of a party; is acting as a lawyer in the proceeding; is known by the judge to have more than a *de minimis* interest that could be substantially affected by the outcome of the proceeding; or is to the judge's knowledge likely to be a material witness in the proceeding. Third degree of relationship includes great-grandparents, grandparents, parents, uncles, aunts, siblings, children, grandchildren, great-grandchildren, nephews and nieces.
6. A lawyer in the proceeding is associated with a law firm with which the judge's spouse is affiliated.

Any party can file a motion to disqualify an ALJ because of bias.[53] This motion is ruled upon by the ALJ whose impartiality is being challenged. An ALJ can also disqualify himself or herself *sua sponte*.

## § 10.11. Substitution of ALJ

OAH regulations provide that if for any reason, an ALJ is unable to continue presiding over a pending hearing or is unable to issue the decision, whether proposed or final, another ALJ may be assigned to conclude the hearing and render the decision.[54] There is no need to reopen the hearing or to recall witnesses who have already testified. The new ALJ can continue the hearing and make the decision based on the existing record. On the other hand, the ALJ in his or her discretion may decide to conduct further proceedings that are "necessary and proper."[55]

53. OAH Rule 11C(2), Md. Code Regs. 28.02.01.11C(2), COMAR 28.02.01.11C(2).
54. OAH Rule 11C(3)(a), Md. Code Regs. 28.02.01.11C(3)(a), COMAR 28.02.01.11C(3)(a).
55. OAH Rule 11C(3)(b), Md. Code Regs. 28.02.01.11C(3)(b), COMAR 28.02.01.11C(3)(b).

## § 10.12. Intervention

A person may seek to intervene in an OAH hearing by filing a motion not later than fifteen days before any pre-hearing conference or the hearing date, whichever is earlier.[56] First, a person will be permitted to intervene if the person has an unconditional right to intervene as a matter of law. One example of where there is an unconditional right to intervene as a matter of law is in a child support case where a tax refund has been intercepted from a child support obligor, and the obligee requests intervention.[57] Secondly, a person may be permitted to intervene if the person claims an interest relating to the subject matter of the hearing that is adversely affected and not adequately represented by existing parties.[58] One example is when intervention is sought in a special education case involving a local public school system, and the request is for a non-public out-of-state placement.

In deciding whether to grant the motion to intervene, the ALJ will consider whether intervention will unduly delay or prejudice the adjudication of the rights of the original parties.[59] The judge's ruling on the motion to intervene should be made "as soon as practicable."[60] An order allowing intervention may place conditions on the intervener's participation.[61] Such conditions may include the intervener being available for existing scheduled hearing dates, supplying memoranda, agreeing to discovery, and obtaining counsel.

If OAH has not been delegated the authority to make the final decision in a case in which intervention has been sought, the denial of a motion to intervene may be appealed to the agency that has the final decisionmaking authority in accordance with the agency's regulations. If the OAH has been delegated the final decisionmaking authority, review of the denial is in "accordance with law,"[62] which apparently has no significance at this time. The ALJ has the discretion to stay the OAH proceedings pending review of a denial of a motion to intervene.

## § 10.13. Pre-Hearing Conferences

The ALJ may hold a pre-hearing conference to resolve matters preliminary to the hearing.[63] The pre-hearing conference may be conducted in person, by telephone, or by video conference. The ALJ may require the parties to submit information before the pre-hearing conference. Although any matter that will promote the orderly and prompt conduct of the hearing may be discussed at the pre-hearing conference, the following matters are expressly listed in the OAH Rules of Procedure as appropriate for discussion at a pre-hearing conference: issuance of subpoenas, factual and legal issues, stipulations, requests

56. OAH Rule 15, Md. Code Regs. 28.02.01.15, COMAR 28.02.01.15.

57. *See* Md. Code Regs. 03.04.05, COMAR 03.04.05. *See also* Chapman v. Kamara, 356 Md. 426, 739 A.2d 387 (1999), Montgomery County v. Bradford, 345 Md. 175, 691 A.2d 1281 (1997).

58. OAH Rule 15A(2), Md. Code Regs. 28.02.01.15A(2), COMAR 28.02.01.15A(2).

59. OAH Rule 15C(1), Md. Code Regs. 28.02.01.15C(1), COMAR 28.02.01.15C(1).

60. OAH Rule 15C(2), Md. Code Regs. 28.02.01.15C(2), COMAR 28.02.01.15C(2).

61. OAH Rule 15C(3), Md. Code Regs. 28.02.01.15C(3), COMAR 28.02.01.15C(3).

62. OAH Rule 15D(2), Md. Code Regs. 28.02.01.15D(2), COMAR 28.02.01.15D(2).

63. OAH Rule 17A, Md. Code Regs. 28.02.01.17A, COMAR 28.02.01.17A.

for official notice, identification and exchange of documentary evidence, admissibility of evidence, identification and qualification of witnesses, motions, discovery disputes, order of presentation, scheduling, and alternative dispute resolution.

When a pre-hearing conference is held, a pre-hearing order must be issued by the ALJ. The pre-hearing order sets forth the actions taken or which will be taken with regard to the matters discussed at the conference. The pre-hearing order becomes part of the record of the case. A pre-hearing order can also be issued even if a pre-hearing conference is not held.

## § 10.14. Discovery

As discussed in Chapter 5, discovery does not play as large a role in administrative litigation as it does in civil litigation in circuit court. The OAH regulation on discovery provides that by written request no later than thirty days before the scheduled hearing, a party may require any other party to produce within fifteen days for inspection and copying any file, memorandum, correspondence, document, object, or tangible item, including electronically stored information, that is relevant to the subject matter of the case and not privileged.[64] Copies of the requested documents and records are made at the expense of the party making the request, although a waiver of copying expenses may be available under the Public Information Act.[65]

A party who has filed a timely discovery request under the OAH regulation but has not received a reply may, after providing reasonable notice to the opposing party, file a motion seeking to compel a response and/or a motion for sanctions.[66] Moreover, based on a party's motion or the ALJ's own initiative, the ALJ may enter an order establishing reasonable limits on the scope of discovery and/or prohibiting specific discovery.[67]

Parties are permitted to enter into other discovery agreements not covered by the OAH regulation on discovery. For example, parties may agree to more extensive discovery including depositions or interrogatories.[68] Parties may also enter into agreements concerning the inadvertent production and handling of privileged material.[69] Moreover, as discussed in Chapter 5, the agencies that have delegated their contested case hearing authority to OAH may have their own discovery regulations which OAH would apply.

## § 10.15. Subpoenas

The principles relating to administrative agency subpoenas in contested cases have been discussed in Chapter 5. OAH has its own regulations that supplement these principles for contested cases held at OAH.

---

64. OAH Rule 13, Md. Code Regs. 28.02.01.13, COMAR 28.02.01.13.
65. Maryland Code Annotated, State Government § 10-611 *et seq.*
66. OAH Rule 13E, Md. Code Regs. 28.02.01.13E, COMAR 28.02.01.13E.
67. OAH Rule 13C, Md. Code Regs. 28.02.01.13C, COMAR 28.02.01.13C.
68. OAH Rule 13B, Md. Code Regs. 28.02.01.13B, COMAR 28.02.01.13B.
69. OAH Rule 13D, Md. Code Regs. 28.02.01.13D, COMAR 28.02.01.13D.

First, it is important to remember that the agency that has delegated its hearing authority to OAH may have its own regulations regarding subpoenas. OAH is bound to follow these regulations. For example, the agency with the largest caseload at OAH, the MVA, has its own subpoena rules.[70] In special education cases heard by OAH, OAH is bound by federal subpoena requirements when hearing special education cases.[71]

The OAH subpoena regulation first provides that on the request of any party, or at the direction of an ALJ, OAH may issue a subpoena requiring the attendance and testimony of witnesses and the production at the hearing of any tangible items in the possession or under the control of the witness.[72] A party's requests for a subpoena must be in writing, and filed "to the extent practicable" at least ten calendar days before the hearing.[73] A request for a subpoena shall specify the name and full address of the person to be subpoenaed, and the name, full address, and telephone number of the party requesting the subpoena.[74] A subpoena that requests the production of tangible items, books, papers and other documents shall describe those items with particularity.[75]

Subpoenas may be served by personal delivery by an individual eighteen years or older who is not a party to the proceeding, or by certified mail to the address specified in the subpoena request.[76] If service of the subpoena is by OAH, service is proper by regular United States Postal Service mail, or by personal or courier delivery.[77] Service by OAH is by regular mail unless the subpoena request specifies otherwise. The costs of certified mailing and personal or courier delivery are the responsibility of the person requesting the subpoena. Return of service when service is by certified mail is by the filing of the original return receipt.[78] When service is by personal delivery, return of service is by the filing of an affidavit signed by the person who made service including the following information: name of person served, date of service, place of service, and a statement that the server is eighteen years old or older and not a party to the proceeding.[79] Proof of service of subpoenas by certified mail or personal delivery is the responsibility of the person requesting the subpoena.[80]

A person may object to a subpoena by filing a motion to quash with OAH or for other relief.[81] The grounds for objecting to a subpoena are discussed in Chapter 5.

The party requesting the subpoena is responsible for notifying the person subpoenaed if the hearing is cancelled or postponed. Once issued, a subpoena remains in effect until the conclusion of the hearing.[82]

OAH is authorized to assess fees to cover administrative expenses to process a subpoena.[83] The fee cannot exceed five dollars. No fee may be charged to a state agency or to petitioners

70. Md. Code Regs. 11.11.03.07, COMAR 11.11.03.07.
71. *See* 20 U.S.C. § 1415(d)(2).
72. OAH Rule 14A, Md. Code Regs. 28.02.01.14A, COMAR 28.02.01.14A.
73. OAH Rule 14B (1),(2), Md. Code Regs. 28.02.01.14B(1),(2), COMAR 28.02.01.14B(1),(2).
74. OAH Rule 14B(3), Md. Code Regs. 28.02.01.14B(3), COMAR 28.02.01.14B(3).
75. OAH Rule 14B(4), Md. Code Regs. 28.02.01.14B(4), COMAR 28.02.01.14B(4).
76. OAH Rule 14C(1), Md. Code Regs. 28.02.01.14C(1), COMAR 28.02.01.14C(1).
77. OAH Rule 14C(1)(c), Md. Code Regs. 28.02.01.14C(1)(c), COMAR 28.02.01.14C(1)(c).
78. OAH Rule 14D(1), Md. Code Regs. 28.02.01.14D(1), COMAR 28.02.01.14D(1).
79. OAH Rule 14D(2), Md. Code Regs. 28.02.01.14D(2), COMAR 28.02.01.14D(2).
80. OAH Rule 14C(5), Md. Code Regs. 28.02.01.14C(5), COMAR 28.02.01.14C(5).
81. OAH Rule 14E, Md. Code Regs. 28.02.01.14E, COMAR 28.02.01.14E.
82. OAH Rule 14C(6), Md. Code Regs. 28.02.01.14C(6), COMAR 28.02.01.14C(6).
83. Maryland Code Annotated, State Government § 9-1604(b)(1)(vi)(2).

who are unable to pay the fee.[84] Pursuant to OAH regulations, OAH will waive the subpoena fee for a party represented by counsel retained through Judicare, Maryland Volunteer Legal Service, Inc., Maryland's Legal Aid Bureau, Inc., or any other legal services program that receives funding from the Maryland Legal Services Corporation.[85] Other parties are also eligible for a waiver under various regulations and statutes. A request for a subpoena fee waiver must be in writing, and submitted with the request for the issuance of the subpoena. Within five working days of OAH's receipt of the fee waiver request, OAH will ask the party seeking the waiver to provide evidence of eligibility for waiver.[86]

If a person fails to comply with a properly served subpoena, OAH may apply to a circuit court for an order to show cause why that person should not be committed to jail for refusal to comply with the subpoena.[87] OAH, however, cannot seek court enforcement unless the subpoena has been served with the formal requirements of a circuit court subpoena.[88] This means that although OAH regulations permit subpoenas to be served by regular mail, if an attorney suspects that the person to whom the subpoena is being mailed may ignore the subpoena, the attorney should use personal service or certified mail with return receipt requested.

## § 10.16. Stipulations

The parties may agree to any stipulations or procedural matters. All stipulations must be filed in writing or entered on the record. Regardless of a stipulation, an ALJ may require additional development of stipulated matters. All stipulations are part of the administrative record.[89]

In *VNA Hospice of Maryland v. Department of Health and Mental Hygiene*,[90] the court noted that at the hearing at OAH, there was "no testimony from witnesses. Instead, the matter was tried on a detailed stipulation of facts submitted by counsel for VNA and counsel for the Department, various exhibits, affidavits, legal memoranda, and oral argument by counsel for each side."[91]

## § 10.17. Prefiled Testimony

OAH regulations permit testimony to be prefiled, although it is in the discretion of the ALJ whether to accept prefiled testimony into the record.[92] If the ALJ agrees to exercise his or her discretion to accept prefiled testimony, the testimony must be filed and served

84. Maryland Code Annotated, State Government § 9-1604(b)(2).
85. Md. Code Regs. 28.03.01.06A(2), COMAR 28.03.01.06A(2).
86. Md. Code Regs. 28.03.01.06B,C, COMAR 28.03.01.06B,C.
87. OAH Rule 14F, Md. Code Regs. 28.02.01.14F, COMAR 28.02.01.14F.
88. OAH Rule 14C(3), Md. Code Regs. 28.02.01.14C(3), COMAR 28.02.01.14C(3).
89. OAH Rule 21G, Md. Code Regs. 28.02.01.21G, COMAR 28.02.01.21G.
90. 406 Md. 584, 961 A.2d 557 (2008).
91. 406 Md. 584, 594, 961 A.2d 557, 563 (2008).
92. OAH Rule 21E(1), Md. Code Regs. 28.02.01.21E(1), COMAR 28.02.01.21E(1).

on all parties not later than ten days before the hearing.[93] This rule is aimed at facilitating the actual hearing. It is not intended to replace the need to bring witnesses to the hearing. At present, prefiled testimony is not used frequently at OAH. Attorneys involved in complex cases, however, should consider using this rule in order to expedite the hearing.

## § 10.18. Official Notice

The OAH regulation on official notice follows the APA provision on official notice.[94] At the request of a party or on the ALJ's own motion, an ALJ may take official notice of a fact that is judicially noticeable or is general, technical, or scientific information within the specialized knowledge of the agency.[95] Because OAH has no specialized knowledge of any substantive area, official notice at OAH would seem to be limited to facts that are judicially noticeable despite the OAH regulation's language.

Before taking official notice of a fact, the OAH ALJ must notify each party of the facts intended to be officially noticed, and give each party an opportunity to contest these facts.[96]

## § 10.19. Waiver of Hearing

OAH regulations permit the parties to agree to the admission of evidence and to waive their rights to appear at a hearing.[97] If all parties so agree, a contested case hearing before an ALJ is not necessary, and the ALJ will proceed to make the proposed or final decision without a hearing.

## § 10.20. Waiver of Right to Appear at Hearing

A party may waive the right to appear personally at the hearing unless prohibited by law.[98] There do not appear to be any statutes or regulations that prohibit such a waiver. Any waiver must be in writing and filed with OAH.[99] A waiver may be withdrawn by written notice not later than five days before the scheduled hearing.[100] If a waiver has been filed, failure of the party to appear at the hearing may not result in a finding of default. Rather, the hearing is held in the absence of the party, and the decision is made.[101]

---

93. OAH Rule 21E(2), Md. Code Regs. 28.02.01.21E(2), COMAR 28.02.01.21E(2).

94. OAH Rule 21F, Md. Code Regs. 28.02.01.21F, COMAR 28.02.01.21F; Maryland Code Annotated, State Government § 10-213(h).

95. OAH Rule 21F(1), Md. Code Regs. 28.02.01.21F(1), COMAR 28.02.01.21F(1).

96. OAH Rule 21F(2), Md. Code Regs. 28.02.01.21F(2), COMAR 28.02.01.21F(2).

97. OAH Rule 20D, Md. Code Regs. 28.02.01.20D, COMAR 28.02.01.20D.

98. OAH Rule 20D(1)(a), Md. Code Regs. 28.02.01.20D(1)(a), COMAR 28.02.01.20D(1)(a).

99. OAH Rule 20D(1)(b), Md. Code Regs. 28.02.01.20D(1)(b), COMAR 28.02.01.20D(1)(b).

100. OAH Rule 20D(1)(c), Md. Code Regs. 28.02.01.20D(1)(c), COMAR 28.02.01.20D(1)(c).

101. OAH Rule 20D(1)(d), Md. Code Regs. 28.02.01.20D(1)(d), COMAR 28.02.01.20D(1)(d).

## § 10.21. Dismissal for Lack of Prosecution

A case pending at OAH cannot be placed on inactive status.[102] After six months from the last docket entry, a case is subject to dismissal for lack of prosecution based on a request by a party or upon the initiative of an ALJ.[103] Upon a party's request or the ALJ's own initiative that dismissal for lack of prosecution is warranted, the ALJ must send a notice to all parties that a final or proposed dismissal for lack of prosecution will be entered after the expiration of thirty days from the date of the notice unless a motion is filed within thirty days from the date of the notice establishing good cause not to dismiss.[104] If good cause is shown, dismissal will be deferred for a specific period and upon specified terms.[105] Whether good cause exists is within the discretion of the ALJ. The burden of providing an explanation for the lack of prosecution is on the party facing dismissal. A court order prohibiting a case from proceeding would constitute good cause.

## § 10.22. Default Order for Failure to Attend or Participate

If, after receiving proper notice, a party fails to attend or participate in a pre-hearing conference, hearing or other stage of the proceeding, the ALJ may proceed in that party's absence or may issue the proposed or final decision against the defaulting party.[106] A party may file a motion to vacate a final order of default within thirty days after the date of the order.[107] The motion shall state the reasons for the failure to attend or participate in the proceeding. If good cause is shown, the default order shall be vacated, and the case set for further proceedings.[108] Whether good cause exists is a matter within the discretion of the individual ALJ. For motions to vacate a default order, good cause generally means something beyond the control of the person who is the subject of the default order that prevented that person from participating and that prevented the person from notifying OAH of that circumstance prior to the scheduled time of the required action. Examples might include documented problems with receiving mail, being out of the country, or being hospitalized. If the default order relates to a proposed decision, the default order is reviewed by the agency with the final decisionmaking power like any other proposed decision from OAH.

## § 10.23. Venue

OAH designates the site of the hearing.[109] Although OAH's main office is in Hunt Valley, OAH conducts hearings throughout the state in various venues. For example, OAH holds

102. OAH Rule 24A, Md. Code Regs. 28.02.01.24A, COMAR 28.02.01.24A.
103. OAH Rule 24B, Md. Code Regs. 28.02.01.24B, COMAR 28.02.01.24B.
104. OAH Rule 24C,D, Md. Code Regs. 28.02.01.24C,D, COMAR 28.02.01.24C,D.
105. OAH Rule 24E(2), Md. Code Regs. 28.02.01.24E(2), COMAR 28.02.01.24E(2).
106. OAH Rule 23A, Md. Code Regs. 28.02.01.23A, COMAR 28.02.01.23A.
107. OAH Rule 23B(1), Md. Code Regs. 28.02.01.23B(1), COMAR 28.02.01.23B(1).
108. OAH Rule 23B(2), Md. Code Regs. 28.02.01.23B(2), COMAR 28.02.01.23B(2).
109. OAH Rule 07, Md. Code Regs. 28.02.01.07, COMAR 28.02.01.07.

hearings at local MVA offices, state and private hospitals, prisons, nursing homes, and various government facilities throughout the state.

## § 10.24. Flexible Due Process and Formality of the Hearing

The concept of flexible due process, as discussed in Chapter 4, is central to the role of OAH. OAH has stated as its mission to "provide flexible due process for any person affected by the action or proposed action of State agencies." Flexible due process is defined by OAH to mean that "each person has a fair opportunity to be heard, and the complexity of the hearing varies according to the nature of the case." The process that is due, therefore, varies.

The formality of the contested case hearings at OAH ranges from one end of the spectrum to the other. Some hearings resemble circuit court trials in their formality. Other hearings bear little resemblance to courtroom trials. OAH ALJs do not wear robes, but are referred to as "Judge ___." There are no bailiffs, and rarely a court reporter. The settings also vary. The main hearing room at OAH's headquarters at Hunt Valley, the John Hardwicke Hearing Room, looks exactly like a courtroom in a courthouse. On the other hand, some hearings, especially at some Motor Vehicle Administration offices, are heard in rooms that resemble storage closets. When ALJs travel to hear cases, they bring along their name plates and a digital recorder. In some settings, the ALJ sits no more than a few feet from the parties. There is therefore no one typical OAH hearing. Each hearing reflects the subject matter involved, whether the parties are represented by counsel, and the setting.

## § 10.25. The Hearing

The ALJ presides at the hearing. In conducting the hearing, the ALJ calls the hearing to order, and explains the purpose and nature of the hearing.[110] The ALJ administers the oaths to witnesses who are sworn or put under affirmation to testify truthfully.[111] The ALJ makes evidentiary rulings, and can examine or even call witnesses to ensure a full and complete record.[112] The ALJ has the duty to make sure that each witness is identified when testifying, and the duty to create a proper record by identifying and cataloging documents and other exhibits. In order to avoid unnecessary delay,[113] the ALJ can limit repetitious testimony, and reasonably limit the time for presentation.[114]

The ALJ has the power to request the parties to submit legal memoranda, proposed findings of fact, and proposed conclusions of law.[115] The ALJ can modify or waive time

110. OAH Rule 20A(2), Md. Code Regs. 28.02.01.20A(2), COMAR 28.02.01.20A(2).
111. OAH Rule 20A(3), Md. Code Regs. 28.02.01.20A(3), COMAR 28.02.01.20A(3).
112. OAH Rule 11B(5), Md. Code Regs. 28.02.01.11B(5), COMAR 28.02.01.11B(5).
113. OAH Rule 11A(2), Md. Code Regs. 28.02.01.11A(2), COMAR 28.02.01.11A(2).
114. OAH Rule 11B(6), Md. Code Regs. 28.02.01.11B(6), COMAR 28.02.01.11B(6).
115. OAH Rule 11B(9), Md. Code Regs. 28.02.01.11B(9), COMAR 28.02.01.11B(9).

periods for good cause, and can impose appropriate sanctions for failure to follow obligations imposed by law or by an order of the ALJ.[116] Overall, the role of the ALJ is to conduct the hearing in a fair manner to ascertain the facts, and safeguard the rights of the parties.

At the hearing, each party has the right to make an opening statement, present witnesses, offer evidence, cross examine witnesses called by others, and make a closing statement.[117]

## § 10.26. Open Hearings

In general, all proceedings conducted at OAH are open to the public.[118] There are classes of cases, however, that are not open to the public based on a statute specific to that type of case. For example, most cases from the Department of Human Resources involving food stamps, emergency assistance, child abuse and neglect, and child support enforcement are closed by law. Cases within the Department of Health and Mental Hygiene involving patients' rights, involuntary admission to psychiatric facilities, medical assistance, and other entitlement programs are not open to the public. By regulation, some cases arising under the state personnel system are not open to the public.[119] An attorney who is concerned with whether the hearing will be open to the public should check with OAH and the relevant agency to determine whether any law provides for a non-public hearing. Even in cases where the law provides for a non-public hearing, the hearing can be opened to the public if all persons, including the State, waive the non-public nature of the hearing. Moreover, even in cases that are generally open to the public, parts of the hearing may be closed to the public upon a request of a party in order to protect matters of a confidential nature, for example, medical information. It would be improper, however, to close a hearing to the public merely because a party would prefer the hearing not to be public. Additionally, an ALJ has the power to remove individuals whose conduct impedes the orderly progress of the hearing,[120] and to restrict attendance because of physical limitations of the hearing room.[121]

All documents, notices, and records in the possession of OAH as a result of a contested case proceeding may be inspected and copied in accordance with Maryland's Public Information Act.[122] Audio recording equipment, cameras, and other electronic or photographic equipment are permitted at the hearing unless a law prohibits their use or unless the ALJ determines that the use of such equipment may impede the orderly progress of the hearing or otherwise interfere with the hearing process.[123] The general practice at OAH is that still photographs may not be taken except prior to the beginning of a hearing or after it has concluded. Usually only one video camera may be used during the hearing. The video camera must be at a fixed location before the start of the hearing and remain at that fixed location. Media are required to share the videotape.

---

116. OAH Rule 11B(13), Md. Code Regs. 28.02.01.11B(13), COMAR 28.02.01.11B(13).

117. OAH Rule 20A(1), Md. Code Regs. 28.02.01.20A(1), COMAR 28.02.01.20A(1).

118. Maryland Code Annotated, State Government § 10-212; OAH Rule 19A, Md. Code Regs. 28.02.01.19A, COMAR 28.02.01.19A.

119. *See* Md. Code Regs. 17.04.07.14B, COMAR 17.04.07.14B.

120. OAH Rule 19C(1), Md. Code Regs. 28.02.01.19C(1), COMAR 28.02.01.19C(1).

121. OAH Rule 19C(2), Md. Code Regs. 28.02.01.19C(2), COMAR 28.02.01.19C(2).

122. OAH Rule 19B, Md. Code Regs. 28.02.01.19B, COMAR 28.02.01.19B.

123. OAH Rule 19D, Md. Code Regs. 28.02.01.19D, COMAR 28.02.01.19D.

## § 10.27. Telephone Hearings

The OAH ALJ may conduct all or part of a hearing by telephone or other similar audio electronic means provided that each party has an opportunity to participate in and hear the entire proceeding.[124] If a party establishes good cause in opposition to the holding of a hearing by telephone, or to other similar audio means, the hearing must be held in person, or by video conferencing or other similar audiovisual means.[125] For a telephone hearing, documentary evidence that will be offered must be mailed or delivered to all parties and OAH at least five days before the hearing.[126] The OAH regulation emphasizes that "all substantive and procedural rights apply to telephone hearings, subject only to the limitations of the physical arrangement."[127]

The OAH regulations do not discuss what would constitute good cause to oppose a telephone hearing. One issue that may arise is when the credibility of a witness testifying solely by telephone is crucial to the case. If credibility is crucial, the proponent of the witness should have a higher burden to justify telephone testimony.

## § 10.28. Video Hearings

A contested case hearing at OAH may also be conducted by video or similar audiovisual electronic means if each party has an opportunity to participate in, hear and see the entire proceeding.[128] If a party establishes good cause in opposition to the holding of a hearing by video or other audiovisual electronic means, the hearing must be held in person.[129] Video hearings are scheduled for Inmate Grievance Office cases and for state personnel system hearings involving correctional employees.[130] Video conferencing is also used to receive testimony from an expert witness located out-of-state, or from a necessary fact witness who is in military service or otherwise unable to attend the hearing.

For a video hearing not involving the Inmate Grievance Office, documentary evidence that will be offered at the hearing must be mailed or delivered to all parties and OAH at least five days before the hearing.[131] At Inmate Grievance Office hearings, documents are faxed between the OAH hearing location and the location of the inmate during the hearing. As with hearings held via telephone, all substantive and procedural rights apply to video hearings, subject only to the limitations of the physical arrangement.[132]

---

124. Maryland Code Annotated, State Government § 10-211(a).

125. Maryland Code Annotated, State Government § 10-211(b); OAH Rule 20B(2), Md. Code Regs. 28.02.01.20B(2), COMAR 28.02.01.20B(2); OAH Rule 20C(2), Md. Code Regs. 28.02.01.20C(2), COMAR 28.02.01.20C(2).

126. OAH Rule 20B(4), Md. Code Regs. 28.02.01.20B(4), COMAR 28.02.01.20B(4).

127. OAH Rule 20B(3), Md. Code Regs. 28.02.01.20B(3), COMAR 28.02.01.20B(3).

128. OAH Rule 20C(1), Md. Code Regs. 28.02.01.20C(1), COMAR 28.02.01.20C(1).

129. OAH Rule 20C(2), Md. Code Regs. 28.02.01.20C(2), COMAR 28.02.01.20C(2).

130. OAH Rule 20C(4), Md. Code Regs. 28.02.01.20C(4), COMAR 28.02.01.20C(4).

131. OAH Rule 20C(4), Md. Code Regs. 28.02.01.20C(4), COMAR 28.02.01.20C(4).

132. OAH Rule 20C(3), Md. Code Regs. 28.02.01.20C(3), COMAR 28.02.01.20C(3).

## § 10.29. ADA Compliance

The Americans with Disabilities Act applies to contested case hearings at OAH. An OAH regulation provides that if "a party or witness requests a reasonable accommodation required by the Americans with Disabilities Act, [OAH] shall provide the accommodation."[133] It is highly recommended that requests for an accommodation be made sufficiently prior to the hearing to permit the accommodation to be made, although a request at the hearing will be honored if possible. Failure to provide adequate notice of the need for an accommodation may lead to the need to postpone the hearing, and possibly change the venue or type of hearing.

## § 10.30. Evidence

The OAH regulations adopt the same evidentiary principles that are set forth in the Maryland APA. These principles are discussed in Chapter 6. Most importantly, hearsay is admissible and can be the sole basis of a finding.[134] Objection to the admission of hearsay evidence at an OAH contested case hearing is the most common mistake made by attorneys unfamiliar with OAH procedure.

## § 10.31. Exclusion of Witnesses

Upon the request of a party, a witness other than a party shall be excluded from the hearing room except when testifying.[135] No party, representative, witness or spectator may disclose to an excluded witness the nature, substance or purpose of testimony, exhibits, or other evidence introduced during that witness's absence.[136] If a potential witness receives information in violation of this regulation, the ALJ may exclude the testimony of that witness or take other appropriate action.[137] For example, in a situation where a sequestered witness received information he or she should not have received, but this was not the fault of the witness or the party for whom the witness is testifying, it would be inappropriate to exclude the witness's testimony. In this situation, "other appropriate action" may include arranging for the appearance of another witness to testify on the same issue, allowing additional evidence regarding the information disclosed, or instructing the witness to disregard the conversation. A party that is not an individual may designate an employee or officer as its representative to remain in the hearing room even though the employee or officer may be a witness.[138] An expert

133. OAH Rule 09C, Md. Code Regs. 28.02.01.09C, COMAR 28.02.01.09C.
134. OAH Rule 21C, Md. Code Regs. 28.02.01.21C, COMAR 28.02.01.21C.
135. OAH Rule 21D(1), Md. Code Regs. 28.02.01.21D(1), COMAR 28.02.01.21D(1).
136. OAH Rule 21D(2), Md. Code Regs. 28.02.01.21D(2), COMAR 28.02.01.21D(2).
137. OAH Rule 21D(5), Md. Code Regs. 28.02.01.21D(5), COMAR 28.02.01.21D(5).
138. OAH Rule 21D(3), Md. Code Regs. 28.02.01.21D(3), COMAR 28.02.01.21D(3).

witness who is to render an opinion based on the testimony given at the hearing is not subject to exclusion.[139]

## § 10.32. Interpreters

As discussed in Chapter 5, the Maryland APA does not require that an agency governed by the APA provide an interpreter for a party or witness who does not understand the English language.[140] Individual agencies, however, can provide for such interpreters, and OAH has such a regulation. This OAH regulation, which supplements the APA provision on interpreters, provides that "upon request of a party or witness who cannot hear, speak, or understand the spoken or written English language, [OAH] shall provide a qualified interpreter during the hearing."[141] The interpreter is required to take an oath that the interpreter will accurately interpret the proceedings.[142] Translation by a relative or friend is not permitted. A state-approved interpreter who is impartial in the matter is required. Interpreters are paid from State funds. It is preferable to provide OAH with notice in advance of the hearing so that an interpreter can be scheduled and available at the beginning of the hearing. However, even without advance notice, OAH is able to provide an interpreter through a telephone interpreter service with which OAH has contracted.

## § 10.33. Motion for Judgment

A party may move for judgment on any or all of the issues at the close of the evidence offered by an opposing party.[143] The moving party must state reasons why the motion should be granted. No objection to the motion is necessary.[144] A party does not waive the right to make the motion by introducing evidence during the presentation of any opposing party's case. When a Motion for Judgment is made, the ALJ may either determine the facts and render a decision against the opposing party, or decline to make any decision until the close of all evidence.[145] If the Motion for Judgment is not granted, the moving party may offer evidence, but by offering evidence, the motion is considered withdrawn.[146]

## § 10.34. The Record

One of the responsibilities of OAH is to create the official administrative record for purposes of judicial review if OAH has been delegated the authority to make the final decision, or for the delegating agency's review if OAH has been delegated the power to

139. OAH Rule 21D(4), Md. Code Regs. 28.02.01.21D(4), COMAR 28.02.01.21D(4).
140. Maryland Code Annotated, State Government § 10-212.1.
141. OAH Rule 09A, Md. Code Regs. 28.02.01.09A, COMAR 28.02.01.09A.
142. OAH Rule 09B, Md. Code Regs. 28.02.01.09B, COMAR 28.02.01.09B.
143. OAH Rule 12E(1), Md. Code Regs. 28.02.01.12E(1), COMAR 28.02.01.12E(1).
144. OAH Rule 12E(1), Md. Code Regs. 28.02.01.12E(1), COMAR 28.02.01.12E(1).
145. OAH Rule 12E(2), Md. Code Regs. 28.02.01.12E(2), COMAR 28.02.01.12E(2).
146. OAH Rule 12E(3), Md. Code Regs. 28.02.01.12E(3), COMAR 28.02.01.12E(3).

make only a proposed decision. The administrative record includes the following items: all pleadings, motions, responses, correspondence, memoranda, proposed findings of fact and conclusions of law, requests filed by parties, all hearing notices, all documentary and other tangible evidence received or considered, a statement of each fact officially noticed, all stipulations, all offers of proof and objections, all rulings, orders, and decisions whether proposed or final, matters placed on the record in connection with an ex parte communication, the recording of the hearing and any pre-hearing proceeding, any transcript of the recording prepared by a court reporting service, and all exhibits marked for identification whether or not the exhibit was offered or admitted into evidence.[147]

## § 10.35. ALJ Decisions

In some contested cases, the ALJ makes a bench decision immediately after the close of the evidence. Most bench decisions are oral decisions. The largest number of oral bench decisions are Motor Vehicle Administration cases. Some bench decisions are written decisions accomplished by the ALJ completing a form. For example, cases involving involuntary commitment to a mental institution are bench decisions. All bench decisions by OAH are cases where OAH has final decisionmaking authority.

Some contested cases require a written opinion by the ALJ. Often, there is a strict deadline by which the decision must be made, imposed by statute or regulation. A written decision by an ALJ is the decision of that ALJ, not the product of an OAH process requiring internal review. Although the ALJ's decision becomes OAH's decision, there is not an institutional decisionmaking process at OAH.

Past written opinions from OAH are available at the library at OAH offices in Hunt Valley. Opinions are not available on-line. An opinion of an OAH ALJ has no precedential value. Because of confidentiality and privacy issues, many OAH opinions are not available without a prior request. Some opinions such as those from cases involving child abuse, medical assistance, and personnel matters will only be made available after information has been redacted. It is recommended that before going to the OAH library, a librarian should be contacted to discuss the availability of a particular opinion or class of opinions.

It is important to note that in all cases, even in those for which OAH has been delegated the final decisionmaking authority, OAH has no policy-making power. OAH must decide the case based on policy established by the agency. The APA provides that in a contested case, OAH "is bound by any agency regulation, declaratory ruling, prior adjudication, or other settled, preexisting policy, to the same extent as the agency is or would have been bound if it were hearing the case."[148]

If OAH is not the final decisionmaker, OAH submits the proposed decision to the agency that has retained final decisionmaking authority, and sends a copy of the proposed decision to each party.[149] A proposed decision is subject to the exceptions process discussed in Chapter 11.

---

147. OAH Rule 22, Md. Code Regs. 28.02.01.22, COMAR 28.02.01.22.
148. Maryland Code Annotated, State Government § 10-214(b).
149. Maryland Code Annotated, State Government § 10-220(b).

## § 10.36. Revision

If OAH has been delegated the final decisionmaking authority, the ALJ's final decision is subject to revision.[150] A final decision may be revised only by the ALJ who rendered the decision for which revision is requested.[151] Revision to correct clerical mistakes is available on the ALJ's own initiative or based on a motion by any party.[152] A party may also file a Motion for Revision in the event of fraud, mistake or irregulatory.[153] One interpretation of this regulation is that an arguably erroneous ruling by an ALJ, even if the ALJ upon reflection concludes that her or his ruling was incorrect, is not subject to revision. Relevant here is that a prior OAH regulation permitted not only revision, but also "reconsideration." Under the current regulations, OAH ALJs do not expressly have the power to reconsider their decisions. As discussed in Chapter 5, the Court of Appeals has held that Maryland agencies have the inherent power to reconsider their decisions even absent any statute or regulation authorizing reconsideration.

## § 10.37. Stays

A request for revision does not automatically stay the action or toll the time for filing for judicial review.[154] OAH ALJs, however, may stay their orders on their own initiative or based on a motion to stay filed by a party.[155] In addition to the grounds for granting a stay discussed in Chapter 13 which apply to all agencies, in light of the OAH apparent position that it cannot revise or reconsider a decision even if the ALJ realizes that it was erroneous, a stay pending judicial review would be appropriate when the ALJ recognizes the possibility that his or her decision was erroneous.

## § 10.38. Cases Remanded to OAH

If a case is remanded to OAH by an agency or a court for further proceedings, the case is considered filed with OAH when the order of the agency or court is received.[156] The OAH regulation provides that OAH will "promptly schedule further proceedings as necessary."[157]

---

150. OAH Rule 27A, Md. Code Regs. 28.02.01.27A, COMAR 28.02.01.27A.
151. OAH Rule 27A, Md. Code Regs. 28.02.01.27A, COMAR 28.02.01.27A.
152. OAH Rule 27C, Md. Code Regs. 28.02.01.27C, COMAR 28.02.01.27C.
153. OAH Rule 27B, Md. Code Regs. 28.02.01.27B, COMAR 28.02.01.27B. The revisory power at OAH is to be exercised in the same manner as courts exercise their revisory power under Maryland Rule 2-535(b). Mistakes of law are not grounds for revision.
154. Md. Rule 7-205; Maryland Code Annotated, State Government § 10-222(e).
155. Maryland Code Annotated, State Government § 10-222(e).
156. OAH Rule 26A, Md. Code Regs. 28.02.01.26A, COMAR 28.02.01.26A.
157. OAH Rule 26B, Md. Code Regs. 28.02.01.26B, COMAR 28.02.01.26B.

## § 10.39. Alternative Dispute Resolution (ADR) at OAH

As well as its primary goal of adjudicating contested cases, OAH is involved with alternative dispute resolution (ADR). ADR is defined in the OAH regulations as the process of resolving matters pending before OAH through a settlement conference, neutral case evaluation, neutral fact finding, mediation, other non-adversarial dispute resolution processes, or a combination of those processes.[158] OAH generally uses two categories of ADR, settlement and mediation, both of which may employ some sort of neutral case evaluation. ADR at OAH is to help the parties achieve resolution of their dispute without a hearing. All OAH ALJs are trained in ADR. Most ADR at OAH is facilitated by ALJs, but some cases are handled by ADR trained paralegals and staff attorneys. Unlike contested case hearing requests, requests by parties for a specific facilitator are honored if possible. Also, unlike hearing assignments, subject matter expertise of the facilitator may be a factor in an ADR assignment through the clerk's office.

An ADR proceeding may be scheduled only if all parties agree.[159] ADR is used most often in special education cases, Home Improvement Commission cases, and the more complex regulatory matters. All ADR proceedings at OAH are closed to the public and are confidential. Discussions in an ADR proceeding may not be made part of the case record in any subsequent proceeding. Additionally, ADR proceedings may not be recorded electronically or in any other manner.[160] An OAH ALJ who presides at an ADR proceeding may not be the ALJ at any pre-hearing conference, hearing on the merits, or any other stage of a contested case.[161] Moreover, an ALJ or other individual who conducts an ADR proceeding may not be called to testify, participate in discovery, or otherwise provide information in any subsequent proceeding related to the ADR proceeding.[162]

## § 10.40. Foreclosure Mediation

In 2010, OAH was given a role in the foreclosure process of residential properties. Pursuant to Maryland Code, Real Property §7-105.1 and Title 14, Chapter 200 of the Maryland Rules of Procedure, a borrower facing foreclosure on residential property that is owner occupied may file a request with the circuit court for foreclosure mediation to be held at OAH. The court then transmits the request for mediation to OAH within five days. Mediation must be scheduled by OAH to occur within sixty days, unless good cause is established for a thirty day extension. The mediations are held at OAH offices in Hunt Valley and in circuit courts throughout the state for the convenience of the parties.

---

158. OAH Rule 18A, Md. Code Regs. 28.02.01.18A, COMAR 28.02.01.18A.

159. OAH Rule 18B, Md. Code Regs. 28.02.01.18B, COMAR 28.02.01.18B.

160. OAH Rule 18D(3), Md. Code Regs. 28.02.01.18D(3), COMAR 28.02.01.18D(3).

161. OAH Rule 18C, Md. Code Regs. 28.02.01.18C, COMAR 28.02.01.18C. *See* Spencer v. Md. State Board of Pharmacy, 380 Md. 515, 846 A.2d 341 (2004) (holding it was improper for two Board members to participate at a case resolution conference and then participate in the decision of the case).

162. OAH Rule 18D(4), Md. Code Regs. 28.02.01.18D(4), COMAR 28.02.01.18D(4).

The homeowner must attend the mediation. The homeowner may be represented by an attorney or be accompanied by a housing counselor. A representative of the lender who has the authority to settle the matter or be able to readily contact a person with authority to settle must also be present at the mediation. All discussions at the mediation are confidential. Discussions at the mediation are not admissible in any administrative or judicial proceeding. Moreover, the mediator cannot be called as a witness to testify at any administrative or judicial proceeding about any discussions at the mediation.

At least twenty days before the mediation, the borrower and lender are required to exchange certain documents. The borrower must provide federal tax returns for the last two years, proof of income including employment income, benefit income such as social security and disability benefits, unemployment benefits, rental income, and alimony and child support. The borrower also must provide a summary of monthly expenses. If the loan does not have an escrow account for taxes and insurance, the borrower must also provide a copy of the most recent property tax bill and proof of payment, and a copy of the current insurance bill and proof of payment. The lender must provide information including payment history, escrow activity, and property valuation documentation.

Within five days after the mediation, OAH must file a report with the court stating the outcome of the foreclosure mediation. If this foreclosure mediation results in an agreement, the court shall take action to implement the agreement. If the foreclosure mediation does not result in an agreement, the secured party may advertise the sale of the property. If the foreclosure mediation was not held or was terminated because the secured party failed to attend or failed to provide required documents, the court may dismiss the secured party's action to foreclosure.

# Chapter 11

# Contested Cases: OAH Proposed Decisions and the Exceptions Process

## § 11.1. Exceptions Regulations

If OAH has not been delegated the power to make the final agency decision, the ALJ's proposed decision is sent to the agency along with the official administrative case record.[1] Each agency which has delegated proposed decisionmaking authority to OAH should have regulations which set forth the exceptions process at the agency. Unfortunately, the exceptions regulations at some agencies are lacking. For example, as discussed in Chapter 2, the Board of Physicians did not have a valid regulation setting forth the maximum number of pages that could be filed as exceptions. When the Board attempted to enforce a fifteen page limit that had never been properly adopted as a regulation, the circuit court enjoined enforcement of the page limit.

## § 11.2. Scope of Exceptions Process

One issue which has caused some discussion is the scope of the exceptions process at the agency. It is not always clear whether the agency will consider new evidence during the exceptions process or whether it will permit (or maybe require) witnesses who testified at OAH to testify at an exceptions hearing. Properly drafted and adopted regulations on the exceptions process should be required for all agencies which have delegated proposed decisionmaking authority to OAH. Some guidance on the exceptions process absent any regulations is found in the Court of Appeals decision *Mehrling v. Nationwide Insurance Company*.[2]

Mehrling filed a complaint with the Maryland Insurance Administration (MIA) challenging the termination of her contract as an insurance agent by Nationwide Insurance Co. MIA had delegated to OAH the power to make a recommended decision. The OAH ALJ dismissed Mehrling's complaint on the ground that she lacked standing because she had filed recently a petition for bankruptcy, and thus the bankruptcy trustee was the proper party to file the complaint. In fact, just prior to the ALJ's decision, Mehrling's bankruptcy petition had been dismissed by the bankruptcy court. The OAH ALJ had not been informed of this dismissal. Pursuant to MIA regulations, Mehrling filed

1. Maryland Code Annotated, State Government § 10-220(a).
2. 371 Md. 40, 806 A.2d 662 (2002).

exceptions with MIA. Her exceptions included evidence that her bankruptcy petition had been dismissed, and thus she did have standing to bring the action against Nationwide. The Associate Deputy Commissioner acting on behalf of MIA adopted the ALJ's decision to dismiss Mehrling's complaint because of lack of standing. Upon judicial review in the circuit court, the MIA decision to dismiss the complaint was upheld. The circuit court judge ruled that because Mehrling had not presented the evidence of the dismissal of her bankruptcy petition to the OAH ALJ, she was precluded from presenting it to MIA in her exceptions. This was affirmed by the Court of Special Appeals. The Court of Appeals ruled that the MIA and the lower courts were wrong on this point. Mehrling was permitted to present new evidence to the MIA as part of her exceptions even though she had not presented this evidence at OAH. Because the agency had retained the authority to make the final decision, judicial review was of the agency's decision, not the ALJ's decision. The court reaffirmed its holding in *Maryland State Police v. Zeigler*,[3] discussed in Chapter 5, that agencies have broad discretion to consider evidence after the close of the evidentiary hearing. Moreover, the APA provides that exceptions are deemed part of the record that the agency must consider in making its final decision.[4] Therefore, the court concluded that new evidence could be presented to the agency in support of the party's exceptions.

## § 11.3. Standard of Review in the Exceptions Process

The general rule is that an agency that has retained the authority to make the final decision has *de novo* power to make the final decision, except if a demeanor based credibility determination was crucial to the OAH proposed decision. The agency owes no deference to the OAH proposed decision. As discussed in Chapter 15, this is different than the standard of review which a reviewing court employs when reviewing the final agency decision.

The principles involving the standard of review in the exceptions process were developed in two cases, *Anderson v. Department of Public Safety and Correctional Services*[5] and *Department of Health and Mental Hygiene v. Shrieves*.[6] These two cases created what is often called the *Anderson-Shrieves* doctrine.

*Anderson* involved a disciplinary action against a state prison guard for alleged excessive force on an inmate. At the time of the case, the Department of Personnel was the agency that decided state personnel matters.[7] The Department had delegated to OAH only the authority to issue a proposed decision in state employee disciplinary cases. After a hearing at OAH, the ALJ issued a proposed decision that concluded that Anderson had not used excessive force, should not be disciplined, and should be reinstated to his former position. Anderson's employer, the Maryland Penitentiary, filed exceptions to the proposed decision with the Secretary of Personnel. The Secretary appointed a designee to conduct a hearing to review the OAH decision. This designee reviewed the administrative record, including the taped recording of the OAH hearing, and heard oral arguments from counsel for both

3. 330 Md. 540, 625 A.2d 914 (1993).
4. *See* Maryland Code Annotated, State Government § 10-220(d)(3).
5. 330 Md. 187, 623 A.2d 198 (1993).
6. 100 Md. App 283, 641 A.2d 899 (1994).
7. This function is now handled by the Department of Budget and Management.

Anderson and the Penitentiary. The designee, although adopting some of the ALJ's findings, in general "renounced" the decision of the ALJ, and ordered that Anderson be separated from state service. In her decision, the designee "complained" that the ALJ had given weight to the testimony of only three witnesses, but had ignored the testimony of other witnesses.

Anderson sought judicial review in the circuit court, and the circuit court affirmed the agency decision. Anderson then appealed to the Court of Special Appeals, but before a decision was rendered by that court, the Court of Appeals issued a writ of certiorari on its own motion. The question presented involved the proper standard of review between the OAH and the agency that had delegated the authority to OAH to make a proposed decision.

The Court of Appeals recognized that the creation of OAH had created a new issue regarding the contested case decisionmaking process in Maryland. The Court of Appeals looked for guidance to the U.S. Supreme Court decision in *Universal Camera Corporation v. National Labor Relations Board*.[8] *Universal Camera* taught a few lessons. First, because the responsibility for the final decision is with the agency, not the ALJ, the agency is not limited to reversing an ALJ's findings of fact only if those findings are clearly erroneous. The power of the agency to reverse the ALJ is broader than what is permissible under the clearly erroneous standard. Second, judicial review of a contested case under substantial evidence review requires review of the "entire record," and the entire record includes the proposed decision of the ALJ. Third, substantial evidence review "is not modified in any way" when the agency has disagreed with the ALJ. Fourth, and perhaps most significant in *Anderson*, is that in evaluating the entire record as part of its substantial evidence review, the significance that is given to the ALJ's proposed decision "depends largely on the importance of credibility in the particular case." The agency should give "appropriate deference to the opportunity of the examiner to observe the demeanor of the witnesses," including how the witness sits or stands, whether the witness is nervous, the witness' coloration, modulation or pace of speech, and other non-verbal communication.[9] The degree of deference due the ALJ's proposed decision is "related to the importance of credibility in a particular case." The "ALJ's decision to give or deny credit to a particular witness' testimony should not be reversed absent an adequate explanation of the grounds for the [agency's] source of disagreement with the ALJ."[10] Although the agency has the power to reject credibility assessments by the ALJ, it must give "strong reasons for doing so." In *Anderson*, the Court of Appeals concluded that the agency had given "no real significance to the ALJ's report," and that "the credibility of the witnesses was of the utmost importance in the circumstances here; it played a dominant role; it was pivotal." The agency's final decision gave no deference to the ALJ's "assessment of the credibility of the witnesses."[11] The agency "gave no strong reasons for rejecting the ALJ's assessments of credibility." The Court of Appeals therefore held that the agency "did not appreciate the proper relationship between [the agency] and the ALJ." The case was remanded to the Department of Personnel.

8. 340 U.S. 474 (1951).

9. Anderson v. Department of Public Safety and Correctional Services, 330 Md.187, 220, 623 A.2d 198, 216 (1993); *see* Schinnerer v. Maryland Insurance Admin., 147 Md. App. 474, 494, 809 A.2d 709, 720–21 (2002), *cert. denied*, 373 Md. 408, 818 A.2d 1106 (2003) (ALJ believed witness's testimony because witness "was unable to look the [ALJ] in the eye while testifying about his version of events.").

10. 330 Md. 187, 217, 623 A.2d 198, 213 (1993).

11. 330 Md. 187, 218–19, 623 A.2d 198, 213 (1993).

One year later, the Court of Special Appeals decided *Department of Health and Mental Hygiene v. Shrieves.*[12] *Shrieves* also involved the discipline of a state employee by the Department of Personnel. Shrieves was charged with sexually harassing a co-worker when he was photographing her for an employee identification card. A hearing was held at OAH where extensive testimony was taken regarding what happened between Shrieves and the co-worker. The OAH ALJ concluded that the agency had not shown by a preponderance of the evidence that Shrieves had sexually harassed the co-worker. The ALJ found Shrieves' account of what happened "credible." Shrieves' employer, the Department of Health and Mental Hygiene, filed exceptions with the Department of Personnel. After hearing oral argument and considering the record, the Secretary's designee issued a thirty-page opinion that concluded that Shrieves had engaged in sexual harassment and should be discharged. On judicial review, the circuit court reversed the agency's decision. The circuit court's interpretation of *Anderson* was it was the circuit court's "job to determine if the ALJ had a rational basis for making the decision she did, i.e., if there was substantial evidence to support the ALJ's decision." Because the ALJ's proposed decision was based on substantial evidence, and because the agency had not adequately stated its reasons for disagreeing with the ALJ, the circuit court ordered Shrieves to be reinstated and receive back pay.

The Court of Special Appeals in *Shrieves* held that the circuit court had misinterpreted *Anderson.* The Court of Special Appeals emphasized that *Anderson* had not set forth a new standard for reviewing agency decisions. *Anderson* did not direct a reviewing court to vacate an agency decision that was contrary to the ALJ's proposed decision if the ALJ's decision was supported by substantial evidence. The proper role of the court is to review the agency's final order for substantial evidence, not the ALJ's decision for substantial evidence. The relevant issue for the reviewing court is not whether the agency erred in overruling the ALJ, but rather whether there is substantial evidence to support the agency's final decision. The Court of Special Appeals in *Shrieves* stated that the ALJ's findings are not entitled to any special deference by the delegating agency except insofar as the findings are based on the ALJ's determination of credibility of the witnesses. The court, however, then made a very important distinction between credibility based on demeanor and credibility based on the evidence itself, what the court called derivative inferences. Only demeanor-based credibility determinations by an ALJ are entitled to deference. As to credibility determinations based on derivative inferences from the record, deference is owed to the agency (not the ALJ) because the agency is presumed to have broad experience and expertise, and because it is the agency to which the legislature has delegated the power to administer the governing statute. As to credibility determinations based on derivative inferences, a reviewing court must affirm the agency unless the inferences are unreasonable. As to credibility determinations based on demeanor, however, the agency has "little or no basis for disputing" the ALJ.

The Court of Special Appeals also discussed that the agency's relationship to the ALJ when the ALJ is making a proposed decision is not equal to the relationship between a reviewing court and the final decision of the agency. A court must affirm the agency even if the court would have reached a different conclusion as long as the agency decision is supported by substantial evidence. When the agency is reviewing the proposed decision of the ALJ, even if the ALJ decision is supported by substantial evidence, the agency can substitute its judgment and decide differently from what the ALJ proposed. The only caveat to this is when the ALJ's decision is based on the demeanor of witnesses. In that situation, the agency can only reject the ALJ's findings if the agency gives strong reasons.

12. 100 Md. App. 283, 641 A.2d 899 (1994).

The Court of Special Appeals then turned to reviewing the Department of Personnel's decision regarding Shrieves. The problem was that it did "not know the basis for the [agency's] decision." The court could not determine to what extent, if any, the agency's disagreement with the ALJ was based on demeanor-based credibility. The court therefore remanded the matter so that the Department of Personnel could provide a "clear statement of the rationale" for its decision.

The *Anderson-Shrieves* doctrine is well established in Maryland. An illustrative case is *Gabaldoni v. Board of Physician Quality Assurance.*[13] This case involved a disciplinary action against a physician for violations of several provisions of the Medical Practice Act. One allegation involved failure to meet the appropriate standard of care in his treatment of an anemic pregnant patient who died during childbirth. After an extensive hearing at OAH, the ALJ concluded that the physician had acted appropriately in his treatment of the patient, and therefore no sanctions were warranted. This proposed decision then went to the Board of Physician Quality Assurance. The Board concluded that the physician had failed to meet the appropriate standard of medical care, and issued a reprimand. The Court of Special Appeals upheld the Board's decision and sanction. After analyzing the evidence presented at the hearing and the Board's written decision, the court concluded that the Board's decision was based on "derivative inferences based on not discredited testimony," in reaching factual conclusions different than those reached by the ALJ, and that "to the extent the Board disagreed with demeanor-based findings of the ALJ, the Board had set forth strong reasons for doing so."[14]

## § 11.4. Expert Witnesses and the Anderson-Shrieves Doctrine

Several cases have involved the application of the *Anderson-Shrieves* doctrine to expert witness testimony at the contested case hearing. In *Consumer Protection Division v. Morgan,*[15] the Consumer Protection Division (CPD) alleged that a real estate appraiser had engaged in unfair and deceptive trade practices in violation of the Consumer Protection Act. Both the CPD and the alleged violator presented expert witnesses at the OAH hearing on various issues regarding the real estate appraisal process to support their respective positions. As part of her proposed decision, the ALJ concluded that the appraiser had not violated the Consumer Protection Act. This conclusion was in part based on her evaluation of the competing expert witnesses. The ALJ's proposed decision was then reviewed by the CPD. The CPD, relying on its own expert witness who had testified at OAH but who was not found persuasive by the ALJ, ruled that the appraiser had violated the Act. Upon judicial review in circuit court, the CPD was reversed. The circuit court's ruling was based on the court's belief that the ALJ's decision "required a demeanor-based assessment of the competing witnesses and that the ALJ, not the CPD Chief, must perform that role." Before

---

13. 141 Md. App. 259, 785 A.2d 771 (2001).

14. 141 Md. App. 259, 263, 785 A.2d 771, 773 (2001). *See also* Community Clinic, Inc. v. Department of Health & Mental Hygiene, 174 Md. App. 526, 922 A.2d 607, *cert. denied*, 400 Md. 647, 929 A.2d 890 (2007) (agency is free to disagree with proposed OAH decision except where credibility is based on demeanor).

15. 387 Md. 125, 874 A.2d 919 (2005).

the Court of Special Appeals considered the appeal from the circuit court, the Court of Appeals granted certiorari on its own initiative. The Court of Appeals stated that:

> This issue revolves around whether the Division's determination of misrepresentation in comparable sales and neighborhood predominant values was a demeanor-based credibility assessment.... An assessment of the appraisers' demeanor is of minimal importance in this technical case. Ordinarily, demeanor had been held to be of little consequences in evaluating the credibility of experts who provide conflicting testimony.... Though credibility of the conflicting experts must play a central role in the [agency] decision, that credibility is a function of logical analysis, credentials, data base, and other factors readily discernible to one who reads the record. [In this case, it has] not [been] demonstrated that this is an issue that turns on conflicting eyewitness reports or evaluations of the witnesses' demeanor or conduct.[16]

The Court of Appeals upheld the decision of the CPD.

*State Board of Physicians v. Bernstein*[17] also involved expert witnesses. A physician was accused of failing to comply with the appropriate standard of care while supervising a patient's anesthesia. A contested case hearing was held before an OAH ALJ. At the hearing, the Board presented two expert witnesses to support the charge. In his defense, the physician called two expert witnesses who supported his position. The ALJ issued an extensive written proposed decision in which the ALJ recommended that the charges be dismissed. Exceptions were filed to the ALJ's decision, and a exceptions hearing was held before the Board. The Board rejected the ALJ's proposed decision and issued a reprimand. Although the Board stated that it did not disagree with many of the ALJ's factual findings, the Board added that "the standard for the provision of quality medical care is determined by appropriate peer review, the opinion of experts in the field, and the Board's own expertise," and that it was "within its province to weigh the opinions given by the expert witnesses in a contested case hearing depending on the experts' training, experience and knowledge, as well as the bases for their opinions." The Board then summarized each expert witness's credentials, background and testimony. The Board in its decision did not address the ALJ's credibility determinations of the expert witnesses.

Upon judicial review, the circuit court reversed the Board's decision on the ground that the Board had not given strong reasons for disagreeing with the ALJ's credibility determinations of the expert witnesses. The Court of Special Appeals disagreed with the circuit court on this point, relying on *Anderson*, *Shrieves* and *Morgan*. The Court of Special Appeals wrote that this case involved "a classic battle of the experts" which did not depend on demeanor-based credibility assessments of any of the testifying experts. Although the ALJ stated several times in her proposed decision that the physician's expert witnesses were "more credible than the Board's expert witnesses, the reasons she gave to support her credibility findings did not involve assessments of the witnesses based on their demeanor."[18] The basis of the ALJ's decision was that the physician's experts were more experienced, more proficient, more knowledgeable and more objective, and thus more persuasive and credible. This conclusion was in no way based on the expert witnesses' "outward appearances"; demeanor played no role in the ALJ's decision. Therefore, pursuant to *Anderson*, *Shrieves*, and *Morgan*, the Board owed no deference to the credibility assessments made by the ALJ, and was not required to state strong reasons for rejecting

16. 387 Md. 125, 197–202, 874 A.2d 919, 962–64 (2005).
17. 167 Md. App. 714, 894 A.2d 621 (2006).
18. 167 Md. App. 714, 760, 894 A.2d 621, 647 (2006).

those assessments.[19] The Court of Special Appeals did remand the case to the Board for reconsideration of its decision because the court held that the opinion of one of the experts relied upon by the Board lacked adequate foundation.

## § 11.5. Approaches in Federal and Other State Cases

The *Anderson-Shrieves* doctrine is consistent with the approach taken by federal courts when reviewing a federal agency's final decision reversing the proposed decision of a federal ALJ. Maryland follows leading federal cases such as *Federal Communications Commission v. Allentown Broadcasting Corporation*,[20] and *Penasquitos Village, Inc. v. NLRB.*[21] The problem with relying on federal cases on this issue is that federal administrative law follows a different adjudicatory model than does Maryland. Federal agencies do not have an independent central hearing agency such as OAH. Federal ALJ's are assigned to hear and make proposed decisions for one agency. The federal model is similar to the pre-1990 approach in Maryland which was found wanting because of concerns of impartiality and fairness. OAH's goal of providing a truly independent ALJ is compromised by an exceptions process that gives no deference to the ALJ's proposed decision.

Other states that have adopted central hearing agencies like Maryland's OAH have adopted approaches different than Maryland in regards to the agency's power to reverse the ALJ's proposed decision. For example, the Florida court in *Gross v. Department of Health*[22] wrote that "although an agency may reject or modify the conclusions of law and interpretation of administrative rules of the hearing officer, it may not reject or modify findings of fact where those findings of fact are based on competent substantial evidence."[23] Consideration should be given to limiting the power of agencies to reverse proposed decisions of OAH. Moving away from the *Shrieves-Anderson* standard will better further the goals of fairness and impartiality which were the basis of the creation of OAH.

## § 11.6. Modification of the Exceptions Process by Regulation or Statute

The standard of review of proposed OAH decisions by the agency with final decisionmaking power as adopted in *Anderson* and *Shrieves* can be changed for a particular

19. A good example of how credibility can be based on a cold record unrelated to demeanor is Rosov v. Maryland State Bd. of Dental Exam'rs, 163 Md. App. 98, 877 A.2d 1111 (2005), where the ALJ discredited an affidavit because it contradicted an earlier account of the same incident, and the affidavit was given after the affiant had received a $1,000 bonus, a paid Caribbean cruise and diamond earrings from the dentist who was being investigated.

20. 349 U.S. 358 (1955).

21. 565 F.2d 1074 (9th Cir. 1977).

22. 819 So. 2d 997 (Fla. Dist. Ct. App. 2002).

23. 819 So. 2d 997, 1001 n.6 (Fla. Dist. Ct. App. 2002). There are numerous law review articles discussing the issue of an agency's review of a proposed decision of a central hearing agency. Among these articles are Jim Rossi, *Final, But Often Fallible: Recognizing Problems With ALJ Finality*, 56 Admin. L. Rev. 53 (2004); James F. Flanagan, *Redefining the Role of the State Administrative Law Judge*, 54 Admin. L. Rev. 1355 (2002); Charles E. Daye, *Powers of Administrative Law Judges, Agencies, and Courts*, 79 N.C.L. Rev. 1571 (2001).

agency or a specific type of case. *Kohli v. LOOC, Inc.*[24] involved a regulation which is no longer in effect, but this opinion is still useful. *Kohli* involved a claim of employment discrimination based on religion by a member of the Sikh religion who was not hired by a Domino's Pizza store because Kohli refused to shave his beard which he wore for religious reasons. The case was brought by the Commission on Human Relations (CHR) which by regulation had delegated to OAH the power to conduct the initial hearing and issue a "provisional order." This provisional order became the agency's final order unless an appeal was taken to an Appeal Board of CHR. In the event of an appeal, the decision of the Appeal Board was the final agency decision. By regulation, the Appeal Board was given the power to "affirm, reverse, or modify the administrative law judge's decision in accordance with the standards as set forth in State Gov't § 10-222(h)."[25] As discussed in Chapter 15, State Gov't § 10-222(h) sets forth the standards by which a court reviews the final agency decision in a contested case. Under the statute, reversal of an agency decision in a contested case is permitted only if the decision is unconstitutional, exceeds the statutory authority or jurisdiction of the agency, resulted from unlawful procedure, is affected by an error of law, is unsupported by substantial evidence, or is arbitrary or capricious. The impact of the CHR regulation was to create the relationship between OAH and CHR identical to the relationship between an agency and a reviewing court—exactly what *Anderson* and *Shrieves* held was not the proper relationship. However, because a specific regulation spoke directly to the issue of the relationship between OAH and CHR, *Anderson* and *Shrieves* did not apply. CHR was bound to follow its own regulation, and thus CHR's review of the OAH provisional order was limited.[26]

24. 103 Md. App. 694, 654 A.2d 922 (1995).

25. Md. Code Regs. 14.03.01.10F(1), COMAR 14.03.01.10F(1). Subsequent to the decision in *Kohli*, the CHR amended its regulations eliminating the provision that limited the Appeals Board's review powers to that of a court reviewing an agency's decision. *See* Md. Code Regs. 14.03.01.10F(1), COMAR 14.03.01.10F(1) (discussed in State Comm'n on Human Relations v. Kaydon Ring & Seal, Inc., 149 Md. App. 666, 818 A.2d 259 (2003)).

26. See also, Berkshire Life Insurance Co. v. Maryland Insurance Administration, 142 Md. App. 628, 791 A.2d 942 (2002).

# Chapter 12

# Contested Cases: MVA Hearings at OAH

The largest number of cases heard at OAH are from the Motor Vehicle Administration (MVA). Of the approximate 55,000 cases that OAH hears each year, about one-half are from the MVA. Of greatest significance are cases involving Maryland's Implied Consent Law, § 16.205.1 of the Transportation Article. These cases involve drivers who have either refused to take or have failed a chemical breath test for alcohol. OAH has been delegated the authority by MVA to hold the contested case hearings and to make the final agency decision in these cases. This chapter will discuss some of the more important features of an MVA hearing at OAH. Of course, this chapter must be read along with the other chapters in this book, as well as the statutes and regulations that set forth the substantive law relevant to these hearings.

## § 12.1. Flexible Due Process

Perhaps nowhere is the concept of flexible due process better illustrated that in MVA hearings at OAH. Although it is well settled that a driver's license is a property interest that may not be suspended or revoked without due process,[1] due process does not require a "full-blown evidentiary hearing" when the state is determining whether a license should be suspended or revoked.[2] MVA hearings at OAH are among the most informal hearings at OAH. Many of the traditional aspects of formal adjudicatory hearings are missing at these hearings. The tone of the hearing is usually somewhat informal and conversational. The ALJ should be referred to as "Judge ____." The ALJ's name will be on a nameplate on the desk behind which the ALJ is sitting.

MVA hearings are heard not only at OAH headquarters in Hunt Valley, but also at locations throughout the state, including local MVA offices.[3] The hearing rooms used at the Hunt Valley location for MVA hearings tend to be the smallest of the hearing rooms. In general, there will be room for the ALJ who will sit behind a desk, and a few persons who will sit in chairs facing the ALJ. At locations other than OAH, the hearing rooms may be even smaller than those at Hunt Valley. Parties and their attorneys should expect cramped quarters.

1. *See* Bell v. Burson, 402 U.S. 535 (1971).
2. *See* Dixon v. Love, 431 U.S. 105 (1977); Plumer v. Maryland, 915 F.2d 927 (4th Cir.1990).
3. Md. Code Regs. 11.11.02.07, COMAR 11.11.02.07.

## § 12.2. The Hearing

The ALJ will begin the hearing by activating a digital voice recorder, usually located in the ALJ's laptop computer. The ALJ will then call the case to order, and identify for the record the nature of the hearing. The ALJ typically will then explain that the ALJ does not work for MVA, but is an independent ALJ with OAH. The ALJ will also explain that no one from MVA will be appearing at the hearing, but that MVA has submitted an electronic file. MVA hearings at OAH no longer rely on paper documents. Rather, MVA electronically transmits all the documents it wants introduced at the OAH hearing. The ALJ pulls up on a computer monitor in the hearing room each document. There is a monitor for the ALJ and a separate monitor for the licensee and his/her attorney. Significantly, MVA is not required to present any live witnesses to prove its case.[4]

The attorney (or pro se litigant) will be asked to state any objections to the documents, whether there are any issues they would like to present, and whether they would like to offer any evidence or argument.

A motion for "no action" can be made. If the motion is denied, evidence can then be presented by the licensee. The ALJ is permitted to question the witnesses, including the licensee. If the evidence presented demonstrates that there is a dispute as to a material issue of fact, for example, in a case involving the licensee's refusal to submit to a chemical breath test, if the licensee testifies that he was not advised of the administrative sanctions for refusing to take the test, a motion can be made to postpone the hearing and subpoena a witness, typically the arresting officer, to present live testimony subject to cross-examination.

In *Motor Vehicle Administration v. Karwacki*,[5] the Court of Appeals held that hearsay evidence alone provided "adequate support" for the driver's license suspension. The court held that the ALJ was entitled to give greater weight to the sworn statement of a police officer who did not testify at the hearing and who was not subpoenaed by the licensee than to live testimony contrary to the sworn statement. The court also stated that the ALJ had no obligation in the face of conflicting evidence to subpoena the police officer on his own motion. It should also be noted that prior to the hearing, the MVA can subpoena the police officer involved in the chemical breath test if upon its review of the written file MVA is concerned that the documents do not establish the elements of the case.

If there are no disputed facts and the documentary evidence establishes the elements to suspend the driving privileges of the licensee, the ALJ will then consider evidence in mitigation of the sanction. For example, evidence of the need to drive to work or during employment may result in a suspension limited to non-employment situations. Evidence of the licensee's participation in an alcohol treatment or education program may also be helpful. An interlock restriction may also be available.

Decisions in MVA cases by OAH are usually bench decisions made at the end of the hearing, although in some cases, the ALJ will take the case under advisement. Decisions in MVA cases are no longer handwritten. When the ALJ issues the decision, the decision is typed on a computer, and the decision is immediately registered on the MVA's computerized database. The ALJ will also inform the licensee of his/her right to seek judicial review of the decision in the circuit court in the county where the licensee resides.

4. Md. Code Regs. 11.11.02.10, COMAR 11.11.02.10.
5. 340 Md. 271, 666 A.2d 511 (1995).

If the licensee is not a Maryland resident, petitions for judicial review of MVA decisions are in the circuit court for Anne Arundel County.

## § 12.3. Implied Consent Cases

As has been stated numerous times in this book, it is imperative that an attorney representing a client in a contested case involving any agency have a full understanding of the substantive law involved, and MVA cases are no exception to this. Because the most significant MVA cases heard at OAH concern a licensee's refusal to take a chemical breath test or a licensee who took a chemical breath test registering a blood alcohol content of over 0.08, it is useful to set forth the substantive issues that are relevant in such cases.

At the MVA hearing to determine whether a driver's license should be suspended for failing a chemical breath test or refusing to take one, the following issues are relevant:

1. Whether the police officer who stopped or detained the person had reasonable grounds to believe that the person was driving or attempting to drive while under the influence of alcohol or drugs. "Reasonable grounds" means "reasonable articulable suspicion," not probable cause or preponderance of the evidence.[6]
2. Whether there was any evidence of the use by the person of alcohol or drugs;
3. Whether the police officer fully advised the person of the administrative sanctions that are imposed for refusing to take the chemical breath test.[7] For example, a person who refuses to take the test for the first time is subject to a forty-five day suspension;
4. Whether the person actually refused to take the test; *Motor Vehicle Administration v. Dove*[8] held that the licensee's fear of needles did not excuse his knowing, voluntary refusal to submit to a blood alcohol concentration test. The fact that the licensee offered to take a breath alcohol concentration test did not rebut his refusal to take the blood test when the statute provides that a blood test shall be used to measure blood alcohol concentration when the licensee has been injured and removal to a medical facility is required. Moreover, the fact that the licensee's preliminary breath test indicated a blood alcohol concentration of 0.00 was irrelevant to the licensee's refusal to take the blood test.
5. Whether the person drove or attempted to drive a motor vehicle while having an alcohol concentration of 0.08 or more at the time of testing; and
6. Whether, if the hearing involves suspension of a commercial driver's license, the person was operating a commercial motor vehicle.[9]

A useful article can be found in the January/February 2006 Maryland Bar Journal entitled "Handling MVA Hearings" by Leonard R. Stamm.

---

6. Motor Vehicle Administration v. Shepard, 399 Md. 241, 923 A.2d 100 (2007).

7. Motor Vehicle Administration v. Delawter, 403 Md. 243, 941 A.2d 1067 (2008), held that a licensee could be referred to the Medical Advisory Board by OAH despite the fact that the DR-15 Advice of Rights form did not give notice that this was a possible consequence of the licensee requesting a hearing at OAH.

8. 413 Md. 70, 991 A.2d 65 (2010).

9. *See* Motor Vehicle Administration v. Jones, 380 Md. 164, 844 A.2d 388 (2004).

# Chapter 13

# Judicial Review: Procedural Matters

This chapter discusses procedural matters relating to judicial review of agency decisions made in contested cases.

## § 13.1. Non-Reviewability and Inherent Power of Review

In Federal Administrative Law, there are two situations where there is no judicial review of an agency decision.[1] First, Congress can enact legislation that denies judicial review of an agency action. Second, the Federal APA provides that there is no judicial review of federal agency decisions which are "committed to agency discretion by law." As discussed below, Maryland does not recognize either federal basis for judicial non-reviewability.

A federal statute can expressly preclude judicial review of a federal agency decision. For example, 38 U.S.C. § 211(a) provided that decisions of the Veterans' Administration providing benefits for veterans and their dependents or survivors shall be "final and conclusive" and no court of the United States shall have "power or jurisdiction to review any such decision."[2] Maryland does not permit its legislature to enact a statute which denies judicial review of an administrative agency decision. The leading case establishing that a Maryland statute cannot preclude judicial review is *Criminal Injuries Compensation Board v. Gould*.[3] *Gould* involved a regulatory scheme that provided compensation to victims of crimes. The relevant statute gave the right to seek judicial review of the Board's decisions only to the Office of the Attorney General (OAG). The statute expressly provided that no other judicial review was available. Gould was a victim of a crime and sought compensation, but his claim was denied by the Board. When he sought to challenge this denial in circuit court, the Board argued that the clear intent of the legislature was to limit judicial review to only the OAG. The Court of Appeals wrote:

> Notwithstanding the clear expressed intention by Article 26A, § 10(a) to exempt the decisions and actions of the Board from judicial review . . . , this Court, in a long line of cases, has consistently held that the Legislature cannot divest the

1. 5 U.S.C. § 701(a).
2. *See* Johnson v. Robison, 415 U.S. 361 (1974); Section 211(a) has since been amended, and judicial review of veterans' benefit claims are now authorized. *See also* McNary v. Haitian Refugee Center, Inc., 498 U.S. 479 (1991).
3. 273 Md. 486, 331 A.2d 55 (1975).

> courts of the inherent power they possess to review and correct actions by an administrative agency which are arbitrary, illegal, capricious or unreasonable.[4]

The "inherent power" of judicial review discussed in *Gould* can be traced to the 1945 Court of Appeals decision in *Heaps v. Cobb*.[5] *Heaps* involved the denial of pension benefits by the Board of Trustees of the Baltimore City Employees Retirement System. When the unsuccessful claimant sought to challenge this denial in court, the Board argued that because the enabling statute did not expressly provide for an appeal from its decision, the court had no power of judicial review. The Court of Appeals rejected the Board's position. The court wrote that the courts have the "inherent power, through the writ of mandamus, by injunction, or otherwise, to correct abuses of discretion and arbitrary, illegal, capricious or unreasonable acts."[6] The court also wrote that "[w]here the statute or ordinance makes no provision for judicial review, an implied limitation upon an administrative board's authority is that its decisions be supported by facts and that they be not arbitrary, capricious or unreasonable."[7]

*Heaps* and *Gould* therefore establish that neither statutory silence nor statutory preclusion of judicial review of an agency decision will deny the court its power to review an agency decision. A more recent example of this is discussed in *Laurel Racing Association, Inc. v. Video Lottery Facility Location Commission*.[8] In drafting the legislation authorizing video lottery terminals (slot machines), a Senate committee had added language providing that decisions of the State Board of Contract Appeals involving slot machine parlor licenses "shall be final and not subject to appeal" to any court. This language was approved by the full Senate, but ultimately deleted from the final bill which became law. As the Court of Appeals commented in *Laurel Racing*, the "deletion was probably the result of a determination that precluding judicial review would be unconstitutional."[9]

Another case illustrating the court's inherent power of review is *South Easton Neighborhood Association v. Town of Easton*.[10] This case involved a request by a hospital to expand its emergency room facilities. A prerequisite to this expansion was the closure and conveyance of part of a public street to the hospital. The Town Council approved the street closing. A citizen's group challenged this decision in circuit court. The Court of Appeals recognized that there was no statutory authority for the circuit court to consider a petition for judicial review of the Town Council's decision to close the street. But the Court wrote in *Easton*, "even absent such statutory authority, [the Court of Appeals has] authorized, in limited, Constitutional circumstances, the judiciary to exercise its inherent authority to review quasi-judicial decisions by administrative agencies ... The courts retain inherent power to review actions of administrative boards shown to be arbitrary, illegal or capricious."[11]

The inherent power of the courts to review administrative decisions applies not only to decisions made in a contested case, but all agency decisions including a Maryland agency's decision not to take action. The leading Maryland case on this point is *Harvey v. Marshall*.[12] Harvey had been declared the biological father of three children by two

4. 273 Md. 486, 500–01, 331 A.2d 55, 65 (1975).
5. 185 Md. 372, 45 A.2d 73 (1945).
6. 185 Md. 372, 379, 45 A.2d 73, 76 (1945).
7. 185 Md. 372, 380, 45 A.2d 73, 76 (1945).
8. 409 Md. 445, 975 A.2d 894 (2009).
9. 409 Md. 445, 464 n.7, 975 A.2d 894, 905 n.7 (2009).
10. 387 Md. 468, 876 A.2d 58 (2005).
11. 387 Md. 468, 477 n.3, 876 A.2d 58, 64 n.3 (2005).
12. 389 Md. 243, 884 A.2d 1171 (2005).

consent decrees in 1986 and 1989. During the time while the children were in the custody of the mother, Harvey accumulated significant child support arrearages as the result of his non-payment of court-ordered child support. The mother applied for welfare assistance because she was not receiving the child support that Harvey owed. Pursuant to a Maryland statute, as a condition of receiving welfare assistance, the mother was required to initiate child support proceedings and assign the children's support rights to the State. As a result of this assignment, Harvey owed the State approximately $30,000. In 1996, the children's mother became ill and unable to care for the children. Harvey then took physical custody of the children. Harvey requested the Child Support Enforcement Administration (CSEA) to forgive or abate his child support arrearages so that his funds could be used for the current and future support of his children. Although the CSEA acknowledged that it had "statutory discretion" to eliminate or reduce the child support arrearages Harvey owed the State, it refused to do so.

One of the issues addressed by the Court of Appeals in *Harvey* was "whether a decision [by an agency] not to exercise statutory discretion ... may be subject to judicial review."[13] The Court's answer was even when there is no statutory provision for judicial review, courts have inherent power to review an agency's inaction.

*Towson University v. Conte*[14] likewise involved the court's inherent power to review an agency decision. *Conte* involved a wrongful discharge suit against Towson University. The contested case provisions of the APA do not apply to Towson University because of its status as a public university under Section 12-101 of the Education Article. Nevertheless, the Court of Appeals recognized that Maryland courts have inherent authority to review administrative decisions alleged to be arbitrary, capricious or unlawful. Moreover, this inherent review authority was not the sole remedy available to a person challenging an administrative action. In *Conte*, a challenge to the university's action could also be brought as a breach of contract action.

It is important to understand that Maryland courts have inherent power of judicial review of administrative decisions. This is illustrated by *Oltman v. Maryland State Board of Physicians.*[15] Oltman was a physician assistant whose license was revoked in 2003. In 2005, Oltman applied to the Board for reinstatement. Without any hearing, Oltman's reinstatement request was denied, and he was told not to reapply for three years. Oltman filed a Petition for Judicial Review of this decision pursuant to Maryland Rule 7-202. Because the Board's decision was not the result of a contested case hearing, there was no statutory right to judicial review under the Rule. What Oltman failed to argue was that the court had inherent jurisdiction to review the denial of his reinstatement request. In a footnote, the court expressly noted this.[16] It seems to me that the court did have jurisdiction to review the Board's denial pursuant to the court's inherent power of judicial review. The court was unwilling, however, to exercise such power unless requested.

---

13. 389 Md. 243, 273, 884 A.2d 1171, 1189 (2005).
14. 384 Md. 68, 862 A.2d 941 (2004).
15. 182 Md. App. 65, 957 A.2d. 611, *cert. denied*, 406 Md. 746, 962 A.2d. 372 (2008).
16. 182 Md. App. 65, 78 n.6, 957 A.2d. 611, 619 n.6 (2008).

## § 13.2. Non-Reviewability and Committed to Agency Discretion by Law

The second situation where there is no judicial review by a federal court of a federal agency decision is when the agency decision is "committed to agency discretion by law."[17] This federal rule of judicial non-reviewability applies when the federal agency's discretion is so broad that a reviewing court would have no meaningful standard to apply to review the agency decision. This federal doctrine has been applied to deny judicial review to an agency's decision not to investigate a possible violation and not bring an enforcement action,[18] as well as to deny judicial review of the termination of an employee of the Central Intelligence Agency.[19] Non-reviewability does not apply, however, to deny judicial review if there is a constitutional challenge to the agency decision.

Although the phrase "committed to agency discretion" was used in *Spencer v. Maryland State Board of Pharmacy*[20] along with citation to *Heckler v. Chaney*,[21] a leading U.S. Supreme Court case on the federal "committed to agency discretion by law" exception, this doctrine of non-reviewability was clearly not adopted by the Court of Appeals in *Spencer*. The *Spencer* court reviewed the Board's decision not to delegate its authority to OAH to hold contested case hearings under the arbitrary or capricious standard.

Further support that Maryland does not deny judicial review of agency decisions committed to agency discretion can be found in *Oltman v. Maryland State Board of Physicians*.[22] The circuit court had ruled that it did not have "jurisdiction to entertain a petition for judicial review from the denial of a petition for reinstatement." In his written decision the circuit court judge stated:

> I think the fact that there are no standards set out in the statute also suggests that it's purely a discretionary ... decision with the Board. There is nothing that a [c]ourt would have before it to determine whether or not the Board exercised discretion appropriately or not. There are no statutory standards. There's no guidelines that say ... so long as somebody meets certain standards they can come back and practice. So I think that is also indicative of the fact that it is purely a matter of grace on the part of the Board and it is not subject to judicial review ... [U]nless there is some statutory authority for judicial review[,] administrative agencies have a certain number of activities that they can engage in that are not subject to judicial review ...

The circuit court judge's language is classic federal "committed to agency discretion by law" analysis. But in its opinion, the Court of Appeals did not rely on this reasoning in agreeing that Oltman's petition was not judicially reviewable. Moreover, as discussed earlier, the circuit court had not been presented with the argument that the court had review power under its inherent power of judicial review.

17. *See* § 701(a)(2) of the Federal Administrative Procedure Act, 5 U.S.C. § 701(a)(2).
18. Heckler v. Chaney, 470 U.S. 821 (1985).
19. *See* Webster v. Doe, 486 U.S. 592 (1988).
20. 380 Md. 515, 846 A.2d 341 (2004).
21. 470 U.S. 821 (1985).
22. 182 Md. App. 65, 957 A.2d 611, *cert. denied*, 406 Md. 746, 962 A.2d 372 (2008).

## § 13.3. Non-Reviewability and Intra-Government Disputes

There is one instance where judicial review is precluded in Maryland. A dispute between two government agencies is not subject to judicial review. This is illustrated by *Maryland v. Board of Education of Montgomery County.*[23] A county board of education sought judicial review of a decision by the State Department of Education relating to overpayments of state support of certain benefits for county school board employees. The Court of Appeals held that the inherent right to judicial review set forth in *Gould* did not apply to intra-governmental disputes, and that judicial review can be precluded for such disputes. The inherent right to judicial review only applies to disputes between government agencies and individuals or private entities where it is claimed that the administrative decision has impaired personal or property rights.[24]

## § 13.4. Original Jurisdiction in the Circuit Court

A request for judicial review of an agency decision is filed with the circuit court for the county where any party resides or has a principal place of business.[25] It may appear curious that review of an administrative decision is filed with a circuit court, which is generally viewed as a trial court, instead of an appellate court such as the Court of Special Appeals. Because judicial review of an agency decision is a review of a record, not a trial involving witnesses, it might seem more appropriate for an appellate court, not a trial court, to review the agency's decision. At the federal level, most agency decisions are reviewed by the courts of appeals. The reason why judicial review of Maryland administrative agency decisions is in the circuit court, and the consequences of this, has been discussed in several cases.

*Shell Oil Co. v. Supervisor of Assessments of Prince George's County*[26] involved a statute that provided for a direct appeal from the Tax Court[27] to the Court of Appeals. The statute was held unconstitutional. The Court of Appeals ruled that judicial review of an agency decision must be initially filed with a circuit court. This was based on the distinction between original jurisdiction and appellate jurisdiction. There can be no appellate jurisdiction until there has been an exercise of original jurisdiction by a court. Because a court's appellate jurisdiction involves review of a decision by a lower court, there must be a lower court decision in existence for an appellate court to review. Because the Tax Court, like every other Maryland agency (including OAH), is not a court, review of its decisions is an exercise of a court's original jurisdiction. The Court of Appeals in *Shell Oil* also rejected the notion that the Tax Court, although not a court, was performing judicial functions, so that review in an appellate court was proper. The Court of Appeals'

23. 346 Md. 633, 697 A.2d 1334 (1997).
24. 346 Md. 633, 697 A.2d 1334 (1997).
25. Maryland Code Annotated, State Government § 10-222(c).
26. 276 Md. 36, 343 A.2d 521 (1975).
27. The Tax Court is an executive branch administrative agency that resolves certain tax law disputes.

response was that the Tax Court's functions were only quasi-judicial, not judicial. Any attempt by an agency to perform judicial functions would be a violation of separation of powers under Article 8 of the Declaration of Rights of the Maryland Constitution. In response to the argument that federal agency decisions are reviewed by federal courts of appeals, the court responded that the Maryland Constitution differs from the U.S. Constitution. In Maryland, the judicial function can only be exercised by those courts enumerated in its Constitution. The U.S. Congress, on the other hand, is empowered to create inferior courts under Article III, section 1, of the U.S. Constitution. *Shell Oil*, therefore, establishes that as a matter of Maryland constitutional law, judicial review of a Maryland agency decision can only be in a court of original jurisdiction, not an appellate court.[28] To change this would require a constitutional amendment.

Despite the fact that judicial review of an administrative decision is not an exercise of appellate jurisdiction, it has been common practice to refer to such judicial review in a circuit court as an "appeal." Until July 1993, the Rules governing judicial review were captioned, "Administrative Agencies—Appeal From."[29] The present rules in Title 7, Chapter 200 of the Maryland Rules are now captioned "Judicial Review of Administrative Decisions." Additionally, Title 7 is now entitled, "Appellate and Other Judicial Review in Circuit Court." Unfortunately, at the top of the right-hand pages of Title 7, Chapter 200 where the relevant rules are set forth, the heading reads, "Appellate Review in Circuit Court." Attorneys should recognize that the use of the term "appeal from an administrative decision" is technically incorrect,[30] although most likely the word "appeal" will continue to be used in everyday conversation when discussing the challenge to an agency decision in circuit court.

Several cases have demonstrated the importance of the distinction between original and appellate jurisdiction. *Kim v. Comptroller of the Treasury*[31] involved a premature filing of a petition to review a decision of the Tax Court. In *Kim*, a hearing was held before a judge of the Tax Court on December 6, 1995, to decide whether Kim owed any state sales and use taxes, and whether any penalty was appropriate. At the end of the hearing, the Tax Court judge orally ruled that the tax assessment was proper, but that no penalty should be imposed. The Tax Court judge directed the Assistant Attorney General who represented the Comptroller to prepare a written order reflecting the oral order. On December 11, Kim filed a Petition for Review in circuit court requesting review of the December 6 oral order. It was not until December 18 that the Tax Court judge actually signed the written order as prepared by the Office of the Attorney General. On January 17, Kim filed a memorandum in support of his December 11 petition. On January 22, the Comptroller filed a motion to dismiss Kim's Petition for Review because it had been prematurely filed, i.e., filed before the December 18 final written order. The circuit court granted the Comptroller's motion to dismiss, relying upon decisions involving premature filings of appeals. The Court of Appeals disagreed, and held that the Petition for Review filed before the written order should not have been dismissed. It wrote:

---

28. *See* Bergmann v. Board of Regents of the Univ. System of Md., 167 Md. App. 237, 892 A.2d 604 (2006); Motor Vehicle Admin. v. Weller, 390 Md. 115, 887 A.2d 1042 (2005).

29. *See* Dep't of Gen. Servs. v. Harmans Assocs. Ltd. Partnership, 98 Md. App. 535, 542 n.2, 633 A.2d 939, 943 n.2 (1993).

30. *See* Driggs Corp. v. Md. Aviation Admin., 348 Md. 389, 398, 704 A.2d 433, 438 (1998) ("[T]he Attorney General's Office has been laboring under the misimpression that an action for judicial review of an administrative agency's final order is in the nature of an 'appeal,' invoking the appellate jurisdiction of the circuit court."); *see also* Armstrong v. Mayor & City Council of Baltimore, 169 Md. App. 655, 906 A.2d 415 (2006).

31. 350 Md. 527, 714 A.2d 176 (1998).

> Although often misinterpreted to be an appeal, this Court has repeatedly emphasized that an action for judicial review of an administrative decision is an original action. It is not an appeal.... Because judicial review is an original action and not an appeal, the Comptroller's and circuit court's reliance on cases dealing with the premature filing of appeals was inappropriate. The time requirements for filing appeals are ordinarily treated as jurisdictional in nature.... Therefore, this Court has held ... that a prematurely filed appeal must be dismissed by an appellate court because the appellate court has no jurisdiction over the matter.... The same cannot be said, however, of a prematurely filed petition for judicial review, because the time requirements for filing a petition for judicial review are not jurisdictional. It is in the nature of a statute of limitations.... Statutes of limitations are not ordinarily jurisdictional, and are generally waivable, including the 30-day time limit for filing a petition for judicial review.[32]

Shortly after *Kim* was decided, the Court of Special Appeals in *Wormwood v. Batching Systems, Inc.*[33] noted that *Kim* should not be interpreted to mean that petitions for judicial review can be filed late and always be effective. If the statute of limitations defense is not waived by the opposing side, the time for filing a Petition for Review "ordinarily will be strictly enforced, as is any limitations defense properly raised." Moreover, if properly raised, the defense is "ordinarily not subject to the exercise of discretion" by the court.[34]

The significance of *Kim* and *Wormwood* is that because judicial review of an administrative decision is an original action, untimely filings of petitions for review are evaluated based on the law relating to statutes of limitations. An untimely filing of a petition for review will lead to dismissal if the late filing is raised by an opposing party. If judicial review of an agency action were an exercise of appellate jurisdiction (which it is not), late filing would not have to be raised as a defense by a party in order for the court to dismiss the action.[35]

Another case illustrating the importance of understanding that judicial review of an agency decision involves the circuit court's original jurisdiction is *Driggs Corp. v. Maryland Aviation Administration*.[36] Driggs petitioned the circuit court to review a decision of the Board of Contract Appeals. The circuit court on January 13, 1997, dismissed the petition on the ground that Driggs had acquiesced in the agency's decision. On January 23, Driggs filed a motion under Md. Rule 2-534, "Motion to Alter or Amend a Judgment," asking the circuit court to amend or alter its order. That motion was denied on February 25. On March 7, Driggs filed a Notice of Appeal with the Court of Special Appeals. The Office of the Attorney General moved to dismiss the appeal pursuant to Md. Rule 8-202(a) because the appeal was filed more than 30 days after the circuit judge's January 13 order. Driggs countered that pursuant to Md. Rule 8-202(c), the Notice of Appeal in his case needed to be filed within 30 days of the date of the denial of his motion to amend or alter under Md. Rule 2-534, i.e., within 30 days from February 25. The Attorney General responded that Md. Rules 2-534 and 8-202(c) had no application because "Drigg's petition to the

---

32. 350 Md. 527, 534–36, 714 A.2d 176, 179–80 (1998).

33. 124 Md. App. 695, 723 A.2d 568, *cert. denied*, 354 Md. 113, 729 A.2d 405 (1999).

34. 124 Md. App. 695, 705, 723 A.2d 568, 573 (1999).

35. *See also* Colao v. County Council of Prince George's County, 346 Md. 342, 697 A.2d 96 (1997) noting that it is incumbent on a defendant to raise an untimely filing as a defense, and that untimely filings of petitions for judicial review are not governed by findings of good faith or exercise of the court's discretion. In Colao, a timely defense was raised, and the case was dismissed.

36. 348 Md. 389, 704 A.2d 433 (1998).

Circuit Court invoked the appellate, rather than the original jurisdiction of that court." The Court of Appeals, displaying a bit of annoyance with the Office of the Attorney General, stated that Md. Rules 2-534 and 8-202(c) did apply because the circuit court's original jurisdiction was involved.

## § 13.5. Forms of Review

Although, as just discussed, all judicial review of administrative decisions begins in the circuit court, different forms of review are used to review different types of agency decisions. In Chapter 3, the Petition for Declaratory Judgment was discussed as the proper method of challenging a regulation. This chapter will discuss three other methods of obtaining judicial review– the Petition for Judicial Review, Administrative Mandamus, and traditional Mandamus.

## § 13.6. The Petition for Judicial Review

A Petition for Judicial Review is filed in the circuit court to obtain judicial review when judicial review is authorized by statute.[37] Since the vast majority of agency decisions in contested cases are judicially reviewable pursuant to a statute, the Petition for Judicial Review is the document filed most often to obtain judicial review of a contested case.

Maryland Rule 7-202(b) requires that the Petition for Review be captioned as follows:

| | | |
|---|---|---|
| IN THE CIRCUIT COURT FOR ____________ | * | |
| | * | |
| PETITION OF ____________ | * | |
| [name and address] | * | CIVIL ACTION NO. __ |
| | * | |
| FOR JUDICIAL REVIEW OF THE DECISION OF THE | * | |
| ____________ | * | |
| [name and address of administrative agency | * | |
| that made the decision] | * | |
| | * | |
| IN THE CASE OF ____________ | * | |
| [caption of agency proceeding, | * | |
| including agency case number] | * | |

37. Md. Rule 7-202(a).

The Court of Appeals has explained that the purposes of requiring the information in the above caption are:

1. to trigger the obligation of the court clerk to send a copy of the petition to the agency;
2. to trigger the agency's obligation to identify the case and to give prompt written notice to all parties at the agency of the filing of the petition and of the time within which a response must be filed; and
3. to trigger the agency's obligation to file the agency record with the court.[38]

In *Colao v. County Council of Prince George's County*,[39] the caption in the petition did not indicate the agency case number, a violation of Md. Rule 7-202(b). According to the Court of Appeals, if the case number had appeared in the body of the petition so that the case number could have been clearly and conveniently ascertained by the court clerk, the omission of the case number from the caption would have been treated as a technical irregularity not affecting the orderly processing of the case, and the petition would have been sufficient. In *Colao*, however, nothing in the petition indicated that review was being sought of the second of two agency decisions. Consequently, judicial review was denied of the agency decision whose case number did not appear either in the caption or in the petition.

The Petition for Judicial Review is a simple document. The petition does not present any legal arguments. Pursuant to Md. Rule 7-202(c), the only matters required to be in the petition are:

(1) A request for judicial review;

(2) Identification of the order or action of which review is sought; and

(3) Whether the petitioner was a party at the agency proceeding. If petitioner was not a party, the petition must state the basis of petitioner's standing to seek judicial review.

## § 13.7. Filing

Along with the original petition, the petitioner must provide to the clerk of the court a copy of the petition. The copy is sent to the agency by the clerk who informs the agency of the date of filing and the civil action number assigned to the case.[40] Upon receipt of the petition from the court clerk's office, the agency must give prompt written notice by ordinary mail to everyone who was a party at the agency proceeding that a petition for judicial review was filed, the date of the filing, the name of the court, and the civil action number. The agency must also notify every party that if it wants to oppose the petition, it must file a response within 30 days after the agency's notice was mailed.[41] Within five days after mailing the notice, the agency must then file with the court clerk a certificate

38. Colao v. County Council of Prince George's County, 346 Md. 342, 697 A.2d 96 (1997).
39. 346 Md. 342, 697 A.2d 96 (1997).
40. Md. Rule 7-202(d)(1).
41. Md. Rule 7-202(d)(3).

of compliance with the notice requirements. Failure to file the certificate of compliance, however, does not affect the validity of the agency's notice.[42]

## § 13.8. Time Limits

Under Rule 7-203, petitioner must file the Petition for Judicial Review with the court within 30 days after the latest of:

(1) the date of the order or action of which review is sought;

(2) the date the administrative agency sent notice of the order or action to the petitioner, if notice was required by law to be sent to the petitioner; or

(3) the date the petitioner received notice of the agency's order or action, if notice was required by law to be received by the petitioner.[43]

An interesting case involving the 30-day time limit is *Kim v. Comptroller of the Treasury*.[44] *Kim* involved a tax dispute heard by a judge of the Tax Court. The judge orally ruled against Kim after the hearing on December 6, and instructed the Assistant Attorney General to prepare the written order. The written order was not signed until December 18. On December 11, Kim had filed a Petition for Judicial Review of the December 6 oral decision. The Court of Appeals ruled that Kim's December 11 petition was ineffective because the relevant date governing the timeliness of an action for judicial review was the date the written order of the Tax Court judge was filed and mailed to the parties. The *Kim* court ruled, inter alia, however, that although the December 11 filing was premature, Kim's filing of a memorandum in support of his Petition for Judicial Review on January 17 was within 30 days of the final order of the Tax Court, and therefore was sufficient to satisfy the time limit. Because the memorandum contained sufficient information to satisfy Md. Rule 7-202(c), the memorandum served as a timely and adequate Petition for Judicial Review.

Another case involving Rule 7-203 is *Centre Insurance Company v. J.T.W.*[45] which focused on whether the 30-day period for filing the Petition for Judicial Review began when the agency decision was mailed or received. Because Rule 7-203 is qualified by the phrase "except as otherwise provided ... by statute," the Court was required to interpret a section of the Insurance Article which required the petition for judicial review to be filed within 30 days after the hearing order "was served on the persons entitled to receive it." The Court held that the "plain language" of the statute required filing within 30 days of when the order was mailed.

The *J.T.W.* case emphasizes the importance of knowing the particular statutes of each agency as well as the general rules set forth in the APA and the Maryland Rules. It also serves as a reminder that unlike in court cases where Maryland Rule 1-203(c) provides an extra three days for service by mail, administrative agency rules may be different, and

42. Md. Rule 7-202(e).
43. Md. Rule 7-203(a).
44. 350 Md. 527, 714 A.2d 176 (1998).
45. 397 Md. 71, 916 A.2d 235 (2007).

must be separately evaluated. Relying on what is true in the district court or circuit court often will create a problem for an attorney unfamiliar with administrative practice.

## § 13.9. Other Petitions for Review

Once one party files a timely Petition for Judicial Review, any other person entitled to file its own Petition has 10 days after the date the agency mailed notice of the filing of the first petition to file its own petition. If this 10-day date is earlier then the 30-day time period provided for the filing of the first petition, the filing deadline is the 30-day period.[46]

## § 13.10. Response to Petition

Rule 7-204(a) provides that "any person, including the agency, who is entitled by law to be a party and who wishes to participate as a party shall file a response to the petition." The response shall state the intent to participate in the action for judicial review, but no other allegations are necessary. The response "shall be filed within 30 days after the date the agency mails notice of the filing of the petition unless the court shortens or extends the time." Only the petitioner needs to be served with the response.

This rule was involved in *Department of Public Safety & Correctional Service v. Neal.*[47] The agency terminated Neal from employment, and Neal appealed her termination. A hearing was held at OAH which had the authority to make the final agency decision. The OAH ALJ reversed the termination, and imposed a four-week suspension. The agency filed a Petition for Judicial Review on June 16, and mailed notice of its filing the same day. Neal did not file a response within 30 days. On July 28, the agency filed a motion to stay the ALJ's decision. On August 13, Neal, acting pro se, filed an opposition to the motion to stay. On August 29, the circuit court granted in part and denied in part the motion to stay. A hearing on the Petition for Judicial Review was held on October 15. At the hearing, the agency moved to preclude Neal from participating at the hearing on the ground that she had never filed a response to the Petition for Judicial Review. The circuit court denied the agency's motion. Although Neal had not filed a timely response to the petition, the court treated Neal's opposition to the agency's motion to stay as a late filed response to the Petition, and extended the time limit for its filing. The Court of Special Appeals affirmed the circuit court. Neal's opposition to the motion to stay "made plain that she intended to participate" in the circuit court's judicial review of the agency decision. Moreover, under Rule 7-204, the court had the discretion to extend the time for filing a response and could do so retroactively after the deadline had passed.

Another case is *Egloff v. County Council of Prince George's County.*[48] Egloff filed a Petition for Judicial Review of a county land use decision. A Petition for Judicial Review was also

46. Md. Rule 7-203(b).
47. 160 Md. App. 496, 864 A.2d 287 (2004), *cert. denied*, 386 Md. 181, 872 A.2d 47 (2005).
48. 130 Md. App. 113, 744 A.2d 1083, *cert. denied*, 358 Md. 381, 749 A.2d 172 (2000).

filed by O'Laughlin. An environmental group, the Beck group, filed a response to O'Laughlin's petition. O'Laughlin then dismissed his petition. The circuit court then held that Egloff lacked standing to file his petition. The issue then became whether the Beck group's response was effective as a Petition for Judicial Review. The Court of Special Appeals ruled no. A person who files a response is a person who opposes a petition for judicial review. There were no petitions to which to respond because O'Laughlin had dismissed his petition and Egloff's petition had been dismissed because he lacked standing. If the Beck group had issues that it wanted reviewed by the court, it needed to file its own Petition for Judicial Review in a timely manner.

## § 13.11. Preliminary Motions

Rule 7-204(b) provides that a "person may file with the response a preliminary motion addressed to standing, venue, timeliness of filing, or any other matter that would defeat a petitioner's right to judicial review." Although not expressly mentioned in the Rule, a preliminary motion to dismiss for failure to exhaust administrative remedies is probably the most popular preliminary motion filed. The Rule further provides that except for a motion to dismiss because of improper venue, the failure to file a preliminary motion does not constitute waiver of an issue. Any preliminary motion must be served on the petitioner and the relevant agency.

An interesting issue involving preliminary motions was raised in *Oltman v. Maryland State Board of Physicians*.[49] The Board issued an order disciplining Oltman. Oltman filed a Petition for Judicians Review challenging this order. After Oltman filed his Petition for Judicial Review, the Board filed a preliminary motion to dismiss on the ground that the circuit court did not have jurisdiction to review the agency decision. The Board had not filed a Response to the original Petition under Rule 7-204(a). Oltman argued that the Board "lacked standing to file its motion to dismiss" because Rule 7-204(b) only permits a person who has filed a Response to the Petition to file a preliminary motion. The court rejected Oltman's argument, writing:

> Md. Rule 7-202 clearly contemplates what happened here, i.e. that the Board may challenge a petitioner's right to obtain judicial review of its decision via a "preliminary motion." Nothing in the language or history of the rule suggests that the right to file such a preliminary motion is contingent on the Board simultaneously filing a separate response to the merits of the petition for judicial review. Moreover, reading the rule to create such a contingency defies common sense. Here, the Board's filing of a motion to dismiss adequately demonstrated that the Board "intends to participate in the action" in order to contest the right to judicial review. "No other allegations are necessary." Md. Rule 7-202(a). Once the Board prevailed on its motion, there was no longer any action for judicial review and therefore, no reason for the Board to file another response for the illogical purpose of indicating an intent to participate in a dismissed case.[50]

The court's conclusion in *Oltman* appears correct, although it is inconsistent with the plain language of Rule 7-202(b).

---

49. 182 Md. App. 65, 957 A.2d. 611, *cert. denied*, 406 Md. 746, 962 A.2d. 372 (2008).
50. 182 Md. App. 65, 79–80, 957 A.2d. 611, 619–620 (2008).

# § 13.12. Stays

It is important to remember that the filing of a Petition for Review does not automatically stay the enforcement of the agency's decision.[51] A party seeking a stay of the agency decision pending judicial review should request a stay from the final agency decision-maker (either the agency or OAH). Alternatively, a party can file a motion with the circuit court requesting the court to stay the agency order. A circuit court's decision on a motion to stay is not an appealable order.[52] Failure to request a stay from the agency should not prohibit the filing of a motion to stay with the court. The exhaustion doctrine does not appear to have been applied to motions for a stay.

In a request to the agency for a stay, the two most important factors are irreparable harm and the public interest. If, for example, the agency order is to suspend a license for one month, failure of the agency to stay its order will effectively deny the aggrieved party the right to judicial review of the suspension because it will have expired before the case is reviewed. The public interest is also of utmost significance. If the matter involves an imminent, continuing threat to the safety, health or welfare of the public, a stay would not be appropriate. When the motion for stay is addressed to the court, an additional consideration is relevant—likelihood of success on the merits. Just as courts consider likelihood of success on the merits in deciding whether to grant a preliminary injunction, a court will consider likelihood of success on the merits when ruling on a motion for a stay.

One issue involving stays is whether a statute or regulation can deny a court from staying an administrative order pending judicial review. I believe there are serious problems with this. First, as a matter of public policy, there are situations where a stay is appropriate. A court applying the traditional tests for equitable relief should always be permitted to consider whether a stay should be granted. Secondly, I believe there is a separation of powers problem when the legislature through a statute, or the executive branch through a regulation, attempts to deny the judiciary the power to grant equitable relief. This is especially true in Maryland which has long recognized the inherent power of the courts to review administrative agency decisions.

# § 13.13. Transmittal of Agency Record

In order for the court to review the agency decision, the record created at the agency must be sent to the court. Maryland Rule 7-206(e) provides that "the agency shall transmit to the clerk of the circuit court the original or certified copy of the record of its proceedings within 60 days after the agency receives the first petition for review." The 60-day time period can be shortened or extended by the court based upon a motion by either the agency or any party. No extension may be made for more than an additional 60 days.[53] The filing of a preliminary motion does not result in an automatic extension of the time to transmit the record.[54]

---

51. Md. Rule 7-205; Maryland Code Annotated, State Government § 10-222(e).
52. Berkshire Life Ins. Co. v. Md. Insurance Admin., 142 Md. App. 628, 791 A.2d 942 (2002).
53. Md. Rule 7-206(d).
54. Committee note to Md. Rule 7-204(b).

What is the "record" that the agency must transmit? The record is defined in the Maryland Rules as the transcript of the testimony, all exhibits, and other papers filed in the agency proceeding.[55] Papers may be omitted that the parties agree to omit by written stipulation. The court may also order certain papers omitted. If the testimony has been recorded but not transcribed before the filing of the petition for judicial review, the first petitioner is responsible to pay the expense of transcription.[56] The cost of transcription may be taxed as a cost to be apportioned as directed by the court.[57] Upon receiving the record from the agency, the clerk of the court notifies the parties of the date the record was filed.[58]

If the agency has not transmitted the record within the time period, the action "shall be dismissed"[59] unless the court finds that the failure to transmit the record was caused by the act or omission of the agency, a stenographer, or a person other than the moving party. In *Wormwood v. Batching System, Inc.*[60] the Court of Special Appeals refused to dismiss the case even though the record had not been timely transmitted to the court. The court in *Wormwood* held that the rule involving the transmittal of the record was not jurisdictional nor in the nature of a statute of limitations. The transmittal rules were subject to substantial compliance. In this case, there was substantial compliance because the delay was not solely attributable to Wormwood, and the entire record including the transcript was before the circuit court prior to when the motion to dismiss had been filed. Additionally, there had been no showing of prejudice.[61]

In *Montgomery County v. Post*,[62] the Animal Matters Hearing Board for Montgomery County (Board) ordered that a dog owned by Post be muzzled because the dog was potentially dangerous. Post filed a Petition for Judicial Review on May 4. On September 10, Post filed a motion to reverse the Board's decision based on the failure of the Board to transmit the record. This motion was granted by the circuit court. The Court of Special Appeals reversed the circuit court. It wrote:

> When the board failed to send notice of the petition for judicial review to the parties before it and failed to transmit the record, the court had the authority to dismiss the petition for judicial review or to extend the time for transmitting the record. Dismissal of the petition would not have been appropriate in light of the fact that the failure to give notice and transmit the record was caused by the Board.[63]

Because, the court wrote, there is "nothing in the Maryland Rules permitting summary reversal of an agency's decision without review of the record," the proper remedy was to extend the time for the agency to comply with the rule. The case was remanded to the circuit court.

---

55. Md. Rule 7-206(a).
56. Md. Rule 7-206(a).
57. Md. Rule 7-206(a).
58. Md. Rule 7-206(e).
59. Md. Rule 7-206(d).
60. 124 Md. App. 695, 723 A.2d 568, *cert. denied*, 354 Md. 113, 729 A.2d 405 (1999).
61. The court also mentioned that because this was a matter from the Workers' Compensation Commission, substantial compliance was "particularly appropriate." This should not be construed, however, as suggesting that substantial compliance for Md. Rule 7-206 is not proper in cases from other agencies. *See also* Hahn Transp., Inc. v. Gabeler, 156 Md. App. 213, 846 A.2d 462 (2004).
62. 166 Md. App. 381, 888 A.2d 1224 (2005).
63. 166 Md. App. 381, 390, 888 A.2d 1224, 1229–30 (2005).

# § 13.14. Memoranda

Within 30 days after the clerk of the court sends the notice of the filing of the agency record, the petitioner must file a memorandum that sets forth:

1. a concise statement of the questions presented for review;
2. a statement of facts material to those questions; and
3. argument on each question, including citations of authority and references to pages of the record and exhibits upon which the petitioner is relying.[64]

The petitioner's memorandum is served on each person who has filed a response. The agency should also be served with the memorandum if it is entitled to be a party. Any person who has filed a response, and the agency if entitled to be a party to the action, may file an answering memorandum within 30 days of being served with the petitioner's memorandum. The petitioner may then file a Reply Memorandum within 15 days after being served with an answering memorandum.[65]

The time periods for filing these memoranda may be shortened or extended by stipulation of the parties or by court order. No stipulation can permit the petitioner's first memorandum and any answering memorandum to be filed less than 30 days before the scheduled hearing. No stipulation can permit any Reply Memorandum to be filed less than 10 days before the scheduled hearing.[66]

The maximum length of any memorandum is 35 pages unless permission is obtained from the court.[67] If there is more than one petitioner or responding party, any petitioner or responding party may adopt by reference any part of the memorandum of another. The intent of the drafters of these Rules is that all issues and allegations of error be raised in the memoranda. An issue not raised in the memoranda "ordinarily" should not be entertained at argument.[68] It was not the intent of the drafters to preclude a person who filed a preliminary motion under Md. Rule 7-204(b), but who did not file an answering memorandum, from arguing the issues raised in the preliminary motion.[69] If the petitioner fails to file a memorandum within the prescribed time periods, the court may dismiss the action if the failure to file or the late filing caused prejudice to the moving party.[70]

A person who has filed a Response to the Petition for Judicial Review but who did not file an Answering Memorandum within the prescribed time limits may not present argument at the hearing except with the permission of the court.[71] In *Department of Public Safety & Correctional Services v. Neal*,[72] Neal had not filed a Response to the Petition for Judicial Review and had not filed any Memorandum. Neal, however, had filed an opposition to the petitioner's motion to stay. The court treated her opposition to the motion to stay as a Response to the Petition for Judicial Review, and granted her permission to present oral argument at the hearing. The court saw no prejudice. The opposing party, the agency,

---

64. Md. Rule 7-207.
65. Md. Rule 7-207.
66. Md. Rule 7-207(c).
67. Md. Rule 7-207(a).
68. Committee Note to Md. Rule 7-207.
69. Committee Note to Md. Rule 7-207.
70. Md. Rule 7-207(d).
71. Md. Rule 7-207(d).
72. 160 Md. App. 496, 864 A.2d 287 (2004), *cert. denied*, 386 Md. 181, 872 A.2d 47 (2005).

had notice of Neal's argument from the Opposition to Motion to Stay which was filed well before the hearing.

## § 13.15. Mandamus

A Petition for Judicial Review is used to obtain judicial review of a contested case when judicial review is provided for by statute.[73] But as discussed earlier in this chapter, even if there is no statute that provides for judicial review of an agency action, a court will still review the agency decision pursuant to the court's inherent power of review. The proper action to file in circuit court to obtain judicial review of an agency action when statutory review is not provided is Mandamus.

In Maryland Administrative Law, there are two different mandamus actions. The first is known as Administrative Mandamus, and is set forth in Chapter 400 of Title 7 of the Maryland Rules. Administrative Mandamus is the proper mandamus action when the agency decision being challenged is the result of the exercise of the agency's quasi-judicial power,[74] i.e., a decision from a contested case. The second type of mandamus in Maryland Administrative Law is known as traditional or common law mandamus. This type of mandamus action is used to review an agency action that is not the product of a contested case and for which there is no statutory right of judicial review.

The distinction between Administrative Mandamus and traditional Mandamus was discussed by the Court of Special Appeals in *Bethel World Outreach Church v. Montgomery County*.[75] A church sought judicial review of the Montgomery County Council's decision to change the water and sewer category description of its property. There is no statute that provides for judicial review of this Council decision. The church filed an action for Administrative Mandamus contesting the legality of the Council's action. The Administrative Mandamus action was dismissed because the Council's decision was an exercise of its quasi-legislative, not quasi-judicial powers. The church refiled the case including a count based on traditional mandamus. The court held that this was the appropriate method to review the quasi-legislative decision of the Council in the absence of any statutory right to judicial review. The church, however, was unsuccessful on the merits.

## § 13.16. Administrative Mandamus

Administrative Mandamus is very similar to an action brought by a Petition for Judicial Review. The intent of the drafters of the Administrative Mandamus rules, which took effect in 2006, was to make clear that judicial review of administrative quasi-judicial decisions is the same whether or not there is a statutory right of judicial review.

An action for a writ of administrative mandamus is brought by filing a complaint whose form, contents and timing are the same as for the filing of Petitions for Judicial Review.[76] The filing of the complaint does not stay the order or action of the administrative

73. Md. Rule 7-202(a).
74. Md. Rule 7-401.
75. 184 Md. App. 572, 967 A.2d 232 (2009).
76. Md. Rule 7-402(a).

agency, but the court may grant a stay under the same circumstances as a stay would be ordered following the filing of a Petition for Judicial Review.[77]

The agency record is filed with the court as in cases where a Petition for Judicial Review has been filed.[78] If no agency record exists, the agency shall provide a verified response that sets forth the grounds for its decision and any written materials supporting the decision. The court may remand the record to the agency for further supplementation of materials supporting the decision.[79] Memoranda are filed just as in cases involving Petitions for Judicial Review.[80]

Administrative mandamus was held to be inappropriate in *Talbot County v. Miles Point Property, LLC*[81] because the challenged action was not quasi-judicial. This case involved the denial by the Talbot County Council to reclassify properties for purposes of eligibility of water and sewer service. In discussing whether the Council's decision was quasi-judicial, the court wrote "the greater a decisionmaker's reliance on general, 'legislative facts,' the more likely it is that an action is legislative in nature. Likewise, the greater a decisionmaker's reliance on property-specific, 'adjudicative facts,' the more reasonable it is to term the action adjudicatory in nature." In this case, the Council's decision did not "indicate a focus on the unique characteristics" of the applicant's property. Because the Council's decision was based "largely on legislative facts," its decision was not quasi-judicial and "administrative mandamus will not lie."

## § 13.17. Traditional Mandamus

An agency decision or action that is not the result of a quasi-judicial proceeding can be reviewed pursuant to a traditional mandamus action brought pursuant to Rule 15-701. An action for a writ of mandamus requires a verified complaint.[82] As explained in *Harvey v. Marshall*,[83] "a petition for mandamus involves two complimentary requirements: (1) a clear right on the part of the petitioner to the relief requested, and (2) a clear duty on the part of the administrative agency to perform the particular duty implicated."[84] If there is any "vestige of discretion" in the agency decision or action, mandamus is not appropriate. The traditional common law writ of mandamus is "one where the relief sought involves the traditional enforcement of a ministerial act (a legal duty) by recalcitrant public officials.[85]

In *South Easton Neighborhood Association v. Town of Easton*,[86] mandamus was not appropriate to challenge a town council's decision to close a street because such a decision

77. Md. Rule 7-402(b); *see* Md. Rule 7-205.
78. Md. Rule 7-402(d), *see* Md. Rule 7-206.
79. Md. Rule 7-402(d).
80. Md. Rule 7-402(e); *see* Md. Rule 7-207.
81. 415 Md. 372, 2 A.3d 344 (2010).
82. Md. Rule 15-701(a).
83. 389 Md. 243, 884 A.2d 1171 (2005).
84. 389 Md. 243, 277 n.18, 884 A.2d 1171, 1191 n.18 (2005).
85. South Easton Neighborhood Ass'n v. Town of Easton, 387 Md. 468, 876 A.2d 58 (2005) (citing Gisriel v. Ocean City Bd. of Supervisors of Elections, 345 Md. 477, 693 A.2d 757 (1997), *cert. denied*, 522 U.S. 1053 (1998); Murrell v. Mayor & City Council of Baltimore, 376 Md. 170, 829 A.2d 548 (2003)).
86. 387 Md. 468, 876 A.2d 58 (2005).

was discretionary. *Talbot County v. Miles Point Property, LLC*[87] emphasized that common law mandamus is appropriate only when the challenge involves a ministerial duty of an agency, not a discretionary one. The County Council's decision not to reclassify certain property to be more quickly eligible for water and sewer service was not a ministerial action, and thus review by a common law mandamus action would not lie. Similarly, in *Harvey v. Marshall*,[88] mandamus was not appropriate because it was within the Child Support Enforcement Administration's discretion whether to forgive child support arrearages.

On the other hand, traditional mandamus was held appropriate in *Hayward v. Department of Human Resources*.[89] In this case, two school employees had been accused of child abuse, but the charges were found to be "unsubstantiated." The employees requested a "conference" to review the agency's redacted investigation record in order to request corrections and/or supplements. When the agency denied the conference request, the employees filed for a Writ of Mandamus in circuit court to order the agency to grant the conference required by the statute. The circuit court's refusal to issue the Writ of Mandamus was reversed by the Court of Special Appeals. The Court of Special Appeals emphasized that the statute "is clear and mandates" a conference—no discretionary act of the agency was being challenged.[90]

## § 13.18. Discovery

In general, discovery does not play a large role in the judicial review of an administrative decision. Judicial review is generally limited to the record created at the agency, and thus there is no need to develop a new factual record. This point was discussed in *Venter v. Board of Education of Howard County*[91] where the chief business officer of the Howard County public school system sought judicial review of the State Board of Education's decision upholding the county board of education's decision to terminate his employment. Venter sought discovery in circuit court as part of the judicial review of his termination. The circuit court judge's denial of discovery was affirmed by the Court of Special Appeals. The court wrote:

> Discovery in circuit court should not be permitted when a remand to the administrative agency is a viable alternative. This general rule is consistent with the very narrow scope of judicial review of administrative appeals.... The reviewing court ordinarily does not render a new judicial decision grounded on the testimony or evidence introduced for the first time before the court.... Accordingly, the focal point for judicial review should be the administrative record already in existence, not some new record made initially in the reviewing court.[92]

The court then noted that Rule 2-504 which authorized the issuance of a scheduling order does not provide a right of discovery when the circuit court is reviewing the decision of an administrative agency. Also, Rule 7-208(c) provides that in judicial review of an agency

87. 415 Md. 372, 2 A.3d 344 (2010).
88. 389 Md. 243, 884 A.2d 1171 (2005).
89. 177 Md. App. 402, 935 A.2d. 493 (2007), *cert. granted*, 403 Md. 304, 941 A.2d 1104 (2008).
90. 177 Md. App. 402, 409, 935 A.2d. 493, 497 (2007).
91. 185 Md. App. 648, 972 A.2d 328, *cert. denied*, 410 Md. 561, 979 A.2d. 709 (2009).
92. 185 Md. App. 648, 684–85, 972 A.2d 328, 349 (2009).

decision, "additional evidence in support of or against the agency's decision is not allowed unless permitted by law."[93]

There is a separate discovery rule when judicial review is obtained through an action for Administrative Mandamus. Under Rule 7-402(c), the court may permit discovery that the court finds to be appropriate, but only in cases where the party challenging the agency action makes a strong showing of the existence of fraud or extreme circumstances that occurred outside the scope of the administrative record, and a remand to the agency is not a viable alternative. Although Rule 7-402(c) technically only applies to actions for Administrative Mandamus, it accurately reflects the law of discovery in judicial review of agency decisions in any context.

## § 13.19. Attempts to Question the Agency Decision-Maker

Most of the discovery disputes in judicial review of administrative decisions have involved attempts by a party to have the circuit court order that agency officials to be questioned through depositions and interrogatories about how the officials made a particular decision. In a series of cases, Maryland courts have held that absent exceptional circumstances, agency officials cannot be compelled to give testimony explaining their decision making process.

In *Boehm v. Anne Arundel County*,[94] an attempt was made to take the deposition of the County Zoning Administrator regarding possible bias in a zoning decision. The Court of Special Appeals refused to order such questioning, stating that "the law is clear that it is improper to probe the mental processes of an administrator in reaching his conclusion. Those legally responsible for a decision must in fact make it, but their method of doing so is largely beyond judicial scrutiny."[95]

In *Public Service Commission v. Patuxent Valley Conservation League*,[96] a circuit court had ordered commissioners of the Public Service Commission (PSC) to appear for depositions. This order was based on the allegation that during the PSC's consideration of a certificate of public convenience and necessity for the construction of a power transmission line, an "ex parte communication may have taken place between the hearing examiner and the Chairman" of the PSC. The basis of the circuit court order was that the allegation of the ex parte contact was an allegation of "bad faith" and "improper procedure" that justified the depositions. The Court of Appeals engaged in a full discussion of when a court could order agency officials to be questioned about their decision. Citing two U.S. Supreme Court cases, *Citizens to Preserve Overton Park, Inc.v. Volpe*[97] and *United States v. Morgan*,[98] the court in *Patuxent Valley* held that "depositions of administrative officials cannot be ordered solely upon a bald allegation of 'bad faith' or 'improper procedure.'" Rather, the party seeking the deposition must make a "strong preliminary showing of bad faith or improper behavior" before the court will order the deposition of an agency

93. 185 Md. App. 648, 685, 972 A.2d 328, 349 (2009).
94. 54 Md. App. 497, 459 A.2d 590 (1983).
95. 54 Md. App. 497, 503, 459 A.2d 590, 595 (1983).
96. 300 Md. 200, 477 A.2d 759 (1984).
97. 401 U.S. 402 (1971).
98. 313 U.S. 409 (1941).

official.[99] Because no such showing had been made, it was improper to order the questioning of the PSC commissioners.

*Montgomery County v. Stevens*[100] involved the discipline of a county police officer for making comments that were deemed to constitute "conduct unbecoming" a police officer. The circuit court had ordered the deposition of the police chief who had ordered the discipline based on allegations of the chief's improper ex parte communications and other procedural irregularities. The Court of Appeals rejected the argument that these allegations justified the "unusual order for discovery." It was a "fundamental principle" that a party challenging an agency action is forbidden to inquire into the mental processes of agency officials. A limited exception applies if the party seeking the deposition can make a strong showing, not just a mere allegation, of fraud or extreme circumstances external to the administrative record. Because there had been no strong showing of impropriety, no deposition was appropriate. The court also stated that even if testimony from agency officials was necessary in order to provide for meaningful judicial review, the appropriate remedy would be a remand to the agency, not court-ordered depositions.

In *Maryland State Board of Dental Examiners v. Fisher*,[101] the circuit court had ordered that members of the Board of Dental Examiners be questioned regarding whether they had been provided a summary of the evidence, whether they had any discussions regarding possible bias of one board member, whether the record had been personally reviewed by each board member prior to making a decision, whether any board member had participated in drafting the charges or had otherwise used information obtained in the investigatory phase in deciding the case, whether standards existed for the imposition of sanctions, and whether each board member was aware of prior sanctions in similar cases. Not surprisingly, the circuit court's order was reversed by the Court of Special Appeals. There had not been "a sufficiently strong showing of fraud or of extreme circumstances that would justify such an intrusion into the Board's deliberative process."[102] More specifically, the allegation that the board had considered only a summary of the evidence was insufficient to "trigger judicial intervention." Additionally, the court emphasized that a strong showing of fraud or extreme circumstances was required before any depositions could be ordered. A litigant is not entitled to depose board members to try to learn of information that would justify the depositions. The Court of Special Appeals in *Fisher* also ruled, however, that an in-camera review by the circuit court of the minutes of a board meeting was justified. The court said that there was an important distinction between board members being questioned and the circuit court examining minutes in camera.

In *Maryland-National Capital Park and Planning Commission v. Mardirossian*,[103] a real estate developer sought discovery from the commissioners of the planning commission which had denied the developer's request to cut down trees near the Potomac River. In refusing to grant a protective order from the discovery request, the Court of Special Appeals was very careful to emphasize, as did the developer's counsel, that the discovery requests were not part of any judicial review of the commission's decision, nor to strengthen the developer's position in any upcoming judicial review proceeding of the commission's decision. Counsel for the developer "stressed that at deposition he was not seeking information that related to how the commissioners arrived at their decision in any case,

99. 300 Md. 200, 216, 477 A.2d 759, 767 (1984).

100. 337 Md. 471, 654 A.2d 877 (1995).

101. 123 Md. App. 322, 718 A.2d 627, *cert. denied*, 352 Md. 355, 722 A.2d 63 (1998).

102. 123 Md. App. 322, 328, 718 A.2d 627, 630 (1998).

103. 184 Md. App. 207, 964 A.2d 713, *cert. granted*, 409 Md. 44, 972 A.2d 859, *dismissed as moot*, 409 Md. 413, 975 A.2d 875 (2009).

nor did counsel have any intent to make inquiry about matters involving quasi-judicial decision-making by the Commission."[104] Rather, the discovery requests were part of a civil lawsuit filed by the developer against a third person for private nuisance, false light invasion of privacy, and interference with prospective advantage. Nothing in the court's opinion in *Mardirossian* is inconsistent with the cases cited above regarding the right of discovery in judicial review proceedings of administrative agency decisions.

## § 13.20. Circuit Court Judicial Review Hearing

When a Petition for Judicial Review has been filed, unless waived in writing by the parties, a hearing is held before a circuit court judge.[105] The hearing is held no earlier than ninety days after the date the agency record is filed with the court.[106] It is the responsibility of the clerk of the court's office to set the date for the hearing upon receipt of the administrative record.[107] When the matter is before the circuit court based on an action for a writ of Administrative Mandamus, Rule 7-402(f) provides that the "court *may* hold a hearing" (emphasis added). In practice, a hearing is held unless waived by the parties.

Judicial review of an agency decision in circuit court is heard by and decided by a judge alone. There is no right to a jury when an agency decision is being reviewed.[108] In *County Council for Montgomery County v. Investors Funding Corp.*,[109] the Court of Appeals expressly held that the lack of a jury trial in judicial review of agency decisions does not violate the constitutional right to a jury under the federal or Maryland Constitutions.

Judicial review by the circuit court is limited to the administrative record already in existence.[110] The circuit court does not base its decision on new information or evidence presented for the first time before the court. The APA, State Gov't § 10-222(f)(1), provides that "judicial review of disputed issues of fact shall be confined to the record." Rule 7-402(f) provides that in actions for Administrative Mandamus, "additional evidence in support of or against the agency's decision is not allowed unless permitted by law."

## § 13.21. De Novo Trial

Except for Worker's Compensation Commission cases, which are governed by their own body of law rather than principles of general Administrative Law, a *de novo* trial before a jury to review an administrative agency decision would be unconstitutional. This conclusion is based on the Court of Appeals' decision in *Department of Natural Resources v. Linchester Sand & Gravel Corp.*[111] *Linchester* involved a statute that provided that the denial by the Department of Natural Resources (DNR) of a permit for dredging in a wetland area was subject to a *de novo* trial in circuit court. Moreover, either party could

104. 184 Md. App. 207, 215, 964 A.2d 713, 718 (2009).
105. Md. Rule 7-208(a).
106. Md. Rule 7-208(b).
107. Md. Rule 7-202(d)(3)(A).
108. Maryland Code Annotated, State Government § 10-222(g)(1).
109. 270 Md. 403, 312 A.2d 225 (1973).
110. Maryland Code Annotated, State Government § 10-222(f)(1).
111. 274 Md. 211, 334 A.2d 514 (1975).

elect a jury trial. After Linchester was denied a permit by DNR, Linchester exercised this statutory right. After a *de novo* trial, the jury, based on instructions from the circuit judge that traced the wetlands statute, granted the permit. The Court of Appeals vacated the jury verdict. The court held that "this type of extensive and nullifying judicial *de novo* review" violated the Maryland Constitution. Such *de novo* review amounted to usurpation by the judicial branch of the executive branch's administrative powers. It was unconstitutional for the circuit court "to empanel a jury and then in effect instruct it to convert itself into an administrative body."[112] The court also noted that if such review were permitted, it "would place this State in the intolerable situation of having as many wetland decision-makers as there are circuit court judges and juries empaneled for this purpose. If this were to be the case, the result would be a destruction of the effectiveness of the department in conserving, for the general public good, the valuable wetlands of this State, and reduce the agency's power, in this field, as a practical matter, to a nullity."[113] The court in *Linchester* stated that a *de novo* trial of workers' compensation cases presented the "singular example" where the agency function was "so essentially judicial" that a *de novo* trial would not be unconstitutional.

Although in light of *Linchester* the phrase "*de novo* review" has no place in describing judicial review of an agency decision, the phrase "*de novo* review" does pop up in legislation and regulations in regards to review by an agency of a decision of a sub-agency or another agency. It is usually unclear what is the intent of such legislation or regulations. For example, an historic preservation board's determination of the historical significance of a property may be subject to "*de novo* review" by a planning and development agency. Does this mean that the planning and development agency ignores the hearing held before the historic preservation board and must hold a full evidentiary hearing with new testimony? Or does it mean that a new record is not created at the second agency proceeding, but that the second agency will decide the matter "*de novo*," i.e., as if no prior agency had rendered a decision. The term "*de novo* review" should be avoided unless it is clearly explained what is intended.

## § 13.22. Presentation of New Evidence at Circuit Court Hearing

Although the general rule is that the circuit court will consider only the evidence that is properly contained in the agency record in reviewing the agency decision, there are two exceptions to this general rule. First, the APA, State Gov't § 10-222(g)(2), provides that a party "may offer testimony on alleged irregularities in procedures before the presiding officer that do not appear on the record." In *Consumer Protection Division v. Consumer Publishing Co.*,[114] a false advertising case, the circuit court had admitted evidence relating to an advertiser's market share and amount of business in Maryland, examples of advertising by competitors, and evidence of consumer satisfaction with the advertiser's products. The Court of Appeals held that the circuit judge erred in admitting this new evidence because none of it related to procedural irregularities.

112. 274 Md. 211, 228, 334 A.2d 514, 525 (1975).
113. 274 Md. 211, 228–29, 334 A.2d 514, 525 (1975).
114. 304 Md. 731, 501 A.2d 48 (1985).

The Court of Special Appeals in *Maryland General Hospital v. Maryland Health Resources Planning Commission*[115] took what seems to be too narrow an approach to State Gov't § 10-222(g)(2) by focusing on the statute's use of the word "testimony." The court stated that "only testimony in its more narrow sense of oral evidence" may be introduced to prove procedural irregularities. Because the petitioners sought to introduce documents, § 10-222(g)(2) had no application. In my opinion, it seems improper to limit § 10-222(g)(2)'s application to oral testimony.

Another exception to the general rule that no new evidence can be presented to the circuit court is that in some circumstances new evidence may be presented to demonstrate that the agency acted in an arbitrary or capricious manner. An agency decision that is arbitrary or capricious must be reversed.[116] One way an agency acts in an arbitrary or capricious manner is when the agency without an adequate explanation acts inconsistently. In order to prove that the agency has acted inconsistently, evidence of decisions by the same agency prior or subsequent to the agency decision being reviewed may be admissible at the circuit court. Arbitrary or capricious review is discussed in detail in Chapter 20.

## § 13.23. Remand for New Evidence at the Agency

To be contrasted to a party's attempt to have new evidence introduced before the circuit court is a party's request for the court to order that new evidence be permitted to be introduced back at the agency. The APA provides that a

> court may order the presiding officer to take additional evidence on terms that the court considers proper if: before the hearing date in court, a party applies for leave to offer additional evidence; and the court is satisfied that the evidence is material; and there were good reasons for the failure to offer the evidence in the proceeding before the presiding officer.[117]

Based on the new evidence presented to the agency, the final agency decision-maker may modify the findings and decision. The additional evidence and any modifications of the findings or the decision become part of the administrative record and are filed with the reviewing court. It is important to remember that this section does not authorize the court to consider new evidence; it only authorizes the court to order the agency to consider new evidence.[118]

## § 13.24. Scope of Circuit Court Review

A very important limitation on the circuit court in reviewing an agency decision is that an agency can only be upheld for the reasons stated and relied upon by the agency in reaching its decision.[119] If there are reasons not relied upon by the agency that support

115. 103 Md. App. 525, 653 A.2d 1029, *cert. denied*, 339 Md. 355, 663 A.2d 72 (1995).

116. Maryland Code Annotated, State Government § 10-222(h)(3)(vi).

117. Maryland Code Annotated, State Government § 10-222(f)(2).

118. *See* Motor Vehicle Admin. v. Mohler, 318 Md. 219, 567 A.2d 929 (1990).

119. *See* Dep't of Health & Mental Hygiene v. Campbell, 364 Md. 108, 771 A.2d 1051 (2001); United Steelworkers v. Bethlehem Steel Corp., 298 Md. 665, 472 A.2d 62 (1984).

the agency decision that are supplied by agency counsel in written submissions or at oral argument, or by the reviewing court's own research or knowledge, the agency decision cannot be sustained based on these reasons.[120] In this regard, judicial review of an agency decision differs from appellate review of a trial court decision. When reviewing a trial court decision, the appellate court is permitted to perform its own search into the trial record, and to consider alternative arguments to support the lower court decision. An appellate court will affirm the lower court if there is any support for the lower court's decision even if such support was not relied upon by the lower court. This is not true when an agency decision is being reviewed by the circuit court.[121]

## § 13.25. Circuit Court Order

When ruling on a Petition for Judicial Review, Maryland Rule 7-209 provides that the circuit court may dismiss the action, or may affirm, reverse or modify the agency's order or action, remand the action to the agency for further proceedings, or "an appropriate combination" of these dispositions. When ruling on a writ of Administrative Mandamus, Maryland Rule 7-403 provides that the circuit court may issue an order "denying the writ of mandamus, or may issue the writ remanding the case for further proceedings, or reversing or modifying the decision."

Dismissal of petitioner's case would be appropriate if the court concludes that there is no standing, an untimely filing, or failure to exhaust administrative remedies. A remand to the agency would be appropriate if the agency's findings were inadequate so that the reviewing court was unable to determine the basis of the agency decision,[122] if the agency decision was based on an error of law,[123] if the agency failed to take into consideration relevant matters, or if the agency relied on an irrelevant factor in reaching its decision.[124] A remand to the agency would not be appropriate if the burden of proof had not been met.[125]

Not entirely clear is the reviewing court's power to "modify" the agency decision. In *Consumer Protection Division v. Consumer Publishing Co.*,[126] a false advertising case involving diet pills, the circuit court vacated the agency's final order and substituted as the new order an agreement that the diet pill maker had entered into with the federal government involving the same diet pills. The agency argued that the circuit court had exceeded its authority by substituting the court's own remedy for that of the agency. The diet pill maker responded that the circuit court had acted within its power to "modify" the agency order. The Court of Appeals reversed the circuit court. It stated that "the authority to 'modify' cannot be stretched to include replacing the agency's order with an entirely distinct one based on an agreement between the Company and the Federal Government."[127] Similarly, in *Motor Vehicle Administration v. Baptist*,[128] the Court of Special Appeals held

120. *See* Md. Racing Comm'n v. Belotti, 130 Md. App. 23, 744 A.2d 558 (1999).

121. *See* Evans v. Burruss, 401 Md. 586, 933 A.2d. 872 (2007), *cert. denied*, 552 U.S. 1187 (2008).

122. *See* Dep't of Health & Mental Hygiene v. Shrieves, 100 Md. App. 283, 641 A.2d 899 (1994).

123. *See* Md. Dep't of Health & Mental Hygiene v. Brown, 177 Md. App. 440, 935 A.2d. 1128 (2007).

124. *See* Eaton v. Rosewood Ctr., 86 Md. App. 366, 586 A.2d 804 (1991); *see also* People's Counsel for Baltimore County v. Country Ridge Shopping Ctr., Inc., 144 Md. App. 580, 799 A.2d 425 (2002).

125. Annapolis Mkt. Place, LLC v. Parker, 369 Md. 689, 802 A.2d 1029 (2002).

126. 304 Md. 731, 501 A.2d 48 (1985).

127. 304 Md. 731, 747, 501 A.2d 48, 56 (1985).

128. 185 Md. App. 56, 968 A.2d 638 (2009).

that the circuit court exceeded its "modification" authority by ordering the MVA to issue a driver who was driving with a blood alcohol concentration of .20 (over twice the legal limit) an ignition-interlock restricted license in lieu of the license suspension ordered by MVA.

These cases indicate that a "modification" which is actually a "substitution" by the reviewing court of what the court believes is a more appropriate sanction is not permitted. No bright line, however, exists as to what may be an appropriate modification.

## § 13.26. Petition for Civil Enforcement

Almost every Administrative Law case in circuit court is brought by the party who has lost at the agency. However, there is another type of Administrative Law case that can be filed by a party who was successful at the agency but has not received the remedy ordered. These cases are initiated by the filing of a Petition for Civil Enforcement pursuant to State Gov't § 10-222.1. Under this section of the APA, a person who was a party to a contested case may seek enforcement of the administrative order in the circuit court in the county where any party resides or has a principal place of business. Named as the defendants in the civil enforcement petition are the persons or perhaps the agency that failed to provide the relief ordered by the agency.

This APA section was involved in *Department of Health & Mental Hygiene v. Rynarzewski*.[129] The Court of Special Appeals emphasized that this matter was before the court not on a Petition for Judicial Review of a contested case order, but as a civil enforcement action. Rynarzewski was a state employee who had been terminated from state employment for failing to report to work in violation of COMAR regulations relevant to his job. Rynarzewski's defense was that he had not reported to work on the advice of his doctor. He challenged his termination, and was provided a hearing at OAH which had been delegated the authority to render a final decision in such cases. The OAH ALJ ruled that the termination was not proper because Rynarzewski's absence from work was "due to his legitimate mental disability," and that there was no violation of any COMAR regulation. The ALJ ordered that Rynarzewski be reinstated with back pay and benefits retroactive to the date he was fit to return to work. Most significantly, the employer, DHMH, did not file a Petition for Judicial Review to challenge the ALJ's decision, although it clearly had the right to do so. DHMH, however, refused to reinstate Rynarzewski, and did not pay him for lost benefits or back pay. The proper course of action by Rynarzewski was the filing of a Petition for Civil Enforcement. The court ordered the agency to reinstate Rynarzewski to his former employment, although the court ruled that the back pay and past benefit issues needed to be resolved by a new grievance.

From a constitutional perspective, civil enforcement actions are needed in cases like *Rynarzewski* because OAH, like all agencies, has no power of contempt. The power of contempt belongs solely to the judicial branch, and any attempt to delegate contempt powers to an executive branch agency would violate separation of powers.[130] Therefore, if a party, including an agency, that is the subject of an administrative order ignores the order, only a court has the full power to enforce the agency order.

129. 164 Md. App. 252, 883 A.2d 205 (2005).
130. Maryland Code Annotated, State Government § 10-623(c)(3)(iii).

## § 13.27. Reimbursement for Litigation Expenses

The Maryland APA provides that in certain very limited circumstances, an agency must reimburse certain small businesses and non-profit organizations for litigation expenses, including attorney's fees, incurred in defending itself against unwarranted administrative charges.[131] This APA provision, found in State Government § 10-224, applies only to businesses that are independently owned and operated and which have fewer than fifty employees, or to an organization that is exempt or eligible for exemption from taxation under § 501(C)(3) of the Internal Revenue Code.

A small business or non-profit organization to be eligible for reimbursement must prove the following:

1. A contested case or civil action was initiated against the small business or non-profit organization by an agency as part of its administrative or regulatory function;
2. The contested case or civil action was initiated without substantial justification or in bad faith; and
3. The contested case or civil action did not result in an adjudication, stipulation, or acceptance of liability by the small business or non-profit organization, or a determination of non-compliance, violation, infringement, deficiency or breach, or a settlement agreement under which the small business or non-profit organization agreed to take corrective action or pay a monetary sum.

If reimbursement is appropriate, the small business or non-profit organization can be awarded all expenses incurred, including attorney's fees and expenses for necessary witnesses. The award may be reduced or denied to the extent that the proceedings were unreasonably delayed by the conduct of the small business or non-profit organization. No award can be for more than $10,000.

The claim for reimbursement must first be filed with the agency. Once the agency denies any award, an action can be filed in circuit court. The agency can appeal an award by the circuit court to the Court of Special Appeals.

## § 13.28. Judicial Review in Court of Special Appeals

State Government § 10-223(b)(1) provides that a party who is aggrieved by a final judgment of the circuit court reviewing an administrative agency decision may appeal to the Court of Special Appeals in the same manner as the appeal of civil cases. State Government § 10-223(b)(2) provides that an agency that was a party at the circuit court is also entitled to seek appellate review in the Court of Special Appeals if it was aggrieved by the circuit court decision.

The most important point about review in the Court of Special Appeals is that the Court of Special Appeals does not review the decision of the circuit court, but rather

131. Maryland Code Annotated, State Government § 10-224.

directly reviews the agency decision. The role of the Court of Special Appeals is identical to the role of the circuit court in reviewing the agency decision. Therefore, questions presented to the Court of Special Appeals should be drafted in terms of whether the agency decision should be reversed, not whether the circuit court erred in its decision.[132] As the Court of Special Appeals wrote in *State Commission on Human Relations v. Kaydon Ring & Seal, Inc.*,[133] "regardless of whether the circuit court applied a correct or incorrect standard of review, it only is necessary that in performing our review, we apply the correct standard."[134] The irrelevance of the circuit court proceeding to judicial review in the Court of Special Appeals is also illustrated in *Patrick v. Secretary, Department of Public Safety & Correctional Services*[135] where the transcript of the circuit court proceeding had not been provided to the Court of Special Appeals. The court saw this to be "of no consequence, ... because we look to the record developed at the agency level."[136]

An interesting issue involves the interplay of the principle that the Court of Special Appeals reviews the decision of the agency not the decision of the circuit court, and Maryland Rule 8-131(a) which provides that except for issues of jurisdiction, the Court of Special Appeals "[o]rdinarily, ... will not decide any other issue unless it plainly appears ... to have been raised in or decided by the trial court." What should be the result if an issue was raised at the agency (to satisfy the exhaustion doctrine), but not raised at the circuit court? It seems that failure to argue a point to the circuit court that was raised at the agency should not serve as a bar against presenting that argument to the Court of Special Appeals.

*Beeman v. Department of Health & Mental Hygiene*[137] cited Rule 8-131(a) in refusing to review an issue presented in Appellant's brief but not presented to the circuit court. This issue, however, had also not been presented to the agency. Rule 8-131(a) was also cited by the Court of Special Appeals in *Maryland Securities Commissioner v. U.S. Securities Corp.*[138] to permit review when an issue had not been ruled upon by the circuit court, but had been presented to it.

In *Colburn v. Department of Public Safety & Correctional Services*,[139] the Court of Appeals was reviewing the agency decision "on bypass." When reviewing a case on bypass, the Court of Appeals considers only those issues that would have been cognizable by the Court of Special Appeals. One issue raised in *Colburn* was that the OAH ALJ who had made the final agency decision had "erred in finding that there was no evidence that appellant's salaries [were] subject to reduction because of variation in the quality or quantity of the work performed." At the Court of Appeals, the agency contended that "this issue was not raised below by appellants, and therefore, is not preserved" for review. The Court of Appeals' response was "In our review of the record, we find that the ALJ addressed the issue of disciplinary deductions in pay in her written opinion. Under Maryland Rule 8-131, we review those issues that have been 'raised in or decided by' the lower tribunal." Therefore, the issue had been properly presented for review.

---

132. *See* Balt. County Licensed Beverage Ass'n v. Kwon, 135 Md. App.178, 761 A.2d 1027 (2000); Md. Racing Comm'n v. Belotti, 130 Md. App. 23, 744 A.2d 558 (1999).

133. 149 Md. App. 666, 818 A.2d 259 (2003).

134. 149 Md. App. 666, 694, 818 A.2d 259, 276 (2003)

135. 156 Md. App. 423, 847 A.2d 450 (2004).

136. 156 Md. App. 423, 434 n.8, 847 A.2d 450, 457 n.8 (2004).

137. 107 Md. App. 122, 666 A.2d 1314 (1995).

138. 122 Md. App. 574, 716 A.2d 290 (1998).

139. 403 Md. 115, 939 A.2d 716 (2008).

In *Maryland Department of Transportation v. Maddalone*,[140] which involved a challenge to the termination of a state employee, the agency "devote[d] a significant part of its brief to advancing the legal argument that Maddalone held a 'special appointment' in the Executive Service, and therefore could be fired for any reason, including an unconstitutional or illegal reason." The Court of Special Appeals refused to consider this argument because it "was not raised before the ALJ (or the circuit court on judicial review), and therefore is not properly before this Court," citing Maryland Rule 8-131.[141]

## § 13.29. No Court of Special Appeals Review

In Maryland, except as constitutionally authorized, appellate jurisdiction is determined entirely by statute. Therefore, to bring an appeal from the circuit court to the Court of Special Appeals there must be a statute providing for such an appeal. The general appellate review statute is Courts and Judicial Proceedings § 12-301. This statute provides that "[c]xcept as provided in § 12 302, ... a party may appeal from a final judgment entered in a civil or criminal case by a circuit court. The right of appeal exists from a final judgment entered by a court in the exercise of original, special, limited, [or] statutory jurisdiction." Courts and Judicial Proceedings § 12-302(a) then provides that "[u]nless a right to appeal is expressly granted by law, § 12-301 ... does not permit an appeal from a final judgment of a court entered or made in the exercise of appellate jurisdiction in reviewing the decision of the District Court, an administrative agency, or a local legislative body." Although as discussed earlier in this chapter, circuit court review of an agency decision is not the exercise of appellate jurisdiction, this statute had been held to apply to circuit court review of agency decisions.[142] Because State Government § 10-223(b) expressly grants appellate review in the Court of Special Appeals, there is statutory appellate review for those decisions covered by section 10-223(b). But importantly, not all administrative agencies in Maryland are covered by section 10-223(b). Section 10-223(b) only covers agencies covered by Subtitle 2 of the Maryland APA. Subtitle 2 does not apply to several state agencies listed in State Gov't § 10-203(a), and significantly does not apply to a local agency that operates in only one county.

For most of the agencies excluded from Subtitle 2, a statute separate from Section 10-223(b) does provide for appellate review in the Court of Special Appeals. For some agencies, however, especially some local agencies, there is no statute providing for appellate review, and thus although there is judicial review in circuit court, there is no judicial review in the Court of Special Appeals. In *South Easton Neighborhood Association v. Town of Easton*,[143] although the Town Council's decision to close a street was reviewed by the circuit court, because no statute provided for appellate court review, there was no Court of Special Appeals review. In *Dvorak v. Anne Arundel County Ethics Commission*,[144] there was no appeal to the Court of Special Appeals from a circuit court decision reviewing a decision from the Anne Arundel County Ethics Commission. Additionally, *Rogers v. Eastport Yachting*

140. 187 Md. App. 549, 979 A.2d 229 (2009).
141. 187 Md. App. 549, 583 n.18, 979 A.2d 229, 250 n.18 (2009).
142. *See* Dvorok v. Anne Arundel County Ethics Commission, 400 Md. 446, 929 A.2d 185 (2007).
143. 387 Md. 468, 876 A.2d 58 (2005).
144. 400 Md. 446, 929 A.2d 185 (2007).

*Center, LLC*[145] held that the Court of Special Appeals lacked jurisdiction to hear an appeal involving a decision of the Port Warden; no statute authorized such an appeal.[146]

There seem to be a couple situations, however, where the Court of Special Appeals will hear the appeal even absent a statute expressly providing for an appeal. First, even absent a statute, if a challenge is made to the circuit court's jurisdiction to review the agency decision, the Court of Special Appeals has jurisdiction to review that jurisdictional issue.[147] Secondly, the Court of Appeals in *Murrell v. Mayor & City Council of Baltimore*[148] held that the Court of Special Appeals had jurisdiction, even absent a statute, when the "substance of the circuit court action was a common law mandamus action."[149]

## § 13.30. Judicial Review in the Court of Appeals

Under Courts & Judicial Proceedings Article § 12-201, any party, including the agency, can seek judicial review in the Court of Appeals by filing a Petition for Certiorari. The petition may be filed either before or after the Court of Special Appeals has rendered a decision.[150] The Court of Appeals also has the power to issue a writ of certiorari on its own motion.[151] The Court of Appeals has a "Bypass Committee" which reviews cases filed in the Court of Special Appeals and decides whether any cases should bypass the intermediate appellate court and be decided by the Court of Appeals prior to a decision from the Court of Special Appeals.

When an appeal is filed with the Court of Special Appeals from a circuit court decision reviewing an agency decision, the Court of Special Appeals reviews the decision of the agency, not the decision of the circuit court. When a decision from an administrative agency is brought to the Court of Appeals, the issue arises as to whether the Court of Appeals should review the agency decision or whether it should review the lower court's review of the agency decision.[152] In terms of judicial economy, it makes more sense to have the Court of Appeals review the lower court's decision, not the agency's decision. Nevertheless, the Court of Appeals has repeatedly stated: "We review an administrative agency's decision under the same statutory standards as the Circuit Court. Therefore, we reevaluate the decision of the agency, not the decision of the lower court."[153] Because the

145. 408 Md. 722, 971 A.2d 322 (2009).

146. *See also* Gisriel v. Ocean City Bd. of Supervisors of Election, 345 Md. 477, 693 A.2d 757 (1997), *cert denied*, 522 U.S. 1053 (1998).

147. *See* Dvorak v. Anne Arundel County Ethics Commission, 400 Md. 446, 929 A.2d 185 (2007); Rogers v. Eastport Yachting Center, LLC, 408 Md. 722, 971 A.2d 322 (2009).

148. 376 Md. 170, 829 A.2d 548 (2003).

149. 376 Md. 170, 196, 829 A.2d 548, 564 (2003).

150. Maryland Code Annotated, Courts & Judicial Proceedings § 12-201.

151. Maryland Code Annotated, Courts & Judicial Proceedings § 12-201.

152. The lower court decision will typically be the decision of the Court of Special Appeals, but there are cases that "bypass" the Court of Special Appeals. In the case of bypass jurisdiction, the lower court decision will be from a circuit court.

153. Gigeous v. Eastern Correctional Inst., 363 Md. 481, 495–96, 769 A.2d 912, 921 (2001); *see also* Bayly Crossing, LLC v. Consumer Protection Division, 417 Md. 128, 9 A.3d 4 (2010); Dep't of Health & Mental Hygiene v. Campbell, 364 Md. 108, 122, 771 A.2d 1051, 1060 (2001) ("[I]t is the final decision of the final decision-maker at the administrative level, not that of the reviewing court, that is subject to judicial review."); Spencer v. Md. State Bd. of Pharmacy, 380 Md. 515, 846 A.2d 341 (2004) (the inquiry is not whether the Court of Special Appeals erred, but whether the administrative agency

Court of Appeals reviews the agency's decision, not the lower court's decision, the questions presented in a petition for writ of certiorari should be drafted in terms of whether the agency erred, not whether the lower court erred in its review of the agency decision.[154]

erred); Annapolis Market Place, LLC v. Parker, 369 Md. 689, 802 A.2d 1029 (2002); Pollock v. Patuxent Inst. Bd. of Review, 374 Md. 463,476, 823 A.2d 626, 634 (2003).

154. Gigeous v. Eastern Correctional Inst., 363 Md. 481, 769 A.2d 912 (2001).

# Chapter 14

# Judicial Review: Proper Parties and Timing

In determining whether judicial review is available and appropriate, the legal principles involving Standing, Finality, Exhaustion, Primary Jurisdiction, and Ripeness must be understood. This chapter will discuss these doctrines.

## § 14.1. Standing

Federal Administrative Law applies a four-part test to determine whether a person has standing to petition for judicial review of an agency decision. To have standing in federal court, a petitioner must allege an (1) actual or threatened injury which is (2) traceable to the agency action, and which will be (3) redressed by a favorable court decision.[1] Additionally, petitioner must be (4) within the zone of interest arguably protected by the relevant statutes.[2] Although a threatened, future injury can satisfy the injury prong of standing in federal court for judicial review of a federal agency decision, the injury prong is not satisfied if the alleged injury is speculative.[3] There are numerous federal cases discussing standing to get review of a federal administrative agency decision. Maryland does not follow federal law on standing. The Maryland cases take a more liberal approach in granting standing.

## § 14.2. Being a Party

In its section on judicial review of a contested case, the Maryland APA first provides that "a party who is aggrieved by the final decision in a contested case is entitled to judicial review of the decision."[4] The two important issues to determine standing in Maryland therefore are whether the petitioner was a "party" and whether petitioner is "aggrieved."

There are several cases discussing who is considered a party at a contested case, all of which provide support for the statement in *Dorsey v. Bethel A.M.E. Church*[5] that in Maryland "one may become a party to an administrative proceeding rather easily."[6] In

---

1. Lujan v. Defenders of Wildlife, 504 U.S. 555 (1992).
2. Clarke v. Securities Industry Ass'n, 479 U.S. 388 (1987); Air Courier Conference v. American Postal Workers Union, 498 U.S. 517 (1991).
3. *See* Northwest Airlines, Inc. v. Federal Aviation Administration, 795 F.2d. 195 (D.C. Cir. 1986).
4. Maryland Code Annotated, State Government § 10-222(a).
5. 375 Md. 59, 825 A.2d 388 (2003).
6. 375 Md. 59, 72, 825 A.2d 388, 395 (2003).

*Morris v. Howard Research & Development Corp.*,[7] the court wrote that "anyone clearly identifying himself to the agency for the record as having an interest in the outcome of the matter being considered by that agency, ... becomes a party to the proceedings."[8] In *Ross v. Mr. Lucky, LLC*,[9] a person who was denied the right to intervene, but who offered oral comments and introduced documents into the record after all witnesses had finished testifying was held to be a party. *Handley v. Ocean Downs, LLC*[10] held that mere presence at the administrative hearing without any active participation was sufficient to establish someone as a party. In *Handley*, petitioner's status as a party was established when his signature appeared on the hearing sign-in sheet. In *Rogers v. Eastport Yachting Center, LLC.*,[11] the circuit court ruled that petitioner was not a party at the agency hearing, and thus had no standing to seek judicial review. Although Rogers had received notice of the hearing, he "chose neither to attend the hearing nor to submit any written opposition."[12] The standing issue was not addressed by the Court of Appeals in its opinion.

Party status has also been granted to a person who submitted his name in writing at the hearing as a protestant,[13] a person who testified at the hearing,[14] a person who submitted a letter of protest into the record,[15] and persons who identified themselves as parties on the record at the hearing.[16] Although some of these persons could more accurately be labeled as witnesses or observers, under Maryland law, they are viewed as parties. Additionally, a person who qualifies as a party at the administrative level remains a party for purposes of judicial review until that person either abandons his or her status as a party or is dismissed as a party.[17]

## § 14.3. Aggrieved

In addition to being a party, to have standing to get judicial review, petitioner must be aggrieved by the agency decision. To be aggrieved, the party must have a specific interest or property right that is personally and specifically affected. A party cannot merely rely on another person's aggrievement which petitioner is asserting in some type of representative capacity. Nor can petitioner rely on an aggrievement that is suffered by the public in general. A few cases illustrate the Maryland approach to standing and the "aggrieved" requirement.

*Bailey v. Maryland State Department of Public Safety & Correctional Services*[18] involved an employee of the Division of Corrections (DOC) who had been denied the right to represent another DOC employee in a personnel grievance hearing. By statute, non-lawyers are permitted to represent employees at these grievance hearings. The agency, however,

7. 278 Md. 417, 365 A.2d 34 (1976).
8. 278 Md. 417, 423, 365 A.2d 34, 37 (1976).
9. 189 Md. App. 511, 985 A.2d 93 (2009), *cert. denied*, 413 Md. 229, 991 A.2d 1274 (2010).
10. 151 Md. App. 615, 827 A.2d 961 (2003).
11. 408 Md. 722, 971 A.2d 322 (2009).
12. 408 Md. 722, 730, 971 A.2d 322, 327 (2009).
13. Baxter v. Montgomery County Board of Appeals, 248 Md. 111, 235 A.2d 536 (1967).
14. Bryniarski v. Montgomery County Board of Appeals, 247 Md. 137, 230 A.2d 289 (1967).
15. Hertelendy v. Montgomery County Board of Appeals, 245 Md. 554, 226 A.2d 672 (1967).
16. DuBay v. Crane, 240 Md. 180, 213 A.2d 487 (1965); Morris v. Howard Research and Development Corporation, 278 Md. 417, 365 A.2d 34 (1976).
17. Medical Waste Associates v. Maryland Waste Coalition, Inc., 327 Md. 596, 612 A.2d 241 (1992).
18. 333 Md. 397, 635 A.2d 432 (1994).

had refused to permit Bailey to represent the other employee at the grievance proceeding because Bailey had recently been promoted to a supervisory position. When Bailey sought judicial review of the agency decision denying him the ability to represent the other employee, the agency argued that Bailey had not been personally aggrieved because the statute that created the right of non-attorneys to represent certain state employees at personnel grievance hearings was a right that belonged solely to the employee who desired the non-attorney representation. The Court of Appeals held that Bailey did have standing. The court stated that Bailey was not asserting the rights of the employee he sought to represent, but was asserting his own right to represent the employee.

In *Medical Waste Associates v. Maryland Waste Coalition, Inc.,*[19] an environmental organization was denied standing to challenge the issuance of construction permits for a medical waste incinerator. The Court of Appeals stated that the organization's interest was not different in "character and kind" from that suffered by the general public. The Court of Appeals also rejected the organization's position that it had standing because it was bringing the case on behalf of its members, and that its members had been aggrieved differently from the general public. The court's response to this argument was that "for an organization to have standing to bring a judicial action, it must ordinarily have a property interest of its own—separate and distinct from that of its individual members."[20]

In a situation where both an organization and an individual member petition for judicial review, judicial review is appropriate based on the individual's petition even if the organization does not have standing. For example, in *Dorsey v. Bethel A.M.E. Church,*[21] although it was not clear whether a community association had been aggrieved separate and apart from its members, it was clear that several individual petitioners did have standing, and thus the court reviewed the agency decision. The court stated that "[w]here there exists a party having standing to bring an action, [the court] shall not ordinarily inquire as to whether another party on the same side also has standing."[22]

In zoning cases, it has been held that to be aggrieved for standing purposes, a person must own property within the sight or sound range of the property that is subject to the zoning request. A member of the community upset by the zoning decision but not a property owner within sight or sound range, would not have standing because of the lack of a personal and specific injury.[23]

## § 14.4. Special Statutory Standing

A person who does not have standing under the APA may have standing under a special statue relevant to the particular situation. For example, the Maryland Environmental

19. 327 Md. 596, 612 A.2d 241 (1992).

20. 327 Md. 596, 612, 612 A.2d 241, 249 (1992); *See also* Md. Ass'n of Health Maint. Orgs. v. Health Services Cost Review Comm'n, 356 Md. 581, 741 A.2d 483 (1999).

21. 375 Md. 59, 825 A.2d 388 (2003).

22. 375 Md. 59, 67 n.1, 825 A.2d 388, 393 n.1 (2003); *See also* Bayly Crossing, LLC v. Consumer Protection Division, 417 Md. 128, 9 A.3d4 (2010).

23. Committee for Responsible Development on 25th Street v. Mayor and City Council of Baltimore, 137 Md. App. 60, 767 A.2d 906 (2001); Bryniarski v. Montgomery County Board of Appeals, 247 Md. 137, 230 A.2d 289 (1967); Maryland-National Capital Park and Planning Commission v. City of Rockville, 269 Md. 240, 305 A.2d 122 (1973).

Standing Act (MESA)[24] provides standing to an organization seeking judicial review in certain environmental cases regardless of whether the organization has suffered an injury separate from that of its members. Additionally, MESA provides standing to any person regardless of whether the harm suffered by that person differs from the harm suffered by the general public. Special statutory standing rules also apply to certain decisions of the Health Services Cost Review Commission[25] and the Public Service Commission.[26] It is essential to remember, however, that these special standing rules only apply to proceedings brought pursuant to the substantive provisions of these special statutes.[27]

## § 14.5. Standing of the Agency to Obtain Judicial Review

The issue of the agency's standing to participate in the judicial review process has generated a fair amount of discussion in Maryland cases. Although this issue has been resolved for agencies subject to the APA, it still requires analysis for those agencies not subject to the APA.

In *Board of Zoning Appeals v. McKinney*,[28] decided in 1938, the Baltimore City Board of Zoning Appeals had initially denied an application for a permit to build a service station because it was located near a church. Upon reconsideration, the board granted the application. The church obtained judicial review in circuit court, which reversed the zoning board. The zoning board then noted an appeal of the circuit court's decision. The church argued that the zoning board had no standing to appeal to the appellate court because the zoning board was not aggrieved by the circuit court's decision. The Court of Appeals in *McKinney* agreed with the church, and held that the zoning board did not have standing. In its decision, the court emphasized that the zoning board's principal duties were to hear and decide appeals from the decisions of the building engineer, and to grant special exceptions and variances. The zoning board only had quasi-judicial powers; it had no policy-making functions or executive duties.

*McKinney* was followed for over forty-five years in many cases, all of which denied standing to the agency.[29] In *Consumer Protection Division v. Consumer Publishing Co.*,[30] however, the Consumer Protection Division (CPD) was granted standing to seek judicial review of a circuit court decision reversing a CPD order. *McKinney* was distinguished because, unlike the zoning board, the CPD was not a non-adversarial, quasi-judicial agency. The CPD exercised a broad range of functions closely identified with the execution of public policy. Thereafter, applying the reasoning employed in *Consumer Publishing Co.*, agencies were held to have standing in many cases including *Maryland Department of*

---

24. Maryland Code Annotated, Natural Resources I §§ 1-501–508.

25. Maryland Code Annotated, Health-General II § 19-227(c).

26. Maryland Code Annotated, Public Utilities Companies § 3-202(a); *see* Mid-Atlantic Power Supply Assoc. v. Public Service Comm'n, 361 Md. 196, 760 A.2d 1087 (2000) (granting standing to an association under the "plain language" of the statute).

27. A statute could also impose a more restrictive test on standing. *See* Sugarloaf v. Department of Environment, 344 Md. 271, 686 A.2d 605 (1996).

28. 174 Md. 551, 199 A. 540 (1938).

29. *See* Maryland Board of Pharmacy v. Peco, Inc., 234 Md. 200, 198 A.2d 273 (1964); Real Estate Comm'n v. Tyler, 268 Md. 641, 303 A.2d 778 (1973).

30. 304 Md. 731, 501 A.2d 48 (1985).

*Human Resources v. Bo Peep Day Nursery*[31] and *Maryland Racing Commission v. Castrenze.*[32] Eventually in *Calvert County Planning Commission v. Howlin Realty Management, Inc.*,[33] the Court of Appeals wrote:

> Although the fundamental precept of *McKinney* has never been expressly overruled, the point of the recent case law is that, when the agency's decision does or can have significance in terms of the agency's broader responsibilities, the confining limitations of *McKinney* are not applicable. In such a case, the agency must be free to intervene in judicial review actions and contest in the appellate courts judgments that may hamper it from effectively implementing the policies ordained by the Legislature.[34]

Today, it is hard to imagine a situation where the agency decision will not have "significance in terms of the agency's broader responsibilities," and therefore, it is highly unlikely that an agency would be denied standing to seek judicial review of a circuit court decision reversing the agency order.

Since 1993, agencies covered by the APA are expressly granted the right to seek judicial review in the Court of Special Appeals, and in circuit courts when a decision is made at OAH adverse to the agency.[35] The 1993 revision relating to the Court of Special Appeals is a flat out rejection of *McKinney*. The revision relating to judicial review in circuit court was based not only on rejection of *McKinney*, but also by the establishment of OAH and OAH's power in certain situations to make the final, judicially reviewable, decision for the agency. For example, the Motor Vehicle Administration (MVA) has delegated to OAH the power to make the final decision in license suspension cases involving drunk driving. Because of this delegation of authority, the OAH decision is the MVA decision. But a situation may occur where the MVA disagrees with the OAH decision. If the OAH had been delegated only the authority to make a proposed decision, MVA could of course reverse the OAH decision, but when OAH has been delegated the final decision making authority, the next step is review in circuit court. With this recognition, the APA since 1993 provides that an "agency, including an agency that has delegated a contested case to [OAH], is entitled to judicial review of a decision ... if the agency was a party before the agency or [OAH].[36]

## § 14.6. Sua Sponte Rulings on Standing

A final issue involving standing is whether the Court of Special Appeals or Court of Appeals can consider the issue of lack of standing when the standing issue was not raised

---

31. 317 Md. 573, 565 A.2d 1015 (1989), *cert. denied sub nom.* Cassilly v. Md. Dep't of Human Resources, 494 U.S. 1067 (1990).

32. 335 Md. 284, 643 A.2d 412 (1994).

33. 364 Md. 301, 772 A.2d 1209 (2001).

34. 364 Md. 301, 319, 772 A.2d 1209, 1219 (2001). *See also* Montgomery County v. Post, 166 Md. App. 381, 888 A.2d 1224 (2005); Hikmat v. Howard County, 148 Md. App. 502, 813 A.2d 306 (2002).

35. Maryland Code Annotated, State Government § 10-223(b)(2).

36. Maryland Code Annotated, State Government § 10-222(a)(2); *see* Motor Vehicle Admin. v. Lytle, 374 Md. 37, 821 A.2d 62 (2003) (MVA has standing to obtain judicial review of its own decision made by OAH pursuant to delegation of final authority from MVA to OAH if MVA is aggrieved by the decision and was party at the OAH hearing); Gwin v. Motor Vehicle Admin., 385 Md. 440, 869 A.2d 822 (2005).

at the circuit court or raised by the parties at the appellate court. The answer is that standing is an issue that an appellate court can address on its own motion, and can be raised even if not presented below. This is true because if the petitioner lacks standing, there may be no interested parties asserting adverse claims, and thus no justiciable controversy.[37]

## § 14.7. Finality

As a general rule, there is judicial review only of final agency decisions.[38] The purpose of this finality requirement is to avoid "piecemeal actions" that create unnecessary litigation. The action of an administrative agency is final if it determines or concludes the rights of the parties, or if it denies the parties means of further prosecuting or defending their rights and interests in the subject matter in proceedings before the agency, thus leaving nothing further for the agency to do.[39] There are several Maryland cases worth noting on finality.

In *Kim v. Comptroller of the Treasury*,[40] at the end of the hearing, the tax court judge orally ruled on the issue being litigated. The tax court judge directed the Assistant Attorney General who had represented the Comptroller to prepare for the judge's signature a written order based on the oral ruling. When the taxpayer filed for judicial review before the written order was signed, the issue of finality arose. The Court of Appeals ruled the oral ruling was not a final order because "more remained for the Tax Court to do, such as filing a written order and mailing it to the parties."[41]

In *Driggs Corp. v. Maryland Aviation Administration*,[42] the Court of Appeals held that when the issues of liability and damages had been bifurcated, there could be no judicial review of the liability issue until the damage phase of the case also had been decided. An administrative order that determines liability, but does not decide damages, is not final for purposes of judicial review. *Lee-Bloem v. Maryland*[43] involved a challenge by a psychiatrist to the peer review process of the Board of Physicians in its investigation of whether the psychiatrist had provided substandard medical care to a patient diagnosed with schizophrenia. Because the peer review panel's role is only to determine whether there is a sufficient basis for the filing of charges, judicial review of the Board of Physician's decision to investigate and conduct peer reviews was not a final decision, and thus not subject to judicial review. Additionally, the Court of Appeals held in *Maryland-National Capital Park and Planning Commission v. Anderson*[44] that a decision under the Law Enforcement Officer's Bill of Rights that a law enforcement officer was "not guilty" was a final decision because "if the board finds the officer innocent of the charge, that ends the proceeding."[45]

37. County Council of Prince George's County v. Offen, 334 Md. 499, 639 A.2d 1070 (1994).
38. Maryland Code Annotated, State Government § 10-222(a)(1).
39. Arroyo v. Bd. of Educ. of Howard County, 381 Md. 646, 851 A.2d 576 (2004); Holiday Spas v. Montgomery County Human Relations Commission, 315 Md. 390, 554 A.2d 1197 (1989); Dorsey v. Bethel A.M.E. Church, 375 Md. 59, 70, 825 A.2d 388, 394 (2003); Danaher v. Dep't of Labor, Licensing & Regulation, 148 Md. App. 139, 161, 811 A.2d 359, 372 (2002).
40. 350 Md. 527, 714 A.2d 176 (1998).
41. 350 Md. 527, 534, 714 A.2d 176, 179 (1998).
42. 348 Md. 389, 704 A.2d 433 (1998).
43. 183 Md. App. 376, 961 A.2d 647 (2008).
44. 395 Md. 172, 909 A.2d 694 (2006).
45. 395 Md. 172, 188, 909 A.2d 694, 703 (2006).

*Willis v. Montgomery County*[46] held that the refusal of the Workers' Compensation Commission to refer a case to the Maryland Insurance Fraud Division was not judicially reviewable because it was not a final order. The court relied not only on the principle that "to be final, the order or decision must dispose of the case by deciding all questions of law and fact and leave nothing further for the administrative body to decide," but also a special statute and several Workers' Compensation cases.

A leading federal case on finality worth noting is *Federal Trade Commission v. Standard Oil Co.*[47] The Federal Trade Commission is authorized by statute to issue an administrative complaint if the agency "has reason to believe" that a violation of the Federal Trade Commission Act has occurred. Standard Oil challenged an FTC complaint against it based on the argument that the FTC had no reason to believe that Standard Oil had violated any law. Standard Oil's argument was that the FTC had filed its complaint based on political pressure from a United States Senator. The Supreme Court held an agency's issuance of a complaint is not a final decision and therefore not judicially reviewable. The Supreme Court left open the possibility that judicial review of the validity of the complaint would be appropriate after the agency had made a final decision on the merits.

## § 14.8. Review of Interlocutory Orders

An exception to the finality rule is that under some circumstances, there can be judicial review of an interlocutory order. The APA provides that:

> Where the presiding officer has final decision-making authority, a person in a contested case who is aggrieved by an interlocutory order is entitled to judicial review if: (1) the party would qualify ... for judicial review of any related final decision, (2) the interlocutory order: (i) determines rights and liabilities; and (ii) has immediate legal consequences; and (3) postponement of judicial review would result in irreparable harm.[48]

This APA provision was involved in *Tamara A. v. Montgomery County Department of Health and Human Services*[49] which involved a hearing at OAH to determine whether Tamara should be placed on a central registry of persons found to have abused or neglected a child. Prior to the administrative process seeking to place Tamara's name on the central registry, there had been circuit court proceedings where Tamara's children had been found to be children in need of assistance (CINA). Shortly before the scheduled hearing at OAH, the Department of Health and Human Services (DHHS) filed a motion with OAH seeking dismissal of the OAH hearing based on collateral estoppel. The OAH ALJ after reviewing the record of the CINA cases, denied DHHS's motion, ruling that collateral estoppel did not apply. Rather than participate at the OAH hearing, DHHS filed a petition for immediate judicial review in circuit court. The sole issue presented to the Court of Appeals was whether the denial of DHHS's motion to dismiss based on collateral estoppel was subject to immediate judicial review under the APA, State Government § 10-222(b).

The Court of Appeals first noted that even though Tamara had conceded at the circuit court that DHHS had the right to immediate judicial review of its motion to dismiss, this

46. 415 Md. 523, 3 A.3d 448 (2010).
47. 355 U.S. 396 (1958).
48. Maryland Code Annotated, State Government § 10-222(b).
49. 407 Md. 180, 963 A.2d 773 (2009).

was not dispositive of the issue. Parties cannot waive the finality requirement or agree to have the court review an interlocutory order. The court then applied the APA requirements for judicial review of an interlocutory order. The court first held that the OAH ALJ who denied the DHHS motion to dismiss had final decision-making authority, and that DHHS, if aggrieved, would qualify for judicial review of any final decision, thus satisfying the first two requirements of the statute. The court next held, however, that the third requirement for immediate judicial review was not satisfied. The ALJ's ruling

> did not determine any rights or liabilities of the parties, but merely kept alive the statutory right that Tamara had to have DHHS's determination of indicated child neglect reviewed by an ALJ; nor did it have any immediate legal consequences. The parties remained in the same legal position and status they occupied when DHHS made its finding and Tamara noted her appeal.... Moreover, we fail to see how postponement of judicial review would cause any irreparable harm to DHHS. Indeed, although the correctness of the ALJ's decision is not presently before us, the statutory construct itself suggests that an appeal of a finding of indicated child abuse or neglect is not necessarily precluded by a CINA determination.[50]

In a footnote, the court remarked that "to the extent that delay" in having Tamara placed on the registry was a "concern" to DHHS, if DHHS had not sought immediate judicial review of the interlocutory order and had participated in the hearing at OAH, the case would have been resolved years earlier.[51]

Although *Tamara A.* involved the Maryland APA provision on judicial review of interlocutory appeals, the same law applies to agencies not covered by the APA. When State Government § 10-222(b) was added to the APA in 1993, the Drafter's Note stated that the new section was intended to codify *Holiday Spas v. Montgomery County Human Relations Commission.*[52] *Holiday Spas* involved an agency not covered by the APA because it operated in only one county. The county commission had found that Holiday Spas had engaged in unlawful gender discrimination. The agency ordered Holiday Spas to alter its operations within ten days. The agency, however, reserved for later determination any damage award. Holiday Spa sought judicial review of the agency order. Even though the agency decision was not a final decision because the damage issue awaited further agency action, the court agreed to review the initial ruling in order to "protect from the irreparable injury threatened in the exceptional case by administrative rulings which attach legal consequences to action taken in advance of other hearings and adjudications that may follow."[53]

## § 14.9. Exhaustion

An important doctrine regarding the availability of judicial review is the exhaustion doctrine. The basic exhaustion doctrine is that a court will not grant review of an agency action unless the party seeking judicial review has gone through, i.e., exhausted, the available agency process and procedures. Exhaustion can be applied to an entire case, thus denying any judicial review, or exhaustion can be applied to only some issues in the case.

50. 407 Md. 180, 194, 963 A.2d 773, 781 (2009).
51. 407 Md. 180, 195 n.9, 963 A.2d 773, 781 n.9 (2009).
52. 315 Md. 390, 554 A.2d 1197 (1989).
53. 315 Md. 390, 398, 554 A.2d 1197, 1201 (1989).

In the latter situation, the court will review the agency action, but will not consider those issues that the party failed to exhaust at the agency. If an issue was raised by one party at the agency, that issue can be raised by a co-party upon judicial review.[54]

In arguing to a court whether the exhaustion doctrine should be applied, it is important to understand the policy reasons upon which exhaustion is based.[55] The policy reasons for requiring exhaustion are:

1. *Expertise.* Agencies possess expertise in the subject area beyond that of the courts. Agencies should be allowed to apply their expertise prior to judicial involvement.
2. *Agency integrity/legislative choice.* The legislature made the decision to delegate to an administrative agency the power to regulate certain matters. The agency should be given the opportunity to handle these matters. By requiring exhaustion of the administrative process before permitting judicial intervention, the legislature's decision to create the agency and delegate powers to it is respected. Moreover, the integrity of the agency is respected by not allowing a party to ignore the process provided by the agency.
3. *Judicial economy.* Legislatures create administrative agencies in part to relieve the workload of the courts. Judicial economy is furthered by the exhaustion doctrine in a few ways. First, if the party is required to pursue the administrative process, it may be successful at the agency, and the matter will never get to the courts. Second, even if the party is not completely successful at the agency, it may be partially successful at the agency, and thus the court will be required to review only some of the original issues. Third, even if the party is not successful at the agency, the matter may be less burdensome for the court when it reviews the case because issues may have been narrowed, facts stipulated, and a factual record created.

The exhaustion argument can be raised by a court *sua sponte* even when not raised by any party.[56] Exhaustion can also be raised by a party for the first time to the Court of Special Appeals or Court of Appeals even when the issue had not been raised to the lower court.[57] The desire to skip the administrative process to get "right into" court is rarely a successful strategy. The following sections will discuss several illustrative cases that have attempted to obtain judicial review without exhausting the administrative process.

## § 14.10. The No Agency Jurisdiction Claim

Even when it is argued that the agency has no jurisdiction over the dispute or over the person involved, exhaustion is generally required. The leading case is *Maryland Commission*

---

54. Carriage Hill-Cabin John, Inc. v. Md. Health Res. Planning Comm'n, 125 Md. App. 183, 724 A.2d 745 (1999); Meadowridge Indus. Ctr. Ltd. P'ship v. Howard County, 109 Md. App. 410, 675 A.2d 138 (1996).

55. *See* Soley v. State Comm'n on Human Relations, 277 Md. 521, 356 A.2d 254 (1976); Heery Int'l, Inc. v. Montgomery County, 384 Md. 129, 862 A.2d 976 (2004).

56. Moose v. Fraternal Order of Police, Montgomery County Lodge #35, Inc., 369 Md. 476, 800 A.2d 790 (2002); Brown v. Fire & Police Employees' Retirement System, 375 Md. 661, 826 A.2d 525 (2003).

57. *See* Furnitureland South, Inc. v. Comptroller of the Treasury, 364 Md. 126, 771 A.2d 1061 (2001).

*on Human Relations v. Mass Transit Administration*.[58] In this case, three women who had unsuccessfully applied to the Mass Transit Administration (MTA) to be hired as bus drivers filed complaints with the Commission on Human Relations (CHR) alleging they had been unlawfully discriminated against because of their weight. After an investigation, CHR concluded that there was probable cause to believe that MTA had engaged in unlawful employment discrimination based on physical handicap. CHR then set the matter for adjudication before a hearing examiner.[59] Rather than defend itself at the agency adjudication, MTA filed a request for declaratory relief in circuit court seeking a judicial declaration that obesity was not a physical handicap within the meaning of Maryland's employment discrimination statute. MTA argued that because obesity was not a physical handicap under the statute, CHR had no jurisdiction over the matter. CHR responded that MTA's judicial request should be dismissed because MTA had failed to exhaust CHR's administrative process.

The Court of Appeals held that a party's argument that an agency will be exceeding its jurisdiction or authority if the agency ultimately interprets a statute in a certain way does not excuse the failure to exhaust the administrative process. The "agency does not have jurisdiction" argument must be presented to the agency first. If the agency decides against the party on the jurisdiction argument, the party must continue with the agency adjudication on the merits before the court will review the "no jurisdiction" argument. The rationale for this exhaustion requirement is that the party challenging the agency's jurisdiction may be successful on the merits at the agency, and thus the court will never become involved with the case.[60]

There is an extremely narrow exception to the rule that the "no jurisdiction" of the agency argument must be exhausted. If it can be established that the agency acted "palpably without jurisdiction," the no jurisdiction argument will be reviewed by a court without requiring exhaustion at the agency level. This exception was exhaustively discussed in *Heery International, Inc. v. Montgomery County*[61] where the court recognized that although this exception had been discussed in several cases,[62] no case had ever concluded that an administrative agency had actually acted "palpably without jurisdiction." In *Heery*, the court stated that this exception only applies if the "underlying fundamental subject matter jurisdiction" of the agency was challenged, and the agency "lacks a clear authority to adjudicate a given class of claims."[63] In *Heery*, the court rejected the argument that the county agency was palpably without jurisdiction to utilize a certain dispute resolution process to litigate a claim against a party with whom it contracted. The contractor therefore was required to participate in the administrative process before obtaining any judicial determination of this dispute.

58. 294 Md. 225, 449 A.2d 385 (1982).

59. This case was before the OAH was created.

60. *See also* State Comm'n on Human Relations v. Freedom Express/Domegold, Inc., 375 Md. 2, 825 A.2d 354 (2003).

61. 384 Md. 129, 862 A.2d 976 (2004).

62. *See* Md. Comm'n on Human Relations v. Mass Transit Admin., 294 Md. 225, 440 A.2d 385 (1982); Maryland v. Md. State Bd. of Contract Appeals, 364 Md. 446, 773 A.2d 504 (2001); State Comm'n on Human Relations v. Freedom Express/Domegold, Inc., 375 Md. 2, 825 A.2d 354 (2003).

63. 384 Md. 129, 143–44, 862 A.2d 976, 985 (2004).

## § 14.11. Statutory Interpretation

A court will also not consider a statutory interpretation argument unless that statutory interpretation argument was presented to the agency. For example, in *Moose v. Fraternal Order of Police, Montgomery County Lodge #35, Inc.*,[64] the Court of Appeals dismissed a declaratory judgment action seeking an interpretation of the Law Enforcement Officers' Bill of Rights (LEOBR) because the police officer had failed to present the statutory interpretation argument to the agency. The court wrote that "normally a party cannot obtain a statutory interpretation involving the application of a statute by the appropriate administrative agency until all administrative remedies have been exhausted."[65] Similarly in *Brodie v. Motor Vehicle Administration*,[66] the court was asked to decide whether the MVA under a statute in the Transportation Article could revoke a driver's license when that license had already been revoked. The court refused to answer this question because it had not been presented at the administrative hearing and had not been addressed by the agency in its decision.[67]

## § 14.12. Constitutional Challenges

The exhaustion of administrative remedies doctrine will even preclude a court from reviewing a constitutional challenge if the petitioner has not exhausted the available administrative remedies. For example, as discussed in Chapter 16, due process requires an unbiased decisionmaker. The argument that the agency is unconstitutionally biased will not be considered by a court unless that issue was presented to the agency. Two cases illustrate this. In *Maryland State Board of Dental Examiners v. Fisher*,[68] on judicial review of the board's order disciplining a dentist, it was alleged that because one board member had a dental office in the same geographic area and in the same dental specialty as Dr. Fisher, Fisher's due process right to an unbiased board was violated. The reviewing court refused to consider this constitutional claim because it had not been adequately presented to the agency.

In *Public Service Commission v. Wilson*,[69] a former employee of the commission challenged her termination of employment. One argument that the employee sought to present to the court was that the chairman who fired her was "unconstitutionally biased against her" because she was a Democrat and the chairman was a Republican. This bias argument had not been presented at the agency. The court held that it would "not reach or decide" the bias claim because it was "premised on the particular facts" and was an "unconstitutional as applied" argument.[70]

64. 369 Md. 476, 800 A.2d 790 (2002).
65. 369 Md. 476, 494–95, 800 A.2d 790, 802 (2002).
66. 367 Md. 1, 785 A.2d 747 (2001).
67. *See also* Schwartz v. Md. Dep't of Natural Res., 385 Md. 534, 870 A.2d 168 (2005).
68. 123 Md. App. 322, 718 A.2d 627, *cert. denied*, 352 Md. 335, 722 A.2d 63 (1998).
69. 389 Md. 27, 882 A.2d 849 (2005).
70. 389 Md. 27, 91–93, 882 A.2d 849, 887–88 (2005).

The *Wilson* court's explanation for its application of the exhaustion doctrine in that case suggests that an unconstitutional on its face argument may not need to be exhausted. Similar language is found in *Insurance Commissioner v. Equitable Life Assurance Society.*[71] This case concerned whether Maryland statutes that authorized differentials in certain insurance rates violated the Equal Rights Amendment to the Maryland Declaration of Rights. The Court of Appeals in *Equitable Life* emphasized that constitutional issues must be exhausted unless the attack is to the constitutionality of the statute as a whole and there is no need to consider evidence and render findings of fact. Because in *Equitable Life,* an evidentiary hearing and findings of fact were required, the constitutional attack first had to be presented to the Insurance Commissioner.

Other constitutional challenges have also been rejected because of failure of the petitioner to exhaust administrative remedies. *Laurel Racing Association, Inc. v. Video Lottery Facility Location Commission*[72] involved the unsuccessful bidder for a license to operate a slot machine parlor at Laurel Race Track. The major dispute arose over whether the initial license fee was refundable to an unsuccessful bidder. Laurel Racing Association argued that because the licensee fee (which in Laurel's case amounted to $28.5 million) was not refundable under the relevant licensing statute, the statute was an unconstitutional taking of Laurel's property in violation of Article III, § 40 of the Maryland Constitution as well as a violation of due process. The Court of Appeals refused to consider these constitutional challenges because Laurel had not exhausted the administrative remedy before the Board of Contract Appeals.

*Prince George's County v. Ray's Used Cars*[73] involved a challenge to the constitutionality of a zoning ordinance that established a 25,000 square feet minimum lot size for used car lots. The Court of Appeals held that because the used car dealers who were impacted by the ordinance had not instituted any administrative proceedings seeking variances or other administrative remedies that could remedy their complaint, the court would not reach the constitutional issues presented. The court emphasized that the administrative remedies that could be pursued and which were still available were "fully adequate." The court also wrote in the opinion, as it does in just about every other case involving exhaustion and constitutional issues, that "Maryland administrative agencies are fully competent to resolve issues of constitutionality and the validity of statues or ordinances in adjudicatory administrative proceedings which are subject to judicial review."[74]

## § 14.13. Inadequate or Unauthorized Procedures

An argument that has had some success in overcoming the exhaustion requirement is that the agency's procedures are either inadequate or unauthorized, and therefore the court should decide the issue presented without requiring the petitioner to go through the flawed administrative process.[75] An example of the unauthorized procedure exception is *Coroneos v. Montgomery County*[76] where the agency required a party who wanted to pursue an appeal from a decision of the Animal Services Division (ASD) of the Montgomery

71. 339 Md. 596, 664 A.2d 862 (1995).
72. 409 Md. 445, 975 A.2d 894 (2009).
73. 398 Md. 632, 922 A.2d 495 (2007).
74. 398 Md. 632, 650–51, 922 A.2d 495, 506 (2007).
75. *See* Magan v. Med. Mut. Liab. Insurance Society of Md., 81 Md. App. 301, 567 A.2d 503 (1989).
76. 161 Md. App. 411, 869 A.2d 410 (2005).

County Police Department to the Montgomery County Animal Matters Hearing Board to either make prepayment of $45,390 per month for the impoundment costs of animals, post a bond, or make arrangements for the care of the animals. Rather than complying with any of these three conditions, the animal owner filed a complaint in circuit court for relief. In response to the argument that the circuit court should dismiss the complaint because of the owner's failure to exhaust the administrative remedies by his failure to appeal the ASD's decision to the Hearing Board, the Court of Special Appeals held that because the agency had no authority to require any of the requirements it had imposed on the animal owner's appeal to the Hearing Board, the exhaustion doctrine did not require dismissal. The court noted that "appellants attempted to pursue their administrative remedy, and resorted to the circuit court only after the agency did not take any action and treated their case as if they had no administrative remedy available."[77]

Similarly, in *Abington Center Associates Limited Partnership v. Baltimore County*,[78] exhaustion was not required at the Tax Court in a tax dispute involving a taxpayer who failed to pay taxes the State claimed were owed. Because the Tax Court only had authority over taxpayer disputes involving refunds, the dispute could be heard in the circuit court without requiring the taxpayer to go through the administrative process.[79] Although the court did not use the phrase "palpably without jurisdiction" in its opinion, *Abington Center* may also be seen as falling within that exception to exhaustion.

## § 14.14. Inadequate Remedy

Exhaustion may also not be required if the agency is unable to provide an adequate remedy. The rationale for the inadequate remedy exception is that the case will most likely require judicial involvement to obtain the proper remedy, and therefore one of the main goals of the exhaustion doctrine—judicial economy—would not be served by requiring exhaustion. There are arguments, however, that exhaustion should still be required even if the agency cannot grant the relief or remedy requested. These counterarguments are also based on the policies that form the foundation of the exhaustion doctrine. Perhaps the agency should be allowed to decide those matters within its expertise even if the agency cannot fully resolve the dispute. Moreover, even if the agency cannot fully resolve the dispute, agency evaluation of the case may reduce the judicial resources that will eventually be required. This would be especially true if fact finding is involved. These considerations indicate that the principle that exhaustion is not required if the agency cannot provide an adequate remedy should not be applied automatically. Consideration on a case-by-case basis is appropriate.

The inadequate remedy exception has arisen in several inmate grievance cases. *McCullough v. Wittner*[80] involved a lawsuit filed in circuit court by a prison inmate seeking monetary damages for personal injuries suffered when he was beaten by a prison guard. The circuit court granted the defendant's motion to dismiss the lawsuit because the inmate,

77. 161 Md. App. 411, 429, 869 A.2d 410, 420 (2005).

78. 115 Md. App. 580, 694 A.2d 165 (1997).

79. *See also* Chestnut Real Estate Partnership v. Huber, 148 Md. App. 190, 811 A.2d 389 (2002) (when remedy of mandatory injunction is not within power of agency, exhaustion not required); Heery Int'l, Inc. v. Montgomery County, 384 Md. 129, 862 A.2d 976 (2004) (no demonstration that administrative process failed to provide an adequate remedy).

80. 314 Md. 602, 552 A.2d 881 (1989).

McCullough, had not filed a grievance with the Inmate Grievance Commission, and thus had failed to exhaust the administrative remedies. In the Court of Appeals, McCullough argued that the Inmate Grievance Commission had no power to award money damages, and thus exhaustion of his claim at the agency level was not necessary. The Court of Appeals rejected McCullough's argument. It held that even assuming that the Commission did lack authority to make a monetary award, McCullough was required to exhaust the Inmate Grievance Commission process before pursuing his tort action in court. An agency's lack of power to grant the particular type of relief should not "necessarily mean" that exhaustion is not required "if the case involves a question within the agency's special competence."[81] The court also noted that the statute regarding the Inmate Grievance Commission contained an express exhaustion requirement.[82] Another reason that supports the holding that exhaustion was required in *McCullough* is that there were factual issues in dispute. Whenever there are many factual issues involved, there should be a preference for having the agency resolve them.

*McCullough* must be compared to two other inmate grievance cases that did not require exhaustion. In *Maryland House of Corrections v. Fields*,[83] an inmate sought release from jail by filing a petition for a writ of habeas corpus claiming that he had already served more time in jail than required. Although the Inmate Grievance Commission did have expertise in this area, and factual issues were involved, exhaustion was not required. The Court based its decision on Field's constitutional right to petition for habeas corpus as trumping the exhaustion requirement.

Exhaustion was also not required in *Adamson v. Correctional Medical Service, Inc.*[84] In *Adamson*, a prisoner sued in circuit court for money damages for breach of contract and negligence against a private medical provider who had a contract with the State of Maryland to provide medical services in prison. Because the case was against a private contractor, not the State, exhaustion with the Inmate Grievance Commission was not required.

## § 14.15. The Constitutional Exception

Maryland cases also recognize an exception to the exhaustion requirement referred to as the "constitutional exception." All cases agree that this is a "very narrow" exception that is applied in very limited situations.

The first step in the constitutional exception analysis is that the attack must be made to the constitutionality of a statute as a whole.[85] Next, the constitutional exception does not apply where there "exists no recognized statutory, common law, or equitable alternative to the statutorily prescribed administrative and judicial review remedies. In other words, where the only recognized avenue for relief is the administrative and judicial review proceedings," exhaustion is required even when a statute is being challenged on its face.[86] Third, the constitutional exception does not apply if the constitutional challenge to the statute involves the need for fact finding.[87] The constitutional exception also does not

81. 314 Md. 602, 608, 552 A.2d 881, 884 (1989).
82. 314 Md. 602, 608–09, 552 A.2d 881, 884 (1989).
83. 348 Md. 245, 703 A.2d 167 (1997).
84. 359 Md. 238, 753 A.2d 501 (2000).
85. Goldstein v. Time-Out Family Amusement Centers, Inc., 301 Md. 583, 483 A.2d 1276 (1984).
86. Montgomery County v. Broadcast Equities, Inc., 360 Md. 438, 456, 758 A.2d 995, 1005 (2000).
87. Montgomery County v. Broadcast Equities, Inc., 360 Md. 438, 456, 758 A.2d 995, 1005 (2000).

apply where the agency might afford the plaintiff relief on non-constitutional grounds, thus making unnecessary a ruling on the constitutional issue.[88] Additionally, the constitutional exception will not be applied if a "judicial determination on the facial validity of an enactment is not likely to terminate the controversy."[89]

The constitutional exception was deemed applicable, and thus the court reviewed petitioner's case even though the administrative process had been ignored, in *Ehrlich v. Perez*.[90] Petitioners were non-citizen, lawful permanent residents, who received a notice from the Department of Health and Mental Hygiene (DHMH) that certain medical benefits they had been receiving would be ending because of a decision of the Governor to eliminate funding for these programs from the upcoming budget. The notice from DHMH informed the petitioners that they had the right to appeal the termination of their benefits to the Office of Administrative Hearings (OAH). Instead of filing with OAH, petitioners filed a complaint in circuit court alleging that the budget decision was unconstitutional in violation of the Maryland Declaration of Rights. The merits of petitioners' challenge were decided by the Court of Appeals which wrote:

> We could find nothing else in the record transmitted in the present litigation to suggest ... an administrative appeal was pursued by any of the Appellees named in the original complaint. Even if an opportunity for an administrative remedy existed, judicial consideration of the present action would not be barred by the doctrine of exhaustion of administrative remedies because the "constitutional exception" to the general rule applies in the present case.... This "constitutional exception" permits an aggrieved litigant to proceed immediately to court to seek a declaratory judgment or equitable remedy, regardless of the existence of an available administrative appeal, where the sole contention raised in the court action is based on a facial attack on the constitutionality of the government action.[91]

The constitutional exception was also accepted, and exhaustion not required, in *Harbor Island Marina v. Board of County Commissioners*,[92] which involved the argument that Calvert County did not have the power under state law to enact a particular zoning ordinance. This facial challenge to the statute as a whole involved no factual issues. Moreover, a resolution favorable to petitioner would terminate the matter and not require any administrative proceedings.

On the other hand, *Prince George's County v. Ray's Used Cars*[93] refused to apply the constitutional exception to the claim that a zoning ordinance which established a 25,000 square feet minimum lot size for used car dealers was unconstitutional in violation of due process and equal protection. The court held that the challenge was not to the zoning ordinance "as a whole," there were factual issues that needed to be determined, and there were non-constitutional grounds that could remedy plaintiff's complaint. Also, in *Montgomery County v. Broadcast Equities, Inc.*,[94] the court refused to apply the constitutional exception because even if the court did rule on the facial attack on the statute, other non-constitutional issues remained which meant administrative proceedings were still necessary.

88. Montgomery County v. Broadcast Equities, Inc., 360 Md. 438, 456, 758 A.2d 995, 1005 (2000).
89. *See* Prince George's County v. Ray's Used Cars, 398 Md. 632, 922 A.2d 495 (2007).
90. 394 Md. 691, 908 A.2d 1220 (2006).
91. 394 Md. 691, 705 n.6, 908 A.2d 1220, 1228 n.6 (2006).
92. 286 Md. 303, 407 A.2d 738 (1979).
93. 398 Md. 632, 922 A.2d 495 (2007).
94. 360 Md. 438, 758 A.2d 995 (2000).

All issues, including the constitutional challenge needed to be presented to the agency before a court would hear any part of the case. Application of the constitutional exception was also rejected in *Goldstein v. Time-Out Family Amusement Centers, Inc.*[95] because the challenge involved how the statute had been applied against petitioner.

## § 14.16. Integral Component Exception

Another situation where a court will address an issue that was not exhausted at the agency level is when resolution of the issue not raised is an integral, and thus unavoidable, component of the court's determination of an issue that was raised at the agency. In *Motor Vehicle Administration v. Weller*,[96] the agency argued that Weller's failure to object to the introduction of results of a preliminary breath test (PBT) at the OAH hearing precluded him from raising this issue on judicial review. Because the issue of whether the suspension of Weller's driver's license was supported by substantial evidence was properly before the court, the admissibility of the PBT result was "a necessary component integral" to the substantial evidence issue, and thus was addressed by the court.

## § 14.17. Exhaustion Doctrine Applied Against the State

The exhaustion doctrine is also applied against state agencies. For example, in *Furnitureland South, Inc. v. Comptroller of the Treasury*,[97] the Comptroller brought an action in circuit court against a North Carolina furniture retailer seeking a declaratory judgment that the retailer was required to collect Maryland sales tax on furniture sales in Maryland because the North Carolina furniture retailer was a "vendor" under Maryland tax law, and thus was responsible for collecting Maryland sales tax. Among the defenses raised by the retailer was that the Commerce Clause of the U.S. Constitution[98] prohibited the application of the Maryland sales tax statutes to it because the retailer did not have a sufficient nexus with Maryland. The Court of Appeals held that the declaratory judgment action filed by the Comptroller must be dismissed because the Comptroller had failed to exhaust the administrative remedies which were available to determine the retailer's tax obligations. The Court reiterated its oft stated position that "under Maryland law, administrative agencies are fully competent to resolve issues of constitutionality and the validity of statutes or ordinances in adjudicatory administrative proceedings which are subject to judicial review.... The presence of constitutional issues does not authorize a party to circumvent the statutorily prescribed administrative remedies."[99]

Exhaustion was applied against the Office of the Attorney General in *Maryland v. Maryland Board of Contract Appeals and Law Offices of Peter G. Angelos.*[100] This case involved

95. 301 Md. 583, 483 A.2d 1276 (1984).
96. 390 Md. 115, 887 A.2d 1042 (2005).
97. 364 Md. 126, 771 A.2d 1061 (2001).
98. U.S. Const., art. 1, § 8, cl. 3.
99. 364 Md. 126, 138, 771 A.2d 1061, 1068 (2001).
100. 364 Md. 446, 773 A.2d 504 (2001).

a contract between the Office of the Attorney General and a private law firm which authorized the law firm to represent the State in litigation against the tobacco industry. When the tobacco companies unexpectedly settled in a relatively short period of time, a dispute over the fee owed to the law firm resulted. After the Attorney General rendered a decision as to how much the law firm would be paid for its legal services, the law firm filed an appeal with the State Board of Contract Appeals. The Attorney General's response on behalf of the State was to file in circuit court an action for a declaratory judgment that the Board had no jurisdiction over the fee dispute. When the case reached the Court of Appeals, the court refused to resolve the dispute or issue a declaratory ruling. Since the Board of Contract Appeals was clearly not "palpably without jurisdiction," the dispute needed to be exhausted at the agency before the court would review the fee dispute.

## § 14.18. Federal Case Law

For the most part, Maryland courts rely on the leading exhaustion cases from the U.S. Supreme Court. For example, *McKart v. United States*,[101] *McGee v. United States*,[102] and *Myers v. Bethlehem Shipbuilding Corp.*[103] have all been cited in Maryland opinions as setting forth the appropriate principles of the exhaustion doctrine. Opinions from lower federal courts would seem useful to research and cite to Maryland courts on the exhaustion doctrine. The exhaustion cases from Maryland and federal courts all point to the conclusion that exhaustion is a discretionary doctrine which the courts apply on a case by case basis depending on the particular facts of each case guided by the policies that form the foundation of the exhaustion doctrine.

## § 14.19. Primary Jurisdiction

The doctrine of primary jurisdiction concerns whether a person can have a court resolve a particular controversy or whether an agency should first be given the opportunity to resolve it.[104] Unfortunately, the doctrine of primary jurisdiction is sometimes confused with exhaustion. Primary jurisdiction, however, is a doctrine separate and apart from exhaustion. Primary jurisdiction, not exhaustion, is the relevant doctrine when (1) it is clear that both a court and an agency have the power, i.e., the jurisdiction, to initially decide the case as a matter of original jurisdiction; (2) a person decides to invoke the court's jurisdiction; and (3) the argument is made that although the court does have the jurisdiction to decide the case, so does the agency, and the agency should be given the right to hear it first. If primary jurisdiction is invoked, the case is not dismissed at the court, but it is stayed pending resolution by the agency.[105]

The primary jurisdiction doctrine seeks to promote several policies which consistently appear in Administrative Law—expertise, judicial economy, and uniformity. Where a

101. 395 U.S. 185 (1969).

102. 402 U.S. 479 (1971).

103. 303 U.S. 41 (1938).

104. *See* United States v. Western Pacific Railroad, 352 U.S. 59 (1956).

105. *See* Maryland v. Md. State Bd. of Contract Appeals, 364 Md. 446, 773 A.2d 504 (2001); Md. Reclamation Assocs. v. Harford County, 382 Md. 348, 855 A.2d 351 (2004).

matter involves greater expertise in the agency than the court, where uniform regulatory decisions are desirable, and where there is a concern that the courts may be burdened with a particular type of case, the primary jurisdiction doctrine provides that the case should be heard at the agency even though the court has the power to hear the case. Primary jurisdiction is a discretionary doctrine that depends on the particular facts of each case and how the policies behind the doctrine would be furthered by its application.

Even if not raised by any party, primary jurisdiction can be applied by a court sua sponte.[106] There are several elaborate Maryland cases discussing primary jurisdiction that are helpful in understanding when it will be applied in Maryland.

*Luskin's Inc. v. Consumer Protection Division*[107] involved whether two advertisements for an electronics store constituted false advertising under Maryland consumer protection law. After the first ad had aired, Luskin's received a letter from the Consumer Protection Division (CPD) that this ad was in violation of the Commercial Law Article. In response to this letter, officials from Luskin's and CPD met to discuss a second ad which had not been aired and which was different from the first ad. CPD officials told Luskin's that the second ad was also in violation of the law. After this meeting, Luskin's filed in circuit court a complaint for declaratory judgment requesting the court to declare that its second ad did not violate the Commercial Law Article. Shortly after Luskin's had filed this declaratory judgment action in court, the CPD filed an administrative complaint against Luskin's charging that the first ad violated Maryland law. The circuit court judge first denied CPD's motion to dismiss Luskin's declaratory judgment action, and then ruled that Luskin's second ad did not violate any law. On the administrative side, the first ad was held to violate the Commercial Law Article. The Luskin's advertising dispute eventually made its way to the Court of Appeals where the court held that the circuit court judge should not have issued a declaratory order on the second ad.

The Court of Appeals in *Luskin's* first provided a useful discussion of the doctrine of primary jurisdiction. Primary jurisdiction is a judicially-created rule that comes into play when a court and agency have concurrent jurisdiction over the same matter, and there is no statutory provision to coordinate the work of the court with that of the agency. Primary jurisdiction is "relevant only ... where the claim is initially cognizable in the courts but raises issues or relates to subject matter falling within the special expertise of an administrative agency."[108] The Court of Appeals then addressed the arguments Luskin's had presented why primary jurisdiction did not apply. First, Luskin's had argued that there were no disputed facts. Whether fact-finding is required is relevant to primary jurisdiction because it relates to judicial economy. If fact-finding is required, it is preferable to invoke primary jurisdiction and have the agency hear the case. The Court of Appeals responded in a few ways to this argument. First, it stated that there was a factual dispute whether the already-aired and the proposed ads were similar and whether they were deceptive. Second, even if facts are undisputed, if different inferences may be drawn from those facts, or where the agency's judgment must be exercised in applying the law to the facts, the case should be heard by the agency. In this case, there was a need for the interpretation of facts and application of the law to these facts. These were better undertaken initially by the agency with special expertise in the area.

The Court of Appeals then discussed § 13-407 of the Commercial Law Article which provides: "If a person is aggrieved by an order or decision of the [CPD], he may institute

106. *See* Towson University v. Conte, 384 Md. 68, 126, 862 A.2d 941, 974 (2004) (dissent).
107. 338 Md. 188, 657 A.2d 788 (1995).
108. 338 Md. 188, 195, 657 A.2d 788, 791 (1995).

any appropriate proceeding he considers necessary." Luskin's argued that this section gave the circuit court exclusive jurisdiction to handle declaratory judgment actions against the CPD, and thus primary jurisdiction was not applicable. The court ruled that the CPD did have jurisdiction over Luskin's advertisements pursuant to various provisions of the Consumer Protection Act, and thus there was concurrent jurisdiction in the CPD and the circuit courts—"precisely the situation for which the primary jurisdiction doctrine was created to coordinate."[109] The court next quickly rejected the argument that primary jurisdiction was not applicable because the CPD was a party at the circuit court proceeding. If this argument were valid, primary jurisdiction would be an almost meaningless doctrine. All a party would need to do to avoid primary jurisdiction would be to sue the agency in court.

The next argument Luskin's presented was that there was no adequate administrative remedy. Adequacy of the administrative remedy is relevant to primary jurisdiction because it relates to the policy of judicial economy. If the administrative remedy is inadequate, the matter will end up in court eventually anyway.[110] In *Luskin's*, the court held that Luskin's had an adequate administrative remedy because of the section of the APA that permits a party to seek a Declaratory Ruling from an agency.[111] The court also noted that the CPD had the power to rule not only on past advertisements, but also on future advertisements; therefore, there was an administrative forum to resolve the proposed advertisement issue. Finally, the Court of Appeals rejected Luskin's argument that because the administrative action was filed after the circuit court case was initiated, primary jurisdiction should not be invoked. The court stated that primary jurisdiction can be invoked even if no administrative action has been filed.

*Zappone v. Liberty Life Insurance Co.*[112] also presented an extensive discussion of primary jurisdiction. Briefly stated, Zappone claimed that he had been the victim of a dishonest life insurance agent. Zappone filed a complaint in circuit court alleging fraud, negligent misrepresentation, and negligence against the agent and the insurance company for which the agent worked. The circuit court dismissed the complaint, holding that the provisions of the Insurance Code constituted the exclusive remedy for claims of unfair or deceptive trade practices by insurers and insurance agents in connection with the sale of insurance. According to the circuit court, Zappone's sole remedy was an administrative one with the Insurance Commissioner.

In discussing the primary jurisdiction issue, the Court of Appeals identified three categories of cases:

1. cases where the administrative remedy is exclusive;
2. cases where the administrative remedy is primary, but not exclusive; and
3. cases where the administrative remedy and the alternative judicial remedy are concurrent.[113]

In the first category of cases, no court case is permitted. In the second category, the moving party must invoke and exhaust the administrative remedy and seek judicial review of the administrative decision before the court can adjudicate the merits of the alternative remedy.

109. 338 Md. 188, 196–97, 657 A.2d 788, 792 (1995).

110. *See* Nader v. Allegheny Airlines. Inc., 426 U.S. 290 (1976).

111. Maryland Code Annotated, State Government § 10-305(c); *see* discussion of Declaratory Rulings in Chapter 25.

112. 349 Md. 45, 706 A.2d 1060 (1998).

113. 349 Md. 45, 60–61, 706 A.2d 1060, 1067–68 (1998).

For cases in this second category, it is appropriate for the trial court for a reasonable period of time to retain jurisdiction over the independent judicial action pending completion of the administrative process. For cases in the third category, the moving party can pursue the judicial remedy without invoking the administrative remedy.

The Court of Appeals then set out principles to determine in which of the three categories a case should be placed. The administrative scheme will be treated as exclusive if the statutory language is clear that it is exclusive[114] or if there exists no other recognized alternative statutory, common law, or equitable cause of action. Where there is a legislatively-created administrative remedy and no recognized statutory, common law, or equitable remedy, the Declaratory Judgment Act itself does not create an alternative remedy.[115] Second, where there is an alternative judicial remedy based upon a statute, the common law, or equitable principles, there is a presumption that the administrative remedy is intended to be primary, and that the alternative judicial action cannot be maintained without first invoking and exhausting the administrative remedy. This presumption can be rebutted based on a consideration of various factors. Among these factors are:

1. The comprehensiveness of the administrative remedy. The more comprehensive the administrative scheme, the more likely the legislature intended it to be primary.
2. The agency's view of its own jurisdiction. An agency's interpretation that its scheme is primary is entitled to weight.
3. Whether the judicial cause of action is wholly or partially dependent upon the statutory scheme which also created the administrative scheme. If it is dependent, the administrative scheme is primary.
4. Whether the judicial cause of action involves the expertise of the agency. If agency expertise is involved, the administrative scheme is primary.[116]

Based on these factors, the court in *Zappone* held that primary jurisdiction should not be invoked. The common law tort actions of fraud, negligent misrepresentation, and negligence could proceed in circuit court without resort to the Insurance Administration. The relevant statutes gave no indication that the Insurance Administration proceedings were exclusive; the common law tort claims were well-recognized causes of action independent of any statutory scheme; no expertise of the Insurance Commissioner was involved; and the Insurance Commissioner had not viewed its administrative remedy as primary.

Several other primary jurisdiction cases are worth discussing. *Bell Atlantic of Maryland, Inc. v. Intercom Systems Corp.*[117] involved a small telephone company which filed a complaint in circuit court alleging that Bell Atlantic had tortiously interfered with one of its contracts, as well as counts for negligence and breach of contract. Compensatory and punitive damages were sought. The Court of Appeals held that the Public Service Commission had primary jurisdiction over the dispute, and therefore the matter first had to be presented to the Public Service Commission.

---

114. *See, e.g.*, Moats v. City of Hagerstown, 324 Md. 519, 597 A.2d 972 (1991) (Law Enforcement Officer's Bill of Rights is exclusive remedy).

115. 349 Md. 45, 63 n.6, 706 A.2d 1060, 1069 n.6 (1998).

116. 349 Md. 45, 64–67, 706 A.2d 1060, 1069–70 (1998).

117. 366 Md. 1, 782 A.2d 791 (2001).

In *Fosler v. Panoramic Design, Ltd.*,[118] a homeowner filed three actions against a home improvement contractor: (1) a declaratory judgment action in circuit court seeking a declaration that services provided to Fosler constituted "home improvement" within the meaning of the Maryland Home Improvement Law; (2) a complaint with the Maryland Home Improvement Commission alleging that Panoramic was performing home improvement work without a license; and (3) a complaint with the Montgomery County Department of Housing and Community Affairs alleging that Panoramic committed a deceptive practice in violation of the County's consumer protection laws. The Court of Appeals, applying *Zappone*, held that the administrative remedies provided by the Home Improvement Law were primary, and therefore, the circuit court erred in ruling on Fosler's declaratory action.

*Converge Services Group, LLC. v. Curran*[119] involved the Consumer Protection Division (CPD) and the issuer of a surety bond product that was marketed as a substitute for residential security deposits. The CPD had been investigating the issuer for violation not only of the Consumer Protection Act (CPA), which the CPD regularly enforces, but also other statutes, including the Security Deposit Law (SDL), about which the CPD did not have any special expertise. Before the CPD filed any administrative charges against the issuer, the issuer filed an action in circuit court seeking a declaration that it had not violated any laws. The Court of Appeals held that the circuit court had properly applied primary jurisdiction when it refused to issue the declaratory judgment. Even though the CPD only had expertise in the CPA and not the SDL, "an administrative determination by the [CPD] as to the charges of alleged violations of the CPA could be helpful to a court in considering the facially related allegations as to violations of the SDL."[120]

A very important point to remember about the primary jurisdiction doctrine is that it does not prohibit the *filing* of the independent judicial action, it merely postpones a judicial decision until after the agency has had the opportunity to rule on that part of the dispute on which the agency has primary jurisdiction. This point was made in *Arroyo v. Board of Education of Howard County*[121] and in *University System of Maryland v. Mooney.*[122] In *Arroyo*, an administrative process before the school board was brought in order to terminate Arroyo as a public school guidance counselor. In response, Arroyo filed a civil complaint in circuit court seeking damages alleging the tort of wrongful discharge. The Court of Appeals wrote that the filing of the tort claim was appropriate; however, a decision on the merits of the tort case had to be postponed until the administrative process was completed. In *Mooney*, assignees of accounts receivable due under a contract with the state university system filed an action in circuit court alleging that the university system had violated the Commercial Law Article when it made a check payable to the assignor. Although the Court of Appeals held that the matter needed to be heard by the Maryland Board of Contract Appeals, the court also wrote after citing *Arroyo*, "If there was any doubt about whether to proceed administratively or through the courts, the Mooneys could have filed their claim administratively and judicially; the circuit court action then could have been stayed pending the administrative decision."[123]

---

118. 376 Md. 118, 829 A.2d 271 (2003).
119. 383 Md. 462, 860 A.2d 871 (2004).
120. 383 Md. 462, 483, 860 A.2d 871, 883 (2004).
121. 381 Md. 646, 851 A.2d 576 (2004).
122. 407 Md. 390, 966 A.2d 418 (2009).
123. 407 Md. 390, 413, 966 A.2d 418, 431 (2009).

The principle that primary jurisdiction results in a stay of the judicial proceeding, but not dismissal, demonstrates a significant difference between exhaustion and primary jurisdiction. When the exhaustion doctrine is properly applied, the court loses all jurisdiction of the dispute and has no power to eventually rule on it. When primary jurisdiction is properly applied, the court retains jurisdiction, and retains the power to rule on the matter after the agency has dealt with the issue.

An issue that was not resolved in *Arroyo* or *Mooney* is the interrelationship between primary jurisdiction and the running of the statute of limitations for the independent judicial proceeding. Left unanswered was whether the limitations period is tolled during the time the administrative action is proceeding. My opinion is that the statute of limitations is not tolled by the administrative process. The independent judicial action should be filed prior to the expiration of the limitations period as if no administrative proceeding existed. This is why the appropriate action of the court when primary jurisdiction is invoked is to stay, not dismiss the judicial action.

Also noteworthy are two companion cases involving attorney discipline, *Attorney Grievance Commission v. Lichtenberg*[124] and *Attorney Grievance Commission v. Davis.*[125] In both cases, the Court of Appeals refused to interpret a provision of the Insurance Article of the Maryland Code because the Insurance Commissioner was not a party to the proceedings. Both cases involved statutory interpretation issues that had never been ruled upon by the Insurance Commissioner, and the court did not want to proceed on an issue of such "significant importance" to the regulation of title insurance agents and brokers without input from the commissioner. Judges Wilner and Harrell disagreed with the majority's decision to avoid interpreting the statute. They viewed this decision as "applying the doctrine of primary jurisdiction, disguised as something else."[126] Judges Wilner and Harrell pointed out (correctly in my opinion) that primary jurisdiction was not the relevant doctrine. Because the Court of Appeals has exclusive, original jurisdiction over attorney disciplinary cases, "[t]his is not a situation in which a court and an administrative agency have concurrent jurisdiction over the same matter."[127]

## § 14.20. Ripeness

In Federal Administrative Law, exhaustion and primary jurisdiction are joined with the ripeness doctrine when discussing the availability and timing of judicial review. Ripeness involves a situation where a person seeks to obtain judicial review of an agency decision before the agency has sought to enforce its decision. For example, in the leading federal case on ripeness, *Abbott Labs. v. Gardner,*[128] drug manufacturers sought to challenge in federal court regulations of the Food and Drug Administration despite the fact that no drug company had been accused of violating these regulations. The Supreme Court developed a two-part test to determine whether a case is ripe for judicial review prior to any enforcement action by the agency. The first prong of the test is whether the issue is fit for review. Under this fitness test, the court considers whether the agency decision

124. 379 Md. 335, 842 A.2d 11 (2004).
125. 379 Md. 361, 842 A.2d 26 (2004).
126. 379 Md. 361, 385, 842 A.2d 26, 40 (2004).
127. 379 Md. 361, 385, 842 A.2d 26, 40 (2004).
128. 387 U.S. 136 (1967).

involves factual or legal issues, and whether the agency decision is final, meaning that compliance is expected. Final decisions that do not involve factual issues are fit for review. The second prong of the test is whether denying immediate judicial review would impose hardship on the party seeking review. If hardship would be created by postponing review of the fit issue, the matter is ripe for judicial review despite its seemingly premature posture.

As discussed in Chapter 3, under the Maryland APA, judicial review of a regulation in a Maryland circuit court prior to the agency's enforcement of the regulation is authorized and proper. The classic ripeness situation as presented in *Abbott Labs* where a regulated party seeks to bring a pre-enforcement challenge to a regulation is therefore not relevant in Maryland. In the context of judicial review of contested cases, a case where ripeness may have been relevant was *Luskin's Inc. v. Consumer Protection Division,*[129] discussed earlier in connection with Primary Jurisdiction. In that case, Luskin's challenged in circuit court "informal advice" given to it by the Consumer Protection Division that a proposed Luskin's advertisement that had not yet been broadcast would be in violation of Maryland consumer protection laws if it were broadcast. An argument could have been made that the complaint should have been dismissed because the case was premature, i.e., not ripe, for judicial review. The Maryland court, however, analyzed the case based on the doctrine of primary jurisdiction, never mentioning ripeness. It does not appear that Maryland cases have developed any meaningful ripeness jurisprudence comparable to what exists in Federal Administrative Law.

129. 338 Md. 188, 657 A.2d 788 (1995).

# Chapter 15

# Judicial Review: Grounds for Reversal and Deference

Many cases seeking judicial review of an agency decision are resolved prior to the reviewing court reaching the merits of the substantive issues presented. However, if the preliminary and procedural matters are decided in favor of the court actually reviewing the agency decision, it is essential to understand the grounds upon which a court can reverse the agency.

## § 15.1. APA and Non-APA Grounds for Reversal

The grounds upon which a court can reverse an agency decision in a contested case are set forth in the APA, the Maryland Rules governing Administrative Mandamus, and in the case law which has developed a common law of judicial review. As discussed in the chapters that follow, the grounds upon which a court can reverse an agency decision in a contested case are as follows:

1. Unconstitutional
2. Excess of Statutory Authority or Jurisdiction
3. Unlawful Procedure
4. Error of Law
5. Unsupported by Substantial Evidence
6. Arbitrary or Capricious
7. Abuse of Discretion

These grounds for reversal apply whether or not the agency being reviewed is governed by the APA, and whether the court is reviewing the case based on a Petition for Judicial Review, an action for a Writ of Administrative Mandamus, a common law writ pursuant to the court's inherent right of judicial review, or a statutory review provision specifically relating to a particular agency. As the Court of Appeals wrote in *Bowen v. City of Annapolis:*[1] "The basis of judicial review of an administrative decision may be by explicit statutory authorization or by a common law or equity writ. Regardless of the basis for judicial review, the standard of review is the same."[2] Likewise, in *Harvey v. Marshall,*[3] the Court of Appeals wrote that "an administrative proceeding even if not subject to judicial review

1. 402 Md. 587, 937 A.2d 242 (2007).
2. 402 Md. 587, 611, 937 A.2d 242, 256 (2007).
3. 389 Md. 243, 884 A.2d 1171 (2005).

under the APA, would be subject to judicial review, of essentially the same scope, in an action for mandamus, certiorari, injunction or declaratory judgment."[4]

## § 15.2. Deference

Whenever a court reaches the merits of the challenge to the agency decision, one of the first issues that must be identified is what degree of deference the court should give the agency. First, when the agency decision is being challenged as unconstitutional or based on unlawful procedure, it is clear that the court will give no deference to the agency. The court when evaluating a constitutional or procedural argument makes its own independent judgment on the issue, and decides the constitutional or procedural issue without any regard to the agency's position.

Second, it is clear that when the agency decision is being challenged as unsupported by substantial evidence, arbitrary or capricious, or an abuse of discretion, deference is owed to the agency decision. When reviewing a challenge to the agency decision based on these three grounds, the court does not independently decide how it would have decided the issue. With these three challenges, the court does not substitute its judgment for that of the agency. The court does not decide the case based on what the court believes is the right or the better decision. Rather, because of the deference owed to the agency under substantial evidence, arbitrary or capricious, and abuse of discretion review, a court can only reverse the agency if the agency decision was unreasonable. To prove an agency decision is unreasonable is a difficult, although not impossible, task.

It is not entirely clear, however, what amount of deference the court owes an agency when the court is reviewing a challenge based on the argument that the agency has committed an error of law, and the argument that the agency has acted in excess of its statutory authority or jurisdiction. As discussed in Chapters 18 and 19, there are some cases that review these two challenges with no deference to the agency. Other cases, however, review these two challenges with some deference, although the amount of deference given is not the same deference given under the substantial evidence, arbitrary or capricious, and abuse of discretion standards. The different deference approaches will be discussed in greater detail in the separate chapters on each ground for reversal.

4. 389 Md. 243, 296, 884 A.2d 1171, 1203 (2005).

# Chapter 16

# Judicial Review: Unconstitutional

An agency decision in a contested case will be reversed if it violates the Maryland Constitution or those parts of the United States Constitution that apply to the states.[1] It is obviously beyond the scope of this book to discuss every possible constitutional challenge that could be brought to reverse an agency decision. This chapter, however, will discuss those issues most relevant to constitutional challenges to agency decisions in contested cases.

## § 16.1. Deference

The first point to emphasize is that when an agency decision is challenged as unconstitutional, the court gives no deference to the agency. Constitutional issues are decided by the court independently just as if the constitutional issue was before the court in a case not involving an administrative agency. When evaluating a constitutional challenge, the courts substitute their own judgment for that of the agency.[2] For example, in *Classics Chicago, Inc. v. Comptroller of the Treasury*,[3] the issue was whether a corporation which had no physical presence in Maryland could be constitutionally required to pay Maryland state income tax. Resolution of this issue depended on whether there was a substantial nexus between the corporation and the State of Maryland so that imposition of the income tax did not violate the Commerce Clause of the U.S. Constitution or principles of Due Process. The Court of Special Appeals wrote that the "extent to which this State has the ability to tax a nonresident under the United States Constitution is a question of law on which we owe no deference."[4] Although the court upheld the agency's imposition of the tax, this was based on the court's own independent evaluation of the constitutional issue. The court did not take into consideration the fact that the agency had ruled that the tax was constitutional.

1. Maryland Code Annotated, State Government § 10-222(h)(3)(i).
2. AT&T Communications of Md., Inc. v. Comptroller of the Treasury, 405 Md. 83, 950 A.2d. 86 (2008), Comptroller of the Treasury v. SYL, Inc., 375 Md. 78, 825 A.2d 399 (2003).
3. 189 Md. App. 695, 985 A.2d 593 (2010).
4. 189 Md. App. 695, 708, 985 A.2d 593, 601 (2010).

## § 16.2. Separation of Powers

A very important constitutional issue in Administrative Law is separation of powers. There are several significant cases challenging an agency's decision in a contested case on the ground the agency decision violated the separation of powers doctrine in Maryland.

As discussed in Chapter 2 on Rulemaking, Article 8 of the Maryland Declaration of Rights provides:

> That the Legislative, Executive, and Judicial powers of Government ought to be forever separate and distinct from each other; and no person exercising the functions of one of said Departments shall assume or discharge the duties of any other.

Because all Maryland agencies are part of the Executive Branch, an agency's quasi-judicial powers to make decisions in a contested case have been challenged as unconstitutional under Article 8. These challenges have generally been unsuccessful.

In *Maryland Aggregates Association v. Maryland*,[5] the Department of Natural Resources (DNR) had been delegated by the legislature the power to regulate surface mining. One section of the Natural Resources Article required mine operators to compensate property owners for sinkhole damage if the DNR determined that the damage was caused by surface mine dewatering. It was argued by a group of mine operators that "the Legislature, in authorizing the [DNR] to sit as the sole fact finder and judge in a dispute between neighboring property owner and quarry operator, has displaced the judicial branch of government in violation of Article 8."[6] The Court of Appeals responded that although "any attempt to authorize an administrative agency to perform what is deemed a purely judicial function or power would violate the separation of powers principle," the power vested in DNR "to determine, in the first instance, factual issues relating to compensation under the Act is not judicial power but quasi-judicial power which may properly be exercised" by DNR.[7] The court stated that it has "long recognized that the tasks of making factual determinations and resolving disputes are not reserved exclusively to the judicial branch of government."[8] This is true in part because "the complexity of governmental obligations has resulted in increasing reliance upon administrative agencies for the performance of both rulemaking and adjudicatory functions."[9] There are limitations, however. First, in order to avoid a separation of powers violation, there must be an opportunity for judicial review of the agency's final determination. A regulatory scheme where the agency decision is not subject to judicial review would be unconstitutional. Second, an executive branch agency cannot be given the power to enforce its decisions because "the essence of judicial power is the final authority to render and enforce a judgment."[10] Only a court can enforce an order of an executive agency.[11] Because the DNR had been given the power to make only an initial determination of a mine operator's liability, and its decision was subject to judicial review, the court held that the separation of powers doctrine had not been violated.

---

5. 337 Md. 658, 655 A.2d 886, *cert. denied sub nom.* Genstar Stone Prods. Co. v. Maryland, 514 U.S. 1111 (1995).
6. 337 Md. 658, 675, 655 A.2d 886, 895 (1995).
7. 337 Md. 658, 676, 655 A.2d 886, 895 (1995).
8. 337 Md. 658, 676, 655 A.2d 886, 895 (1995).
9. 337 Md. 658, 677, 655 A.2d 886, 895 (1995).
10. 337 Md. 658, 674, 655 A.2d 886, 895 (1995).
11. *See* Dep't of Natural Resources v. Linchester Sand & Gravel Corp., 274 Md. 211, 334 A.2d 514 (1975); Interstate Commerce Comm'n v. Brimson, 154 U.S. 447 (1894).

Another case involving separation of powers and an agency's exercise of quasi-judicial powers is *County Council for Montgomery County v. Investors Funding Corp.*[12] Pursuant to legislation, the Montgomery County Commission on Landlord-Tenant Affairs was conferred various powers in landlord-tenant disputes, including the power to impose a civil penalty not exceeding $1,000, the power to award money damages not exceeding $1,000, the power to award payment for temporary substitute housing, the power to terminate leases, the power to order repairs, and the power to order the return of security deposits and rental monies paid. It was contended that these powers were powers that belonged exclusively to the judicial branch. After a rather lengthy discussion, the Court of Appeals upheld all the powers delegated to the Commission. There was no violation of the separation of powers because:

> the function of the Commission is primarily administrative and the power vested in it to hear and determine controversies involving landlords and tenants is granted only as an incident to its administrative duty; in other words, the Commission's function is not primarily to decide questions of legal rights between private parties, but is merely incidental, although reasonably necessary, to its regulatory powers.[13]

The Court of Appeals also upheld the agency's power to impose a civil penalty because it was "not a power beyond constitutional delegation to an administrative agency."[14] However, the court was troubled by the "discretion vested in the Commission to fix the amount of the penalty in any amount up to $1,000, for any violation of the Act, in the total absence of any legislative safeguards or standards to guide it in exercising its discretion."[15] The court held that this "constitutes an invalid delegation of legislative powers."[16] The lack of standards meant that no meaningful judicial review of the amount of the penalty was possible. Therefore, the court held that "because of the complete lack of any legislative safeguards or standards, the grant of unlimited discretion to the Commission to fix civil penalties in any amount up to $1,000 is illegal."[17]

Judge Barnes wrote a separate opinion in *Investors Funding*. Judge Barnes' position was that all legislative powers granted to the Commission were unconstitutional. Judge Barnes pointed out (correctly) that Maryland's express separation of powers provision as set forth in Article 8 of the Declaration of Rights was a stronger statement of separation of powers than that expressed in the U.S. Constitution and in the vast majority of states. Judge Barnes wrote that the majority opinion failed "to appreciate fully the unusual and almost unique legal position Maryland occupies, so far as the delegation of judicial powers and functions is concerned, as a result of relevant provisions of the Maryland Constitution."[18] He maintained that in light of Maryland's express separation of powers provision, a stricter approach was warranted.

A case subsequent to *Investors Funding*, *Lussier v. Maryland Racing Commission*[19] indicates that Judge Barnes' position is clearly not the accepted view. In fact, *Lussier* suggests that even the flexible fine struck down in *Investors Funding* is valid. *Lussier* involved the validity of a regulation adopted by the Racing Commission giving it the authority to impose a

12. 270 Md. 403, 312 A.2d 225 (1973).
13. 270 Md. 403, 441, 312 A.2d 225, 245 (1973).
14. 270 Md. 403, 441, 312 A.2d 225, 246 (1973).
15. 270 Md. 403, 441, 312 A.2d 225, 246 (1973).
16. 270 Md. 403, 441, 312 A.2d 225, 246 (1973).
17. 270 Md. 403, 442, 312 A.2d 225, 246 (1973).
18. 270 Md. 403, 448, 312 A.2d 225, 249 (1973).
19. 343 Md. 681, 684 A.2d 804 (1996).

fine up to $5,000. Nothing in any statute provided how the Commission should determine the amount of the fine. The Commission, however, did adopt a regulation that set forth four standards to guide the agency in setting the amount of the fine. These four standards were: the seriousness of the violation; the harm caused by the violation; the good faith or lack of good faith of the violation; and the licensing history of the violator. If *Investors Funding* was followed, the Racing Commission's power to impose a fine up to $5,000 would be unconstitutional. But in *Lussier*, the flexible fine was upheld. *Investors Funding* was distinguished in *Lussier* on the basis that *Investors Funding* involved an express legislative authorization for the agency to impose monetary penalties up to a certain limit, while in *Lussier*, there was no such authorization. But, the fact that there was no statutory authority for the flexible fine in *Lussier* should make the Racing Commission's regulation more vulnerable to attack, not less vulnerable, under separation of power concerns. The separation of powers concern expressed in *Investors Funding* seems to have been shortlived.

Maryland case law indicates that although Article 8 of the Maryland Declaration of Rights expresses a strict view of separation of powers, Maryland agencies can exercise quasi-judicial powers to decide disputes which have been traditionally viewed as belonging to the judicial branch. It does not matter whether the dispute is between two private parties, such as in *Maryland Aggregates*, or whether it is the more typical administrative law dispute between the agency and a private person, such as in a professional discipline case. Maryland agencies can provide remedies similar to that of the courts including the power to fine and to order injunctive relief. However, two judicial powers have always traditionally been denied to agencies—the power of contempt and the power to imprison. These two powers belong exclusively to the judicial branch.

In Maryland, the key to separation of powers and administrative agency powers is the availability of judicial review. As discussed in Chapter 13 regarding the inherent power of judicial review, any attempt to deny judicial review of an agency decision would be unconstitutional as a violation of separation of powers. But as long as there is judicial review, Maryland agencies can exercise broad quasi-judicial powers despite the fact that the agencies are within the executive branch.

## § 16.3. Due Process — Bias

It is well established that due process requires an impartial decisionmaker.[20] In general, there are three types of bias: financial bias, personal bias, and prejudgment bias. Financial bias involves the situation where the agency decisionmaker has a financial stake in the outcome of the case. Personal bias involves the situation where the agency decisionmaker is personally involved with either the parties or the subject matter of the case. Prejudgment bias involves the situation where the agency decisionmaker has prejudged the facts of the case.

An ALJ or agency official who is biased under any of the three bias standards must be disqualified from participating in the contested hearing and decision. A motion should be filed with the agency requesting disqualification based on bias. Because bias is an issue that must be exhausted, failure to request disqualification at the agency level will mean

20. Schweiker v. McClure, 456 U.S. 188 (1982).

that bias cannot be raised on judicial review.[21] If a motion to disqualify based on bias is made with the agency but denied, the bias argument can be presented to the reviewing court to reverse the agency decision.

## § 16.4. OAH ALJ Bias

It is clear that if OAH has been delegated the authority to make the final agency decision, bias of the OAH ALJ who refused to disqualify himself or herself and who issued the final agency decision would constitute a basis for the court to reverse the agency decision.[22] What is not clear is whether the denial of a motion to disqualify an OAH ALJ in a case where OAH has been delegated only the power to make a proposed decision is a ground to reverse the final agency decision. The OAH regulation on Disqualification and Substitution of an ALJ, discussed in Chapter 10, does not draw a distinction between cases where OAH has been delegated final or proposed decision-making authority. However, my opinion is that a final agency decision is not subject to successful challenge on judicial review when the final agency decision followed a proposed OAH decision made by an ALJ who should have, but refused, to disqualify himself or herself from making the proposed decision. Because it is the agency's decision that is subject to judicial review, not the proposed decision of the OAH ALJ, the final agency decision should not be reversed because of improper bias of the OAH ALJ who issued the proposed decision. Although bias at any level should be avoided, it is doubtful that the agency decision would be vulnerable to attack because of bias of the proposed decisionmaker.

## § 16.5. Financial Bias

A decision-maker cannot be impartial if the decision-maker has a financial interest in the case. An obvious example of disqualifying financial bias would be if a zoning board member owned land that was the subject of a zoning request. The reported cases involve financial bias claims based on less direct financial interest.

*Eichberg v. Maryland Board of Pharmacy*[23] involved an administrative proceeding to revoke a pharmacist's license. It was argued that a fair and impartial hearing could not be granted by the Board because it was "made up of practicing pharmacists [who] have an economic interest in reducing the number of their competitors."[24] The Court of Special Appeals rejected this argument. It cited a Wisconsin case for the proposition that "membership in or connection with the same profession or occupation as that of the accused licensee does not alone indicate a disqualifying bias or interest on the part of the questioned tribunal member sufficient to violate due process."[25] Only if there is "evidence

21. See Public Service Commission v. Wilson, 389 Md. 27, 882 A.2d 849 (2005); Maryland State Board of Dental Examiners v. Fisher, 123 Md. App. 322, 718 A.2d 627, *cert. denied*, 352 Md. 335, 722 A.2d 63 (1998).

22. Md. Code Regs. 28.02.01.11(C), COMAR 28.02.01.11(C).

23. 50 Md. App. 189, 436 A.2d 525 (1981).

24. 50 Md. App. 189, 197–98, 436 A.2d 525, 531 (1981).

25. 50 Md. App. 189, 189, 436 A.2d 525, 531 (1981), *citing* Kachian v. Optometry Examining Bd., 170 N.W.2d 743 (Wis. 1969).

of an actual, direct or substantial pecuniary interest on the part of any of the pharmacists" would disqualification be required. In this case, the allegation of financial bias was "indirect and speculative," and thus no disqualification was warranted.

*Maryland State Board of Dental Examiners v. Fisher*[26] involved a disciplinary proceeding against a dentist. The dentist, Fisher, claimed that one board member should have recused himself because this board member had a dental office in the same geographic area and in the same specialty. The Court of Special Appeals did not reach the merits of the claim. It held that Fisher's counsel's request at the hearing "that anyone on the Board with an interest in the case recuse himself or herself" was insufficient to preserve the issue for judicial review.[27]

In *Regan v. Board of Chiropractic Examiners*,[28] it was argued to the circuit court and the Court of Special Appeals that two board members operated their chiropractic offices in the same geographic area as Regan's office and would therefore "benefit economically by an adverse decision to Dr. Regan." The disqualification argument was rejected as "speculative and baseless." The bias claim was not pursued in the Court of Appeals.

## § 16.6. Personal Bias

There are several Maryland cases involving personal bias. *Regan v. State Board of Chiropractic Examiners*[29] involved a disciplinary proceeding against a chiropractor, Regan. The Board of Chiropractic Examiners hears its cases itself; it does not use OAH in any manner. Prior to the administrative hearing before the Board, Regan moved to disqualify four members for personal bias. One Board member, an attorney, agreed to recuse himself because his law firm had previously handled a criminal matter involving Regan's office manager who was to testify at the hearing. The other three board members refused to recuse themselves. The personal bias claim against Lewis, a chiropractor member of the Board, was that Regan had told a female employee, Gee, to try to have a "sexual liaison" with Lewis if Gee wanted to keep her job. Gee in fact did go to Lewis's office, but did not try to seduce him. Regan argued that because of the seduction plot, Lewis had a personal bias and should be disqualified. Regan sought the recusal of Klinger, another chiropractor on the Board, because Klinger had purportedly telephoned Regan to inform him that one of Regan's advertisements did not comply with the board's regulations. Regan claimed he changed the advertisement based on Klinger's representation to him that no enforcement action would be brought if the advertisement were changed. Because Klinger was personally involved in disputed facts, Regan sought Klinger's disqualification. Regan moved to disqualify another board member, Blanck, because Regan planned to call her as a witness to testify about the Board's proposed regulations governing chiropractic assistants.

The Board denied Regan's motions to disqualify Lewis, Klinger, and Blanck. Regarding Lewis, the board wrote that "Dr. Lewis, like all other Board members, has pledged to carry out his responsibilities as a public official; part of those responsibilities, as a Board member, is to participate in hearings; in so doing, all of the members have pledged to listen to all

26. 123 Md. App. 322, 718 A.2d 627, *cert. denied*, 352 Md. 335, 722 A.2d 63 (1998).
27. 123 Md. App. 322, 328, 718 A.2d 627, 631 (1998).
28. 120 Md. App. 494, 707 A.2d 891 (1998), *aff'd in part*, 355 Md. 397, 735 A.2d 991 (1999).
29. 355 Md. 397, 735 A.2d 991 (1999).

of the evidence presented and render a fair and impartial decision."[30] The Board also ruled that Klinger and Blanck would not testify at the hearing, and therefore there was no need to disqualify them. Upon judicial review, Regan challenged the failure of Lewis and Klinger to be disqualified. At the Court of Appeals, Regan contended that "actual bias is not necessary to recuse an administrative fact finder; instead, a fact finder may just as well be recused based on his appearance of impropriety in a particular case."[31] Regan argued that Lewis's participation was "particularly improper because there can be no reasonable dispute that someone who is allegedly the target of a blackmail plot may not sit in judgment of the individual accused of masterminding that plot without giving rise to an appearance of impropriety."

The Court of Appeals "assume[d], for the purposes of this case, that the appearance of impropriety standard" applied. The court then stated a few points. There is a strong presumption of impartiality on the part of agency decisionmakers. A decision by board members refusing to disqualify themselves will not be reversed unless it constitutes an abuse of discretion. When applying the appearance of impropriety standard, the test is an "objective one" which assumes that a "reasonable person" knowing and understanding all the relevant facts would recuse the judge. Applying this standard, the Court of Appeals concluded that neither Lewis nor Klinger were required to be disqualified. As to Klinger, the court held that "[i]t is difficult to imagine that a reasonable person, knowing all of the facts, would believe that Dr. Klinger was biased, particularly since the charge was promptly dismissed before the hearing ever began and since no evidence was heard on the matter."[32] Regarding Lewis, the court held that no reasonable person knowing and understanding all the relevant facts would believe that Lewis was prejudiced because of the alleged seduction plot. This was true for a few reasons: Lewis was unaware of the plot; Gee made no attempt to sexually entice Lewis; no evidence was taken on the charge; and the charge was dismissed. Moreover, none of the allegations involved behavior by Lewis, and "courts have been most reluctant to find an appearance of impropriety on the basis of a litigant's actions.... A litigant ordinarily should not be permitted to create an appearance of impropriety in order to disqualify a judge."[33]

A personal bias challenge was successful in *Spencer v. Maryland State Board of Pharmacy*.[34] At the contested case hearing before the Board of Pharmacy, an agency which hears its own cases and does not delegate to OAH any authority, Spencer's attorney accused some members of the Board of sleeping and not paying attention to the testimony. These accusations were followed by heated conversations between Board members and the attorney, finger pointing, and the attorney being called a "bold-faced liar" by a Board member. The Court of Appeals held that these events established that Spencer had not been provided a fair and unbiased hearing. The matter was remanded to the Board.

Another personal bias case involved an ALJ at OAH who while a case was pending before him was interviewing for a job with the agency that was a party to the case. In *Gigeous v. Eastern Correctional Institution*,[35] ALJ McCloud had issued several written decisions denying various prehearing motions filed by Gigeous, who was challenging his termination of employment by the Department of Corrections. At the same time, McCloud

30. 355 Md. 397, 403, 735 A.2d 991, 994 (1999).
31. Regan conceded that there has been no showing of actual bias.
32. 355 Md. 397, 413, 735 A.2d 991, 999 (1999).
33. 355 Md. 397, 414–15, 735 A.2d 991, 1000 (1999).
34. 380 Md. 515, 846 A.2d 341 (2004).
35. 363 Md. 481, 769 A.2d 912 (2001).

was discussing his own potential employment with the Department of Corrections. By the time Gigeous' termination case reached the Court of Appeals, McCloud's prior involvement had become moot because a different ALJ had replaced McCloud in the case and had reviewed all the issues previously ruled upon.

## § 16.7. Prejudgment Bias

If a decisionmaker has prejudged the facts of the case, the decisionmaker must be disqualified. The prejudgment must relate to the facts of the case, not merely a predilection toward a certain policy. The Court of Special Appeals in *Board of Education of Somerset County v. Somerset Advocates for Education*[36] quoted from an earlier book of mine where I had written: "An administrative official who has expressed concern over the water quality of the Chesapeake Bay would not necessarily be disqualified in a proceeding involving an application for construction of a medical waste incinerator near the bay unless the official had stated his/her position on the particular facts of that application."[37] In the *Somerset* case, a corporation established for the purpose of creating and operating a charter school challenged the denial of its application to operate a charter school by the Somerset County Board of Education. One of the challenges to the denial was that the Board of Education had a general bias against charter schools. One allegation was that members of the local school board had engaged in "fear mongering" by commenting to the media on the tax impact of a charter school. The charter school applicant also tried to rely on the "general resistance" which public school boards have to charter schools. The Court of Special Appeals ruled that nothing demonstrated bias or impartiality on the part of the local school board. The court wrote that "in determining whether there is either actual bias or an appearance of impropriety on the part of a decision maker in a judicial or quasi-judicial proceeding, we begin with the presumption of impartiality."[38] The court next noted that the applicant "did not allege matters which involved financial, personal or prejudgment bias, ... but rather generally alleged that the Local Board was opposed to the establishment of charter schools. That, in itself, would not constitute a basis for recusal."[39] The court then added "assuming, arguendo, that the Local Board was generally opposed to granting a charter, there is no evidence in the record ... that demonstrates that such 'bias' influenced the Local Board's decision to deny appellee's application. Professor Rochvarg has explained that merely possessing a 'predilection toward a certain policy' does not render an administrative decisionmaker unfit to render an impartial decision."[40]

Another prejudgment bias claim was presented in *Consumer Protection Division v. Consumer Publishing Co.*[41] Bias was based on a press release issued by the Office of the Attorney General on the day false advertising charges were filed against a mail order company that sold diet pills. The company contended that the press release was "inflammatory" and revealed a "clear prejudgment ... that the Company was guilty of the charges

36. 189 Md. App. 385, 984 A.2d 405 (2009).

37. 189 Md. App. 385, 410, 984 A.2d 405, 420 (2009), *citing* Arnold Rochvarg, Maryland Administrative Law 94 (MICPEL 2d ed. 2007).

38. 189 Md. App. 385, 409, 984 A.2d 405, 419 (2009).

39. 189 Md. App. 385, 409–10, 984 A.2d 405, 419–20 (2009).

40. 189 Md. App. 385, 410, 984 A.2d 405, 420 (2009).

41. 304 Md. 731, 501 A.2d 48 (1985).

alleged." The Court of Appeals rejected this argument. It cited cases which indicated that "[c]ourts have repeatedly held that the issuance of press releases announcing charges by the agency that will ultimately decide the case does not violate due process guarantees."[42] The Attorney General had a duty to protect and warn consumers, and a press release was one method of doing this. The court also held that the press release did not give the impression that any facts had been prejudged. The press release only set forth that charges had been filed, and that a hearing officer would decide whether there had been a violation of law.

In *Spencer v. Maryland State Board of Pharmacy*,[43] a case resolution conference (CRC) was held in an attempt to resolve a pharmacist disciplinary matter without the necessity of a contested case hearing. Two members of the Board of Pharmacy participated at the CRC on behalf of the Board. The parties could not resolve the matter at the CRC, and a contested case hearing was held. The two Board members who had participated at the CRC refused to disqualify themselves from the case claiming that even though they had been involved in the settlement negotiations, they had not prejudged the case. Upon judicial review, it was held that the two Board members should have recused themselves. The Court of Appeals wrote that "it was improper for those members who participated in the settlement negotiations to remain as panel members adjudicating [the] case, and those members may not constitute a part of the panel if or when [the] case is reheard."[44] The Court did note in a footnote, however, that it was not adopting a "per se rule of recusal," but was rather relying on "the overall appearance of impropriety in this case."[45]

Prejudgment bias was also argued in *Public Service Commission v. Wilson*[46] which involved a Public Service employee challenging the legality of her firing. Her bias claim was based on the fact that the Chairman of the PSC had initiated the firing and then later served as the appeals officer in the intra-agency appeals process. The court did not decide this claim because the employee had not presented the bias argument to the agency, and thus had not exhausted her administrative remedies on this issue.

## § 16.8. Rule of Necessity

The Rule of Necessity is an exception to bias. The Rule of Necessity is a common law doctrine that permits a judge, ALJ, or other administrative decisionmaker to decide a case despite the decisionmaker's bias if there is no provision for appointment of another person to decide the case.[47] The Maryland Court of Appeals first recognized the Rule of Necessity as applicable to members of administrative agencies in 1954 in *Board of Medical Examiners v. Steward*[48] where the court wrote that although "every person is entitled to a fair and

42. 304 Md. 731, 764, 501 A.2d 48, 65 (1985).
43. 380 Md. 515, 846 A.2d 341 (2004).
44. 380 Md. 515, 534, 846 A.2d 341, 352 (2004).
45. 380 Md. 515, 534 n.7, 846 A.2d 341, 352 n.7 (2004).
46. 389 Md. 27, 882 A.2d 849 (2005).
47. The leading case is United States v. Will, 449 U.S. 200 (1980), which involved a challenge by federal district court judges to statutes that had the effect of reducing the compensation of all federal judges by changing the formula for annual cost of living increases. Even though every federal judge had a personal financial interest in the outcome of the case, the Rule of Necessity was invoked, and the case was decided by judges whose salaries would be affected.
48. 203 Md. 574, 102 A.2d 248 (1954).

impartial hearing…, disqualification will not be permitted to destroy the only tribunal with power" to decide the case.[49] The rule of necessity was also discussed by the Court of Special Appeals in *Regan v. State Board of Chiropractic Examiners*[50] where an attempt was made to disqualify the entire Board of Chiropractic Examiners. Regan argued that because it was impossible to convene an impartial board, the court should order that the case be heard by OAH even though the Board of Chiropractor Examiners had not delegated any hearing authority to OAH. The Court of Special Appeals refused to order the Board to delegate its hearing authority to OAH. The Court of Special Appeals relied on both the agency's discretion to delegate to OAH and upon the Rule of Necessity. The Rule of Necessity issue was not addressed when *Regan* reached the Court of Appeals.

In an article I wrote, *Is the Rule of Necessity Really Necessary In State Administrative Law: The Central Panel Solution*,[51] I criticized the use of the Rule of Necessity in state administrative hearings. Although Maryland has not employed the Rule of Necessity in recent years, other states have. Too many cases in other states have permitted biased agency officials to issue final decisions because no alternative decisionmaker was available. In Maryland and about one half of the states, however, the creation of a central hearing panel such as OAH can always provide an alternative tribunal. The Rule of Necessity should never be applied when referral to a central panel is an option.[52]

## § 16.9. Due Process — Combination of Functions

Related to the bias issue is the combination of functions within one administrative agency. Typically, one agency is responsible for investigating, prosecuting, and deciding the case. It has been argued that the combination of these functions is a violation of due process because the agency, by investigating and prosecuting the case, will be biased to decide the case in the agency's favor. This argument has been presented in several Maryland cases.

In *Consumer Protection Division v. Morgan*,[53] the Consumer Protection Division alleged unfair and deceptive trade practices by several property investors and appraisers. One argument made on judicial review of the cease and desist order was that due process had been violated because "there is no separation of the prosecutorial and adjudicatory process within the Division." Morgan claimed that the "combination of prosecutorial and adjudicatory functions makes the adjudicatory process farcical, as the Division's adjudicator can overturn the ALJ's proposed decision and issue an order in accord with the Division

49. 203 Md. 574, 582, 102 A.2d 248, 252 (1954).

50. 120 Md. App. 494, 707 A.2d 891 (1998), *aff'd in part,* 355 Md. 397, 735 A.2d 991 (1999).

51. 19 J. Nat'l Assoc. Admin. Law Judges 35 (1999).

52. *Cf.* Spencer v. Md. State Board of Pharmacy, 380 Md. 515, 846 A.2d 341 (2004), where the Court of Appeals held that it was not arbitrary or capricious for the Board to refuse to delegate the case to OAH even though the court also held that some Board members were not impartial and had improperly participated at the earlier administrative hearing. The Board was not "required to send the case to the OAH, because logically there existed other options to the Board, such as recusing the offending members and replacing them with different members." 380 Md. 515, 532–33, 846 A.2d 341, 351 (2004).

53. 387 Md. 125, 874 A.2d 919 (2005).

prosecutor's charges." The Court of Appeals rejected this due process argument. The court relied on the U.S. Supreme Court's decision in *Withrow v. Larkin*[54] which had rejected the argument that due process is violated when one agency is empowered to investigate, prosecute, and decide a case. In *Withrow*, the Supreme Court wrote:

> The contention that the combination of investigative and adjudicative functions necessarily creates an unconstitutional risk of bias in an administrative adjudication ... must overcome a presumption of honesty and integrity in those serving as adjudicators; and it must convince that, under a realistic appraisal of psychological tendencies and human weakness, conferring investigative and adjudicative powers on the same individuals poses such a risk of actual bias or prejudgment that the practice must be forbidden if the guarantee of due process is to be adequately implemented.[55]

*Withrow v. Larkin* was further cited for the proposition that it is "very typical for the members of administrative agencies to receive the results of investigations, to approve the filing of charges or formal complaints instituting enforcement proceedings, and then to participate in the ensuing hearings."[56] This "does not violate due process of law."[57] The Court of Appeals in *Morgan*, however, did recognize that in a particular case, "special facts and circumstances" may create a "risk of unfairness [that is] intolerably high." In this case, there was "no evidence in the record of special facts and circumstances posing an intolerably high risk of unfairness."

The combination of functions/due process argument was also raised in *Consumer Protection Division v. Consumer Publishing Co.*,[58] *State Board of Physicians v. Bernstein*,[59] *Rosov v. Maryland State Board of Dental Examiners*,[60] *Nationwide Mutual Insurance Co. v. Insurance Commissioner*,[61] and *Eichberg v. Maryland Board of Pharmacy*.[62] In each case, the court relying on *Withrow v. Larkin* rejected the due process claim.

Although the caselaw makes clear that due process is not violated by the combination of functions within one agency, the lack of separation of functions continues to be a major criticism of the administrative process. The creation of OAH was in part a response to the unfairness of the combination of functions problem. But this problem has not been resolved by OAH's creation. When OAH is delegated only the power to make proposed decisions for the agency that has investigated and prosecuted the case, the combination of functions problem remains. Only when OAH is delegated final decision making authority is there no combination of functions problem. I believe that OAH should be statutorily granted the power to make the final decision in most, if not all, contested cases. By granting final authority to OAH, thus separating the decisionmaking function from that of the investigating and prosecuting functions, the perceived, if not actual, unfairness created by the combination of these functions within one agency would be eliminated.

54. 421 U.S. 35 (1975).
55. 421 U.S. 35, 47 (1975).
56. 421 U.S. 35, 56 (1975).
57. 421 U.S. 35, 56 (1975).
58. 304 Md. 731, 501 A.2d 48 (1985).
59. 167 Md. App. 714, 894 A.2d 621 (2006).
60. 163 Md. App. 98, 877 A.2d 1111 (2005).
61. 67 Md. App. 727, 509 A.2d 719, *cert. denied*, 307 Md. 433, 514 A.2d 1211 (1986).
62. 50 Md. App. 189, 436 A.2d 525 (1981).

## § 16.10. Equal Protection — Selective Enforcement

There have been a few cases in Maryland where it was argued that the court should vacate an agency order in a contested case because the agency had improperly targeted a company or person for selective enforcement in violation of equal protection. Although selective enforcement is a possible ground upon which to reverse an agency decision, no Maryland case has found an agency to have engaged in such improper selective enforcement.

*Consumer Protection Division v. Consumer Publishing Co.*[63] involved a false advertising case against a company that sold diet pills through the mail. One argument presented was that the administrative complaint should be dismissed because the Consumer Protection Division (CPD) "improperly targeted [Consumer Publishing] for selective enforcement" and thus violated its right to equal protection under the law. Consumer Publishing argued that other companies marketed similar products by substantially similar advertising, but that the CPD had not taken any action against them. The Court of Appeals held, assuming arguendo, that competitors did have substantially similar advertising, Consumer Publishing's equal protection argument was without merit. The court cited two U.S. Supreme Court cases, *Oyler v. Boles*[64] and *Snowden v. Hughes*,[65] for the proposition that

> the conscious exercise of some selectivity in enforcing a statute fair on its face does not in and of itself amount to a constitutional violation.... In order to establish a violation of the Fourteenth Amendment's Equal Protection Clause, the Company must prove that the Division's selective enforcement 'was deliberately based upon an unjustifiable standard or arbitrary classification.'[66]

Even though Consumer Publishing was the only firm against whom the CPD had proceeded, it had not been shown that the CPD deliberately chose not to prosecute other firms in the industry. The court further stated that an agency "cannot be expected to bring simultaneous proceedings against all of those engaged in identical practices," and that "it is surely rational for an agency to target resources against one violator and rely on the success of that action to induce voluntary compliance or ease subsequent enforcement against others."[67] There was no evidence that the CPD had "intentionally and purposely decided to prosecute only Consumer Publishing and not to prosecute other industry violators." Moreover, there was no showing that the enforcement action against Consumer Publishing was based on an unjustifiable standard or arbitrary classification such as race, sex, organizational membership, or in retaliation for the exercise of constitutional or statutory rights. Consumer Publishing had come to the CPD's attention because it had placed full-page ads in Maryland newspapers and ranked second in national market share in mail order companies selling diet pills.

Selective enforcement was also argued in *Consumer Protection Division v. Luskin's Inc.*[68] which involved an advertisement that offered free airline tickets with the purchase of a television, stereo or other appliance. Luskin's argued that other companies were employing

---

63. 304 Md. 731, 501 A.2d 48 (1985).
64. 368 U.S. 448, 456 (1962).
65. 321 U.S. 1, 8–10 (1944).
66. 304 Md. 731, 751, 501 A.2d 48, 59 (1985).
67. 304 Md. 731, 752, 501 A.2d 48, 59 (1985).
68. 120 Md. App. 1, 706 A.2d 102 (1998), *rev'd in part on other grounds*, 353 Md. 335, 726 A.2d 702 (1999).

the same type of advertising, but no action had been taken against them. The Court of Special Appeals held that the Consumer Protection Division (CPD) had not engaged in improper selective enforcement. Luskin's had not shown that CPD deliberately chose not to prosecute other companies. Moreover, Luskin's advertisement promised a gift of greater value than what was offered in the majority of the other advertisements. Additionally, Luskin's had "nationwide recognition," and thus the CPD's decision to take action against Luskin's was "a rational one." This issue was not discussed by the Court of Appeals in its decision in this case.

Selective enforcement was also briefly discussed in *Hurl v. Board of Education of Howard County*[69] which involved the involuntary transfer of a public school teacher. In rejecting the teacher's challenges, the Court of Special Appeals observed that the teacher "never alleged facts indicating that she was somehow being improperly, discriminatorily, randomly, or unjustly singled out or targeted by the Superintendent."[70]

## § 16.11. Due Process — Void for Vagueness

Another due process constitutional challenge to an agency decision in a contested case is based on the void for vagueness doctrine. There are two components to this doctrine. First, due process requires fair notice. As the court wrote in *Blaker v. State Board of Chiropractic Examiners*,[71] due process requires that "persons of ordinary intelligence and experience be afforded a reasonable opportunity to know what is prohibited, so that they may govern their behavior accordingly."[72] The second component of the void for vagueness doctrine is whether there are "legally fixed standards and adequate guidelines for ... triers of fact and others whose obligation it is to enforce, apply, and administer" the law. The purpose of this second criterion is to avoid arbitrary or discriminatory application of the law. However, the "vagueness doctrine does not require absolute precision or perfection." Moreover, void for vagueness is not established merely because it allows the agency to exercise some discretion. The doctrine applies only when the discretion is so broad as to be "susceptible to irrational and selective patterns of enforcement."[73]

*Blaker* involved a challenge to the discipline of a chiropractor after the Board found the chiropractor (Blaker) to be "professionally incompetent." Blaker argued that the term "professionally incompetent" was void for vagueness, and thus Blaker's discipline was a violation of his due process rights. The Court of Special Appeals held that the term "professionally incompetent" as used in the statute relating to the discipline of chiropractors "is plain language commonly understood by members of the chiropractic community and, as such, does not render the statute void for vagueness." The court continued: "In common parlance, 'incompetence' means a lack of the learning or skill necessary to perform, day in and day out, the characteristic tasks of a given calling in at least a reasonably effective way."[74] Blaker's argument that the agency's decision was unconstitutional, therefore, was rejected. Similarly, in *Finucan v. Maryland Board of Physician Quality Assurance*,[75] the

69. 107 Md. App. 286, 667 A.2d 970 (1995).
70. 107 Md. App. 286, 310, 667 A.2d 970, 982 (1995).
71. 123 Md. App. 243, 717 A.2d 964, *cert. denied*, 351 Md. 662, 719 A.2d 1261 (1998).
72. 123 Md. App. 243, 256, 717 A.2d 964, 970 (1998).
73. 123 Md. App. 243, 257, 717 A.2d 964, 971 (1998).
74. 123 Md. App. 243, 258, 717 A.2d 964, 971 (1998).
75. 380 Md. 577, 846 A.2d 377, *cert. denied*, 543 U.S. 862, *reh'g denied*, 543 U.S. 1016 (2004).

court rejected the argument that the term "immoral or unprofessional conduct" as used in the statute which set forth grounds for disciplining doctors was unconstitutionally vague.

## § 16.12. Avoidance of Constitutional Issues

Although agency decisions are subject to constitutional challenges, the courts have repeatedly stated that the "strong and established policy is to decide constitutional issues only when necessary."[76] To the extent a case can be resolved on a non-constitutional basis, the court will avoid discussing the constitutional challenge.

76. VNA Hospice of Maryland v. Department of Health and Mental Hygiene, 406 Md. 584, 604, 961 A.2d 557, 569 (2008).

# Chapter 17

# Judicial Review: Substantial Evidence Review

The Maryland APA provides that a court reviewing an agency decision in a contested case may reverse or modify the decision if a finding, conclusion or decision of the agency is "unsupported by competent, material, and substantial evidence in light of the entire record as submitted."[1] The same standard applies to review under Administrative Mandamus.[2] Substantial evidence review is a term of art in Administrative Law. It is applied in judicial review of quasi-judicial decisions of federal agencies as well as agencies in every state. As discussed in Chapter 3, substantial evidence review does not apply to judicial review of a regulation. As discussed in this Chapter, substantial evidence review applies to an (1) agency's findings of fact, (2) the inferences which the agency draws from the facts, and (3) mixed questions of fact and law.

## § 17.1. Findings of Fact

Substantial evidence review applies to the agency's findings of fact. If any fact upon which the agency has based its decision is not supported by substantial evidence, the agency decision must be reversed, unless no prejudice resulted.[3]

A court reviewing an agency decision to determine whether the agency's findings of fact are supported by substantial evidence must review the entire (or whole) record. This means the court must consider not only what in the record supports the agency's findings, but also those parts of the record that are contrary to the agency's findings. Although at an early stage in Administrative Law it was argued that a court when engaged in substantial evidence review should only concern itself with whether the evidence in the record that supported the agency was substantial without any regard to the evidence that was contrary to the agency decision, this position was rejected by the U.S. Supreme Court in its 1951 decision *Universal Camera Corp. v. National Labor Relations Board.*[4] *Universal Camera* has been adopted in every state, including Maryland.

After the reviewing court considers the entire agency record, the court must decide whether the agency's findings of fact were reasonable. Only if the petitioner can convince the reviewing court that no reasonable person could have made the same findings of fact based on the same record as the agency did, can a court reverse the agency's findings of fact for not being supported by substantial evidence.

1. Maryland Code Annotated, State Government § 10-222(h)(3)(v).
2. Md. Rule 7-403 (2)(E).
3. *See* Chapter 24.
4. 340 U.S. 474 (1951).

Whenever a reviewing court can only reverse an agency decision if it is "unreasonable," this indicates that judicial review is deferential to the agency. Because substantial evidence review is a "reasonableness" review, a reviewing court in applying substantial evidence review gives deference to the agency's findings of fact. Such deferential review of finding of facts is justified by one of the most important goals of Administrative Law—relieving the burden on the judicial system. The time-consuming process of hearing evidence and finding facts is why these hearings are held at administrative agencies, not in courts.

The deferential "reasonableness" review nature of substantial evidence review means that a court cannot reverse the agency's findings of fact on the basis that the court on the same record would have reached a different conclusion. Even if the court disagrees with the agency's findings of fact, if the agency's findings of fact are reasonable, the court must affirm. Under substantial evidence review, a court does not decide what are the "correct" findings of fact. Under substantial evidence review, a court does not rule on whether the agency made a "mistake" or made an "error" or came to an "erroneous conclusion" in its findings of fact. Rather, again, the issue is whether the agency was reasonable in its findings of fact. When discussing substantial evidence review, the distinction is often noted between "rightness" and "reasonableness." Under substantial evidence review, the court does not decide whether the agency's findings of fact were right, only whether they were reasonable.[5]

All of these just-stated principles about substantial evidence review are well accepted in Administrative Law on the federal level and among the states. Unfortunately, in discussing substantial evidence review, Maryland courts have at times used other language which in my opinion is either unnecessary or in some circumstances wrong. For example, in *Board of Physician Quality Assurance v. Banks*,[6] when discussing substantial evidence review, the court stated it reviewed the agency decision "in the light most favorable to the agency" because the agency was "prima facie correct" and the agency decision was "presumed valid."[7] These statements logically flow from the fact that substantial evidence review is a reasonableness review with the burden of proving unreasonableness on the petitioner. Whenever a decision only can be reversed if it is unreasonable, that decision by the very nature of reasonableness review is presumed valid, is prima facie correct, and is reviewed in the light most favorable to the agency. Therefore, these additional phrases in no way change the nature of substantial evidence review to make such review more deferential than traditional substantial evidence review.

Some Maryland opinions when discussing substantial evidence review have also used the phrase "fairly debatable." These opinions state that an "issue is fairly debatable if reasonable persons could have reached a different conclusion on the evidence."[8] In my opinion, the "fairly debatable" language adds nothing to traditional, well-accepted, understood notions of substantial evidence review. "Fairly debatable" is nothing more than "reasonable." I know of no opinions in Federal Administrative Law or in other states that use "fairly debatable" when discussing substantial evidence review, and I see no reason

---

5. *See* Montgomery County v. Butler, 417 Md. 271, 9 A.3d 824 (2010).

6. 354 Md. 59, 729 A.2d 376 (1999).

7. 354 Md. 59, 68, 729 A.2d 376, 381 (1999).

8. *See, e.g.*, Anne Arundel County v. 2020C West St., Inc., 104 Md. App. 320, 326, 656 A.2d 341, 344, *cert. denied*, 339 Md. 166, 661 A.2d 700 (1995); Lewis v. Dep't of Natural Resources, 377 Md. 382, 833 A.2d 563 (2003).

why that term should continue to be used in Maryland opinions. The fairly debatable test in no way makes substantial evidence review more (or less) deferential to the agency.

More troublesome is the statement that the "fairly debatable" test is analogous to the clearly erroneous standard under Maryland Rule 8-131(c).[9] The clearly erroneous standard should have no place when discussing judicial review of agency factual findings. The clearly erroneous standard is appropriate when an appellate court is reviewing the factual findings of a trial court sitting without a jury. Judicial review by a Maryland circuit court of an agency decision is not appellate review, but rather the exercise of the circuit court's original jurisdiction.[10] Moreover, there is a substantive difference between substantial evidence review and clearly erroneous review. In *Mayor of Rockville v. Walker*,[11] the court wrote, "if there is any competent, material evidence to support the factual findings below, [the appellate] court cannot hold findings to be clearly erroneous."[12] Clearly erroneous review clearly differs from substantial evidence review in that substantial evidence review requires the court to review the entire record and consider evidence both for and against the agency conclusion. Defining substantial evidence review as "clearly erroneous" review should be avoided.

Also to be avoided because it is not a correct explanation of substantial evidence review is the statement that substantial evidence means "more than a scintilla."[13] "Scintilla of evidence rule" is defined in *Black's Law Dictionary* (6th edition) as "a spark of evidence. A metaphorical expression to describe a very insignificant or trifling item or particle of evidence." This is obviously not what substantial evidence review involves. If there is only a "very insignificant particle of evidence" that supports the agency's factual finding, it cannot be affirmed as supported by substantial evidence.

## § 17.2. Successful Substantial Evidence Challenges

There are many cases where the argument is made that the agency's findings of fact are not supported by substantial evidence. Most of these challenges are not successful. This is a consequence not only of the deference owed to the agency, but also a consequence of the quality of the fact-finding process at OAH and most agencies. But some substantial evidence challenges have been successful, proving that even under a deferential reasonableness review, judicial review can be meaningful. A few of these cases are discussed in this section.

*Maryland Department of Transportation v. Maddalone*[14] involved a state employee (Maddalone) who had been terminated from state employment. Maddalone challenged his termination, and after a hearing at OAH which had been delegated the authority to

9. *See* Tochterman v. Baltimore County, 163 Md. App. 385, 880 A.2d 1118 (2005).

10. *See* discussion of Original Jurisdiction in Circuit Court in Chapter 13; *see also* William F. Fox, Understanding Administrative Law §76 ("One of the most dangerous practices in administrative lawyering is drawing too many analogies to court litigation.").

11. 100 Md. App. 240, 640 A.2d 751 (1994).

12. 100 Md. App. 240, 256, 640 A.2d 751, 759 (1994).

13. *See, e.g.*, Md. State Dep't of Educ. v. Shoop, 119 Md. App. 181, 196, 704 A.2d 499, 506, *cert. denied*, 349 Md. 495, 709 A.2d 140 (1998).

14. 187 Md. App. 549, 979 A.2d. 229 (2009).

make the final agency decision, the ALJ overruled the agency's termination decision. The ALJ concluded that Maddalone had been improperly terminated for a purely political motive. As part of his decision, the ALJ had made some purely factual findings, what the Court of Special Appeals referred to as "first-level factual findings relating to the issue of sole motive for dismissal." Among these purely factual findings were that the Secretary of Transportation (Porcari) knew of Maddalone only from media coverage and only as a political figure; that Porcari had no information about Maddalone's job performance; and that Porcari did not have any individualized personnel information about Maddalone. Upon judicial review, the Court of Special Appeals reversed the OAH decision. The court found that some of the "first-level findings ... are not supported by evidence in the agency record."[15] For example, the "evidence in the agency record does not support a reasonable finding that what Secretary Porcari knew about Maddalone ... was limited to Maddalone's political associations and belief, and did not include his lack of qualifications for the positions he held."[16]

*Consumer Protection Division v. Morgan*[17] involved judicial review of an order of the Consumer Protection Division (CPD) that found several property investors and real estate appraisers to have violated the Consumer Protection Act by engaging in unfair and deceptive practices to take advantage of unsophisticated, first-time home buyers in Baltimore City. There had been eighteen days of administrative hearings at OAH with many witnesses, including several expert witnesses. Several issues raised on judicial review dealt with whether some of the CPD's factual findings were supported by substantial evidence. In a careful, thorough opinion, the Court of Appeals reviewed the evidence in the record in support of the agency's findings and balanced this evidence against the evidence contrary to the agency's findings. On the issues of whether there was substantial evidence that Morgan had misrepresented prior sales histories by failing to note in his appraisals whether a property had been transferred within twelve months before the proposed sale, and whether there was substantial evidence that Morgan had misrepresented comparable sales, the court upheld the agency's findings as supported by substantial evidence. On the issue of whether Morgan had misrepresented neighborhood predominant values, however, the court ruled that the CPD's finding was not supported by substantial evidence. On this issue, the Court of Appeals evaluated the testimony of the one witness upon which the agency had based its finding. The court noted that the witness had

> presented only general testimony about the calculation of neighborhood predominant values. He did not produce any evidence showing how he arrived at his values for any of the properties.... [H]e acknowledged that he had not brought any documents to the hearing to show how he arrived at his values.... [H]is reports merely state his conclusion.[18]

*VanDevander v. Voorhaar*[19] involved the discipline of a sheriff's deputy arising from allegations that the deputy had used excessive force while performing an off-duty security job, and had made untruthful statements about the incident during an internal investigation. The Court of Special Appeals in its review of the evidence held that the finding that an untruthful statement had been made was not supported by substantial evidence.

15. 187 Md. App. 549, 577, 979 A.2d. 229, 246 (2009).
16. 187 Md. App. 549, 578, 979 A.2d. 229, 246 (2009).
17. 387 Md. 125, 874 A.2d 919 (2005).
18. 387 Md. 125, 209, 874 A.2d 919, 968–69 (2005).
19. 136 Md. App. 621, 767 A.2d 339, *cert. denied*, 364 Md. 463, 773 A.2d 514 (2001).

## §17.3. Inferences from the Facts

Substantial evidence review applies not only to agency findings of "raw facts" or "first-level facts" (the who, what, when, where facts), but also to the agency's drawing of inferences from the facts. Judicial review of the agency's inferences therefore is limited to whether the agency's inferences were reasonable. As the Maryland Court of Special Appeals wrote in *Travers v. Baltimore Police Department*:[20]

> A reviewing court may, and should, examine any inference, drawn by an agency, of the existence of a fact not shown by direct proof, to see if that inference reasonably follows from other facts which are shown by direct proof. If it does, even though the agency might reasonably have drawn a different inference, the court has no power to disagree with the fact so inferred.[21]

A useful case here is *Bond v. Department of Public Safety & Correctional Services*[22] which involved the termination of a state employee who had tested positive for marijuana. Significant to this case is that termination was only appropriate if the employee had used marijuana at work. The record contained no direct evidence that Bond used or possessed marijuana at work. The Court of Special Appeals correctly identified its task: "Giving due deference to the agency's fact-finding role, we must decide whether a reasonable inference that appellant smoked, possessed, or was under the influence of marijuana can be drawn from the bare fact that she tested positive for marijuana use."[23] The agency had "theorize[d] that the ALJ reasonably inferred, based on appellant's failed drug test, that it is more likely than not that appellant used or possessed marijuana at work."[24] The court reversed the termination. The court concluded that the "inference that appellant used or possessed marijuana at work cannot reasonably be drawn from the bare fact that she tested positive for marijuana use. Rather than drawing a permissible inference, the ALJ engaged in speculation."[25]

In *Maryland Department of Transportation v. Maddalone*,[26] the ALJ who had the final decisionmaking authority in a case involving the termination of a state employee had "deduced" that the Secretary of Transportation when he fired Maddalone "could not have known" whether Maddalone "possessed the qualifications he was seeking in employees." The Court of Special Appeals held that even though some of the first-level facts were supported by substantial evidence, this inference from those facts was not supported by substantial evidence. The termination decision was reversed.

*Anderson v. General Casualty Insurance Co.*[27] involved the issue whether a notice of insurance cancellation which was mailed to the insured "care of" a third party listed in the declarations page constituted proper notice sufficient to satisfy the statutory notice requirement of the Insurance Article of the Maryland Code. The ALJ made several pure factual findings, for example, that for twenty-six years, the insured had used the third party to receive notices and obtain insurance policies on his behalf. Based on "these facts,

20. 115 Md. App. 395, 693 A.2d 378 (1997).
21. 115 Md. App. 395, 420, 693 A.2d 378, 390 (1997).
22. 161 Md. App. 112, 867 A.2d 346 (2005).
23. 161 Md. App. 112, 125, 867 A.2d 346, 353 (2005).
24. 161 Md. App. 112, 125, 867 A.2d 346, 354 (2005).
25. 161 Md. App. 112, 125, 867 A.2d 346, 354 (2005).
26. 187 Md. App. 549, 979 A.2d. 229 (2009).
27. 402 Md. 236, 935 A.2d. 746 (2007).

and reasonable inferences drawn therefrom," the court upheld the agency finding that notice had been properly sent.

## § 17.4. Mixed Questions of Law and Fact

Substantial evidence review also applies to judicial review of an agency decision in a contested case that involves a mixed question of law and fact. Often, agency decisions are not purely factual or purely legal, but rather involve the application of the law, usually a statutory term, to the particular facts presented in the case. When the agency has applied the facts to a legal term in making its decision, a court will reverse the agency's decision on this mixed question of law and fact only if the decision is not supported by substantial evidence, i.e., unreasonable in light of all the facts in the record.[28]

Application of substantial evidence review to mixed questions of law and fact is well established in both federal and state administrative law. The leading federal case is the U.S. Supreme Court's *National Labor Relations Board v. Hearst Publications, Inc.*[29] which concerned whether vendors who sold newspapers on the street were employees or independent contractors of the publisher under the Federal Labor Management Relations Act. The Supreme Court wrote

> where the question is one of specific application of a broad statutory term in a proceeding in which the agency administering the statute must determine it initially, the review court's function is limited.... The Board's determination that specified persons are employees under this Act is to be accepted if it has warrant in the record and a reasonable basis.[30]

There are many cases in Maryland where the agency decision in a contested case is one of mixed fact and law. In some of these cases, the court identifies the issue being reviewed as one of mixed fact and law. In others, however, the court merely applies substantial evidence review without labeling the issue as mixed fact and law. Before discussing a sampling of some cases that apply substantial evidence reasonableness review to mixed questions of law and fact, one point needs to be made. In *Consumer Protection Division v. Luskins, Inc.*[31] the Court of Special Appeals wrote that "Maryland courts have not relied on federal law when determining what deference should be given to an agency's application of law to fact."[32] That is not an accurate statement; Maryland cases do follow the federal court's approach on this issue.

*Bayly Crossing, LLC v. Consumer Protection Division*[33] involved whether owners of undeveloped residential lots were unregistered "home builders" under the Home Builders Registration Act. Although the parties and the lower reviewing courts had viewed the issue as one of pure statutory interpretation, the Court of Appeals recognized that the issue involved application of the facts to the statutory term which presented a mixed

---

28. *See* Montgomery County v. Butler, 417 Md. 271, 9 A.3d 824 (2010).

29. 322 U.S. 111 (1944).

30. 322 U.S. 111, 131 (1944).

31. 120 Md. App. 1, 706 A.2d 102 (1998), *rev'd in part on other grounds*, 353 Md. 335, 726 A.2d 702 (1999).

32. 120 Md. App. 1, 24, 706 A.2d 102, 113 (1998), *rev'd in part on other grounds*, 353 Md. 335, 726 A.2d 702 (1999).

33. 417 Md. 128, 9 A.3d 4 (2010).

question of law and fact. The Court held that the agency's finding that the owner held itself out as a home builder was not supported by substantial evidence.

*Colburn v. Department of Public Safety & Correctional Services*[34] involved the issue whether correctional supervisors were exempt from the overtime requirements of the Fair Labor Standards Act (FLSA). One of the issues relevant to this determination was whether the supervisors were "salaried" employees. There were several pure factual findings, none of which were challenged. For example, the agency found that the supervisors were paid only for hours worked and had no set minimum amount they received regardless of the number of hours worked. These pure factual findings then had to be applied to the term "salaried employee" as used in the FLSA. The Court of Appeals held that the agency conclusion that the supervisors were salaried employees was supported by substantial evidence. Another issue of mixed question of law and fact in *Colburn* was whether the supervisors qualified for the administrative employee exemption under the FLSA. The court again held that there was substantial evidence to support the agency's application of the pure facts of the supervisors' job duties (which were generally undisputed) to the FLSA exemption.

*Trinity Assembly of God of Baltimore City, Inc. v. People's Counsel for Baltimore County*[35] involved a challenge to a local board of appeals denial of a church's request for a variance to erect a sign on its property which exceeded size limitations. One of the legal standards for a variance is that the property is "unique." The application of this statutory term "unique" to the facts in the church's variance request presented a mixed question of law and fact. The reviewing court correctly applied the substantial evidence standard, and upheld the board's denial.

In *Schwartz v. Maryland Department of Natural Resources*,[36] the issue was whether a vessel was "held for maintenance or repair" for purposes of whether an excise tax was owed. This presented a mixed question of law and fact which was reviewed under the substantial evidence standard. After reviewing the evidence in the administrative record, the agency decision was upheld as supported by substantial evidence.

The following cases also all upheld the agency's decision on a mixed question of law and fact as supported by substantial evidence:

- *Consumer Protection Division v. Morgan*.[37] This case involved a challenge to the imposition of a $34,000 fine. The factors for setting the fine were set forth in the statute. The agency's application of the facts in this case to the statutory criteria was supported by substantial evidence.
- *Charles County Department of Social Services v. Vann*.[38] The agency found that a father was responsible for indicated child abuse when the father hit a child with a belt buckle. This presented a mixed question of law and fact which was supported by substantial evidence.
- *Bergmann v. Board of Regents of the University System of Maryland*.[39] The decision whether a student qualifies for in-state tuition is a mixed question of law and fact reviewable under substantial evidence analysis.

34. 403 Md. 115, 939 A.2d 716 (2008).
35. 407 Md. 53, 962 A.2d 404 (2008).
36. 385 Md. 534, 870 A.2d 168 (2005).
37. 387 Md. 125, 874 A.2d 919 (2005).
38. 382 Md. 286, 855 A.2d 313 (2004).
39. 167 Md. App. 237, 892 A.2d 604 (2006).

- *Marzullo v. Kahl.*[40] The issue whether a facility for breeding, raising and marketing snakes was a "farm" under the zoning laws was a mixed question of law and fact which was supported by substantial evidence.
- *State Department of Assessments & Taxation v. North Baltimore Center, Inc.*[41] Whether an organization is a "charitable organization" exempt from the local property tax is a mixed question of law and fact. The agency decision was upheld since it was supported by substantial evidence.

On the other hand, there are cases where the court has reversed the agency's decision on a mixed question of law and fact because it was not supported by substantial evidence. For example, *Travers v. Baltimore Police Department*[42] involved several charges against a police officer, one of which was that Officer Travers had failed to obey an "order" from a superior officer when Travers did not leave the scene of an alleged domestic violence dispute involving Travers and his girlfriend. The Court of Special Appeals applied the facts to the legal term "order," and held that the finding that Travers had disobeyed an order was not supported by substantial evidence.

*Heard v. Foxshire Associates, LLC*[43] involved a decision by a county board of appeals to grant a special exception to permit a commercial shopping center in a residential area. The legal standard that was required to be applied to the exception request involved "adverse effect." Properly treating the issue of whether the applicant's request would have an adverse effect as a mixed question of law and fact, the Court of Special Appeals held that the agency's decision was not supported by substantial evidence.

## § 17.5. The Banks Case

An important case for the wrong reason is *Board of Physician Quality Assurance v. Banks.*[44] *Banks* involved a mixed question of law and fact which, as has been discussed, is subject to deferential substantial evidence review. *Banks*, however, has been cited as a case involving judicial review of a purely legal issue and that courts when reviewing an agency decision for an error of law should be highly deferential to the agency's legal conclusion. This is an incorrect reading of *Banks*.

Dr. Banks worked in the emergency room in a hospital. Banks was accused of sexually harassing several hospital employees. The Board of Physician Quality Assurance sought to discipline him. Pursuant to the Board's enabling statute, the Board can only discipline a physician if the misconduct occurred while the doctor was engaged "in the practice of medicine." Banks' defense included the argument that any sexual harassment or other misconduct that took place did not occur "in the practice of medicine." The court discussed the evidence involving Banks' conduct, and Banks' role and job responsibilities as a doctor in the emergency room. The court reviewed the Board's application of the facts specific to Dr. Banks to the statutory term "practice of medicine," and upheld the Board's decision. This is a classic example of a mixed question of law and fact which is reviewed by substantial

40. 366 Md. 158, 783 A.2d 169 (2001).
41. 361 Md. 612, 762 A.2d 564 (2000).
42. 115 Md. App. 395, 693 A.2d 378 (1997).
43. 145 Md. App. 695, 806 A.2d 348 (2002).
44. 354 Md. 59, 729 A.2d 376 (1999).

evidence, reasonableness review. To the extent that other Maryland cases, such as *Noland*,[45] cite *Banks* to support highly deferential review of pure issues of law, I disagree.

45. *See* discussion in Chapter 19.

# Chapter 18

# Judicial Review: Exceeds Statutory Authority or Jurisdiction

An agency decision in a contested case will be reversed by a reviewing court if the agency acted in excess of its statutory authority or jurisdiction.[1] It is axiomatic that an agency only has the powers delegated to it by the legislature, and any decision that exceeds the statutory grant of authority or jurisdiction from the legislature to the agency is invalid. Like the other grounds for reversal, this ground for reversal applies whether or not the agency is governed by the APA, and whether or not judicial review is provided by statute.

An easy example of an agency acting in excess of its statutory authority or jurisdiction would be if the agency's decision involved a subject area different than the subject area that the agency regulates. For example, if the Board of Pharmacy issued a decision disciplining a social worker, that decision would obviously be invalid. The actual cases, of course, are not so obvious, and sometimes involve close issues of statutory interpretation or mixed questions of law and fact.

## § 18.1. Mixed Questions of Law and Fact and Excess of Statutory Authority or Jurisdiction

Some challenges alleging that the agency has acted in excess of its statutory authority or jurisdiction involve mixed questions of law and fact. As discussed in Chapter 17 on Substantial Evidence Review, a mixed question of law and fact is reviewed under a substantial evidence standard which involves the court's review of the entire administrative record to determine whether the agency decision was reasonable. Judicial review of all issues involving a mixed question of law and fact is deferential to the agency, including issues involving excess of statutory authority or jurisdiction. An example of this type of case is *Board of Physician Quality Assurance v. Banks*,[2] discussed in Chapter 17, which involved the issue of the Board's jurisdiction over a doctor for misconduct during a period of time that the doctor asserted he was not engaged "in the practice of medicine." If Dr. Banks was not engaged in the practice of medicine at the time of misconduct, the Board would have no authority or jurisdiction to discipline him because under the Board's enabling statute, misconduct outside the practice of medicine is not within the Board's authority or jurisdiction. Because the Board's decision in *Banks* involved application of the particular

1. Maryland Code Annotated, State Government § 10-222(h)(3)(2).
2. 354 Md. 59, 729 A.2d 376 (1999).

facts involving Dr. Banks' job responsibilities at the hospital to the statutory phrase "in the practice of medicine," the Board's decision that Banks was engaged in the practice of medicine at the relevant time was subject to reversal only if the reviewing court found that the Board's decision was not supported by substantial evidence, that is, it was not a reasonable decision.

## § 18.2. Pure Issues of Law

Another category of cases arguing that the agency has acted in excess of statutory authority or jurisdiction involve pure issues of law. In these cases, there are no facts that need to be applied for the court to make its decision. These cases involve statutory interpretation of agency enabling statutes. The major debate in this type of case is the degree of deference, if any, the reviewing court should give to the agency's interpretation of its own statutory authority or jurisdiction. As the discussion below will demonstrate, some cases give no deference to the agency interpretation, while others do give some, perhaps even considerable, deference to the agency's own view of its statutory authority or jurisdiction.

## § 18.3. The No Deference Approach

In some cases involving whether the agency has exceeded its statutory authority or jurisdiction in its decision in a contested case, the Maryland courts have reviewed the agency decision with no deference. In these cases, the court independently decides the statutory issue. An early case is *Gutwein v. Easton Publishing Co.*[3] *Gutwein* involved review of the Commission on Human Relations' (CHR) interpretation that its statutory authorization to "take affirmative action" authorized it to award compensatory damages to a victim of employment discrimination. The Court of Appeals in *Gutwein* independently decided whether such authority existed by analyzing various statutes and cases from federal and state courts. This independent analysis led the court to conclude that the CHR did not have the statutory authority the agency claimed it did. No deference was given to the agency interpretation.

*Consumer Protection Division v. George*[4] also dealt with an agency's authority to "take affirmative action." The Consumer Protection Division interpreted this statutory phrase to include the authority to require a person who had been adjudicated in violation of the Consumer Protection Act to post a surety bond before the violator could engage in future business transactions. The Court of Appeals analyzed this statutory interpretation issue without any deference to the agency's interpretation. The court relied on the "plain language of the statute [which] specifically addresses the steps to take in the case of noncompliance with the Act."[5] The court also cited other cases that had construed "affirmative action" in the context of consumer protection laws. In its opinion, the Court of Appeals did not defer to the agency's interpretation of its own enabling statute.

3. 272 Md. 563, 325 A.2d 740 (1974), *cert. denied*, 420 U.S. 991 (1975).
4. 383 Md. 505, 860 A.2d 896 (2004).
5. 383 Md. 505, 521, 860 A.2d 896, 905 (2004).

The "no deference" approach was also deemed appropriate in *Consumer Protection Division v. Morgan.*[6] Among the many issues raised in this case was whether the Consumer Protection Division (CPD) had the power under the Consumer Protection Act (Act) to order joint and several liability. The Act did not provide expressly for joint and several liability. In resolving this issue, the Court of Appeals engaged in a statutory interpretation analysis no different than the analysis it would apply in a case not involving an agency's interpretation of a statute. The court looked at the purpose of the Act, and reviewed federal cases involving the Federal Trade Commission. The court concluded that the CPD could award restitution on a joint and several basis. The court's affirmance of the CPD's position was based on the court's independent interpretation of the statute; it was not based on any deference to the agency.

In affirming the Tax Court's decision that the Tax Court had the authority to order the Comptroller to pay interest on a tax refund, the Court of Appeals in *Comptroller of the Treasury v. Science Applications International Corporation*[7] applied traditional canons of statutory interpretation to make its own independent judgment on the statute's meaning. The court discussed plain meaning, definitions from several dictionaries, and "commonsense understanding"[8] to reach its decision. Although the Tax Court was affirmed, this was not based on any deference given to the Tax Court's interpretation of its statutory authority.

One issue presented in *Talbot County v. Miles Point Property, LLC*[9] was whether a county board of appeals had jurisdiction to hear a property owner's appeal from the county council's decision not to reclassify property for purposes of water and sewer service. The court identified the issue as pertaining "solely to conclusions of law respecting jurisdiction" which the court would review "de novo" with "no deference."

The no deference approach has also been employed by the Court of Special Appeals. For example, in *Linkus v. Maryland State Board of Heating, Ventilation, Air Conditioning & Refrigeration Contractors,*[10] Linkus had been denied a Masters HVAC license because he had been convicted of rape six years before his license application. The Board's justification for denying the license was based on what it understood to be its "broad discretionary authority to protect the public" through the licensing of HVAC contractors. Linkus challenged the denial of his Master's HVAC license on the ground that the Board had exceeded its statutory authority in relying on his rape conviction. Linkus argued that because his rape conviction was unrelated to any building or electrical code, it was outside the Board's jurisdiction. The Court of Special Appeals undertook its own independent evaluation of the relevant statutes and legislative history. It did not limit its determination to whether the Board was reasonable in its interpretation of its jurisdiction as set forth in its enabling statute. Based on its own independent evaluation, the court held that the Board was not empowered to consider moral character or criminal convictions unrelated to building and electrical codes.

*Blaker v. State Board of Chiropractic Examiners*[11] involved a disciplinary action against a chiropractor. The final order of the Board placed Blaker on probation for two years with four conditions. These conditions were his taking a course in record keeping, passing an examination, being monitored by a mentor, and submitting records for random review.

6. 387 Md. 125, 874 A.2d 919 (2005).
7. 405 Md. 185, 950 A.2d 766 (2008).
8. 405 Md. 185, 203, 950 A.2d 766, 776 (2008).
9. 415 Md. 372, 2 A.3d 344 (2010).
10. 114 Md. App. 262, 689 A.2d 1254 (1997).
11. 123 Md. App. 243, 717 A.2d 964, *cert. denied*, 351 Md. 662, 719 A.2d 1261 (1998).

Blaker argued that the Board exceeded its authority when it imposed these four conditions. At the time of Blaker's case, the relevant statute did not expressly provide that the Board could impose conditions on probation. The Board, however, interpreted the statute to grant it the power to impose such conditions. Significantly, although the Court of Special Appeals upheld the Board's interpretation, the court independently arrived at its conclusion based on general principles of statutory interpretation. The court did not limit its inquiry to whether the Board had acted reasonably in its interpretation of its enabling statute.

## § 18.4. Liquor Board Cases

There have been a few cases involving the jurisdiction and authority of liquor boards and their interpretation of their enabling statutes. Because liquor board cases are usually viewed sui generis, they are discussed separately here. In each of these cases, the court reviewed the liquor board's decision without any deference.

In *Board of Liquor License Commissioners for Baltimore City v. Hollywood Productions, Inc.*,[12] one issue was whether the liquor board had exceeded its authority by restricting the hours of a nightclub. Responding to complaints by area residents, the liquor board had ordered the nightclub to close at 7:00 p.m. on Sundays. Although the sanction of an early closing was not expressly authorized by statute, the liquor board argued that it had such authority because the restriction promoted the welfare and safety of the community. The Court of Appeals rejected the liquor board's position without giving any deference to the liquor board position. Because the legislature had set specific closing times for liquor licensees, as well as specific sanctions that the liquor board was authorized to impose, the liquor board did not have the implied authority to restrict hours of operation.

In *Board of Liquor License Commissioners for Baltimore City v. Fells Point Café, Inc.*,[13] an applicant for a liquor license had voluntarily agreed to certain conditions, e.g., type of music and percentage of revenue from sales of food, in order to avoid opposition from a neighborhood citizens group. The liquor license was granted on these conditions. When the café violated these agreed upon conditions, the liquor board imposed additional restrictions, e.g., no D.J. or live entertainment. The issue presented was whether it was within the liquor board's authority to have imposed the original conditions and then the subsequent conditions. The Court of Appeals reviewed these issues without any deference to the liquor board. The original conditions were upheld, but not the additional ones.

*Hollywood Productions* and *Fells Point Café* were applied by the Court of Special Appeals in *Board of Liquor License Commissioners for Baltimore County v. J.R. Brothers, Inc.*[14] where the court held that the board exceeded its statutory authority by ordering removal of a deck bar, and in *Blackburn v. Board of Liquor License Commissioners for Baltimore City*,[15] where the court held that the board did not exceed its statutory authority in prohibiting after-hours consumption of alcoholic beverages at a private membership club. In both

12. 344 Md. 2, 684 A.2d 837 (1996).
13. 344 Md. 120, 685 A.2d 772 (1996).
14. 119 Md. App. 308, 705 A.2d 16 (1998).
15. 130 Md. App. 614, 747 A.2d 725 (2000).

these liquor license cases, the courts independently analyzed the statutory authority and jurisdiction of the board giving no deference to the board's interpretation.[16]

* * *

The preceding discussion demonstrates that there is significant support in cases from different agencies for the principle that when a court is reviewing an agency's interpretation of its enabling statute in a challenge that the agency decision exceeds its authority or jurisdiction, the court will engage in its own independent statutory interpretation without any deference to the agency interpretation. But, as discussed next, not all cases follow this approach.

## § 18.5. Deferential Approach

There are some Maryland cases that contain language that supports a deferential approach by a court when reviewing an agency's interpretation of its statutory authority or jurisdiction, although in some of these opinions, it is unclear whether the grant of deference was significant to the outcome.

*Opert v. Criminal Injuries Compensation Board*[17] involved the denial of compensation by the Board to a motorcyclist who was injured when he swerved and lost control of his motorcycle to avoid hitting a pedestrian who was illegally walking on the Baltimore Beltway. In general, the Criminal Injuries Compensation Board is authorized by statute to compensate victims of a crime. The word "crime" is defined in the relevant statute to not include "an act involving the operation of a ... motor vehicle," except in certain situations such as when the operator of a motor vehicle causes intentional injury.[18] The Board denied the motorcyclist's claim because it interpreted the word "crime" to not include illegally walking on the Beltway, and thus the motorcyclist was not a "victim of a crime." In its opinion, the Court of Appeals first noted that "both parties acknowledged that there were no material facts in dispute and that the issue was one of statutory construction," and "therefore one of law."[19] The court then stated that:

> in construing statutes, our primary goal is always to discern the legislative purpose, the ends to be accomplished, or the evils to be remedied by a particular provision.... If the language is clear and unambiguous, we ordinarily need not look beyond the statute's provisions and our analysis ends.... If, upon this preliminary analysis, however, we conclude that the language is subject to more than one interpretation, it is ambiguous, and we resolve that ambiguity by looking to the statute's legislative history, case law, and statutory purpose.... To the extent relevant, we look as well to the statute's structure, including the title, and how the statute relates to other laws.[20]

All this is clearly consistent with a no-deference, independent review by the court of issues of law. The court continued, again consistent with a no-deference approach that:

16. *See also* Thanner Enters., LLC v. Baltimore County, 414 Md. 265, 995 A.2d 257 (2010).
17. 403 Md. 587, 943 A.2d 1229 (2008).
18. Maryland Code Annotated, Criminal Procedure § 11-801(d)(2).
19. 403 Md. 587, 593, 943 A.2d 1229, 1232 (2008).
20. 403 Md. 587, 593, 943 A.2d 1229, 1232–33 (2008).

> In a judicial review action in which an administrative agency's interpretation of the statute it is charged with implementing is challenged, it is ultimately for the court to determine whether the agency's interpretation of the statute is legally correct.[21]

The court then wrote, however, "in making that determination, the court generally gives considerable weight to the agency's view."[22] The court then embarked on an elaborate analysis of the statutory provision at issue employing a no-deference analysis, and concluded that the Board was wrong in its interpretation. At the very end of the opinion in a footnote the Court added: "Because this appears to be a case of first impression, we discern no long-standing or consistent practice by the Criminal Injuries Compensation Board to which particular deference would be due."[23] This statement is an application of the deference discussion in *Baltimore Gas & Electric*, discussed in Chapter 19, although that case was not cited in the footnote.

Three judges dissented in *Opert*. The dissenters wrote:

> By reversing the decision of the Criminal Injuries Compensation Board, the majority gives no deference to the interpretation of law offered by the agency charged with interpreting the Criminal Injuries Compensation Act and, thus, fails to apply the appropriate standard when reviewing an administrative agency adjudicatory decision, thereby confusing our jurisprudence, which we recently correctly explicated in *Maryland Aviation Administration v. Noland*.[24]

The dissent then quoted from footnote 3 in *Noland*. As discussed in Chapter 19 in the discussion of Judicial Review of Errors of Law, *Noland* does not support a highly deferential standard of review of legal issues. To further underscore why the dissent in *Opert* is not persuasive is its discussion of "applying the substantial evidence test" which is totally irrelevant to the review of pure issues of law such as the one involved in *Opert*. The dissent also cited as support for its deferential position *Board of Physician Quality Assurance v. Banks*,[25] which as discussed in Chapter 17 involved a mixed question of law and fact.

Although the majority in *Opert* gave no deference to the Commission's interpretation of the statute at issue, the majority did state that some deference may be appropriate in judicial review to challenges alleging that the agency has acted in excess of its statutory jurisdiction or authority.

Another case that mentions deference in regards to a pure issue of law involving a challenge to the agency's statutory jurisdiction or authority is *McCullough v. Wittner*.[26] McCullough was a prisoner who brought a lawsuit in circuit court seeking monetary damages for personal injuries he suffered as the result of being assaulted by a prison guard. The sole issue before the Court of Appeals was whether McCullough needed to exhaust the administrative process at the Inmate Grievance Commission before the court would consider his common law tort action. As discussed in Chapter 14, exhaustion may not be required if the agency cannot provide an adequate remedy. In its discussion of this exception to the exhaustion doctrine, the court addressed whether the Commission had the statutory authority to award monetary damages. The majority in *McCullough* on this issue first wrote "In our view, the Commission and Secretary have statutory authority to award

21. 403 Md. 587, 593, 943 A.2d 1229, 1233 (2008).
22. 403 Md. 587, 594, 943 A.2d 1229, 1233 (2008).
23. 403 Md. 587, 604 n.8, 943 A.2d 1229, 1239 n.8 (2008).
24. 403 Md. 587, 608–09, 943 A.2d 1229, 1241–42 (2008).
25. 354 Md. 59, 68, 729 A.2d 376, 381 (1999).
26. 314 Md. 602, 552 A.2d 881 (1989).

monetary damages as long as funds are appropriated or otherwise properly available for this purpose."[27] This "view" was based on the "language of the Inmate Grievance Commission statute itself." The statute's authorization of the Commission "to entertain any grievance or complaint against any official or employee of the Division of Corrections.... would seem to encompass one requesting a monetary award." The majority continued: "Moreover, there is no language in the statute which, even arguably, limits the remedial authority of the Commission," and "the Secretary is empowered to put the Commission's order into effect or to take whatever action he deems appropriate in light of the Commission's findings."[28]

After resolving the relevant issue based on a no-deference, independent statutory analysis, the majority added two sentences on deference:

> "In addition, the Commission and the Secretary of Public Safety and Correctional Services, soon after the enactment of the Inmate Grievance Commission statute, took the position that orders for the payment of money to inmates were authorized, and several monetary awards were made.... The interpretation of a statute by those officials charged with administering the statute is, of course, entitled to weight."[29]

The majority cited, inter alia, *Baltimore Gas & Electric Co.*[30]

Three judges filed a concurring opinion agreeing that exhaustion was required, but disagreeing that the Commission had the authority to award monetary damages. The concurring judges noted that this statutory authority discussion was "wholly unnecessary" since there were other reasons for requiring exhaustion stated in the majority opinion with which the concurring judges agreed. On the statutory authority issue, the concurring judges wrote that the majority "badly misconstrue[d] the legislative intent when it concludes that the words 'any grievance or complaint' in the statute vest authority in the Commission to make such a monetary personal injury damage award."[31] The concurring opinion then engaged in its own statutory analysis. At the end of their opinion, the concurring judges added its comment on deference:

> And, finally, I think the [majority] has failed to give due consideration to the well-recognized rule that the consistent view taken of a statute by administrative officers charged with its enforcement should be afforded persuasive influence in determining the proper judicial construction ... that the Commission is not empowered to grant monetary awards for personal injuries.[32]

What is especially interesting about the *McCullough* majority and concurring opinions is that both the majority and concurring judges first analyzed the excess of statutory authority issue based on their own independent statutory construction evaluation with no-deference to the Commission. Only at the end of their respective opinions did both add the deference point to support their different conclusions. When engaging in a truly deferential judicial review, such as substantial evidence review, the court begins with the presumption that the agency is correct, and then evaluates whether the agency decision is unreasonable. In *McCullough*, however, the court began its analysis with its own independent evaluation, and used deference to the agency to add support to its own in-

27. 314 Md. 602, 610, 552 A.2d 881, 885 (1989).
28. 314 Md. 602, 611, 552 A.2d 881, 885 (1989).
29. 314 Md. 602, 611–12, 552, A.2d 881, 886 (1989).
30. 305 Md. 145, 501 A.2d 1307 (1986).
31. 314 Md. 602, 614, 552 A.2d 881, 887 (1989).
32. 314 Md. 602, 617, 552 A.2d 881, 888 (1989).

dependent conclusion. Although both the majority and concurring opinions in *McCullough* did argue for some deference to the agency position, neither opinion took the position that the commission should be affirmed as long as the commission interpretation was reasonable. Both opinions relied on the sliding deference analysis set forth in *Baltimore Gas & Electric Co.*,[33] although the application of this deference standard led to opposite conclusions.

Even when the court discusses deference in its review of an agency decision challenged as being in excess of the agency's statutory authority or jurisdiction, this deference is not the same deference given to an agency when the court is reviewing an agency decision for lack of substantial evidence. On issues of law, the court will always retain the right to make its own independent decision as to the proper interpretation of a statute. More on the issue of judicial deference and pure issues of law is included in Chapter 19 on "Errors of Law."

33. 305 Md. 145, 501 A.2d 1307 (1986). *See* discussion in Chapter 19.

# Chapter 19

# Judicial Review: Errors of Law

An agency decision in a contested case can also be reversed if the decision is "affected by any other error of law."[1] The phrase "any other error of law" reflects that challenges to the constitutionality of the agency's decision and to the jurisdiction or authority of the agency are also legal challenges. This ground for reversal therefore covers legal challenges other than constitutional challenges and other than jurisdictional and authority challenges. In truth, many legal challenges are not easily categorized as "errors of law" or challenges to the "jurisdiction or authority" of the agency, and practically, in most cases, it does not matter which ground is alleged. In most situations, multiple grounds for reversal will be argued. This chapter will discuss cases that have been decided under the "affected by any other error of law" ground, with special focus on the deference which the courts give to the agency decision.

## § 19.1. Deference

When a court is reviewing an agency decision for an error of law, there are three different standards of deference that the court could possibly use. First, a court could give no deference to the agency decision on the issue of law. Under the no deference approach, the court reviews the legal issue independent of the agency's interpretation of the law. Under this approach, the court's role in interpreting the law is the same as the court's role in interpreting the law as if no agency decision had been issued. Using traditional principles of statutory interpretation relying on factors such as plain meaning and legislative history, the court decides what it believes is the correct interpretation of the law. This approach is the approach courts take in reviewing constitutional challenges to an agency decision. This deference approach has also been employed in Maryland cases reviewing an agency decision based on "other errors of law." For example in *Evans v. Burrus*,[2] the Court of Appeals wrote that a "reviewing court is under no constraints in reversing an administrative decision that is premised solely upon an erroneous conclusion of law."[3]

On the other hand, the courts could use a "great deference" approach, which would allow the court to reverse the agency based on an error of law only if the agency's interpretation of the law was unreasonable. This approach is similar to the approach courts take in reviewing agency findings of fact, inferences from the facts, and mixed questions of law and fact under substantial evidence review. It appears that no Maryland case has applied this "great deference" approach in its review whether the agency decision

1. Maryland Code Annotated, State Government § 10-222(h)(3)(iv).
2. 401 Md. 586, 933 A.2d 872 (2007), *cert. denied*, 552 U.S. 1187 (2008).
3. 401 Md. 586, 592, 933 A.2d 872, 875 (2007).

was affected by an error of law. No Maryland court equates its judicial review role for an error of law to its role when engaging in substantial evidence review.

Another approach is where the court when reviewing a challenge to the agency decision based on an error of law gives "some deference" to the agency's interpretation of the law, but still decides the issue of law based on the court's own independent evaluation of what the court believes is the proper legal interpretation. Under this approach, the court will substitute its judgment and decide what is the correct interpretation, like the no-deference approach, but in performing its review function, the court is mindful and gives some deference to the agency's interpretation. There are Maryland cases that have taken this "some deference" approach when reviewing an agency decision based on an error of law.

When this "some deference" approach is taken, an important issue is "how much" deference should the court give to the agency. In deciding this issue, the most helpful statement is found in *Baltimore Gas & Electric Co. v. Public Service Commission*,[4] which involved the meaning of the statutory term "reasonable level." The Public Service Commission (PSC) had interpreted "reasonable level" to mean a "level that compares favorably with a statistical reference standard and that has not been reduced as a result of managerial imprudence."[5] In reviewing the PSC's interpretation of this statutory term, the Court of Appeals wrote:

> The weight to be accorded an agency's interpretation of a statute depends upon a number of considerations. Although never binding upon the courts, the contemporaneous interpretation of a statute by the agency charged with its administration is entitled to great deference, especially when the interpretation has been applied consistently and for a long period of time.... Another important consideration is the extent to which the agency engaged in a process of reasoned elaboration in formulating its interpretation of the statute. When an agency clearly demonstrates that it has focused its attention on the statutory provisions in question, thoroughly addressed the relevant issues, and reached its interpretation through a sound reasoning process, the agency's interpretation will be accorded the persuasiveness due a well-considered opinion of an expert body.... In addition, the nature of the process through which the agency arrived at its interpretation is a relevant consideration in assessing the weight to be accorded the agency's interpretation. If the interpretation is the product of neither contested adversarial proceedings nor formal rule promulgation, it is entitled to little weight.[6]

Based on these principles, the Court of Appeals held that the PSC "correctly interpreted" the statute.[7]

The deference analysis set forth in *Baltimore Gas & Electric Co.* is similar to the deference analysis used by federal courts in reviewing federal agency decisions based on *Skidmore v. Swift & Co.*[8] ("*Skidmore* deference"). The Supreme Court in *Skidmore* discussed the deference due to interpretations of the Fair Labor Standards Act by the Administrator of the Wage and Hour Division of the Department of Labor. The Court stated that while an agency's interpretation of its enabling statute was "not controlling," it did "constitute a

4. 305 Md. 145, 501 A.2d 1307 (1986).
5. 305 Md. 145, 159, 501 A.2d 1307, 1314 (1986).
6. 305 Md. 145, 161–62, 501 A.2d 1307, 1315 (1986).
7. *See* Bayly Crossing, LLC v. Consumer Protection Division, 417 Md. 128, 9 A.3d 4 (2010).
8. 323 U.S. 134 (1944).

body of experience and informed judgment to which courts and litigants may properly resort for guidance."[9] According to *Skidmore*, the weight a court will give an agency interpretation "will depend upon the thoroughness evident in its consideration, the validity of its reasoning, its consistency with earlier and later pronouncements, and all those factors which give it power to persuade, if lacking power to control."[10] Some Maryland cases which accord deference to agency interpretations of law rely on this type of analysis to determine in each case how much deference should be given to the agency position.

## § 19.2. The No-Deference Cases

There are many Maryland cases where a court reviews an agency decision in a contested case to determine if the decision was affected by an error of law and gives no deference to the agency. This section will discuss some of these cases.

*VNA Hospice of Maryland v. Department of Health & Mental Hygiene*[11] involved the issue whether a section of the Health General Article of the Maryland Code which used the phrase "home-based hospice services to a patient" included home-based bereavement services to the family members of dying or deceased persons. VNA argued that bereavement services did qualify under the statute; DHMH interpreted the statute differently. The Court of Appeals emphasized that there were no facts in dispute; the issue was a purely legal one. The Court without any deference to the agency interpretation, independently interpreted the statute, and concluded that the statute included bereavement services. The agency decision was reversed as affected by an error of law.

Among the issues presented in *Reier v. State Department of Assessments and Taxation*[12] was whether State-offered benefits were included in an award under the statutory phrase "full back pay" in a case involving the reinstatement of a state employee whose termination had been rescinded. On this issue, the Court of Appeals wrote: "We conduct a de novo review of the ALJ's legal conclusion that benefits are not included in 'full back pay' as the question is one of statutory interpretation and, therefore, a purely legal inquiry."[13] The court then applied techniques of traditional statutory analysis including the plain language of the statue, various dictionary definitions of the word "full," and legislative history. Without giving or even discussing any deference to the agency's conclusion of law, the Court of Appeals independently decided that the agency had not properly interpreted the statute.

*Gwin v. Motor Vehicle Administration*[14] involved the argument that the MVA had made an error of law in its interpretation of two sections of the Transportation Article of the Maryland Code. The MVA had interpreted the two statutes to permit it to recognize out-of-state revocations as a basis for denying a Maryland drivers license. The Court of Appeals undertook its own independent analysis of the statutes relying on traditional principles of statutory construction. The court affirmed the MVA because the court "agreed" with

9. 323 U.S. 134, 140 (1944).
10. 323 U.S. 134, 140 (1944).
11. 406 Md. 584, 961 A.2d 557 (2008).
12. 397 Md. 2, 915 A.2d 970 (2007).
13. 397 Md. 2, 26, 915 A.2d 970, 984 (2007).
14. 385 Md. 440, 869 A.2d 822 (2005).

the MVA's interpretation, i.e., the court considered whether the agency was "correct." The court did not base its holding on any deference to the MVA's interpretation of the statute.

Other cases also support the position that on questions of law, the agency receives no deference. In *Giant Food, Inc. v. Department of Labor, Licensing & Regulation*,[15] the Court of Appeals independently determined the meaning of "stoppage of work" as used in the Maryland unemployment benefits statute. It reversed the agency decision because it disagreed with the agency's interpretation of the statutory term. No deference was given to the agency. In *Maryland Insurance Administration v. Maryland Individual Practice Association*,[16] the Court of Special Appeals independently interpreted a statute involving a medical health plan's obligation to pay claims incurred because of a workplace injury. The Court of Special Appeals held that the agency had improperly interpreted the statute. In *Department of Health & Mental Hygiene v. Dillman*,[17] the relevant issue was the meaning of the word "available" in a statute involving placement for mentally disabled persons in a private residential setting. The court held that "the interpretation of 'available'... is an issue of law which we review *de novo*."[18] In *Maryland Department of the Environment v. Ives*,[19] the issue was whether a statute permitted state employees to use work-related accident leave for treatment of an occupational disease. The Court of Special Appeals decided this issue without any deference to the agency's interpretation.

Further support for the no deference approach is found in *Landsman v. Maryland Home Improvement Commission*[20] where the Commission had ruled that an amendment to its enabling statute increasing the maximum amount of an award from the Home Improvement Guaranty Fund did not apply retroactively to a home improvement contract signed before the amendment became law. The Court of Special Appeals held that no deference was owed to the Commission's interpretation of the statute. After its independent review of the statute, the court held that the statute did have retroactive application.

In *Seminary Galleria, LLC v. Dulaney Valley Improvement Ass'n*,[21] one issue was whether the agency should have applied res judicata in making its decision. The Court of Special Appeals rejected the argument that an agency's determination of the application of res judicata was a mixed question of law and fact reviewed by the substantial evidence reasonableness standard. The court held that application of res judicata was an issue of law which the court reviews *de novo* with no deference to the agency.

There are other cases which can be found where the court when reviewing an agency decision in a contested case to determine if the decision was affected by an error of law gave no deference to the agency and decided the matter *de novo* based on what the court decided was the proper interpretation or application of the law. The crucial factor in these cases is that the court was reviewing an issue of law not dependent on any disputed facts. No distinction was made whether the law being interpreted was the agency's enabling statute, a statute which the agency regularly administers, a law which the agency applies occasionally, or a law that the agency had never interpreted. As the cases indicate, there is strong support for the no-deference approach to judicial review based on an error of law.

---

15. 356 Md. 180, 738 A.2d 856 (1999).
16. 129 Md. App. 348, 742 A.2d 22 (1999).
17. 116 Md. App. 27, 695 A.2d 211 (1997).
18. 116 Md. App. 27, 34, 695 A.2d 211, 215 (1997).
19. 136 Md. App. 581, 766 A.2d 657, *cert. denied*, 364 Md. 462, 773 A.2d 514 (2001).
20. 154 Md. App. 241, 839 A.2d 743 (2003).
21. 192 Md. App. 719, 995 A.2d 1068 (2010).

## § 19.3. The "Some Deference" Approach

Even though there are many cases that accord no deference to the agency when its decision in a contested case is being challenged based on an error of law, there are a significant number of cases where the court does accord deference to the agency's interpretation of law, although the amount of deference given varies from case to case. *Comptroller of the Treasury v. Blanton*[22] involved the Tax Court's interpretation of a section of the Tax-General Article of the Maryland Code to limit a certain tax credit only to certain taxes paid to the state, but not to local jurisdictions. In its review, the Court of Appeals wrote that "an administrative agency's interpretation and application of the statute which the agency administers should ordinarily be given considerable weight by reviewing courts."[23] The court then affirmed the agency interpretation based on the court's reading of the plain language of the statute.

*Kushell v. Department of Natural Resources*[24] involved a dispute over the proper interpretation of a section of the State Boat Act. The Court of Appeals wrote that it reviewed errors of law "*de novo*," applying cardinal rules of statutory interpretation to ascertain and effectuate legislative intent.[25] These rules of statutory interpretation do not differ if a statute is being interpreted in the first instance by a court or whether the court is reviewing an agency's interpretation. The court, however, also wrote that "it will frequently give weight to an agency's experience in interpretation of a statute that it administers," but then quickly added that it is always the court's "prerogative to determine whether an agency's conclusions of law are correct."[26] *Kushell* was explained in *Adventist Health Care Inc. v. Maryland Health Care Commission*[27] as involving an issue "of statutory construction, as to which our review is *de novo*.... [ N]otwithstanding the deference due the interpretation of the administrative agency, after reviewing the applicable canons of construction, we concluded under ordinary rules of English grammar, the plain text supports Kushell's reading."[28] In *Adventist Health*, the court continued, "In *Kushell*, the statute was so plain, and clear, that the Department's expertise in the matter could not, and did not, make a difference."[29]

*Bowen v. City of Annapolis*[30] involved a city civil service board's denial of an increase in pension benefits to retired firefighters and police officers. The dispute involved the interpretation and application of a section of the Code of the City of Annapolis. In its opinion, the Court of Appeals wrote:

> In reviewing the Civil Service Board's legal conclusions, we shall determine if the administrative decision is premised upon an erroneous conclusion of law. In doing so, we give the administrative agency's interpretation and application of

22. 390 Md. 528, 890 A.2d 279 (2006).
23. 390 Md. 528, 534, 890 A.2d 279, 283 (2006).
24. 385 Md. 563, 870 A.2d 186 (2005).
25. 385 Md. 563, 576, 870 A.2d 186, 193 (2005). Rules of statutory interpretation discussed in *Kushell* included relying on the plain language of the statute; relying on ordinary, popular understanding of words; making no word, clause, sentence, or phrase superfluous or nugatory; not interpreting words in isolation; attempting to harmonize provisions so that each may be given effect; and presuming that unambiguous words mean what they say.
26. 385 Md. 563, 576, 870 A.2d 186, 193 (2005).
27. 392 Md. 103, 896 A.2d 320 (2006).
28. 392 Md. 103, 124–25, 896 A.2d 320, 333 (2006).
29. 392 Md. 103, 125, 896 A.2d 320, 333 (2006).
30. 402 Md. 587, 937 A.2d 242 (2007).

> the statute which it administers considerable weight. In other words, we accord a degree of deference to the position of the administrative agency in our review of the administrative agency's legal conclusion, especially when the statutory language ... is ambiguous. Despite this considerable deference granted to the administrative agency, it is still within our prerogative to determine whether an agency's interpretations and conclusions are correct, and to remedy the situation if found to be wrong. On the other hand, when statutory language is clear and unambiguous, administrative constructions, no matter how well entrenched, are not given weight by [the] Court.[31]

Because the court found that "the plain text of [the statute] to be clear and unambiguous," the entire deference discussion was not significant to the court's ruling.

*Anderson v. General Casualty Insurance Co.*[32] also included a discussion of deference and judicial review of an error of law. The Court of Appeals wrote that "[a]s to conclusions of law, we give significant weight to an agency's experience in interpreting a statute the agency administers" unless the language of the statute is unambiguous. If the statute is unambiguous, "our analysis ends there."[33]

*AT&T Communications of Maryland, Inc. v. Comptroller of the Treasury*[34] involved a tax assessment by the Comptroller against AT&T for collection of sales and use tax from out-of-state vendors for "900" numbers. Under the relevant tax statute, if AT&T was merely a common carrier, it was not responsible for the tax. The Comptroller had been successful in the Tax Court. On judicial review, the Comptroller argued that this issue was a mixed question of fact and law which could only be reversed if the court found the agency's decision unreasonable. The Court of Appeals, however, deemed the issue to be "a purely legal question." The Court wrote that "[w]ith regard to its resolution of purely legal issues, a degree of deference to the Tax Court's interpretation and application of a statute that it administers is often appropriate to be accorded by a reviewing court.... It should be noted, however, that although we frequently give weight to an agency's experience in interpretation of a statute it administers, it is always within our prerogative to determine whether an agency's conclusions of law are correct, and to remedy them if wrong."[35] The Court of Appeals reversed the Tax Court decision as affected by an error of law.

*Brown v. Handgun Permit Review Board*[36] involved the denial of an application to renew a permit for a handgun. The denial was based on the agency's interpretation and application of the term "disqualifying crime" in the Maryland Code, Public Safety Article. The Court of Special Appeals wrote that "We review questions of law *de novo*, although we give weight to an agency's interpretation of a statute it is charged with enforcing where the interpretation is longstanding and falls within the agency's area of expertise." In this case, the court "decline[d] to give significant weight to the Board's present interpretation" because it was "not long-standing."[37] The court then decided based on its own application of canons of statutory interpretation that the agency had properly interpreted the statute.

* * *

---

31. 402 Md. 587, 612–13, 937 A.2d 242, 257 (2007).
32. 402 Md. 236, 935 A.2d 746 (2007).
33. 402 Md. 236, 244–45, 935 A.2d 746, 751 (2007).
34. 405 Md. 83, 950 A.2d 86 (2008).
35. 405 Md. 83, 92–93, 950 A.2d 86, 92 (2008).
36. 188 Md. App. 455, 982 A.2d 830 (2009), *cert. denied*, 412 Md. 495, 988 A.2d 1008 (2010).
37. 188 Md. App. 455, 467, 982 A.2d 830, 837 (2009).

The cases in this section demonstrate that some Maryland cases when reviewing whether an agency decision is affected by an error of law give some deference to the agency. Deference is given if the error of law challenge is based on the agency's interpretation of a statute (1) which the agency regularly administers, (2) which involves agency expertise, or (3) which is long-standing. No Maryland case seems to accord any deference to an agency's interpretation of a statute which the agency does not regularly administer or enforce. Even when some deference is accorded, the courts still independently decide the correct interpretation of the law based on its independent application of traditional canons of statutory interpretation. If the statutory language is unambiguous, no deference is ever given.

## § 19.4. Chevron Deference

Administrative Law practitioners who also deal with judicial review in federal courts of federal agency decisions involving errors of law are undoubtedly familiar with *Chevron USA, Inc. v. Natural Resources Defense Council, Inc.*[38] *Chevron* involved the federal Environmental Protection Agency's interpretation of the Clean Air Act's term "stationary source." In *Chevron*, the U.S. Supreme Court set forth a two-step approach that federal courts use when reviewing a federal agency's interpretation of a statute the agency administers. The court first determines whether Congress has "spoken to the precise question at issue." If Congress has spoken to the precise question, that resolves the matter. Neither an agency nor a court can alter the clear intent of the legislature. However, if legislative intent is either missing or ambiguous, the court will defer to the agency's interpretation of its own statute, and uphold the agency's interpretation if the agency's interpretation is reasonable. In this second step of *Chevron*, the court does not engage in its own independent evaluation of the statute as it would if there had been no agency interpretation.

*Chevron* deference only applies when the federal agency is interpreting its own enabling statute or a statute which it regularly enforces or administers. Moreover, subsequent U.S. Supreme Court cases have limited *Chevron* deference to agency interpretations that are the result of rulemakings that follow the Federal APA notice and comment procedures or formal adjudications. Agency interpretations contained in opinion letters, policy statements, manuals, or other formats not the product of a formalized process do not warrant *Chevron* deference.[39] Such informal interpretations may be entitled to *Skidmore* deference. Moreover, agency interpretations advanced for the first time in litigation,[40] or which concern issues not within the agency's expertise are not entitled to *Chevron* deference.[41]

*Chevron* deference goes well beyond the deference Maryland courts have given to agency interpretations of law. No Maryland case applies the two-step approach of *Chevron*, and no Maryland case has upheld an agency decision on a pure issue of law based on merely a reasonableness standard.

38. 467 U.S. 837 (1984).

39. *See* Christensen v. Harris County, 529 U.S. 576 (2000); United States v. Mead Corp., 533 U.S. 218 (2001).

40. *See* Bowen v. Georgetown Univ. Hosp., 488 U.S. 204 (1988).

41. *See* Collins v. National Transportation Safety Board, 351 F.3d 1246 (D.C. Cir. 2003).

## § 19.5. Agency Interpretation of Its Regulations

As discussed in Chapter 2, a regulation is a law equal to a statute. An agency's interpretation of a regulation could be the basis of an error of law challenge to an agency decision in a contested case. If the agency decision is based on its interpretation of a regulation of another agency, the court should give no deference to the agency's interpretation; the court should independently use its own judgment to interpret the regulation. The more typical situation involves an agency interpreting and applying its own regulation. What should the court's role be in reviewing this agency interpretation? There are a few Maryland cases that address this.

*Crofton Convalescent Center, Inc. v. Department of Health and Mental Hygiene, Nursing Home Appeal Board*[42] involved the agency's refusal to reimburse a nursing home under Medicaid for certain interest payments. The agency's refusal to reimburse was based on its interpretation of a regulation in COMAR involving the proper definition of "mortgage interest," and whether the nursing home's "swap payments" qualified as mortgage interest. The majority opinion wrote:

> An agency's interpretation of a regulation is a conclusion of law. Yet even when reviewing an agency's legal conclusions, an appellate court must respect the agency's expertise in its field. Likewise, a great deal of deference is owed to an administrative agency's interpretation of its own regulation. Despite the deference, it is always within our prerogative to determine whether an agency's conclusions of law are correct.... Although we keep in mind the considerable weight afforded an agency's interpretation of its regulations, we may not abdicate our responsibility to examine independently the regulations upon which the Board relied ... to determine if the administrative decision is premised upon an erroneous conclusion of law.[43]

The majority's review of the COMAR regulation led to its affirmance of the agency's denial of the reimbursement. In dissent, Judge Adkins joined by Judge Harrell, accused the majority of "abdicating our responsibility to examine independently the regulations upon which the Board relied.... The deference we give to agency determinations of law has limits. As the majority recognizes, it is always within our prerogative to determine whether an agency's conclusions of law are correct."

*Department of Health and Mental Hygiene v. Campbell*[44] involved the interpretation of the phrase "personal needs allowance" in a COMAR section. The agency's interpretation was that personal needs allowance meant expenses for incidental items used for clothing or grooming such as haircuts, pedicures, shampoos, and chewing gum. The agency rejected an interpretation that personal needs allowance included commissions payable to a guardian of the property. In addressing the proper role of a court when reviewing an agency's interpretation of its own regulation, the court wrote the following:

> The question whether guardianship commissions are an allowable deduction ... under COMAR as a personal needs allowance is solely one of law. As to the review of questions of law, we have pointed out ... that questions of law are completely subject to review by the courts, although the agency's interpretation of a statute

42. 413 Md. 201, 991 A.2d 1257 (2010).
43. 413 Md. 201, 215–16, 991 A.2d 1257, 1265 (2010).
44. 364 Md. 108, 771 A.2d 1051 (2001).

> may be entitled to some deference.... We have noted also that the deference under these circumstances is by no means dispositive, nor otherwise as great as that applicable to factual findings or mixed questions of law and fact.... Accordingly, [the] Court is not bound by the agency's legal conclusions; we are, in short, under no constraints in reversing an administrative decision which is premised solely upon an erroneous conclusion of law.[45]

The Court of Appeals then "agreed" that guardianship commissions were not the kind of personal needs contemplated by the COMAR provision.

To be compared to the language in *Campbell* is *Adventist Health Care, Inc. v. Maryland Health Care Commission*.[46] This case involved the agency's interpretation of a section of COMAR providing that a relocation of a portion of an existing cardiac surgery program was subject to the same Certificate of Need process that was required to approve a new program. Several hospitals challenged this interpretation of COMAR claiming that a different process was required for a relocation. In upholding the agency, the Court of Appeals stated that

> [A] great deal of deference is owed an administrative agency's interpretation of its own regulation.... A question concerning the interpretation of an agency's rule is as central to its operation as an interpretation of the agency's governing statute. Because an agency is best able to discern its intent in promulgating a regulation, the agency's expertise is more pertinent to the interpretation of an agency's regulation than to the interpretation of its governing statute.[47]

The court also cited *Maryland Transportation Authority v. King*[48] for the proposition that "an agency's interpretation of an administrative regulation is of controlling weight unless it is plainly erroneous or inconsistent with the regulation," and that the agency's interpretation should be given "considerable weight."[49] The court then added that "[d]eference to the interpretation of the agency, however, does not mean acquiescence or abdication of our construction responsibility. Despite the deference, it is always within our prerogative to determine whether an agency's conclusions of law are correct."[50] In this case, because the language of the regulation was "at best, ambiguous ... giving deference to the Department's interpretation of its regulation ... may be appropriate to resolve ambiguity, as long as there is a substantial basis ... for that interpretation." Although the court in *Adventist Health* used the terms "considerable weight" and "great deference" in its opinion, the court view did not view its role merely to decide whether the agency acted reasonably.

Although there are valid reasons to give an agency's interpretation of its own regulation some deference, I have a concern as suggested in *Adventist Health* that more deference should be given to an agency interpretation of a regulation which is ambiguous. It is the agency itself that drafts and adopts the regulation. It is a classic maxim of contract law that ambiguities in a contract are resolved against the drafter. By giving more deference to an agency interpretation of its own regulation when the agency has adopted an ambiguous regulation is rewarding the agency for its lack of clarity. Denying deference to an agency interpretation of an ambiguous regulation could act as an incentive to agencies to draft

45. 364 Md. 108, 118, 771 A.2d 1051, 1057 (2001).
46. 392 Md. 103, 896 A.2d 320 (2006).
47. 392 Md. 103, 119–20, 896 A.2d 320, 330 (2006).
48. 369 Md. 274, 799 A.2d 1246 (2002).
49. 369 Md. 274, 288–89, 799 A.2d 1246, 1254 (2002).
50. 392 Md. 103, 121, 896 A.2d 320, 331 (2006).

regulations that provide clear guidance to regulated persons and the public.[51] Rather than considering whether the regulation is ambiguous in deciding what deference is appropriate, a better approach would be to apply the factors adopted in *Baltimore Gas & Electric* as discussed earlier in this chapter.

## § 19.6. Deference and Auer

In judicial review of a federal agency's interpretation of its own regulation, federal courts apply what is known as *Auer* deference based on the U.S. Supreme Court decision in *Auer v. Robbins*.[52] In *Auer*, the Court stated that a federal agency's interpretation of its own regulations will be upheld unless it is "plainly erroneous or inconsistent with the regulations." The exact meaning of *Auer* is still evolving especially whether to what extent, if any, it differs from *Chevron* deference. No Maryland court has applied *Auer* in its review of an agency's interpretation of its own regulations, and to the extent that *Auer* suggests a reasonableness standard of judicial review of an agency interpretation of its own regulations, Maryland caselaw is contrary to *Auer*.

## § 19.7. Noland Footnote 3

Before we leave the discussion of judicial review of agency decisions involving errors of law, a discussion of footnote 3 in *Maryland Aviation Administration v. Noland*[53] is warranted. *Noland* has been cited by Maryland courts—too often in my opinion—for the proposition that judicial review of an agency interpretation of law should be highly deferential, almost to the point of non-renewability. Let me comment.

*Noland* involved judicial review of the Maryland Aviation Administration's decision to terminate a state employee. None of the issues raised in this case involved an agency's interpretation of any statute or regulation. No errors of law were alleged. Nevertheless, in a lengthy footnote, several statements were made about judicial review of issues of law. The first part of footnote 3 focused on the phrase "substituted judgment." The footnote states that although other Maryland cases have stated that a court may substitute its judgment for that of the agency's on issues of law, this was "unfortunate," "misleading," and "inaccurate," because it "suggests, with respect to legal issues, that no deference whatsoever is owed to the agency decision." The footnote then states, "That is not the law."[54] Throughout the footnote, the only case cited as support is *Board of Physician Quality Assurance v. Banks*.[55] But as discussed in Chapter 17, Substantial Evidence Review, *Banks* involved a mixed question of law and fact, not an issue of pure law. Moreover, as discussed in this chapter and in Chapter 18, there are many cases which hold that when a court is

51. *See* Carven v. State Retirement and Pension System of Maryland, 416 Md. 389, 7 A.3d 38 (2010), where Judges Bell, Harrell and Murphy wrote in dissent that because the "ambiguous COMAR regulation at issue applies to a remedial statute, the regulation should be liberally construed in favor of the claimant." 416 Md. 389, 416, 7 A.3d 38, 54 (2010).

52. 519 U.S. 452 (1997).

53. 386 Md. 556, 873 A.2d 1145 (2005).

54. 386 Md. 556, 573 n.3, 873 A.2d 1145, 1154 n.3 (2005).

55. 354 Md. 59, 729 A.2d 376 (1999).

reviewing an agency decision on a purely legal issue, the court reviews the legal issue with no deference, and independently decides the proper interpretation of the law.

A further problem with footnote 3 in *Noland* is that after citing *Banks*, it continues to state that the words "substituted judgment" are "inappropriate" in judicial review of an agency decision because the "term 'judgment' is often used to mean the exercise of discretion, such as an official exercising 'good judgment'.... Obviously, a court may not substitute its exercise of discretion for that exercised by the Executive Branch agency or official." I agree with this statement, but I disagree that it is relevant to the issue of the court's review of an agency's interpretation of law. An agency's interpretation of a statute or regulation is not an exercise of agency discretion.

My disagreement with *Noland* footnote 3 continues with its position that if a court does not give strong deference to an agency's interpretation of law, separation of powers would be violated. But it is the judiciary, not the executive branch, which is the branch of government that interprets the law. I agree with Judge Wilner's statement in his dissent in *Comptroller of the Treasury v. Citicorp International Communications, Inc.*[56] where he wrote:

> I recognize that great deference is to be paid to the factual determinations of the Tax Court and that some deference is to be paid to its legal determinations. If the Tax Court, which, despite its name, is an administrative agency and not a court, has misconstrued either a statute or a contract, however, it has made a legal error, and we are not obliged to give any deference at all to that kind of error. Indeed, we would be violating Art. 8 of the Maryland Declaration of Rights and Art. IV of the Maryland Constitution if, under the guise of deference to administrative expertise we effectively abrogated, through delegation to an Executive Branch agency, our Constitutional responsibility to construe statutes and contracts and interpret the law.[57]

After seemingly attempting to adopt a highly deferential approach to review of issues of law, footnote 3 in *Noland* concludes with a standard that, in my opinion, is not highly deferential. The footnote ends with the following sentence: "If there is a need to articulate a 'standard' for judicial review of an agency's legal rulings, it is sufficient to say that a reviewing court must determine if the administrative decision is premised upon an erroneous conclusion of law." This standard authorizes the court to engage in a "rightness" review—whether an *error* has been made. Whenever a court focuses on error, its review entails an independent evaluation of the agency decision. Such an independent review could give some deference to the agency position based on various factors such as the agency's expertise and thoroughness of consideration (as discussed earlier in this chapter), but "erroneous" review is not highly deferential.

56. 389 Md. 156, 884 A.2d 112 (2005).
57. 389 Md. 156, 184, 884 A.2d 112, 129 (2005).

# Chapter 20

# Judicial Review: Arbitrary or Capricious

An agency decision in a contested case that is arbitrary or capricious will be reversed by a reviewing court. The APA provides that a court may reverse or modify the agency decision "if any substantial right of the petitioner may have been prejudiced because a finding, conclusion, or decision is arbitrary or capricious."[1] The same arbitrary or capricious review applies to judicial review under Administrative Mandamus,[2] and the court's inherent power of review.[3] Arbitrary or capricious review applies to APA agencies and non APA agencies in an identical manner.

## § 20.1. A Case-by-Case Reasonableness Review

The arbitrary or capricious standard is a reasonableness standard. If the agency has acted unreasonably without a rational basis, the agency has acted in an arbitrary or capricious manner. In its application to contested cases, arbitrary or capricious review is similar to substantial evidence review in that both are deferential to the agency. Under both substantial evidence and arbitrary or capricious review, the court does not decide whether it agrees with the agency decision or whether it believes the agency reached the correct decision; rather the court is limited to deciding whether the agency acted reasonably. Although similar in this respect, arbitrary or capricious review and substantial evidence review are different standards. An agency decision can be supported by substantial evidence, yet be arbitrary or capricious.[4] This is true for a couple of reasons. First, substantial evidence review is limited to whether the evidence in the formal record created at the hearing reasonably supports the agency's findings of fact. Arbitrary or capricious review, on the other hand, applies not only to the agency's findings of fact, but also applies to all components of the agency decision. Secondly, arbitrary or capricious review is not limited to the factual record created at the hearing. Arbitrary or capricious review permits the court to consider any argument that the agency has acted unreasonably, even if the argument is based on information outside the agency record.

It is impossible to catalogue every circumstance when an agency acts in an arbitrary or capricious manner that would justify reversal of the agency decision. Attorneys and judges should understand that this standard requires rational conduct by the agency in all respects. Each case must be evaluated on an individual basis. With this understanding,

---

1. Maryland Code Annotated, State Government § 10-222(h)(3)(vi).
2. Md. Rule 7-403(2)(F).
3. See Harvey v. Marshall, 389 Md. 243, 884 A.2d 1171 (2005).
4. *See* Harvey v. Marshall, 389 Md. 243, 304, 884 A.2d 1171, 1202–08 (2005).

there are several cases in Maryland that are helpful in understanding judicial review under the arbitrary or capricious standard.

Some Maryland cases when engaging in arbitrary or capricious review refer to the definitions of the words "arbitrary" and "capricious" found in different editions of *Black's Law Dictionary* and in non-legal dictionaries.[5] Dictionary definitions of arbitrary relied upon by the courts include:

1. Something done without adequate determining principle; non-rational and willful and unreasoning action, without consideration and regard for facts and circumstances presented.
2. Founded on prejudice or preference rather than on reason or fact.
3. In an unreasonable manner, as fixed or done capriciously or at pleasure. Without adequate determining principle; non-rational; not governed by any fixed rules or standard.
4. Willful and unnecessary action, without consideration and regard for facts and circumstances presented.

*Black's Law Dictionary* (6th ed.) defines "arbitrary and capricious" to mean "willful and unreasonable action without consideration or in disregard of facts or law or without determining principle."[6] Although slightly different words are used in different dictionaries and different editions of the same dictionary, all point to one standard: reasonableness. An agency action will be held to be arbitrary or capricious if the agency has acted unreasonably.

In deciding reasonableness under arbitrary or capricious review, the courts have identified several ways in which an agency would be acting in an arbitrary or capricious manner. Courts have focused on the following factors:

1. Has the agency considered all relevant factors in making its decision, or has it ignored relevant factors?
2. Has the agency based its action on any irrelevant factors?
3. Is the agency action consistent with the policy goals of its enabling statute and other relevant statutes?
4. Has the agency acted in a manner consistent with its earlier decisions, and if not, has the agency provided an adequate explanation for the different results?
5. Has the agency treated similarly situated persons differently?
6. Has the agency provided an adequate explanation of its decision?

*Hurl v. Board of Education of Howard County*[7] involved a challenge to the involuntary transfer of a public school teacher by the school board. The Court of Special Appeals rejected various arguments that the school board's decision was arbitrary or capricious. The court held that the school board had provided "rational reasons" for the transfer that were not "contrary to sound educational policy," the statutory standard for transferring a teacher.[8] The school board had not ignored the teacher's "crystalline work record" which

5. A discussion of the various dictionary definitions can be found in *Harvey v. Marshall*, 389 Md. 243, 298–99, 884 A.2d 1171, 1204–05 (2005).

6. Blacks Law Dictionary 898 (6th ed. 1990).

7. 107 Md. App. 286, 667 A.2d 970 (1995).

8. 107 Md. App. 286, 309, 667 A.2d 970, 981 (1995).

was a relevant factor for the board to consider. Nor had the school board based its decision on an irrelevant factor when it relied on the school superintendent's "subjective professional judgment" that the teacher should be transferred. Additionally, the court rejected the teacher's argument that the school board had failed to provide an adequate explanation for the transfer.

*Montgomery County v. Anastasi*[9] involved the argument that the Montgomery County Police Department had deviated from its long established practice of promoting police officers in a strict test score order. In *Anastasi*, a police officer was successful in his challenge to the new promotion practice which considered factors other than test scores. The Court of Special Appeals, citing the U.S. Supreme Court's *Motor Vehicle Manufacturers Association v. State Farm Mutual Auto Insurance Co.*[10] and cases from the U.S. Court of Appeals for the District of Columbia,[11] stated that courts "must scrutinize inconsistent administrative decisions to insure that the decisions represent an intentional change and not merely evidence of arbitrary and capricious enforcement."[12] Therefore, "an agency changing its course must supply a reasoned analysis indicating that prior policies and standards are being deliberately changed, not casually ignored, and if any agency glosses over or swerves from prior precedents without discussion, it may cross the line from tolerably terse to intolerably mute."[13] In *Anastasi*, a rational explanation had not been provided.

*Anastasi* was argued in *Blaker v. State Board of Chiropractic Examiners*[14] when a chiropractor sought access to non-public orders of the Board of Chiropractic Examiners relating to prior charges of incompetence against other chiropractors. Blaker sought those records in order to determine if "the action taken against him constitutes an unexplained deviation from prior Board decisions." Although Blaker was denied access to the records because a statute expressly prohibited their release, the principle that an agency is acting in an arbitrary or capricious manner when it deviates from established precedent without a reasonable explanation for the change was in no way questioned. *Anastasi* was also argued in *Christopher v. Montgomery County Department of Health and Human Services.*[15] Christopher's claim was that the agency had "singled [her] out, in an arbitrary and capricious manner" because she chose to appeal an earlier administrative decision. The court rejected this claim. There was "no evidence in the record that the ALJ treated Christopher any differently from any other applicant, ... acted inconsistently, or deviated from prior policies."[16]

*Swoboda v. Wilder*[17] involved a challenge by neighbors and a community association to a decision by the Baltimore County Board of Appeals approving a building permit in a townhouse community. Two arbitrary or capricious arguments were presented and rejected. First, the Court of Special Appeals rejected the argument that the Board had considered irrelevant factors in making its decision. The Board acted properly in considering factors other than the foundation wall and garage. Secondly, the court rejected the argument

9. 77 Md. App. 126, 549 A.2d 753 (1988).

10. 463 U.S. 29 (1983) (the air bag case).

11. Local 32, American Fed'n of Gov't Employees v. Federal Labor Relations Authority, 774 F.2d 498 (D.C. Cir. 1985); Greater Boston Television Corp. v. Federal Communications Commission, 444 F.2d 841 (D.C. Cir. 1970), *cert. denied*, 403 U.S. 923 (1971).

12. 77 Md. App. 126, 138, 549 A.2d 753, 758 (1988).

13. 77 Md. App. 126, 137, 549 A.2d 753, 758 (1988).

14. 123 Md. App. 243, 717 A.2d 964, *cert. denied*, 351 Md. 662, 719 A.2d 1261 (1998).

15. 381 Md. 188, 849 A.2d 46 (2004).

16. 381 Md. 188, 215, 849 A.2d 46, 62 (2004).

17. 173 Md. App. 615, 920 A.2d. 518, *cert. denied*, 400 Md. 649, 929 A.2d. 891 (2007).

that the Board had acted inconsistently with a past decision. The court's response to this allegation was:

> We do not find the Board's decision in this case to be inconsistent with its decision in *Milligan*. Although both decisions concern corner lots, the Stoneleigh case involved a separate accessory structure for a single family home, rather than an addition to a townhouse end unit. Most importantly, in both cases, the Board cited the factors of mail and package delivery as evidence that supported its orientation decision. Similarly, in both cases, the Board relied on architectural expert opinion that it found persuasive.[18]

## § 20.2. MTA v. King

All of the cases discussed above are consistent with traditional arbitrary or capricious review in Federal Administrative Law and Administrative Law in other states. Arbitrary or capricious review is widely accepted as an overall reasonableness review performed on an individual case by case basis. Unfortunately, there is one Maryland case which sets forth a different standard for arbitrary or capricious review, and whose language has been cited in some other opinions. As discussed below, this case, *Maryland Transportation Authority v. King*,[19] presents an incorrect statement of arbitrary or capricious review.

In *King*, a state employee challenged the MTA's decision to terminate his employment. King argued that termination was improper because the MTA had failed to follow its own regulation which required progressive discipline prior to termination. The Court of Special Appeals had reversed the termination sanction based on the *Accardi* doctrine.[20] The State petitioned the Court of Appeals for certiorari to "decide when, if at all, the *Accardi* doctrine applies to an executive agency's actions." Although certiorari was granted on the *Accardi* issue, in its opinion, the Court of Appeals held that the MTA had not violated any of its regulations, and therefore the court did not "explore the *Accardi* doctrine." No issue involving arbitrary or capricious review had been granted certiorari in *King*, and no issue involving arbitrary or capricious review was presented. Nevertheless, the majority opinion included a discussion of arbitrary or capricious review, which was not only irrelevant to the case, but also substantively not correct in two respects—in its discussion of abuse of discretion, and in its definition of arbitrary or capricious. This chapter section will discuss the incorrect substantive standard for arbitrary or capricious review set forth in *King*; the abuse of discretion issue will be discussed in Chapter 21.

In *King*, the majority defined arbitrary or capricious review to require the court to determine whether the agency had acted in an "extreme and egregious" manner.[21] No authority was cited for this "extreme and egregious" standard. I know of no case from any state or federal court that defines arbitrary or capricious as meaning extreme and egregious. The extreme and egregious standard is inconsistent with the universally accepted definition of arbitrary or capricious review as being a reasonableness review. Reasonableness is a deferential review, and it is undisputable that arbitrary or capricious review is deferential to the agency decision. It is quite clear that a court cannot substitute its judgment for that

18. 173 Md. App. 615, 644, 920 A.2d. 518, 535 (2007).
19. 369 Md. 274, 799 A.2d 1246 (2002).
20. *See* Chapter 22.
21. 369 Md. 274, 291, 799 A.2d 1246, 1255–56 (2002).

of the agency under arbitrary or capricious review. But "extreme and egregious" sets the bar far too high. It suggests that an agency decision that is unreasonable and without any rational basis must be affirmed unless it is extreme and egregious. That is not what arbitrary or capricious means.

It bears repeating that no issue involving arbitrary or capricious was involved in *King* nor was certiorari granted on any question involving arbitrary or capricious review. The entire discussion of arbitrary or capricious review was irrelevant to decide the case. Nevertheless, the majority in *King* decided to use this case to redefine arbitrary or capricious review in a manner unsupported by any authority. Subsequent to *King*, some other Maryland cases have discussed arbitrary or capricious review in terms of extreme and egregious. The only authority cited by these cases is *King*. *King* and those cases that cite *King* should be rejected. A reviewing court would not only be applying the wrong standard when employing an extreme and egregious test to arbitrary or capricious review, but, in my opinion, it also would be abdicating its constitutional responsibility if it were only willing to reverse an agency under the arbitrary or capricious standard for extreme and egregious conduct.

## §20.3. Agency Refusal to Act

Arbitrary or capricious review is the appropriate standard when a court is asked to review an agency's refusal to act. This principle was first stated in *Harvey v. Marshall*[22] which includes a very detailed discussion of arbitrary or capricious review.

*Harvey v. Marshall* involved the refusal of the Child Support Enforcement Administration (CSEA) to forgive child support arrearages that Harvey owed the State. The arrearages were incurred before Harvey had gained custody of his children. When Harvey obtained custody, he argued that it would be "in the best interests" of his children to waive the arrearages so that his funds could be used for the children's current needs.[23] Although CSEA recognized that it had the authority to waive the arrearages, it refused to do so.

The Court of Appeals stated the issue to be "whether a decision not to exercise statutory discretion ... may be subject to judicial review, and, if so, what standard of review should apply."[24] The court's answer was that "when an agency, in the face of a formal invocation of its discretion by an affected person coming within the class of persons contemplated by the statute, fails to act on a matter committed to its discretion by that statute," the matter is subject to judicial review pursuant to the court's inherent power, and the applicable standard of review is whether the agency decision is "arbitrary, illegal, capricious or unreasonable."[25] The court then addressed the merits of Harvey's claim that the CSEA's refusal to exercise its discretion to eliminate his child support arrearages was arbitrary, illegal, capricious, or unreasonable because the agency failed to consider the "best interests of the child." The court held that CSEA's decision was not arbitrary or capricious because the CSEA under its statute is not authorized to consider the best interests of the child in deciding whether to forgive arrearages. In other words, the agency had not failed to consider

22. 389 Md. 243, 884 A.2d 1171 (2005).

23. Harvey claimed that the arrearages adversely affected his credit rating, prevented him from buying a home, and undermined his ability to save for his children's education.

24. 389 Md. 243, 273, 884 A.2d 1171, 1189 (2005).

25. 389 Md. 243, 277, 884 A.2d 1171, 1191 (2005).

a relevant factor in making its decision. Harvey also argued that the CSEA's decision was arbitrary, illegal, capricious or unreasonable because by failing to consider the best interests of the child, the CSEA was acting contrary to its "stated guiding principle." The court responded that although it recognized an agency decision may be deemed "arbitrary or capricious" if it ignores the expressly stated policy goals of the agency, "we find that the CSEA was not obligated to apply ... the best interest of the child standard in deciding to forgive Harvey's child support arrearages. In situations in which courts have determined that stated policy goals may influence a finding of arbitrary, illegal, capricious or unreasonable action, the stated policy goal has referred explicitly and specifically to the particular action or exercise of discretion being challenged."[26]

The *Harvey* opinion then set forth a detailed discussion of arbitrary or capricious review based on many past cases. The Court of Appeals in *Harvey* made the following points:

1. The arbitrary or capricious standard is best understood as a reasonableness standard.
2. Each case must be evaluated on an individual basis because it is impossible to catalogue every circumstance when an agency acts in an arbitrary or capricious manner.
3. Dictionary definitions of "arbitrary" and "capricious" support the position that "so long as the actions of administrative agencies are reasonable or rationally motivated, those decisions should not be struck down as arbitrary or capricious."
4. Arbitrary or capricious decisionmaking occurs when decisions are made impulsively, at random, or according to individual preference rather than motivated by a relevant or applicable set of norms.
5. An agency decision may be deemed arbitrary or capricious if it is contrary to or inconsistent with an enabling statute's language or policy goals.[27]
6. An agency action may be arbitrary or capricious if it is irrationally inconsistent with previous decisions.
7. An agency action may be arbitrary or capricious if individuals are given substantially different sanctions for identical conduct.

The opinion in *Harvey* also noted that beginning with *Maryland Transportation Authority v. King*,[28] arbitrary or capricious had been at times described as requiring agency action to be "extreme and egregious." The opinion then noted that I had written in an earlier book that this definition of arbitrary or capricious is much too deferential, and that such a definition amounts to an abdication of the court's responsibility.

Another case involving arbitrary or capricious review of an agency refusal to act is *Board of License Commissioners for Prince George's County v. Global Express Money Orders, Inc.*[29] In this case, the Board refused to report to the circuit court that two witnesses who had been subpoenaed failed to appear at the administrative hearing. The relevant statute permitted the Board to report to the court a witness' failure to appear at the administrative hearing, but it did not require the agency to do so. The Court of Special Appeals applied

26. 389 Md. 243, 294 n.31, 884 A.2d 1171, 1202 n.31 (2005), *citing* Hurl v. Board of Education of Howard County, 107 Md. App. 286, 667 A.2d 970 (1995).

27. *See* Office of the Public Defender v. Maryland, 413 Md. 411, 993 A.2d 55 (2010).

28. 369 Md. 274, 799 A.2d 1246 (2002).

29. 168 Md. App. 339, 896 A.2d 432 (2006).

the arbitrary or capricious standard to the Board's refusal. The court upheld the Board's decision because the Board had explained its action which was based on relevant factors such as there had been no proffer that the witnesses had been properly served, and the subpoena request had been made only one day before the hearing.

# Chapter 21

# Judicial Review: Abuse of Discretion

Despite some controversy caused by one opinion, which will be addressed shortly, a court reviewing an agency decision in a contested case will reverse the agency if its decision constitutes an abuse of discretion. Abuse of discretion review applies whenever the agency decision involves some measure of discretion. Abuse of discretion review is available whether judicial review is obtained by statute or the inherent review power of the court, and whether or not the agency is governed by the APA. Abuse of discretion review in Maryland appears as both an independent ground for reversal as well as a component of arbitrary or capricious review. In all situations, judicial review of an agency's exercise of discretion is highly deferential.

## § 21.1. Reasonableness

Substantively, abuse of discretion review is a reasonableness review. An agency abuses its discretion when it exercises its discretion in an unreasonable way. In *Wilson-X v. Department of Human Resources*,[1] the Court of Appeals offered the following explanations of abuse of discretion:

(1) A failure to consider the proper legal standard in reaching the decision.

(2) Discretion exercised in a manifestly unreasonable manner.

(3) Discretion exercised which no reasonable person would exercise.

(4) Discretion which is exercised in an arbitrary or capricious manner.

## § 21.2. MTA v. King

Some controversy exists over abuse of discretion judicial review because of *Maryland Transportation Authority v. King*.[2] *King* involved a state employee who had violated several workplace conduct rules over a period of several years. The agency ordered his termination from state employment. On judicial review to the circuit court, the employee argued that his termination should be reversed for three reasons: the findings were not supported by substantial evidence; the decision was arbitrary or capricious; and the agency had failed

1. 403 Md. 667, 944 A.2d 509 (2008).
2. 369 Md. 274, 799 A.2d 1246 (2002).

to follow its own regulations which allegedly required progressive discipline before termination. The circuit court rejected all three arguments and upheld the termination. All three arguments were then presented to the Court of Special Appeals. The Court of Special Appeals affirmed the agency on the substantial evidence and arbitrary or capricious arguments,[3] but reversed the termination sanction on the progressive discipline regulation argument relying on the *Accardi* doctrine.[4] The *Accardi* doctrine, discussed in Chapter 22, requires agencies to follow their own regulations. The State filed a petition for certiorari, which was granted by the Court of Appeals solely on the *Accardi* issue.

The Court of Appeals unanimously held in *King* that the agency had not violated any of its regulations, and therefore would not rule on the *Accardi* issue—the only issue upon which certiorari had been granted and the only issue which had been briefed and argued. Nevertheless, the majority opinion included in its discussion that a court was not authorized to review an agency decision for abuse of discretion.[5] According to the majority, although arbitrary or capricious review was appropriate, abuse of discretion review was not. Both Judges Wilner and Harrell felt compelled to respond to this point in separate concurring opinions.

In his concurring opinion, Judge Wilner wrote that he disagreed that "there is some substantive difference between an abuse of discretion and an arbitrariness and capriciousness standard of review."[6] Wilner criticized the majority opinion for "suggesting a distinction that really does not exist."[7] Wilner added that the "fact that the words 'abuse of discretion' do not appear in the judicial review section of the Maryland APA does not mean that agencies are immune from judicial review when, in fact, they abuse their allowable discretion, either under common law principles or under the APA."[8] Judge Wilner then cited various cases that held that the difference between an abuse of discretion standard and arbitrary and capricious standard was "only a semantic, not a substantive difference."[9]

Judge Harrell in his separate concurring opinion wrote that "[i]t has long been established that Maryland courts have inherent power to correct abuses of discretion and arbitrary, illegal, capricious, or unreasonable acts of administrative agencies,"[10] and that "[t]o the extent ... [the majority opinion's] words would be construed as suggesting that 'abuse of discretion' in no way plays a role in review by courts of agency action through legal modalities other than a petition for judicial review, I would caution the reader."[11]

## § 21.3. Cases Reviewing Agency's Discretion

Strong support exists for the position that judicial review for abuse of discretion is appropriate when a Maryland court reviews an agency decision. First, it is significant that Maryland Rule 7-403(2)(G) expressly provides that a court may issue a writ of mandamus reversing an agency decision if the decision constitutes an abuse of the agency's discretion.

3. 369 Md. 274, 280, 799 A.2d 1246, 1249 (2002).
4. 369 Md. 274, 281, 799 A.2d 1246, 1249–50 (2002).
5. 369 Md. 274, 290–91, 799 A.2d 1246, 1255–56 (2002).
6. 369 Md. 274, 292, 799 A.2d 1246, 1256 (2002).
7. 369 Md. 274, 292, 799 A.2d 1246, 1256 (2002).
8. 369 Md. 274, 293, 799 A.2d 1246, 1256–57 (2002).
9. 369 Md. 274, 295, 799 A.2d 1246, 1258 (2002).
10. 369 Md. 274, 299, 799 A.2d 1246, 1260 (2002).
11. 369 Md. 274, 299, 799 A.2d 1246, 1260 (2002).

The Committee Notes to the Rules of Administrative Mandamus state that the "intent of the new rules is to clarify that judicial review of quasi-judicial actions is the same whether or not a statute provides for judicial review."

Further support for abuse of discretion review in Maryland is found in Federal Administrative Law. The Federal APA provides that a court will reverse an agency decision that is "arbitrary, capricious, an abuse of discretion or otherwise not in accordance with law."[12] This standard has always been recognized as one standard. It is hornbook law that "these three terms [arbitrary, capricious, abuse of discretion] do not have independent significance; arbitrary, capricious, or abuse of discretion review is one standard."[13] Substantively, all three terms mean the same thing—an agency decision that is unreasonable must be reversed.

Perhaps the strongest support that abuse of discretion judicial review is appropriate and available in Maryland Administrative Law is that Maryland cases have reviewed an agency's exercise of discretion employing a reasonableness standard. Sometimes this reasonableness review is labeled arbitrary or capricious review, and sometimes it is labeled abuse of discretion review. It makes no difference which label is used, the substantive standard is the same—reasonableness. It seems to make more sense to label the review "abuse of discretion" when the agency decision involves an exercise of discretion by an agency, instead of labeling it arbitrary or capricious review, but this semantic debate is not significant. Discussed below are cases all of which would need to be reversed if in fact the majority opinion in *King* was correct that Maryland courts have no power to review an agency's exercise of discretion for abuse of that discretion.

As discussed in Chapter 9, under the APA, most agencies have the discretion to delegate their authority to hold and decide contested case hearings to OAH or to retain this authority within the agency.[14] Moreover, if the agency exercises its discretion to delegate the hearing to OAH, the agency has the discretion to delegate either the final or proposed decisionmaking authority.[15] The Board of Pharmacy is one of those agencies that has exercised its discretion not to use OAH. In *Spencer v. Maryland State Board of Pharmacy*,[16] one of the arguments presented was that the Board should be required to delegate the case to OAH. The Court of Appeals in reviewing this discretionary power of the Board, applied the arbitrary or capricious standard, and refused to require the Board to delegate any power to OAH.

*Maryland State Police v. Zeigler*[17] also involved an agency that held its own hearings. This case involved a decision by the agency to reopen the hearing and call additional witnesses. The court held that this decision was within the discretion of the agency. The court reviewed this discretionary decision of the agency by applying the arbitrary or capricious standard. The agency's exercise of its discretion was upheld.

As discussed in Chapter 5, an agency cannot enforce its own subpoenas because under separation of powers, an agency cannot be delegated the power of contempt. An agency must file a request with a court to enforce its subpoenas. In *Board of License Commissioners for Prince George's County v. Global Express Money Orders, Inc.*,[18] a person ignored the

12. 5 U.S.C. § 706(2)(A).
13. W. Funk & Seamon, Administrative Law 287 (Aspen 2d ed. 2006).
14. Maryland Code Annotated, State Government § 10-205.
15. Maryland Code Annotated, State Government § 10-205(b).
16. 380 Md. 515, 846 A.2d 341 (2004).
17. 330 Md. 540, 625 A.2d 914 (1993).
18. 168 Md. App. 339, 896 A.2d 432 (2006).

subpoena of the Board. The Board decided not to seek judicial enforcement of its subpoena, and issued a final decision without the testimony of this subpoenaed witness. One of the grounds argued to the court to reverse the final agency decision involved the Board's decision not to seek circuit court enforcement of the subpoena. This discretionary act of the Board was upheld by the court. The court reviewed the reasons why the agency did not seek judicial enforcement, and found the Board's decision a reasonable exercise of the agency's discretion.

The Board of Physician Quality Assurance (now the Board of Physicians) was given the statutory authority to proceed by a process known as "summary suspension." It is within the Board's discretion to decide when summary suspension should be utilized. In *Board of Physician Quality Assurance v. Mullan*,[19] one issue presented for review was the Board's decision to proceed by summary suspension. This discretionary decision of the Board was upheld as not arbitrary or capricious.

All these cases demonstrate that an agency's exercise of discretion is judicially reviewable under a reasonableness standard. It is not accurate to say that Maryland law does not permit judicial review for abuse of discretion.

## § 21.4. Agency Decision to Proceed by a Contested Case Instead of Rulemaking

Review for abuse of discretion is also used in challenges to the agency's decision to resolve a matter by holding a contested case proceeding instead of a rulemaking proceeding. Some background is useful in order to understand the cases.

As discussed in Chapter 1, administrative agencies usually are granted by the legislature both quasi-legislative power, the power to adopt regulations, and quasi-judicial power, the power to decide contested cases. When faced with an issue within its jurisdiction, the agency can decide to resolve that issue by initiating the rulemaking process or by initiating a contested case. For example, if the Consumer Protection Division (CPD) was interested in prohibiting the advertisement of new cars without disclosure of the cost of freight, the CPD could draft a proposed regulation prohibiting such an advertisement, and eventually adopt that regulation after complying with the procedures required by the APA for adopting regulations. The focus of the rulemaking proceeding would be whether such advertisements are deceptive. On the other hand, the CPD could decide not to propose a regulation, but to file an administrative complaint (Notice of Agency Action) against a car dealer that had placed an advertisement for a new car that did not list the cost of freight. A contested case would be held where the focus would be whether the advertisement was deceptive. Whatever process the agency selected—rulemaking or contested case—would lead to the determination whether an advertisement for a new car that did not include the cost of freight was deceptive.

Even though most agencies have been delegated both the power to use adjudication or the power to use rulemaking to resolve issues within their jurisdiction, the general view is that it is preferable for the agency to use rulemaking. This preference is based on a few factors. Once a rule is adopted, it is binding on the entire industry and there is no need to relitigate the matter for each member of the industry. Contested case orders, on the

19. 381 Md. 157, 848 A.2d 642 (2004).

other hand, bind only the parties to the case. Rulemaking is also viewed as fairer because it provides wider notice and permits wider participation than an adjudication. Moreover, rulemaking is fairer because rules apply only to future conduct; adjudications apply to past conduct. Even though rulemaking is the preferred method, the issue still exists whether a losing party at a contested case can get a court to vacate the agency's order on the ground that the agency should have proceeded by rulemaking. This issue, which has also been raised in Federal Administrative Law and in other states, involves abuse of discretion review.

This issue was first presented to a Maryland court in *Consumer Protection Division v. Consumer Publishing Co.*[20] which involved a claim of false advertising of diet pills. A contested case proceeding against Consumer Publishing led to a final order adverse to it. Upon judicial review, Consumer Publishing made various arguments, one of which was that the Consumer Protection Division (CPD) was required to proceed by rulemaking rather than by a contested case because the allegedly deceptive advertising practices were industry-wide. The Court of Appeals, relying on a line of federal cases, first held that "administrative agencies are not precluded from announcing new principles in adjudicative proceedings, and that the choice between rulemaking and adjudication lies in the first instance within the agency's discretion."[21] The court concluded that the agency's choice of a contested case should not be reversed. The court also noted that some states and federal courts followed a "more restrictive view" that saw an abuse of discretion if the agency used a contested case to "change the law and establish rules of widespread application."[22] Without adopting this more restrictive view, the court in *Consumer Publishing* held that even under this view, the CPD's discretionary decision to use a contested case proceeding instead of a rulemaking proceeding should be upheld.

The rulemaking versus contested case issue was also discussed in *Baltimore Gas & Electric Co. v. Public Service Commission.*[23] The Public Service Commission (PSC) in a contested case permitted BG&E to recover only 50 percent of certain costs it incurred in purchasing supplemental power during an outage because BG&E had failed to demonstrate that the outage was not the result of imprudent management. BG&E argued that this policy could only be developed in a rulemaking. The court rejected BG&E's argument that the PSC had abused its discretion in adopting this standard in a contested case. The court stated that the PSC had not developed a new standard that was being retroactively applied to the detriment of a company that had relied upon past pronouncements. The court seemed influenced by the fact that the three other companies affected by the order had participated in the PSC proceeding and had made known their positions.

The only case where a Maryland court did vacate an agency's adjudicatory order as an abuse of discretion and order the agency to engage in rulemaking is *CBS, Inc. v. Comptroller of the Treasury.*[24] In audits of CBS for years prior to 1980, CBS's treatment of its advertising receipts were not challenged by the Comptroller. In the audits for 1980 and 1981, however, the Comptroller applied a new approach that led to a higher tax liability. CBS argued that this new policy could only be accomplished through a rulemaking proceeding. The Court of Appeals agreed with CBS, stating that while it would "not attempt to make an all-en-

---

20. 304 Md. 731, 501 A.2d 48 (1985).

21. 304 Md. 731, 753–54, 501 A.2d 48, 60 (1985), *citing* Nat'l Labor Relations Bd. v. Bell Aerospace Co., 416 U.S. 267 (1974).

22. 304 Md. 731, 755, 501 A.2d 48, 60–61 (1985), *citing* Ford Motor Co. v. Federal Trade Commission, 673 F.2d 1008 (9th Cir. 1981), *cert. denied*, 459 U.S. 999 (1982).

23. 305 Md. 145, 501 A.2d 1307 (1986).

24. 319 Md. 687, 575 A.2d 324 (1990).

compassing statement" when rulemaking would be required, "when a policy of general application, embodied in or represented by a rule, is changed to a different policy of general application, the change must be accomplished by rulemaking."[25] Critical to the court's holding in *CBS* was that the adjudicatory order "reversed" an existing rule published in COMAR. It is a well-established principle that a regulation can only be changed through rulemaking. The holding in *CBS*, therefore, in my opinion, is not contrary to the principle that an agency when adopting a new policy, i.e., one not already adopted as a regulation, has the discretion to proceed either by rulemaking or contested case.

In *Comptroller of the Treasury v. SYL, Inc.*,[26] the court held that rulemaking was not required because the case did not involve a change in the agency's policy. Prior to this contested case, the agency had no policy regarding the matter; the issue was a fairly recent development.[27]

In *Maryland Association of Health Maintenance Organizations v. Health Services Cost Review Commission*,[28] it was argued that *CBS* required the Health Services Cost Review Commission to engage in rulemaking if it wanted to implement an inflation adjustment system (IAS) for HMO's. The Court of Appeals held that the "*CBS* decision furnished no support" to order rulemaking because the "use of the IAS does not represent a change in the policies or standards applied by the Commission. It is not being applied retroactively to the detriment of the regulated hospitals. The IAS is simply a methodology, long in use, to effectuate the law."[29]

In *Delmarva Power & Light Co. v. Public Service Commission*,[30] the major issue presented was whether certain standards regulating utilities were valid when the standards were adopted without following either the procedures for rulemaking or adjudication. The PSC argued that it had the ability to adopt new policy without proceeding by rulemaking. The PSC cited *Consumer Publishing Co.* and *Maryland Ass'n of Health Maintenance Organizations* to support its position. The court responded that these cases

> stand merely for the proposition that agencies have some measure of, though not unlimited, freedom to develop and apply standards that interpret or implement statutes that they administer through contested-case adjudications rather than through the adoption of regulations. They do not hold that an agency, through a mechanism other than contested-case adjudications, may adopt standards that constitute regulations under the APA without complying with the APA requirements.[31]

In an article that I wrote in the *Maryland Bar Journal* in 1992,[32] I argued that an agency's decision to adopt new policy within the context of a contested case should not be a ground upon which an agency decision in that contested case should be vacated. I still maintain that position although it is contrary to the case law. The major reason for my position is that the person that is the subject of the agency's final order in a contested case has been provided more procedural rights than what would have been provided in a rulemaking proceeding. For example, a party in a contested case has the right to cross-examine

25. 319 Md. 687, 696, 575 A.2d 324, 328 (1990).
26. 375 Md. 78, 825 A.2d 399, *cert. denied*, 540 U.S. 984 (2003).
27. 375 Md. 78, 825 A.2d 399, *cert. denied*, 540 U.S. 984 (2003).
28. 356 Md. 581, 741 A.2d 483 (1999).
29. 356 Md. 581, 602, 741 A.2d 483, 494 (1999).
30. 370 Md. 1, 803 A.2d 460 (2002).
31. 370 Md. 1, 34, 803 A.2d 460, 479 (2002).
32. Arnold Rochvarg, *Rulemaking vs. Adjudication*, 25 Md. Bar J. 12–18 (1992).

witnesses, and to have the agency decision be based exclusively on the record created at the hearing. These two protections do not apply in a rulemaking proceeding. It seems strange to me that a party can complain about being granted the greater procedural protections of a contested case.

In truth, attacks on the agency's choice of contested case over rulemaking are made not because of any preference for rulemaking, but because of displeasure with the final agency adjudicatory order. Rather than focus on the type of proceeding, however, I believe there are better arguments to avoid any unfairness that may be created when an agency develops new policy in contested cases. First, it may be unfair to retroactively apply the new policy created in a contested case. For example, it seems unfair to discipline a dentist for failing to order an x-ray in a particular situation when the failure to order such an x-ray had never in the past been a reason to discipline a dentist. The response to this unfairness, however, is not that rulemaking must be used. The better response is that the Dental Board's decision should not be applied retroactively to the dentist who is the subject of the disciplinary proceeding. The law is well-established in Federal Administrative Law under what circumstances an agency's adjudicatory order will be denied retroactive application. If the new policy is an abrupt departure from present policy, defeats reasonable reliance by the party, and places an unfair burden on the party, it will not be applied retroactively unless there is an essential government interest in retroactive application.[33] Arguments such as improper selective enforcement, and whether the adjudicatory order is arbitrary or capricious because it is inconsistent with prior agency policy are also available when an agency proceeds by a contested case to create new policy. I see no compelling reason to change the law as it stands in this area despite my misgivings. My observations, however, may be appropriate in evaluating whether an agency has abused its discretion in deciding to use the contested case process rather than the rulemaking process.

33. *See* Retail, Wholesale & Dep't Store Union v. Nat'l Labor Relations Bd., 466 F.2d 380 (D.C. Cir. 1972).

# Chapter 22

# Judicial Review: Improper Procedure

Another ground on judicial review to challenge an agency decision from a contested case is that the agency failed to follow the proper procedures required by statute or regulation. Like the other grounds that authorize a court to reverse an agency decision, this ground applies whether or not the agency is governed by the APA and whether the case is being reviewed based on a Petition for Judicial Review, an action for Administrative Mandamus, or a common law writ such as a writ of mandamus. The improper procedure challenge is reviewed by the court *de novo* with no deference to the agency position.

## § 22.1. APA Agencies

The Maryland APA in State Gov't § 10-222(h)(iii) provides that a court can reverse or modify an agency decision if any substantial right of the petitioner has been prejudiced if any finding, conclusion or decision results from an unlawful procedure. The unlawful procedure challenge first can be based on procedures required by the APA. For example, as discussed in Chapter 5, at the contested case hearing, the parties have the right to present their own witnesses and to cross examine other witnesses. If the agency did not permit these procedures, the agency decision is subject to reversal. Moreover, the enabling statute for a particular agency could set forth procedures which the agency would be required to follow.

Additionally, the procedures which the agency must follow are set forth in the agency's regulations. This is illustrated by *Kohli v. LOOC, Inc.*[1] which involved a claim of employment discrimination based on religion when a pizza business refused to hire a member of the Sikh religion because he refused to shave the beard he wore for religious purposes. The administrative process began with a contested case hearing at OAH. The ALJ's recommended decision was that the pizza business had failed to demonstrate that it would suffer undue hardship if it were required to accommodate the job applicant's religious practices. The next step in the process was an appeal to the Appeal Board of the Commission on Human Relations (CHR). As discussed earlier in Chapter 11, the agency usually enjoys wide latitude in disagreeing with the recommended decision of an OAH ALJ. In this case, however, the CHR had adopted a regulation that provided that the Appeal Board of CHR could reverse the decision of the OAH ALJ only on the same grounds that a court could reverse a final agency decision. The CHR regulation thus changed the Appeal Board's power to reverse the proposed decision of the OAH ALJ from the normal power an agency possesses to

1. 103 Md. App. 694, 654 A.2d 922 (1995), *remanded*, 347 Md. 258, 701 A.2d 92 (1997).

reverse an OAH ALJ. When it reversed the OAH ALJ in *Kohli*, the Appeal Board of CHR had not complied with this regulation. The Court of Special Appeals wrote that an agency "must ordinarily and scrupulously observe the rules, regulations, and procedures that it has established.... When the agency fails to follow its own rules, its action is invalid and courts will strike it down.... The purpose of the doctrine is to prevent the arbitrariness which is inherently characteristic of an agency's violation of its own procedures."[2]

The court emphasized that although the agency was under no obligation to have imposed this limitation upon its power to review the proposed decision of the OAH ALJ, once CHR did adopt this regulation limiting its review power, it was bound to follow it, even though not required by any statute.[3]

## § 22.2. Non-APA Agencies

Maryland Rule 7-403 (2)(C) which applies to actions for Administrative Mandamus provides that the court may issue a writ of mandamus reversing or modifying the decision of an agency in a contested case if any substantial right may have been prejudiced because a finding, conclusion, or decision of the agency "results from an unlawful procedure." The unlawful procedure challenge in an action for Administrative Mandamus is no different than a challenge under the APA.

Additionally, for agencies not governed by the APA, the unlawful procedure challenge can be based on the "*Accardi* doctrine," named for the U.S. Supreme Court case, *United States ex rel. Accardi v. Shaughnessy*.[4] Although the *Accardi* doctrine was once thought to be a constitutionally-based right inherent in due process, the modern view is that it does not have a foundation in the due process clause, but is a principle of Administrative Law that state courts are free to adopt or reject.[5] Maryland, after some years of debate, adopted the *Accardi* doctrine as part of Maryland Administrative Law in *Pollock v. Patuxent Institution Board of Review*.[6] *Pollock* involved whether a positive result for drugs in a urine drug test should be excluded at a parole revocation hearing because the sample had been collected contrary to agency "directives" governing urine collection. First, the court wrote that "in respect to agencies governed under the APA, if a court finds that substantial rights of a petitioner had been improperly prejudiced by a departure from procedures, then it is the function of the court to reverse or modify the order."[7] This holding did not resolve the issue in *Pollock*, however, because the Patuxent Institution Board of Review is excluded from the contested case subtitle of the APA. The court in *Pollock* therefore was faced squarely with whether to adopt *Accardi*. In *Pollock*, the Court of Appeals expressly adopted the *Accardi* doctrine for non-APA cases. The Court of Appeals held, however, that a court

2. 103 Md. App. 694, 718, 654 A.2d 922, 934 (1995), *citing* United States v. Hefner, 420 F.2d 809 (4th Cir. 1969).

3. The Commission on Human Relations subsequently amended its regulations to permit fuller review of proposed decisions by OAH. Other agencies, however, have regulations similar to the regulation at issue in Kohli. *See* Berkshire Life Ins. Co. v. Md. Ins. Admin., 142 Md. App. 628, 791 A.2d 942 (2002).

4. 347 U.S. 260 (1954).

5. Bd. of Sch. Comm'rs of Balt. City v. James, 96 Md. App. 401, 425 n.5, 625 A.2d 361, 374 n.5, *cert. denied*, 332 Md. 382, 631 A.2d 452 (1993).

6. 374 Md. 463, 823 A.2d 626 (2003).

7. 374 Md. 463, 469, 823 A.2d 626, 630 (2003).

will not vacate the agency action for failure to follow its procedural rules unless the complaining party can show prejudice. Because Pollock did not demonstrate that the agency's failure to follow its urine collection directives had prejudiced him, the parole revocation was upheld.

There are some Maryland cases that discuss *Accardi* even though the agency action is governed by the APA. Although reliance on *Accardi* is not needed in APA cases, it does indicate that there is no substantive difference between the APA and *Accardi* on the unlawful procedure challenge to an agency decision.

## § 22.3. Agency Failure to Adopt Procedural Regulations

Because an agency decision can be challenged on the ground that the agency making that decision did not follow its own procedural regulations, the issue has arisen whether an agency decision can be challenged on the ground that the agency followed procedures that had never been adopted as valid regulations. The resolution of this issue is not entirely clear.

In *Calvert County Planning Commission v. Howlin Realty Management, Inc.*,[8] an earlier approval of a subdivision was reconsidered and eventually rescinded by the county planning commission. The Commission had no formal written regulations governing the reconsideration of its decisions despite a statute that provided that the Commission "shall adopt rules for transaction of business." The opponent of the reconsideration and rescission argued that the Commission was precluded from reconsidering its earlier approval in the absence of any formal written regulations concerning reconsideration. The Court of Special Appeals had held that there had been no violation of the statutory requirement because the statute did not require the adoption of written regulations. Moreover, there had been an announcement of some rules that would apply to the reconsideration request at the beginning of the proceeding. The Court of Appeals disagreed. It held that the statutory requirement to "adopt rules for transactions of business" did not permit "ad hoc oral rules." Written regulations adopted in accordance with the relevant procedural requirements were required in order to provide "some assurance against arbitrary and capricious conduct on the part of the agency." Despite holding that the Commission's failure to promulgate procedural rules was a violation of the statute, the Court of Appeals did not vacate the rescission order. The court held that due process had not been violated. The court wrote that "due process is concerned with fundamental fairness in the proceeding, not with whether the agency has failed in some way to comply with a statutory requirement."[9] Because prior case law established the Commission's power to reconsider its decisions upon a showing of mistake, the Commission had acted within its authority even absent written regulations governing reconsideration.

*Howlin* was distinguished in *Engineering Management Services v. Maryland State Highway Administration*.[10] In *Engineering Management*, the Maryland State Board of Contract Appeals (MSBCA) applied a summary disposition process without adopting written pro-

8. 364 Md. 301, 772 A.2d 1209 (2001).
9. 364 Md. 301, 322, 772 A.2d 1209, 1221 (2001).
10. 375 Md. 211, 825 A.2d 966 (2003).

cedures authorizing such summary dispositions. The Court of Appeals held that "[c]ontrary to the conduct of the MSBCA, procedural rules must be promulgated by formal rulemaking," and thus the summary disposition was invalid. The court said that *Howlin* was "fairly limited to [its] specific facts,"[11] and that since the APA did not apply in *Howlin* (because it involved a county agency), *Howlin* was not controlling. *Howlin* did not stand for the proposition that an agency can avoid its obligation to promulgate procedural rules by merely announcing them prior to a contested case.[12]

Agencies should be required to adopt procedural rules that govern its decisionmaking powers. Agencies should not be permitted to decide which procedures it can follow on an ad hoc basis. Even if the agency has consistently followed certain procedures in all its cases, proper rulemaking procedures under the APA or other relevant statutes should be followed. The most effective way to enforce an agency's obligation to adopt procedural regulations is to reverse an agency decision that was made following procedures that were not validly adopted.[13]

Interestingly, the APA does not require agencies other than OAH to adopt procedural regulations. Although State Government § 10-206(a)(1) provides that OAH "shall adopt regulations to govern the procedures and practice in all contested cases delegated" to OAH, State Government § 10-206(b) provides that "Each agency may adopt regulations to govern procedures under this subtitle and practice before the agency in contested cases." The justification why *Howlin* was distinguished in *Engineering Management Services* on the basis that the APA did not apply in *Howlin* is somewhat unclear in light of these APA sections.

Although the case law is not clear, two principles seem fair to state. An agency decision will not be reversed by a court based on the agency's failure to adopt procedural regulations that might have been employed, but which were not. On the other hand, if the agency actually applied a procedure in a contested case without properly adopting that procedure as a regulation, the agency decision should be reversed if petitioner can prove prejudice.

11. 375 Md. 211, 234, 825 A.2d 96, 979 (2003).
12. 375 Md. 211, 234 n.29, 825 A.2d 96, 979 n.29 (2003).
13. *See* Chapter 2.

# Chapter 23

# Judicial Review of the Sanction

## §23.1. Grounds to Challenge the Sanction

The sanction imposed by the agency is part of the agency decision. Therefore, all of the grounds for reversing an agency decision should apply to judicial review of the sanction.

First, the sanction could be unconstitutional. For example, a physician who was found to have engaged in misconduct in the practice of medicine could be suspended from the practice of medicine by the Board of Physicians with conditions on reinstatement. If one of the conditions of reinstatement was that the doctor attend church services, the sanction would be unconstitutional, and would be invalidated by the court.

The sanction could also be invalid because it exceeds the statutory authority or jurisdiction of the agency. This was argued in *Blaker v. State Board of Chiropractic Examiners*[1] where the sanction imposed was probation plus the requirement that Blaker comply with four conditions, e.g., take a course in recordkeeping. Blaker challenged the sanction as being in excess of the agency's authority or jurisdiction. He argued that the statute authorized the Board to place a chiropractor on probation, but did not authorize the Board to impose conditions on the probation. The Court of Special Appeals rejected Blaker's argument. Because the Board had been delegated the authority to regulate and monitor the practices of chiropractors, the Board had the authority to place conditions on probation as part of the sanction. This also illustrates that a sanction can be challenged as affected by an error of law.

If the sanction is based on an unlawful procedure, the sanction should be reversed. This was the crux of *Pollock v. Patuxent Institution Board of Review*[2] where Pollock's parole was revoked because his urine sample tested positive for a controlled substance. Pollock argued that his urine sample had been collected without the agency following the proper procedures for urine collection. Although the court agreed that the agency had violated its procedures, the court held that such error was not prejudicial.[3]

A sanction can be challenged as not supported by substantial evidence. This was one of the arguments presented in *Consumer Protection Division v. Morgan*.[4] In *Morgan*, a real estate appraiser was fined $34,000 based on the Consumer Protection Division's finding that he had engaged in unfair and deceptive trade practices in his appraisal of residential properties in Baltimore City. The Court of Appeals held that the fines were supported by substantial evidence.

---

1. 123 Md. App. 243, 717 A.2d 964, *cert. denied*, 351 Md. 662, 719 A.2d 1261 (1998).
2. 374 Md. 483, 823 A.2d 626 (2003).
3. *See* discussion in Chapter 24.
4. 387 Md. 125, 874 A.2d 919 (2005).

A sanction is also subject to challenge as arbitrary or capricious or as an abuse of discretion. These grounds, however, have been the subject of some controversy and debate in Maryland because of two opinions from the Court of Appeals, both of which in my view are incorrect.

## § 23.2. Delambo

To understand the controversy that exists in Maryland regarding judicial review of administrative sanctions, we start with the case of *Maryland State Retirement Agency v. Delambo*.[5] Delambo was a twenty-year state employee who improperly released the identity of the new executive director of the Maryland State Retirement Agency prior to the formal announcement of the hiring. Administrative hearings were initiated against Delambo to remove her from state employment for this misconduct. A hearing was held at OAH which issued a proposed decision to terminate Delambo. Exceptions were filed with the Secretary of the Department of Personnel who issued the final decision removing Delambo from her job. Upon judicial review, the circuit court judge reduced the sanction to suspension without pay for a period of approximately eighteen months. The agency appealed to the Court of Special Appeals which vacated the circuit court decision, but remanded back to the agency for new consideration of the sanction.

The Court of Special Appeals first noted that under the relevant COMAR regulations, the agency was entitled to impose a number of disciplinary sanctions ranging from reprimand to demotion, suspension or removal. The rationale for each sanction under COMAR was "quite different." The court wrote:

> On the issue of punishment, the administrative agency has discretion to impose remedies and penalties.... In this case, [the agency] failed adequately to articulate why removal of [Delambo] was an appropriate exercise of discretion. Instead, [the agency] merely adopted the ALJ's finding that [Delambo's] exceedingly poor judgment, resulting in her misconduct, reflects that she is unfit to hold a position in this agency. There is no indication that either the ALJ or the Secretary (1) considered any of the other relevant factors that must be considered in determining the severity of [Delambo's] punishment, or (2) considered imposing any of the alternative sanctions that might have been appropriate under the circumstances.... For all that appears in the record before us, [Delambo] was fired because she could be fired. We cannot determine what—if any—consideration was given to [Delambo's] (1) overall employment history in State service, (2) attendance record during that period of time, (3) disciplinary record at the present agency and at other State agencies as well, (4) work habits, and (5) relations with fellow employees and supervisors. All these factors should have been considered by the ALJ and the Secretary. Appropriate consideration should also have been given to making the punishment fit the crime.[6]

However, the Court of Special Appeals continued, because a reviewing court does not have "the power to replace the agency's order with an entirely different one," the circuit

5. 109 Md. App. 683, 675 A.2d 1018 (1996).
6. 109 Md. App. 683, 690–91, 675 A.2d 1018, 1022 (1996).

court had overstepped its bounds. The appropriate order at this stage was a remand to the agency. Upon remand,

> the agency must prepare findings of fact and conclusions of law that are adequate for judicial review.... We recommend that the agency's bottom line sanction be accompanied by a statement that explains (1) precisely what (written or unwritten) law, procedure, rule or regulation has been violated by the employee; and (2) why the agency has decided against imposing any of the other sanctions that it has discretion to impose, i.e., why, under the circumstances, the punishment fits the misconduct.[7]

No petition for certiorari was filed with the Court of Appeals. For years, the *Delambo* opinion was accepted as established law in Maryland. It is consistent with federal administrative law and with the law in other states. Its holding is consistent with why there is a findings requirement in administrative law in general.[8]

## § 23.3. Noland

Nine years after *Delambo*, the Court of Appeals decided *Maryland Aviation Administration v. Noland*.[9] Noland was a paramedic employed by the Maryland Aviation Administration (MAA). While responding to a call to transport a combative psychiatric prisoner to a hospital, Noland twice hit the prisoner in the face after the prisoner had spit on Noland and threatened to kill him while Noland was attempting to place the prisoner on a stretcher. A hearing was held at OAH on charges brought by MAA to terminate Noland's employment. After two days of hearings, the ALJ filed an "extensive opinion" recommending suspension rather than termination. The MAA filed exceptions with the Secretary of the Department of Budget and Management. The Secretary adopted almost all of the ALJ's findings of fact and conclusions of law, but disagreed with the ALJ's recommended sanction. The Secretary concluded that termination was appropriate. In support of the termination sanction, the Secretary wrote:

> Penalty determinations are judgment calls within the discretion of the employing agency. We will not disturb a choice of penalty within the agency's discretion unless the severity of the agency's action appears unwarranted in light of all factors. That choice does not appear unwarranted here. I recognize that Mr. Noland's performance was satisfactory or better, and indeed exceeded standards in recent years. It was uncontested that Mr. Noland had a good overall history, had a good attendance record, had a good disciplinary record, had good work habits, and got along well with his co-workers. It is clear that all of these factors are in his favor. However, they do not outweigh the severity of what he did. It was the testimony of Dr. Phillips that it is never warranted to strike a patient. Chief Allen said the same thing. While Noland's record was unquestionably good, and would mitigate ordinary misconduct, what management in effect was saying was that even a stellar record was irrelevant based on the facts of the incident.[10]

7. 109 Md. App. 683, 692, 675 A.2d 1018, 1022 (1996).
8. *See* discussion in Chapter 7.
9. 386 Md. 556, 873 A.2d 1145 (2005).
10. 386 Md. 556, 565–66, 873 A.2d 1145, 1151 (2005).

The Secretary's decision also discussed *Delambo*:

> I also have given my own consideration to the factors specified in *Delambo*. Unquestionably, each of the five factors weighs in Mr. Noland's favor. However, the stubborn fact remains that he twice struck a restrained and handcuffed medical patient, with unwarranted and excessive force. This is not outweighed by the five *Delambo* factors. In this case, a reasonable employer could impose the punishment imposed. The punishment fits the crime, and it is clear that the employee was not punished simply because he could be punished: he was terminated for extreme misconduct. None of the alternative sanctions would have been appropriate.[11]

Upon judicial review, the circuit court reversed the agency's decision to terminate Noland. The circuit court stated that "in determining the appropriate sanction, the Secretary's designee gave insufficient consideration to ... substantial mitigating factors," in particular the fact that Noland was working with the police at the request of the police, and that he was acting in self defense and in defense of others. The MAA appealed the circuit court decision to the Court of Special Appeals. The Court of Special Appeals, relying on *Delambo*, affirmed the circuit court. The Court of Special Appeals held that the "one sentence stating that appropriate consideration was given to [the *Delambo*] factors is not adequate to permit meaningful judicial review."[12]

The Court of Appeals granted MAA's certiorari request, upheld the agency's sanction of termination, and overruled *Delambo* "in its entirety." The Court of Appeals wrote that the "requirements imposed upon administrative agencies in the *Delambo* opinion ... find no support in the Maryland Administrative Procedure Act or in Maryland administrative law generally."[13] Although the court in *Noland* recognized that the findings requirement is a "fundamental right of a party" and is essential to "meaningful judicial review," the court held that the findings requirement only required the agency "to make findings of fact with respect to *factual* matters." The court summarized its position by writing "when the discretionary sanction imposed upon an employee by an adjudicatory administrative agency is lawful and authorized, the agency need not justify its exercise of discretion by findings of fact or reasons articulating why the agency decided upon the particular discipline."[14]

## §23.4. Why Noland Should Be Abandoned

For several reasons, I strongly disagree with *Noland's* holding that an agency can impose a sanction and give no reasons why that sanction was imposed. First, this holding destroys the right of judicial review. As discussed in Chapter 13, an agency can only be affirmed on the grounds upon which the agency relied. A reviewing court cannot supply its own reasons for why the agency decision should be upheld. How can a court review the agency decision on the reasons relied upon by the agency if the agency is not required to explain the basis of its decision? The sanction is just as significant a part of the agency decision as any findings of fact. In many cases, the sanction is the only significant part of the

11. 386 Md. 556, 566–67, 873 A.2d 1145, 1151 (2005).
12. 386 Md. 556, 569, 873 A.2d 1145, 1153 (2005).
13. 386 Md. 556, 579, 873 A.2d 1145, 1159 (2005).
14. 386 Md. 556, 581, 873 A.2d 1145, 1160 (2005).

decision. *Noland* is inconsistent with the many Maryland opinions touting the inherent power of the court to review administrative agencies and the importance of judicial review.

In order for a court to engage in arbitrary or capricious and abuse of discretion judicial review, the agency must explain the basis of its sanction. This is illustrated by *Neutron Products, Inc. v. Department of the Environment*,[15] where the Court of Special Appeals was asked to review a $40,700 fine for a pollution violation. At the OAH hearing, one argument presented by Neutron was that the Department of the Environment had provided no explanation for the amount of the fine. The OAH ALJ rejected Neutron's argument. The ALJ ruled that "as long as it's within their discretion, it doesn't have to be disclosed as to how they came up with their figure."[16] Upon judicial review in circuit court, the attorney for Neutron argued that the agency had "presented absolutely no justifications" for the fine. "[P]art of the judicial review process for imposition of a sanction is arbitrary and capriciousness.... We have no way to be able to argue whether it was arbitrary or capricious."[17] The Court of Special Appeals upheld the fine by holding that the agency was not required to assign a particular dollar amount for each category of violation or individual violation.

A second reason I urge repudiation of *Noland* is that it threatens the quality of agency decisionmaking. If agencies are not required to give any reason for the sanction imposed, I am concerned that agencies will not be as careful and accurate in their decisions as compared to when the *Delambo* framework was employed. Instructive here is an article by Professor Douglas E. Abrams with the title "But Will It Write: How Writing Sharpens Decision-making."[18] The basic premise of the article is that "the discipline of committing arguments to paper can focus thinking more clearly." Perhaps the most appropriate comment was made by the United States Supreme Court in *United States v. Merz*:[19] "Laymen, like judges, will give more careful consideration to the problem if they are required to state not only the end result of their inquiry, but the process by which they reached it."[20]

Another reason *Noland* should be rejected is that it invites distrust of the administrative process. *Noland* lends support to those who attack the administrative process on grounds of bias, discrimination, favoritism and ill-informed decisions. In the famous *Greater Boston Television Corp. v. FCC*[21] opinion, Judge Leventhal, a giant in the area of Administrative Law, made some comments relevant here. Judge Leventhal wrote that "the function of the court is to assure that the agency has given reasoned consideration to all the material facts and issues. This calls for insistence that the agency articulate with reasonable clarity its reasons for decision, and identify the significance of the crucial facts, a course that tends to assure that the agency's policies effectuate general standards, applied without unreasonable discrimination."[22] The opinion emphasized that a reviewing court must rigorously insist on articulated standards and reflective findings which will "enable the public to repose confidence" in the administrative process.

---

15. 166 Md. App. 549, 890 A.2d 858, *cert. denied*, 392 Md. 726, 898 A.2d 1005 (2006).
16. 166 Md. App. 549, 568, 890 A.2d 858, 869 (2006).
17. 166 Md. App. 549, 578–579, 890 A.2d 858, 875 (2006).
18. Douglas E. Abrams, *But 'Will it Write'? How Writing Sharpens Decision-Making*, Precedent, Vol. 3, No. 2, pp. 61–63, Spring 2009; University of Missouri School of Law Legal Studies Research Paper No. 2009-07, available at http://ssrn.com/abstract=1420165.
19. 376 U.S. 192 (1964).
20. 376 U.S. 192, 199 (1964).
21. 444 F.2d 841 (D.C. Cir. 1970), *cert. denied*, 403 U.S. 923 (1971).
22. 444 F.2d 841, 851 (1970).

Another reason *Noland* should be rejected is that it is inconsistent with cases from the federal courts and other state courts.

Federal Administrative Law has long required adequate findings and an adequate explanation for the sanction imposed by an administrative agency. A classic case is the 1946 U.S. Supreme Court decision, *Jacob Siegel Co. v. Federal Trade Commission*.[23] Jacob Siegel Co. (Siegel) manufactured and sold overcoats and topcoats. The FTC found that Siegel had misrepresented that its coats contained imported angora and guanaco hair. The FTC also found that the name under which the coats were marketed, Alpacuna, was deceptive and misleading because it implied that the coats contained vicuna fiber. The FTC imposed a sanction that included a ban on the use of the word "Alpacuna" to describe Siegel's coats. Siegel argued that the prohibition of the use of the name Alpacuna "was far too harsh." The Supreme Court first stated that the FTC "has wide discretion in its choice of a remedy," and that "judicial review is limited," extending "no further than to ascertain whether the Commission made an allowable judgment in its choice of the remedy.... The Commission is the expert body to determine what remedy is necessary."[24] But, the Court continued, the FTC's order must be reversed because "the Commission seems not to have considered whether in what way the ends of the Act could be satisfied and the trade name at the same time saved. We find no indication that the Commission considered the possibility of such an accommodation.... [W]e are left in the dark whether some change of name short of excision would in the judgment of the Commission be adequate."[25] Because the FTC had not explained the basis of its sanction, the case was remanded back to the agency for an explanation.

Other federal cases require findings and explanation of the agency sanction. For example, in *Steadman v. SEC*,[26] the Fifth Circuit of the United States Court of Appeals wrote the "greater the sanction ... the greater is [the agency's] burden of justification."[27] The Fifth Circuit required the SEC to "specifically articulate compelling reasons" for its sanction of permanent exclusion of a broker. The agency had a duty to explain why a lesser sanction would not suffice to discourage others from engaging in the unlawful conduct the SEC sought to avoid. Because the SEC had failed to explain in sufficient detail its reason for the sanction, the court remanded to the agency for an adequate explanation.

Similarly in *Papercraft Corp. v. FTC*,[28] the Seventh Circuit Court of Appeals in an opinion written by future Supreme Court Justice John Stevens wrote that although the court was conscious of the deference accorded to the expertise of agencies, especially when fashioning an appropriate remedy, the FTC in this case had failed to make an adequate demonstration of the need for the sanction it imposed.

The most compelling evidence that *Noland* is inconsistent with Federal Administrative Law are the cases that review discipline of federal workers. (*Noland* involved discipline of a state employee). The federal courts require the federal agency involved in federal worker discipline, the Merit System Protection Board, to consider twelve factors, developed in *Douglas v. Veterans Administration*[29] in deciding the sanction. The *Douglas* factors are very

23. 327 U.S. 608 (1946).
24. 327 U.S. 608, 611–12 (1946).
25. 327 U.S. 608, 613 (1946).
26. 603 F.2d. 1126 (5th Cir. 1979), *aff'd on other grounds*, 450 U.S. 91 (1981).
27. 603 F.2d. 1126, 1139 (1979).
28. 472 F.2d 927 (7th Cir. 1973).
29. 5 M.S.P.B. 313 (1981).

similar to the *Delambo* factors that *Noland* did away with.[30] There are many federal cases where although there was substantial evidence supporting the sanction and the sanction was authorized, the federal court reviewed the sanction to determine if the sanction was arbitrary, capricious or an abuse of discretion. In its review of the sanction, the federal courts consistently require the agency to explain and make findings on its application of the *Douglas* factors. In each case, there is meaningful judicial review of the sanction imposed on a federal employee.[31]

*Noland* is also inconsistent with decisions in other states. Although this book is not the appropriate place for a full review of cases from all the states on the issue of whether an agency should be required to explain the basis of the sanction it has imposed in order to permit meaningful judicial review, a sampling of cases is helpful. In the New Jersey case of *Division of Alcoholic Beverage Control v. Maynards, Inc.*,[32] the court reversed the revocation of a liquor license by analyzing aggravating and mitigating factors such as the petitioner's long history of charitable and civic minded activities, and the training system he developed for employees. The important point is not that the revocation was reversed, but that the court engaged in meaningful review based on a *Delambo* type analysis.

In Illinois, in *Department of Revenue v. Smith*,[33] the court reviewed factors such as the employee's past work record in deciding whether an employee should be suspended or discharged. In Washington, in *Butler v. Lamont School District*,[34] which involved judicial review of the termination of a school bus driver, the court stated that its role was to first determine whether any sanction was appropriate, and then to review the choice of sanction. The court recognized that the choice of sanction was reviewable under arbitrary or capricious review requiring consideration of factors such as work history and impact on other workers.

Continued application of *Noland* is inconsistent with principles of judicial review and of fundamental fairness. *Noland* should be abandoned either by judicial decision or legislative action.

---

30. The 12 *Douglas* factors are: 1. The nature and seriousness of the offense, and its relation to the employee's duties, position, and responsibilities, including whether the offense was intentional or technical or inadvertent, or was committed maliciously or for gain, or was frequently repeated; 2. the employee's job level and type of employment, including supervisory or fiduciary role, contacts with the public, and prominence of the position; 3. the employee's past disciplinary record; 4. the employee's past work record, including length of service, performance on the job, ability to get along with fellow workers, and dependability; 5. the effect of the offense upon the employee's ability to perform at a satisfactory level and its effect upon supervisors' confidence in the employee's ability to perform assigned duties; 6. consistency of the penalty with those imposed upon other employees for the same or similar offense; 7. consistency of the penalty with any applicable agency table of penalties; 8. the notoriety of the offense or its impact upon the reputation of the agency; 9. the clarity with which the employee was on notice of any rules that were violated in committing the offense, or had been warned about the conduct in question; 10. potential for the employee's rehabilitation; 11. mitigating circumstances surrounding the offense such as unusual job tensions, personality problems, mental impairment, harassment, or bad faith, malice or provocation on the part of others involved in the matter; and 12. the adequacy and effectiveness of alternative sanctions to deter such conduct in the future by the employee or others, 5 M.S.P.B. 313, 305–06 (1981).

31. *See e.g.*, Bryant v. National Science Foundation, 105 F.3d 1414 (Fed. Cir. 1997); Newton v. Dep't of the Air Force, 85 F.3d 595 (Fed. Cir. 1996); Schuck v. Frank, 27 F.3d 194 (6th Cir. 1994); Webster v. Dep't of Army, 911 F.2d 679 (Fed. Cir. 1990), *cert. denied*, 502 U.S. 861 (1991).

32. 927 A.2d 525 (N.J. 2007).

33. 501 N.E.2d 1370 (Ill. App. 1986).

34. 745 P.2d 1308 (Wash. App. 1987).

## § 23.5. MTA v. King and Disproportionality

The other case besides *Noland* that has caused controversy in the judicial review of administrative sanctions is *Maryland Transportation Authority v. King*.[35] As will be recalled from the discussion on *King* in Chapter 21 discussing Abuse of Discretion, certiorari was granted by the Court of Appeals on only one issue—whether Maryland should adopt the *Accardi* doctrine. After ruling that there was no need to discuss the *Accardi* issue, *King* offered a discussion of two issues—both irrelevant to the case—abuse of discretion, and judicial review of the agency sanction.

The focus of *King's* unnecessary discussion of judicial review of an agency sanction was the concept of disproportionality. In *King*, the majority opinion made the following points:

1. Judicial review of a sanction does not encompass proportionality review.[36]
2. The grounds set forth in the APA for reversing or modifying an agency sanction do not include disproportionality.[37]
3. As long as the sanction or decision does not exceed the agency's authority, is not unlawful, and is supported by competent, material and substantial evidence, there can be no judicial reversal or modification based on disproportionality unless the disproportionality was so extreme or egregious that the reviewing court can properly deem the decision to be arbitrary or capricious.[38]

Both Judges Wilner and Harrell in separate concurring opinions questioned why this discussion was presented in the majority opinion. Both stated that more was being said about disproportionality than was necessary.

Because the disproportionality discussion in *King* was not relevant to the case before the court, and thus is only dicta, the significance of the disproportionality discussion in *King* based on the *King* opinion alone is unclear. One reading of *King* is that it does not change traditional arbitrary or capricious review of a sanction. To prove a sanction is arbitrary or capricious, it must be proven unreasonable. If a sanction is so disproportionate that it is unreasonable, it is arbitrary or capricious and must be reversed. I agree with Judge Wilner who wrote in his concurring opinion in *King* that challenges "should be stated in the statutory language that the ruling or decision is arbitrary or capricious, and the court's ruling on the challenge should also use that terminology."[39] On the other hand, Judge Eldridge's majority opinion's comments on disproportionality could be read as attempting to change traditional arbitrary or capricious review of sanctions. Judge Eldridge's intent in *King*, I believe, is demonstrated by his subsequent opinion in *Maryland Aviation Administration v. Noland*.[40] Citing extensively his own language in *King*, Judge Eldridge in *Noland* not only reiterated his position that disproportionality is not a legitimate argument to present on judicial review of a sanction, but, as discussed in the previous section, *Noland* eliminated the requirement that an agency justify its sanction by articulating the basis of the particular sanction.

---

35. 369 Md. 274, 799 A.2d 1246 (2002).
36. 369 Md. 274, 290, 799 A.2d 1246, 1255 (2002).
37. 369 Md. 274, 291, 799 A.2d 1246, 1255 (2002).
38. 369 Md. 274, 291, 799 A.2d 1246, 1255 (2002).
39. 369 Md. 274, 293, 799 A.2d 1246, 1257 (2002).
40. 386 Md. 556, 873 A.2d 1145 (2005).

My position is that both *Noland* and *King* are wrong. It is well established that a sanction that is unreasonable must be reversed under either arbitrary or capricious or abuse of discretion analysis, and that disproportionality is part of that review. As discussed in the following sections, *King* is inconsistent with cases from the federal courts, other state courts, and even Maryland cases decided before and after *King*.

## § 23.6. Federal Cases and Disproportionality

Federal courts review sanctions imposed by federal agencies by applying the arbitrary, capricious or abuse of discretion standard. In this review, federal courts consider disproportionality in relation to both the seriousness of the conduct, and in relation to other sanctions imposed by the agency for similar conduct. These federal cases involve federal employee discipline, fines, and equitable remedies. A short discussion of several of these federal cases will illustrate how the *Noland-King* view of judicial review of an administrative sanction is inconsistent with federal law.

*Ward v. Derwinski*,[41] involved a nurse who was fired from her employment at a Veteran's Administration Hospital for mistreatment of a psychiatric patient. The argument was presented that other nurses had received less severe penalties for conduct that was more egregious than Ward's. In its review of the sanction, the federal district court first viewed its role to inquire whether the agency had articulated a rational connection between the facts found and the remedy imposed. The court vacated the sanction. Ward's one instance of verbal taunting was not serious enough to warrant termination especially when the record contained numerous instances where much more severe conduct of others did not result in termination.

In *Jones v. Secretary, Department of the Army*,[42] a federal employee's removal from public service was challenged because the sanction was "too severe" considering that his behavior was involuntary and resulted from a temporary mental illness. The court stated that a reviewing court should defer to the agency's choice of penalty unless it exceeds the range of permissible punishment or unless the penalty is so harsh and unconscionably disproportionate to the offense that it amounts to an abuse of discretion. The *Jones* court continued that the penalty imposed must be reasonable in light of the misconduct, and that reasonableness meant not grossly disproportionate. The court reviewed the agency's findings under *Douglas*, and affirmed the sanction.

*Schuck v. Frank*[43] involved the removal of a federal employee for selling a controlled substance to a co-worker. It was argued that removal was excessive in light of Schuck's work history and other *Douglas* factors. The Court of Appeals for the Sixth Circuit stated that deference to the agency was appropriate unless the penalty was so harsh and unconscionably disproportionate to the offense that it amounted to an abuse of discretion. Because the agency had failed to consider all of the *Douglas* factors, the court reversed the sanction and remanded back to the agency.

*Abaqueta v. United States*[44] involved a doctor terminated from employment at a Veteran's Hospital. The federal district court judge wrote that deference was owed to the agency's

41. 837 F. Supp. 517 (W.D.N.Y. 1992).
42. 912 F. Supp. 1397 (D. Kan. 1995).
43. 27 F.3d 194 (6th Cir. 1994).
44. 255 F. Supp.2d 1020 (D. Ariz. 2003).

choice of sanction unless the penalty is so harsh or disproportionate to the misconduct as to constitute an abuse of discretion. The administrative sanction must be reviewed to determine whether the agency conscientiously considered relevant factors such as past work history, the connection between the job duties and the improper conduct, and the strength of the proof that the misconduct occurred. In this case, the major relevant factor from *Douglas* was the consistency of the penalty with those imposed on others for similar conduct. To make out a claim for disparate treatment, the charges and the circumstances must be substantially similar. In *Abaqueta*, the sanction was affirmed.

In *Power v. United States*,[45] the Court of Claims emphasized that even if the penalty is within the range of penalties permitted by statute, if the penalty is so harsh and unconscionably disproportionate to the offense, it constitutes an abuse of discretion and must be reversed. In this case, the court held that dismissal was so out of proportion to Power's conduct, the agency had abused its discretion. The court wrote, "the punishment does not fit the crime."[46]

*Webster v. Department of Army*[47] affirmed the removal of an employee who worked for the Army. The majority recognized that an agency penalty that was so harsh and grossly disproportionate to the offense would amount to an abuse of discretion, but did not believe that removal in this case was grossly disproportionate. The dissenting judge would have remanded the case because the agency failed to consider a relevant factor—the animus of Webster's supervisor.

Federal cases have also reviewed agency fines. In *Interstate Erectors, Inc. v. Occupational Safety and Health Review Commission*,[48] it was argued that the commission had abused its discretion in assessing penalties of $28,000 and $35,000 for two workplace safety violations. The court wrote that it will not disturb a sanction imposed by the agency unless the punishment exceeds the range of sanction permitted by law, or if the sanction is so harsh that it amounts to an abuse of discretion. In this case, the history of non-compliance by managers and officers of Interstate indicated there was not an abuse of discretion. *Saberi v. Commodity Futures Trading Commission*[49] reviewed a fine to determine if it was excessive or an abuse of discretion. In this case, a fine that was roughly twice the amount profited by an intentional violation of a Commission regulation was affirmed.

Sanctions other than fines and employee discipline have also been reviewed by federal courts for abuse of discretion. The sanction imposed by the Securities Exchange Commission was upheld in *Atlanta-One, Inc. v. SEC*[50] under an abuse of discretion standard, as was the sanction in *LaCrosse v. CFTC*.[51] In both cases, despite the fact that both sanctions were within the statutory limit and supported by substantial evidence, the federal courts considered whether the sanction constituted an abuse of discretion.

The purpose of this last section is not to recite holdings from various federal courts reviewing various sanctions from various federal agencies, but to demonstrate that the *Noland-King* approach to judicial review of administrative sanctions is inconsistent with the approach taken by federal courts. The federal approach is consistent with *Delambo* which Maryland courts followed until *Delambo* was reversed by *Noland*.

---

45. 209 Ct. Cl. 126, 531 F.2d 505 (1976).
46. 531 F.2d 505, 509 (1976).
47. 911 F.2d 679 (Fed. Cir. 1990).
48. 74 F.3d 223 (10th Cir. 1996).
49. 488 F.3d 1207 (9th Cir. 2007).
50. 100 F.3d 105 (9th Cir. 1996).
51. 137 F.3d 925 (7th Cir. 1998).

## § 23.7. Other State Cases and Disproportionality

The *Noland-King* approach to judicial review of administrative sanctions is also inconsistent with the approach taken by a majority of the other states. Although it is beyond the scope of this chapter to discuss every state and every case, some examples will prove this conclusion.

*In re Alpha Directions, Inc.*,[52] the New Hampshire court reviewed a fine of $42,000 against a business that provided insurance brokerage and consulting services without being licensed. The court wrote that an administrative penalty can be set aside if it is so harsh or excessive as to be unreasonable or an unsustainable exercise of discretion. The court concluded that the fine did not establish an abuse of discretion.

New York has many cases that review agency sanctions by applying the standards of arbitrary or capricious, abuse of discretion, and disproportionality. For example, in *Krasowski v. State Education Department*,[53] the court wrote that a court will intervene if the administrative penalty is overly harsh and excessive in comparison to the gravity of the proven charges. In *Krasowski*, the court reversed a sanction against a school teacher that included a requirement of psychiatric treatment. The court said it was "irrational" to require psychiatric treatment when the issue of psychiatric impairment had been litigated at the agency, and the teacher had been found to be free of any impairment. The court in *Zuntag v. City of New York*[54] reversed the agency's sanction of permanent revocation of visitation rights of a prisoner who was caught passing contraband. The court said this sanction was disproportionate to the misconduct committed. Moreover, Zuntag's prior prison record was spotless, and his contraband violation was not performed knowingly. In a physician license revocation case, *Moran v. Chassin*,[55] the court reviewed the sanction by asking whether it was so disproportionate to the offense as to be shocking to one's sense of fairness. *Martindale v. Novello*[56] considered whether a fine against a real estate developer for drilling improper water wells was "grossly disproportionate to the violation as to constitute abuse of discretion."[57] This sanction was upheld; the ALJ had made detailed findings as to the risks inherent in the different types of wells and on the developer's intent and motive.

New Jersey has a consistent line of cases reviewing the sanction for disproportionality that requires the agency to make express findings on mitigating factors such as past work record.[58] Even if the sanction imposed is authorized, New Jersey courts recognize their duty to reverse the agency sanction if it is not proportional to the offense in light of all the circumstances and is shocking to one's sense of fairness.[59] In *Division of Alcoholic Beverage Control v. Maynards, Inc.*,[60] the agency ignored the state of mind of the licensee. This was "not in keeping with the proportionate imposition of penalties." The agency's failure to consider a mitigating factor constituted an abuse of discretion.

52. 880 A.2d 380 (N.H. 2005).
53. 132 A.D.2d 120, 521 N.Y.S.2d 820 (1987).
54. 18 Misc. 3d 210, 853 N.Y.S.2d 469 (2007).
55. 225 A.D.2d 814, 638 N.Y.S.2d 835 (1996).
56. 13 A.D.3d 761, 786 N.Y.S.2d 616 (2004).
57. 13 A.D.3d 761, 763, 786 N.Y.S.2d 616, 618 (2004).
58. *See* In re Herrmann, 192 N.J. 19, 926 A.2d 350 (2007).
59. *See* In re Polk, 90 N.J. 550, 449 A.2d 7 (1982).
60. 192 N.J. 158, 927 A.2d 525 (2007).

In Pennsylvania, in a case involving the revocation of the license of a veterinarian, *Kyu Son Yi v. State Board of Veterinary Medicine*,[61] the sanction was reversed as an abuse of discretion. The court wrote that it may be manifestly unreasonable for an agency to choose the most severe penalty to punish a single and relatively minor violation.

The Delaware court in *Warmouth v. State Board of Examiners in Optometry*[62] when asked to reverse a sanction against an optometrist on the ground that the Board had abused its discretion in imposing a sanction far more severe than warranted by the facts, agreed that it would be an abuse of discretion requiring reversal if the sanction is so disproportionate to the offense in light of all the circumstances as to be shocking to one's sense of fairness. This was not true in this case, and the sanction was affirmed.

The abuse of discretion standard and disproportionality review was employed in an Arizona case involving revocation of a liquor license. In *Shaffer v. Arizona State Liquor Board*,[63] it was argued that the revocation was an abuse of the agency's discretion because the liquor store owner did not consciously violate the law, had a long history of a clean record, and this violation was an isolated incident. The court upheld the sanction since it was not so disproportionate to the offense as to shock one's sense of fairness.

Also illustrating that the approach taken around the country is contrary to that espoused for Maryland in *Noland* and *King* is the Colorado case of *News & Film Service, Inc. v. Public Utilities Commission*.[64] The court commented that the imposition of an administrative sanction involves the weighing of various factors including the culpability of the violator, the seriousness of the offense, and the effect of the sanction upon the violator. If the sanction is clearly disproportionate to the violation, the sanction must be set aside.

Illinois courts consistently apply the following test when reviewing an administrative sanction: A court may overturn a sanction imposed by an agency if it is overly harsh in view of mitigating circumstances. In *Graham v. Illinois Racing Board*,[65] the court reversed the Racing Board's lifetime suspension of a horse trainer. The court relied on the trainer's unblemished prior record, and the fact that the Racing Board had imposed sanctions of a 90-day and a 270-day suspension in two other cases. In applying the same analysis, *Pelling v. Illinois Racing Board*[66] upheld a six-year suspension of a jockey as not unduly excessive based on the finding that the jockey's conduct was intentional.

Consistency and proportionality are also relevant to judicial review of administrative sanctions in Utah. *Lunnen v. Utah Department of Transportation*[67] stated the principle that the agency has the initial burden of showing the sanction is not disproportionate to the misconduct. If the agency fulfills this initial burden, the petitioner can raise the issue of inconsistent treatment. When a sanction is disproportionate, it amounts to an abuse of discretion that the court must reverse.

In the Arkansas case of *Collie v. State Medical Board*,[68] a doctor had his medical license revoked for being romantically and sexually involved with a patient who he eventually married. The doctor argued that the revocation was overly harsh considering that he had never been subject to discipline in thirty five years of practice. The court stated that even

61. 960 A.2d 864 (Pa. Commw. Ct. 2008).
62. 514 A.2d 1119 (Del. Superior Ct.1985).
63. 4 P.3d 460 (Ariz. Ct. App. 2000).
64. 787 P.2d 169 (Colo.1990).
65. 495 N.E.2d 1013 (Ill. App. 1986).
66. 574 N.E.2d 116 (Ill. App. 1991).
67. 886 P.2d 70 (Utah Ct. App.1994).
68. 258 S.W.3d 367 (Ark. 2007).

if a sanction is supported by substantial evidence, a court can still overturn the sanction as arbitrary or capricious if it is too harsh in light of all attendant circumstances, including the nature of the conduct and sanctions given to others. In *Collie*, the Arkansas court reduced the sanction to a one-year suspension.

All of these cases from other states are consistent with *Delambo* and contrary to *Noland* and *King*. Although obviously Maryland need not follow the law of any other state, these cases do indicate that the *Noland-King* approach of not requiring the agency to provide any reasons for the sanction, and not permitting judicial consideration of disproportionality is not supported by cases in other states.

## § 23.8. Maryland Cases and Review of the Sanction

Even after *King*, Maryland courts have recognized that arbitrary or capricious review of a sanction encompasses disproportionality. For example, in *Cohen v. Maryland State Board of Physician Quality Assurance*,[69] the court considered the argument that the "penalty of revocation [of the doctor's license] was unreasonably severe and arbitrary."[70] Although the court recognized that "substantial deference" was owed to the agency, the court reviewed the record to see whether the Board's decision was reasonably based on relevant factors—a classic arbitrary or capricious analysis. The court did not respond that "severity" was not a reviewable issue because it was really "disproportionality." Similarly, in *Department of Public Safety & Correctional Services v. Neal*,[71] the court concluded that the "sanction decision was reasonable ... not too harsh but not too lenient ... and certainly was not arbitrary or capricious."[72] The court noted that the sanction was based on consideration of relevant factors such as the severity of the misconduct and the number of infractions committed within the past year. In *Motor Vehicle Administration v. Weller*,[73] the circuit court had reversed the agency's decision to suspend Weller's driving license because the agency had failed to consider his employment as an insurance adjuster, and it had been eight years since his prior refusal to take a chemical breath test. The Court of Appeals reversed the circuit court because the Court of Appeals believed that the agency had in fact given proper consideration to these two factors, and therefore had not acted "illegally, or in an arbitrary, capricious, oppressive of fraudulent manner." Again, this is traditional arbitrary or capricious analysis applied to review of a sanction.

*Consumer Protection Division v. Morgan*[74] involved, inter alia, a challenge to the CPD's imposition of $34,000 in civil fines. In upholding the sanction, the court looked at a section of the statute with the heading "Factors affecting penalty amount" which set forth the relevant factors the agency was required to apply in deciding the sanction. Because the agency had properly applied the relevant factors, the sanction was upheld.

Also significant is *Maryland State Board of Social Work Examiners v. Chertkov*.[75] Although *Chertkov* was decided before *King*, it has been cited subsequent to *King*, and even after

69. 160 Md. App. 277, 863 A.2d 358 (2004).
70. 160 Md. App. 277, 284, 863 A.2d 358, 362 (2004).
71. 160 Md. App. 496, 864 A.2d 287 (2004), *cert. denied*, 386 Md. 181, 872 A.2d 47 (2005).
72. 160 Md. App. 496, 518, 864 A.2d 287, 300 (2004).
73. 390 Md. 115, 887 A.2d 1042 (2005).
74. 387 Md. 125, 874 A.2d 919 (2005).
75. 121 Md. App. 574, 710 A.2d 391 (1998).

*Noland*. Chertkov was a social worker who had engaged in a fraudulent billing scheme. She argued that it was arbitrary or capricious for her sanction to be more severe than the sanction imposed on another social worker involved in the same scheme. The Court of Special Appeals held that it was proper to apply the arbitrary or capricious standard to review the severity of a sanction even when the sanction was supported by substantial evidence. The court wrote that "[i]t is impossible to catalogue just what would or would not constitute arbitrary action on the part of an agency ... in imposing sanctions, since each situation must be judged on its own facts."[76] The court added that "[o]ther viable theories of arbitrary or capricious sanctions may involve taking improper information into consideration in selecting the sanction ... or deviating unexplainedly from prior established precedents."[77] The Court of Special Appeals also rejected the allegation that the sanction was based on a "desire to punish Chertkov for failing to engage in bargaining." Even if this were the case, that would not constitute an arbitrary or capricious decision because willingness to bargain was not an irrelevant factor to consider. The court also found that Chertkov and the other social worker had engaged in "very different types of misconduct and were not necessarily being sanctioned based on the same acts."[78] This is significant to arbitrary or capricious review because an agency decision that treats equally-situated persons differently without a rational basis would be an arbitrary or capricious decision.

## §23.9. Proper Analysis

*Chertkov*, not *Noland* and *King*, sets forth the proper analysis for judicial review of an administrative sanction. Agencies should be required to explain the basis of the imposed sanction. Courts should apply the same standards of review and the same grounds of reversal when reviewing the sanction as courts apply to other components of the agency decision.

In applying arbitrary or capricious review as well as abuse of discretion review to the sanction, a court should not substitute its judgment for that of the agency. The court should not impose the sanction the court thinks is appropriate or the sanction the court would have imposed if it were the initial decisionmaker of the sanction. Rather, the court must affirm a sanction even if the court disagrees with the agency's choice of sanction as long as the sanction imposed is a reasonable sanction taking into account all relevant factors. These relevant factors will vary from case to case, but they will include the nature of the misconduct, mitigating factors such as lack of intent and past record, and sanctions imposed on others who engaged in similar misconduct. The agency should be required to make findings on all relevant factors. A sanction that is disproportionate to either the misconduct or disproportionate to sanctions in similar cases is not reasonable, and should be reversed. This approach to judicial review of the administrative sanction respects the agency's right to impose a sanction which furthers the policy goals of the agency, while still guaranteeing meaningful judicial review and fairness to regulated parties.

---

76. 121 Md. App. 574, 585–86, 710 A.2d 391, 396 (1998), *citing* Restar v. State Bd. of Educ., 284 Md. 537, 399 A.2d 225 (1979).

77. 121 Md. App. 574, 586, 710 A.2d 391, 396 (1998).

78. 121 Md. App. 574, 588, 710 A.2d 391, 397 (1998).

# Chapter 24

# Judicial Review: Prejudicial Error

## §24.1. The Prejudice Requirement

All of the grounds for reversal of an agency decision in a contested case require that the petitioning party prove that it "may have been prejudiced" in order for the court to reverse the agency.[1] There is no case discussing the degree of harm required by the "may have been prejudiced" language. It is not clear whether the words "may have been" indicate a lower threshold of prejudice than if the standard in the Maryland APA or Rules of Administrative Mandamus required proof that petitioner "was prejudiced." Nor is it clear whether the "may have been prejudiced" standard is different than the Federal APA's requirement that when a federal court is deciding whether to reverse a federal agency decision, "due account must be taken of the rule of prejudicial error."[2] These possible distinctions have not arisen in any case. The cases that do exist seem to have been fairly easy decisions on prejudicial error.

*Blaker v. State Board of Chiropractic Examiners*[3] discussed prejudice and the admission of evidence at the hearing not related to any charge in the charging document. Blaker was a chiropractor who was accused of improper record keeping. The records of several patients whose records were allegedly inaccurate were listed in the charges against him. At the hearing, records relating to other patients were also introduced. It was agreed that the introduction of these other patients' records was improper. The Court of Special Appeals, however, declined to reverse the Board's sanction of Blaker. The court first wrote that whether an error is prejudicial depends on whether it affected the outcome of the case. Because there was ample evidence in the record of inadequate record keeping on those patients listed in the charging document, the improper evidence relating to other patients had no affect on the sanction imposed.

In *Department of Economic & Employment Development v. Propper*,[4] the agency decision included several findings of fact. One of the findings of fact was held not supported by substantial evidence. The Court of Special Appeals, however, did not reverse the agency decision because the court concluded that the unsupported finding of fact was not relied upon by the agency in reaching its final decision.

*Propper* should be compared to *State Board of Physicians v. Bernstein*[5] where the court did reverse the Board's discipline of a doctor. In *Bernstein*, the Board had based its decision

1. Maryland Code Annotated, State Government § 10-222(h)(3).
2. 5 U.S.C. § 706.
3. 123 Md. App. 243, 717 A.2d 964, *cert. denied*, 351 Md. 662, 719 A.2d 1261 (1998).
4. 108 Md. App. 595, 673 A.2d 713 (1996).
5. 167 Md. App. 714, 894 A.2d 621 (2006).

on the expert testimony of two doctors. The Court of Special Appeals held that one of the expert witnesses relied upon by the Board did not qualify as an expert. The issue then became whether the testimony of the one qualified expert would have been sufficient for the Board to impose the same sanction. In *Bernstein*, the Court of Special Appeals held that given the importance of the expert witness testimony, the evidence of bias, and the need to prove the case by clear and convincing evidence, the improper expert witness testimony was prejudicial. The case was remanded to the Board.

*Department of Public Safety & Correctional Services v. Scruggs*[6] involved an allegation that a correctional officer at a woman's prison had engaged in sexual relations with three female prison inmates. Scruggs denied the prisoners' allegations. At the hearing, results of polygraph tests taken by the prisoners indicating that sexual contact had taken place were admitted into evidence. The Court of Special Appeals first held that the admission into evidence of the polygraph tests was error. The court then held that such error was "sufficiently prejudicial" to warrant reversal of the termination sanction. The court's ruling was based on its belief that witness credibility was crucial.

Prejudicial error analysis has also been applied in cases where the agency failed to follow its own procedures. In *Board of School Commissioners of Baltimore City v. James*,[7] the agency failed to follow the required procedures at the initial hearing. However, a new *de novo* hearing was held where the proper procedures were followed. Because the procedural errors at the first hearing had no affect on the outcome of the case, there was no showing of prejudice.

*Pollock v. Patuxent Institution Board of Review*[8] involved the agency's failure to properly follow the procedures for the collection of urine in a parole revocation case. Pollock's parole was revoked when his urine tested positive for a controlled substance. Although the court acknowledged that the agency had violated its urine collection procedures, no prejudice resulted from these procedural violations because there was substantial evidence that the urine sample was that of Pollock.

## § 24.2. Must the Agency Prove Prejudice?

If a party must prove prejudice in order to have a court reverse an agency decision for failure of the agency to follow the agency's procedures, should the agency be required to prove prejudice to impose a sanction on a party who does not follow the agency's procedures? Consider this example: An agency has a procedural regulation requiring that five signed copies of any expert witness report be submitted thirty days prior to the contested case hearing. The sanction for failing to comply with this regulation is that the party will not be permitted to call the expert as a witness at the hearing. Unsigned copies of the report are filed thirty-two days before the hearing. Signed copies are filed one week later. My experience is that the agency will undoubtedly argue that the expert witness whose report was technically not in compliance with the regulation should be prohibited from testifying at the hearing despite the fact that the agency was not prejudiced in any manner. The agency position will be that "a rule is a rule," and that it must be followed. There are no cases to my knowledge expressly discussing whether the agency must prove

6. 79 Md. App. 312, 556 A.2d 736 (1989).
7. 96 Md. App. 401, 625 A.2d 361, *cert. denied*, 332 Md. 382, 631 A.2d 452 (1993).
8. 374 Md. 463, 823 A.2d 626 (2003).

prejudice in this type of example. The cases only discuss the need for the party challenging the agency to prove prejudice when the agency has violated its own procedures. Fairness dictates, however, that the prejudice requirement go both ways. A party's failure to follow the agency's procedural regulation should only lead to a sanction if the agency can prove prejudice.

# Chapter 25

# Declaratory Rulings

## § 25.1. APA Provisions

This chapter discusses the law relating to the issuance of Declaratory Rulings as authorized by Subtitle 3 of the Maryland APA.[1]

As discussed throughout this book, Maryland agencies are given quasi-legislative powers to adopt regulations subject to Subtitle 1 of the Maryland APA, and quasi-judicial powers to decide contested cases subject to Subtitle 2 of the Maryland APA. Most agencies governed by APA Subtitles 1 and 2 are also given the power by Subtitle 3 of the Maryland APA to issue Declaratory Rulings. Several agencies, however, are expressly excluded from Subtitle 3 and thus have no power to issue Declaratory Rulings. The excluded agencies include the Department of Assessment and Taxation, the Board of Appeals of the Department of Labor, Licensing and Regulation, the Insurance Administration, the Injured Workers' Insurance Fund, the Parole Commission, the Public Service Commission, the Tax Court, and the Workers Compensation Commission.[2]

The APA Declaratory Rulings subtitle provides that an "interested person may submit to [an agency] a petition for a declaratory ruling with respect to the manner in which the [agency] would apply a regulation or order of the [agency] or a statute that the [agency] enforces to a person or property on the facts set forth in the petition."[3] There is no definition of "interested person" in the APA except for the section that provides that a "political subdivision of the State or an instrumentality of a political subdivision is entitled, to the same extent as other legal entities, to be an interested person, party, or petitioner in a matter under [the Declaratory Ruling] subtitle, including an appeal."[4] It does not seem, therefore, that a petitioner for a Declaratory Ruling needs to allege that it will be aggrieved in any manner by the regulation or order which is the subject of the requested Declaratory Ruling.

If the agency issues a Declaratory Ruling, the Ruling binds the agency and petitioner on the facts set forth in the petition.[5] Moreover, a Declaratory Ruling is judicially reviewable in circuit court in the same manner as judicial review of contested cases.[6]

The Declaratory Ruling provisions of the APA at first blush seem to provide a very useful tool for persons to get a binding opinion from an agency. Such opinions can lead to greater compliance by regulated persons. But the actual usefulness of a petition for Declaratory Ruling is greatly reduced, perhaps almost defeated, by the fact that it is within

1. Maryland Code Annotated, State Government § 10-301.
2. Maryland Code Annotated, State Government § 10-302.
3. Maryland Code Annotated, State Government § 10-304(a).
4. Maryland Code Annotated, State Government § 10-303.
5. Maryland Code Annotated, State Government § 10-305(b).
6. Maryland Code Annotated, State Government § 10-305(c).

the discretion of the agency whether to issue a Declaratory Ruling in response to a petition.[7] Because a Declaratory Ruling is subject to judicial review, agencies may be unwilling to issue a Declaratory Ruling. For example, in *Comptroller of the Treasury v. Citicorp International Communications, Inc.*,[8] the Assistant Legal Director of the Office of the Comptroller in response to a petition for Declaratory Ruling requesting whether a fee paid to terminate a lease was taxable, "declined to issue a formal declaratory ruling, but did agree to answer the question informally."[9]

The decision by an agency in response to a petition to not issue a Declaratory Ruling is not subject to any judicial review under any provisions of the APA or the Courts and Judicial Proceedings Article. Moreover, because an agency's decision whether to issue a Declaratory Ruling is a matter within the agency's discretion, an action for mandamus is not appropriate to seek an order from a court requiring an agency to issue a Declaratory Ruling.[10]

## § 25.2. When Is a Declaratory Ruling Appropriate?

Putting aside the issue of an agency's possible hesitancy to issue a Declaratory Ruling because of the agency's concern over litigation in circuit court, there are situations where a Declaratory Ruling would not be appropriate even if the agency was inclined to issue one. For example, in *Insurance Commissioner v. Equitable Life Assurance Society*,[11] it was stated that a Declaratory Ruling would not be appropriate to rule on the constitutionality of a statute the agency administered. In *Board of Education of Prince George's County v. Secretary of Personnel*,[12] a Declaratory Ruling was seen as inappropriate when the question at issue was being decided in an upcoming hearing.

In an Opinion of the Attorney General,[13] the Physical Therapy Board was advised by the Attorney General not to issue a Declaratory Ruling when the Board had been asked whether "manipulation" was within the scope of physical therapy. In its Opinion, the Attorney General stated that the purpose of the declaratory ruling procedure is to provide an "efficient, low-cost procedure for individuals to resolve uncertainty about whether a particular plan of action does or does not come within the purview of a regulatory statute." It is not intended to be an alternative to rulemaking when the issue applies generally to all those subject to the agency's jurisdiction. Declaratory Rulings are meant to enable persons concerned with a more narrowly focused issue to obtain binding advice about their particular situation. They are not useful if the issue affects persons not directly subject to the agency's jurisdiction, if the facts presented are insufficient to allow informed resolution of the issue, or if legislative facts are essential to resolving the issue. The Opinion also noted that an agency should decline to issue a declaratory ruling where the ruling,

7. Maryland Code Annotated, State Government § 10-305(a) (agency "may issue" a declaratory ruling).

8. 389 Md. 156, 884 A.2d 112 (2005).

9. 389 Md. 156, 161, 884 A.2d 112, 115 (2005).

10. Harvey v. Marshall, 389 Md. 243, 884 A.2d 1171 (2005), *citing* Bd. of Educ. of Prince George's County v. Sec'y of Personnel, 317 Md. 34, 562 A.2d 700 (1989).

11. 339 Md. 596, 664 A.2d 862 (1995).

12. 317 Md. 34, 562 A.2d 700 (1989).

13. 76 Op. Att'y Gen. 3 (1991).

although technically binding only on the agency and petitioner, would also determine the legal rights of others who are not represented in the declaratory ruling procedure. Based on these factors, the Attorney General gave his opinion that the Physical Therapy Board should not use the declaratory ruling process to determine whether "manipulation" was within the scope of physical therapy.

On the other hand, a situation where a declaratory ruling was deemed appropriate was discussed in *Luskin's, Inc. v. Consumer Protection Division*.[14] Luskin's officials met with officials of the Consumer Protection Division (CPD) to discuss whether an advertisement that it planned to broadcast was in compliance with the Consumer Protection Act. After being told by CPD officials that the proposed ad did not comply, Luskin's filed a complaint in circuit court challenging this informal advice. This complaint was eventually dismissed, but not before the case made its way to the Court of Appeals. In its opinion, the Court of Appeals commented that the appropriate action by Luskin's would have been to file a petition for a Declaratory Ruling.

A Declaratory Ruling issued by the Board of Physicians was challenged in *Potomac Valley Orthopaedic Associates v. Maryland State Board of Physicians*.[15] Several medical practices had requested a Declaratory Ruling from the Board of Physicians on whether the Maryland Patient Referral Law prohibited in certain situations an orthopaedic surgeon from furnishing patients with MRI or CT diagnostic services within his or her office or group. After the Board issued the Declaratory Ruling, the medical practices sought judicial review. The court reviewed the Declaratory Ruling to determine if it was affected by an error of law. The court relied on two Opinions of the Attorney General and legislative history in reaching its decision that the Board's Declaratory Ruling was not premised upon an erroneous conclusion of law.

## § 25.3. Declaratory Ruling or Rulemaking?

*Baltimore City Board of School Commissioners v. City Neighbors Charter School*[16] involved three Declaratory Rulings that had been issued by the State Board of Education. This case originated with an application by a non-profit community group, City Neighbors, to open a public charter school. The application was conditionally approved, but there was disagreement on whether public funds would be paid to help operate the school. The City Board's position was that it could require charter schools to accept certain categories of expenses in the form of services rather than cash. City Neighbors filed a petition for Declaratory Ruling with the State Board of Education requesting an interpretation of the relevant charter school statute. Although the City Board moved to dismiss the petition, the State Board issued a Declaratory Ruling concluding that the City Board's interpretation of the statute was wrong. The City Board then petitioned for judicial review in circuit court. The City Board argued that the State Board had misconstrued the charter school statute, that the State Board's declaratory rulings constituted impermissible rulemaking, and various procedural deficiencies. The Court of Appeals first discussed that special deference was owed to the State Board of Education in its interpretation of public education

14. 338 Md. 188, 657 A.2d 788 (1995).
15. 417 Md. 622, 12 A.3d 84 (2011).
16. 400 Md. 324, 929 A.2d 113 (2007).

law. This deference is more than the deference given to other state agencies.[17] The court then undertook a rather detailed analysis of the relevant statute. It found that the statute was "patently ambiguous," and that the legislative history was "especially pertinent." It concluded that the State Board's interpretation in its Declaratory Ruling should be affirmed.

In regards to the argument that the State Board's Declaratory Ruling was invalid because it was not adopted in conformance with the rulemaking procedures required by the Maryland APA, the majority emphatically responded that this was "wrong." The majority accurately recognized that the "law very clearly recognizes a declaratory ruling under § 10-305 as something different from a regulation."[18] The definition of regulation in Subtitle 1 of the APA expressly excludes a Declaratory Ruling.[19]

A dissent was filed by Judges Raker and Bell. They wrote that the Declaratory Rulings "resulted in regulations in effect, if not name."[20] Their position was that the policies adopted in the Declaratory Rulings were meant to have "general and widespread application," and should have been adopted by rulemaking procedures. The dissent then discussed the case law involving when an agency abuses its discretion by proceeding via a contested case instead of rulemaking, and the 1991 Opinion of the Attorney General, which noted that Declaratory Rulings are "not intended as an alternative to rulemaking." The dissent noted that the court had "never addressed when, if, or to what extent agencies may implement policies through declaratory rulings." Earlier cases, however, "demonstrate that administrative agencies do not possess unfettered discretion to issue policies through whatever procedure they chose." In this case, because the charter school Declaratory Ruling created "new policies of general and widespread application where none existed before," the State Board of Education "should have engaged in formal rulemaking procedures."

The dissent in *City Neighbors* raises an interesting issue. In Chapter 21, I expressed my opinion that an agency's choice of proceeding (rulemaking or contested case) should not be reversed by a reviewing court as long as the agency fully complied with one of the procedural mechanisms authorized by the APA. We now see that the Maryland APA gives agencies the power to create policy by three processes: rulemaking, contested cases, and Declaratory Rulings. There are advantages and disadvantages to both the agency and the public in each of these three methods. As long as the agency properly follows one of the three methods, a court should not be ordering the agency to use a different method. On the other hand, I am sympathetic to the concerns expressed by the dissent that the procedures involved with Declaratory Rulings pale in comparison to the procedures required in rulemaking and contested cases. Maryland agencies have not, however, been relying on Declaratory Rulings to defeat procedural protections. If such a situation ever does occur, a legislative response would be appropriate.

It should also be noted that an agency only has the power to issue a Declaratory Ruling if the agency is petitioned by someone outside the agency. Unlike rulemaking and contested case proceedings, the agency has no power to initiate the Declaratory Ruling process. The choice of having an agency decide a matter by rulemaking or a Declaratory Ruling is one which is made by the interested person, although in both situations, the agency has the discretion to refuse the request.

---

17. "The paramount role of the State Board of Education in interpreting the public education law sets it apart from most administrative agencies." 400 Md. 324, 343, 929 A.2d 113, 125 (2007).

18. 400 Md. 324, 345, 929 A.2d 113, 125 (2007).

19. Maryland Code Annotated, State Government § 10-101(g)(2)(iii).

20. 400 Md. 324, 357, 929 A.2d 113, 133 (2007).

## § 25.4. Declaratory Ruling Regulations

The Maryland APA requires each agency covered by the Declaratory Ruling subtitle to adopt regulations that set forth the form for a petition, and procedures for the submission, consideration, and disposition of the petition.[21] These regulations need to be adopted pursuant to the APA rulemaking procedures and published in COMAR. For example, the Declaratory Ruling regulations of the State Board of Education can be found at COMAR 13A.01.05.02.

There are some agencies that have not adopted Declaratory Ruling regulations. Because of the mandatory, non-discretionary nature of the APA on the agency's obligation to adopt such regulations, a mandamus action would seem appropriate. Without such regulations, any Declaratory Ruling from that agency might be held invalid.

21. Maryland Code Annotated, State Government § 10-304(b)(1) & (2).

# Appendix I

Annotated Code of Maryland
State Government
Title 10. Government Procedures
Subtitle 1. Administrative Procedure Act- Regulations
§ 10-101 to § 10-129

**§ 10-101. Definitions.**

(a) *In general.*- In this subtitle the following words have the meanings indicated.

(b) *Administrator.*- "Administrator" means the Administrator of the Division of State Documents.

(c) *Committee.*- "Committee" means the Joint Committee on Administrative, Executive, and Legislative Review.

(d) *Local government unit.*- "Local government unit" means:

(1) a county;

(2) a municipal corporation;

(3) a special district that is established by State law and that operates within a single county;

(4) a special district that is established by a county pursuant to public general law; or

(5) an office, board, or department that is established in each county under State law and that is funded, pursuant to State law, at least in part by the county governing body.

(e) *Mandate.*- "Mandate" means a directive in a regulation that requires a local government unit to perform a task or assume a responsibility that has a discernible fiscal impact on the local government unit.

(f) *Register.*- "Register" means the Maryland Register.

(g) *Regulation.*-

(1) "Regulation" means a statement or an amendment or repeal of a statement that:

(i) has general application;

(ii) has future effect;

(iii) is adopted by a unit to:

1. detail or carry out a law that the unit administers;

2. govern organization of the unit;

3. govern the procedure of the unit; or

4. govern practice before the unit; and

(iv) is in any form, including:

1. a guideline;

2. a rule;

3. a standard;

4. a statement of interpretation; or

5. a statement of policy.

(2) "Regulation" does not include:

(i) a statement that:

1. concerns only internal management of the unit; and

2. does not affect directly the rights of the public or the procedures available to the public;

(ii) a response of the unit to a petition for adoption of a regulation, under § 10-123 of this subtitle; or

(iii) a declaratory ruling of the unit as to a regulation, order, or statute, under Subtitle 3 of this title.

(3) "Regulation", as used in §§ 10-110 and 10-111.1 of this subtitle, means all or any portion of a regulation.

(h) *Substantively.*- "Substantively" means in a manner substantially affecting the rights, duties, or obligations of:

(1) a member of a regulated group or profession; or

(2) a member of the public.

(i) *Unit.*- "Unit" means an officer or unit authorized by law to adopt regulations.

**§ 10-102. Scope of Title.**

(a) *In general.*- Except as otherwise expressly provided by law, this subtitle applies to: -

(1) each unit in the Executive Branch of the State government; and

(2) each unit that:

(i) is created by public general law; and

(ii) operates in at least 2 counties.

(b) *Exclusions.*- This subtitle does not apply to:

(1) a unit in the Legislative Branch of the State government;

(2) a unit in the Judicial Branch of the State government;

(3) the Injured Workers' Insurance Fund;

(4) a board of license commissioners; or

(5) the Rural Maryland Council.

**§ 10-103, § 10-104- Reversed.**

**§ 10-105. Scope of Part.**

This Part II of this subtitle does not apply to a regulation of a bicounty commission that county governing bodies appoint.

**§ 10-106. Citation of Statutory Authority.**

A regulation is not effective unless it contains a citation of the statutory authority for the regulation.

**§ 10-107. Unit counsel defined; submission to Attorney General or unit counsel.**

(a) *"Unit counsel" defined.*- "Unit counsel" means the unit counsel for the Human Relations Commission, the Public Service Commission, and the State Ethics Commission.

(b) *Approval as to legality.*- Unless a proposed regulation is submitted to the Attorney General or to the unit counsel for approval as to legality, the regulation:

(1) may not be adopted under any statutory authority; and

(2) if adopted, is not effective.

**§ 10-108. Use of "African American" preferred.**

In the preparation of a regulation, a unit shall use the term "African American" instead of "Black", "Negro", "Afro-American", or similar terms.

**§ 10-109. Scope of part.**

This Part III of this subtitle applies only to a unit in the Executive Branch of the State government.

**§ 10-110. Preliminary review.**

(a) *Scope of section.*- Except for subsection (c) of this section, this section does not apply to a regulation adopted under § 10-111(b) of this subtitle.

(b) *Preliminary review - State Children's Environmental Health and Protection Advisory Council.*- At least 15 days before the date a proposed regulation is submitted to the Maryland Register for publication under § 10-112 of this subtitle, the promulgating unit shall submit to the State Children's Environmental Health and Protection Advisory Council established under § 13-1503 of the Health - General Article for review any proposed regulations identified by the promulgating unit as having an impact on environmental hazards affecting the health of children.

(c) *Preliminary review - In general.*-

(1) At least 15 days before the date a proposed regulation is submitted to the Maryland Register for publication under § 10-112 of this subtitle, the promulgating unit shall submit the proposed regulation to the Committee and the Department of Legislative Services.

(2) (i) If the proposed regulation, either in whole or in part, submitted to the Committee and the Department of Legislative Services in accordance with paragraph (1) of this subsection includes an increase or decrease in a fee for a license to practice any business activity, business or health occupation, or business or health profession licensed or otherwise regulated under State law, the promulgating unit shall include clearly written explanatory reasons that justify the increase or decrease in the fee.

(ii) If a regulation submitted under subparagraph (i) of this paragraph proposes an increase in a fee for a license, the written justification also shall include information about:

1. the amount of money needed by the promulgating unit to operate effectively or to eliminate an imbalance between the revenues and expenditures of the unit;

2. the most recent year in which the promulgating unit had last increased its fees;

3. the structure of the promulgating unit as to whether it is one that retains the license fees it receives or passes them through to a national organization or association that creates and administers a uniform licensing examination that is taken by anyone in the United States who is seeking a license to practice a particular occupation or profession or business activity issued by the promulgating unit;

4. measures taken by the promulgating unit to avoid or mitigate the necessity of a fee increase and the results of those measures;

5. special circumstances about the activities and responsibilities of the promulgating unit, including investigations of individuals licensed by the unit, that have had an adverse impact on the unit's operating expenses;

6. consideration given by the promulgating unit to the hardship a license fee increase may have on individuals and trainees licensed or regulated by the unit; and

7. actions taken by the promulgating unit to elicit the opinions of the individuals who are licensed by the promulgating unit and the members of the public as to the effectiveness and performance of the promulgating unit.

(d) *Preliminary review - Action by Committee.-*

(1) The Committee is not required to take any action with respect to a proposed regulation submitted to it pursuant to subsection (c) of this section.

(2) Failure by the Committee to approve or disapprove the proposed regulation during the period of preliminary review provided by subsection (c) of this section may not be construed to mean that the Committee approves or disapproves the proposed regulation.

(3) During the preliminary review period, the Committee may take any action relating to the proposed regulation that the Committee is authorized to take under §§ 10-111.1 and 10-112 of this subtitle.

(e) *Preliminary review - Consultation with Committee.-* Prior to the date specified in subsection (c) of this section, the promulgating unit is encouraged to submit the proposed regulation to the Committee and to consult with the Committee concerning the form and content of that regulation.

**§ 10-111. Time limitations; public hearings.**

(a) *In general.-*

(1) Except as provided in subsection (b) of this section, a unit may not adopt a proposed regulation until:

(i) after submission of the proposed regulation to the Committee for preliminary review under § 10-110 of this subtitle; and

(ii) at least 45 days after its first publication in the Register.

(2) (i) If the Committee determines that an appropriate review cannot reasonably be conducted within 45 days and that an additional period of review is required, it may delay the adoption of the regulation by so notifying the promulgating unit and the Division of State Documents, in writing, prior to the expiration of the 45-day period.

(ii) If notice is provided to the promulgating unit pursuant to subparagraph (i) of this paragraph, the promulgating unit may not adopt the regulation until it notifies the Committee, in writing, of its intention to adopt the regulation and provides the Committee with a further period of review of the regulation that terminates not earlier than the later of the following:

1. the 30th day following the notice provided by the promulgating unit under this subparagraph; or

2. the 105th day following the initial publication of the regulation in the Register.

(3) The promulgating unit shall permit public comment for at least 30 days of the 45-day period under paragraph (1)(ii) of this subsection.

(b) *Emergency adoptions.*-

(1) The unit may adopt a proposed regulation immediately if the unit:

(i) declares that the emergency adoption is necessary;

(ii) submits the proposed regulation to the Committee and the Department of Legislative Services, together with the fiscal impact statement required under subsection (c) of this section; and

(iii) has the approval of the Committee for the emergency adoption.

(2) (i) Subject to subparagraphs (ii), (iii), and (iv) of this paragraph, the approval of the Committee may be given:

1. by a majority of its members who are present and voting at a public hearing or meeting of the Committee; or

2. if staff of the Committee tries but is unable to contact a majority of the members of the Committee in a timely manner and immediate adoption is necessary to protect the public health or safety, by its presiding Chairman or, if its presiding Chairman is unavailable, by its cochair.

(ii) If a member of the Committee requests a public hearing on the emergency adoption of a regulation, the Committee shall hold a public hearing.

(iii) 1. If a public hearing is held on the emergency adoption of a regulation, the Committee may not approve the emergency adoption except by a majority vote of the members present and voting at the hearing or at a meeting of the Committee subsequent to the hearing.

2. If a vote on the emergency regulation is not taken at the public hearing or immediately thereafter, the Committee members shall be provided at least 1 week's notice of the scheduling of any subsequent meeting to vote on the regulation.

(iv) Unless the Governor declares that immediate adoption is necessary to protect the public health or safety, the Committee may not approve the emergency adoption of a regulation earlier than 10 business days after receipt of the regulation by the Committee and the Department of Legislative Services.

(3) If there is no request for a public hearing, the staff of the Committee may poll, in person, by telephone, or in writing:

(i) the members of the Committee; or

(ii) if staff of the Committee tries but is unable to contact a majority of the members of the Committee in a timely manner and immediate adoption is necessary to protect the public health or safety, the presiding Chairman or the cochair.

(4) (i) The Committee may impose, as part of its approval, any condition.

(ii) The Committee shall impose, as part of its approval, a time limit not to exceed 180 days on each request for emergency status.

(iii) If the unit does not adopt the regulation finally before the time limit expires, the status of the regulation reverts to its status before the emergency adoption.

(5) The Committee may rescind its approval by a majority of its members present and voting at a public hearing or meeting of the Committee.

(c) *Fiscal impact statement.*-

(1) The fiscal impact statement, prepared by the unit and submitted under subsection (b) of this section, shall state:

(i) an estimate of the impact of the emergency regulation on the revenues and expenditures of the State;

(ii) whether the State budget for the fiscal year in which the regulation will become effective contains an appropriation of the funds necessary for the implementation of the emergency regulation;

(iii) if an appropriation is not contained in the State budget, the source of the funds necessary for the implementation of the emergency regulation; and

(iv) whether the emergency regulation imposes a mandate on a local government unit.

(2) If the emergency regulation imposes a mandate on a local government unit, the fiscal impact statement shall:

(i) indicate whether the regulation is required to comply with a federal statutory or regulatory mandate;

(ii) if the information may be practicably obtained given the emergency circumstances of the regulations, include an estimate of the impact of the emergency regulation on the revenues and expenditures of local government units; and

(iii) if applicable, and if the required data is available, include the estimated effect on local property tax rates.

**§ 10-111.1. Opposition to adoption.**

(a) *In general.-*

(1) Prior to the expiration of any period of review granted to or reserved by the Committee pursuant to § 10-111(a) of this subtitle, the Committee, by a majority vote, may oppose the adoption of any proposed regulation.

(2) Unless waived by both of the presiding officers, at least 2 weeks prior to acting pursuant to subsection (a)(1) of this section with respect to any proposed regulation, the Committee shall notify the presiding officers who shall notify the appropriate standing committees that the special procedure established by this section may be exercised.

(b) *Factors considered.-* In its review of a proposed regulation pursuant to this section, the factors the Committee shall consider shall include whether the regulation:

(1) is in conformity with the statutory authority of the promulgating unit; and

(2) reasonably complies with the legislative intent of the statute under which the regulation was promulgated.

(c) *Notice to Governor and promulgating unit.-*

(1) Within 5 working days after the Committee votes to oppose the adoption of a proposed regulation, it shall provide written notice to the Governor and the promulgating unit of its action.

(2) Upon receipt of such notice, and with written notice to the Committee and as otherwise required by law, the promulgating unit may:

(i) withdraw the regulation;

(ii) modify the regulation, but only in accordance with § 10-113 of this subtitle; or

(iii) submit the regulation to the Governor with a statement of the justification for the unit's refusal to withdraw or modify the regulation.

(3) Following the receipt of notice under paragraph (2)(iii) above, the Governor may consult with the Committee and the unit in an effort to resolve the conflict. After written

notice has been provided to the presiding officers and to the Committee, the Governor may:

(i) instruct the unit to withdraw the regulation;

(ii) instruct the unit to modify the regulation, but only in accordance with § 10-113 of this subtitle; or

(iii) approve the adoption of the regulation.

(d) *Approval of Governor.*- A proposed regulation opposed by the Committee pursuant to this section may not be adopted, and is not effective unless approved, by the Governor pursuant to subsection (c)(3) of this section.

**§ 10-111.2. Proposed and emergency regulations - Posting and notice.**

(a) *Website list of emergency regulations.*-

(1) The website of the General Assembly shall include a list of all emergency regulations the Committee has received but has not approved.

(2) For each regulation, the list shall include:

(i) the date the Committee received the regulation;

(ii) whether a member of the Committee has requested a public hearing;

(iii) the date of any public hearing scheduled;

(iv) the date and a summary of any action the Committee has taken; and

(v) the name and telephone number of a member of the Committee's staff who can provide further information.

(3) A regulation shall be added to the list within 3 business days after receipt of the regulation by the Committee and the Department of Legislative Services.

(b) *Notice of proposed regulations; fees.*-

(1) The Department of Legislative Services shall maintain a list of members of the public who have requested to receive notice when the Department of Legislative Services receives proposed regulations for which the promulgating unit has requested emergency adoption.

(2) A member of the public who requests notice under this subsection shall specify:

(i) whether the individual wants to receive notice by United States mail or electronic mail; and

(ii) which agencies' regulations the individual wants to receive notice of receipt.

(3) Within 2 business days of receipt of a proposed regulation, the Department of Legislative Services shall provide notice to members of the public who have requested notice, as specified in paragraph (2) of this subsection.

(4) The Department of Legislative Services:

(i) may impose a reasonable fee for sending notice under this subsection by United States mail; and

(ii) may not impose a fee for sending notice under this subsection by electronic mail.

(5) Upon request, a promulgating unit shall provide copies of emergency regulations to members of the public.

**§ 10-112. Procedures for publication.**

(a) *In general.*-

(1) This subsection does not apply to the emergency adoption of a regulation.

(2) To have a proposed regulation published in the Register, a unit shall submit to the Administrator:

(i) the proposed regulation; and

(ii) a notice of the proposed adoption.

(3) The notice under this subsection shall:

(i) state the estimated economic impact of the proposed regulation on:

1. the revenues and expenditures of units of the State government and of local government units; and

2. groups such as consumer, industry, taxpayer, or trade groups;

(ii) include a statement of purpose;

(iii) satisfy the requirements of § 2-1505.2 of this article;

(iv) comply with § 7-113(c) of the Human Services Article; and

(v) give persons an opportunity to comment before adoption of the proposed regulation, by:

1. setting a date, time, and place for a public hearing at which oral or written views and information may be submitted; or

2. giving a telephone number that a person may call to comment and an address to which a person may send comments.

(4) (i) The estimated economic impact statement required under paragraph (3)(i) of this subsection shall state whether the proposed regulation imposes a mandate on a local government unit.

(ii) If the proposed regulation imposes a mandate, the fiscal impact statement shall:

1. indicate whether the regulation is required to comply with a federal statutory or regulatory mandate; and

2. include, in addition to the estimate under paragraph (3)(i)1 of this subsection, the estimated effect on local property tax rates, if applicable, and if the required data is available.

(b) *Emergency adoption.*- As soon as the Committee approves emergency adoption of a regulation, the Committee shall submit the regulation to the Administrator.

(c) *Form.*- If a regulation under this section amends or repeals an adopted regulation, the text of the regulation under this section shall show the changes with the symbols that the Administrator requires.

**§ 10-113. Changes in proposed regulations.**

(a) *In general.*- If a unit wishes to change the text of a proposed regulation so that any part of the text differs substantively from the text previously published in the Register, the unit may not adopt the proposed regulation unless it is proposed anew and adopted in accordance with the requirements of §§ 10-111 and 10-112 of this subtitle.

(b) *Symbology.*- If the regulation is proposed anew, the changes in the text shall be shown with the symbols that the Administrator requires.

(c) *Certification of Attorney General.*-

(1) The Administrator shall refuse to publish the notice of adoption of a regulation that differs from the text previously published unless the notice is accompanied by a certification

from the Attorney General that the provisions of subsections (a) and (b) of this section are not applicable.

(2) The certification shall:

(i) be prepared in the form and according to guidelines specified by the Administrator;

(ii) contain a description of the nature of each change and the basis for the conclusion; and

(iii) be published in the Register as part of the notice of adoption.

**§ 10-114. Notice of adoption.**

(a) *Required.*- After adopting a regulation, a unit shall submit to the Administrator a notice of adoption, for publication in the Register.

(b) *Contents.*- If the text of the adopted regulation is the same or substantially similar to the proposed regulation, the notice shall:

(1) state that the texts are the same or substantially similar;

(2) cite the date of the Register in which the proposed regulation was published; and

(3) show each change in the text with the symbols that the Administrator requires.

**§ 10-115. Reprints.**

(a) *Restricted.*- A unit may not reset or reprint a regulation in the Code of Maryland Regulations, the permanent supplements to the Code of Maryland Regulations, or the Register without the written permission of the Committee.

(b) *Comparison of texts.*- Before reprinting a regulation under this section, a unit shall submit the proposed text of the regulation to the Division of State Documents for comparison with the official text.

**§ 10-116. Withdrawal of proposed regulation.**

(a) *In general.*- A unit:

(1) may withdraw a proposed regulation at any time before its adoption; but

(2) may not adopt the proposed regulation unless it is proposed anew and adopted in accordance with the requirements of §§ 10-111 and 10-112 of this subtitle.

(b) *Failure to adopt.*-

(1) The failure to adopt a proposed regulation within 1 year after its last publication in the Register constitutes withdrawal under this section.

(2) The Administrator shall publish in the Register notice of a withdrawal of a proposed regulation under this subsection.

**§ 10-117. Effective date of regulations.**

(a) *In general.*-

(1) Except as otherwise provided in subsection (b) of this section or in other law, the effective date of a regulation is:

(i) the 10th calendar day after notice of adoption is published in the Register; or

(ii) a later date that the notice sets.

(2) For calculation of the effective date under this subsection:

(i) Article 1, § 36 of the Code does not apply;

(ii) the issue date of the Register in which the notice is published is not counted; and

(iii) each other calendar day, including Saturdays, Sundays, and legal holidays, is counted.

(b) *Emergency adoption.*- The effective date of a regulation after its emergency adoption is the date that the Committee sets.

**§ 10-118. Committee powers over emergency or proposed regulations or portion thereof.**

The Committee may exercise a power granted under this subtitle over an emergency or proposed regulation or a specific, distinct, and severable provision of an emergency or proposed regulation.

**§ 10-119- Reversed.**

**§ 10-120. Scope of part.**

(a) *General exclusions.*- This Part IV of this subtitle does not apply to:

(1) the Governor;

(2) the Department of Assessments and Taxation;

(3) the Board of Appeals of the Department of Labor, Licensing, and Regulation;

(4) the Insurance Administration;

(5) the Maryland Parole Commission of the Department of Public Safety and Correctional Services;

(6) the Public Service Commission;

(7) the Maryland Tax Court; or

(8) the State Workers' Compensation Commission.

(b) *Maryland Automobile Insurance Fund.*- If the Insurance Commissioner states in writing that, as to a particular matter, the Maryland Automobile Insurance Fund need not comply with this Part IV of this subtitle, this Part IV does not apply to the Fund with respect to that matter.

(c) *Applicability to property tax assessment appeals boards.*- This subtitle does apply to the property tax assessment appeals boards.

**§ 10-121. Political subdivisions and instrumentalities.**

A political subdivision of the State or an instrumentality of a political subdivision is entitled, to the same extent as other legal entities, to be an interested person, party, or petitioner in a matter under this subtitle, including an appeal.

**§ 10-122. Procedural regulations.**

(a) *Required.*- Each unit shall adopt regulations to govern procedures under this Part IV of this subtitle, including the related forms that the unit requires and the instructions for completing the forms.

(b) *Descriptive statement.*- To help persons deal with the unit, the unit shall supplement, so far as practicable, the regulations under this section with a description of the procedures of the unit.

**§ 10-123. Petition for adoption of regulation.**

(a) *Petition by interested person.*- An interested person may submit to a unit a petition for the adoption of a regulation.

(b) *Response by unit.*- Within 60 days after the petition is submitted, the unit shall:

(1) in writing, deny the petition and state the reasons for the denial; or

(2) initiate the procedures for adoption of the regulation.

**§ 10-124. Evaluation of impact.**

(a) *"Business" defined.*- In this section, "business" means a trade, professional activity, or other business that is conducted for profit.

(b) *Required.*-

(1) Before a unit adopts a proposed regulation, the unit shall evaluate whether the proposed regulation has any impact on businesses.

(2) To evaluate the impact, the unit shall:

(i) on the basis of the sizes of the businesses that the proposed regulation might affect, divide those businesses into any classes that the unit considers appropriate for the proposed regulation; and

(ii) particularly consider:

1. the costs that the proposed regulation would impose on each class; and

2. the difficulty of compliance for each class.

(c) *Action after evaluation.*- On the basis of the evaluation, the unit may adopt 1 or more regulations that apply differently to classes of businesses.

**§ 10-125. Declaratory judgment.**

(a) *Petition authorized.*-

(1) A person may file a petition for a declaratory judgment on the validity of any regulation, whether or not the person has asked the unit to consider the validity of the regulation.

(2) A petition under this section shall be filed with the circuit court for the county where the petitioner resides or has a principal place of business.

(b) *Authority to consider.*- A court may determine the validity of any regulation if it appears to the court that the regulation or its threatened application interferes with or impairs or threatens to interfere with or impair a legal right or privilege of the petitioner.

(c) *Unit as party.*- The unit that adopted the regulation shall be made a party to the proceeding under this section.

(d) *Finding of invalidity.*- Subject to § 10-128 of this subtitle, the court shall declare a provision of a regulation invalid if the court finds that:

(1) the provision violates any provision of the United States or Maryland Constitution;

(2) the provision exceeds the statutory authority of the unit; or

(3) the unit failed to comply with statutory requirements for adoption of the provision.

**§ 10-126, § 10-127- Reversed.**

**§ 10-128. Severability.**

(a) *In general.*- Unless a regulation expressly states otherwise, its provisions are severable.

(b) *Finding of court.*- The finding of a court that a provision of a regulation is invalid invalidates only any other provision of the regulation that the court finds then is so incomplete that it cannot be carried out in accordance with the purpose of the regulation.

**§ 10-129. Publications of notices.**

(a) *Scope of section.*- This section applies only to a unit in the Executive Branch of the State government.

(b) *Required.*- Whenever a court of final appeal declares all or any part of a regulation invalid and unconstitutional:

(1) the unit that adopted the regulation shall have notice of that fact published in the Register; and

(2) the Administrator shall publish notice of that fact in the permanent supplements or otherwise in the Code of Maryland Regulations.

# Appendix II

Annotated Code of Maryland
State Government
Title 10. Government Procedures
Subtitle 2. Administrative Procedure Act- Contested Cases
§ 10-201 to § 10-226

**§ 10-201. Declaration of policy.**

The purpose of this subtitle is to:

(1) ensure the right of all persons to be treated in a fair and unbiased manner in their efforts to resolve disputes in administrative proceedings governed by this subtitle; and

(2) promote prompt, effective, and efficient government.

**§ 10-202. Definitions.**

(a) *In general.*- In this subtitle the following words have the meanings indicated.

(b) *Agency.*- "Agency" means:

(1) an officer or unit of the State government authorized by law to adjudicate contested cases; or

(2) a unit that:

(i) is created by general law;

(ii) operates in at least 2 counties; and

(iii) is authorized by law to adjudicate contested cases.

(c) *Agency head.*- "Agency head" means:

(1) an individual or group of individuals in whom the ultimate legal authority of an agency is vested by any provision of law; or

(2) the secretary of the State department that is responsible for State programs that are administered by the Montgomery County Department of Health and Human Services.

(d) *Contested case.*-

(1) "Contested case" means a proceeding before an agency to determine:

(i) a right, duty, statutory entitlement, or privilege of a person that is required by statute or constitution to be determined only after an opportunity for an agency hearing; or

(ii) the grant, denial, renewal, revocation, suspension, or amendment of a license that is required by statute or constitution to be determined only after an opportunity for an agency hearing.

(2) "Contested case" does not include a proceeding before an agency involving an agency hearing required only by regulation unless the regulation expressly, or by clear implication, requires the hearing to be held in accordance with this subtitle.

(e) *License.*- "License" means all or any part of permission that:

(1) is required by law to be obtained from an agency;

(2) is not required only for revenue purposes; and

(3) is in any form, including:

(i) an approval;

(ii) a certificate;

(iii) a charter;

(iv) a permit; or

(v) a registration.

(f) *Office.*- "Office" means the Office of Administrative Hearings.

(g) *Presiding officer.*- "Presiding officer" means the board, commission, agency head, administrative law judge, or other authorized person conducting an administrative proceeding under this subtitle.

**§ 10-203. Scope of subtitle.**

(a) *General exclusions.*- This subtitle does not apply to:

(1) the Legislative Branch of the State government or an agency of the Legislative Branch;

(2) the Judicial Branch of the State government or an agency of the Judicial Branch;

(3) the following agencies of the Executive Branch of the State government:

(i) the Governor;

(ii) the Department of Assessments and Taxation;

(iii) the Insurance Administration except as specifically provided in the Insurance Article;

(iv) the Injured Workers' Insurance Fund;

(v) the Maryland Parole Commission of the Department of Public Safety and Correctional Services;

(vi) the Public Service Commission;

(vii) the Maryland Tax Court;

(viii) the State Workers' Compensation Commission;

(ix) the Maryland Automobile Insurance Fund; or

(x) the Patuxent Institution Board of Review, when acting on a parole request;

(4) an officer or unit not part of a principal department of State government that:

(i) is created by or pursuant to the Maryland Constitution or general or local law;

(ii) operates in only 1 county; and

(iii) is subject to the control of a local government or is funded wholly or partly from local funds;

(5) unemployment insurance claim determinations, tax determinations, and appeals in the Department of Labor, Licensing, and Regulation except as specifically provided in Subtitle 5A of Title 8 of the Labor and Employment Article; or

(6) any other entity otherwise expressly exempted by statute.

(b) *Applicability to property tax assessment appeals boards and correction of death certificates.*- This subtitle does apply to:

(1) the property tax assessment appeals boards; and

(2) as to requests for correction of certificates of death under § 5-310 (d) (2) of the Health-General Article, the office of the Chief Medical Examiner.

(c) *Public hearings.*- A public hearing required or provided for by statute or regulation before an agency takes a particular action is not an agency hearing under § 10-202 (d) of this subtitle unless the statute or regulation:

(1) expressly requires that the public hearing be held in accordance with this subtitle; or

(2) expressly requires that any judicial review of the agency determination following the public hearing be conducted in accordance with this subtitle.

(d) *Contested cases arising from State program administered by Montgomery County Department of Health and Human Services.*-

(1) Subject to paragraphs (2) and (3) of this subsection, this subtitle does apply to a contested case that arises from a State program administered by the Montgomery County Department of Health and Human Services in the same manner as the subtitle applies to a county health department or local department of social services.

(2) For purposes of this subtitle, the Office of the Attorney General, after consultation with the County Attorney for Montgomery County, shall determine if the Montgomery County Department of Health and Human Services administers a State program.

(3) This subsection is not intended to extend or limit the authority of the Montgomery County Department of Health and Human Services to administer State programs in the manner of a county health department or local department of social services.

**§ 10-204. Political subdivisions and instrumentalities.**

A political subdivision of the State or an instrumentality of a political subdivision is entitled, to the same extent as other legal entities, to be an interested person, party, or petitioner in a matter under this subtitle, including an appeal.

**§ 10-205. Delegation of hearing authority.**

(a) *To whom delegated; limitation.*-

(1) Except as provided in paragraph (2) of this subsection, a board, commission, or agency head authorized to conduct a contested case hearing shall:

(i) conduct the hearing; or

(ii) delegate the authority to conduct the contested case hearing to:

1. the Office; or

2. with the prior written approval of the Chief Administrative Law Judge, a person not employed by the Office.

(2) A hearing held in accordance with § 4-608(f) or § 5-610(f) of the Business Occupations and Professions Article may not be delegated to the Office.

(3) With the written approval of the Chief Administrative Law Judge, a class of contested case hearings may be delegated as provided in paragraph (1)(ii)2 of this subsection.

(4) This subsection is not intended to restrict the right of an individual, expressly authorized by a statute in effect on October 1, 1993, to conduct a contested case hearing.

(b) *Scope of authority delegated.*- An agency may delegate to the Office the authority to issue:

(1) proposed or final findings of fact;

(2) proposed or final conclusions of law;

(3) proposed or final findings of fact and conclusions of law;

(4) proposed or final orders or orders under Title 20 of this article; or

(5) the final administrative decision of an agency in a contested case.

(c) *Procedure upon receipt of hearing request.*- Promptly after receipt of a request for a contested case hearing, an agency shall:

(1) notify the parties that the authorized agency head, board, or commission shall conduct the hearing;

(2) transmit the request to the Office so that the Office shall conduct the hearing in accordance with the agency's delegation; or

(3) request written approval from the Chief Administrative Law Judge to appoint a person not employed by the Office to conduct the hearing.

(d) *Delegation final; exception.*-

(1) Except as provided in paragraph (2) of this subsection, an agency's delegation and transmittal of all or part of a contested case to the Office is final.

(2) If an agency has adopted regulations specifying the criteria and procedures for the revocation of a delegation of a contested case, delegation of authority to hear all or part of a contested case may be revoked, by the agency head, board, or commission, in accordance with the agency's regulations, at any time prior to the earlier of:

(i) the issuance of a ruling on a substantive issue; or

(ii) the taking of oral testimony from the first witness.

(e) *Duties of the Office.*-

(1) The Office shall:

(i) conduct the hearing; and

(ii) except as provided in paragraph (2) of this subsection or as otherwise required by law, within 90 days after the completion of the hearing, complete the procedure authorized in the agency's delegation to the Office.

(2) The time limit specified in paragraph (1)(ii) of this subsection may be extended with the written approval of the Chief Administrative Law Judge.

**§ 10-206. Procedural regulations.**

(a) *Adoption by Office; conflict.*-

(1) The Office shall adopt regulations to govern the procedures and practice in all contested cases delegated to the Office and conducted under this subtitle.

(2) Unless a federal or State law requires that a federal or State procedure shall be observed, the regulations adopted under paragraph (1) of this subsection shall take precedence in the event of a conflict.

(b) *Adoption by agencies.*- Each agency may adopt regulations to govern procedures under this subtitle and practice before the agency in contested cases.

(c) *Expedited hearings.*- Regulations adopted under this section may include procedures and criteria for requesting and conducting expedited hearings.

(d) *Prehearing procedures.*- Each agency and the Office may adopt regulations that:

(1) provide for prehearing conferences in contested cases; or

(2) set other appropriate prehearing procedures in contested cases.

(e) *Explanatory materials.*- To assist the public in understanding the procedures followed by an agency or the Office in contested cases, an agency or the Office may develop and distribute supplemental explanatory materials, including the related forms that the agency or Office requires and instructions for completing the forms.

**§ 10-206.1. Legal practice.**

(a) *Practice before agency.*- An agency may not:

(1) grant the right to practice law to an individual who is not authorized to practice law;

(2) interfere with the right of a lawyer to practice before an agency or the Office; or

(3) prohibit any party from being advised or represented at the party's own expense by an attorney or, if permitted by law, other representative.

(b) *Publicly provided legal services.*- Subsection (a) of this section may not be interpreted to require the State to furnish publicly provided legal services in any proceeding under this subtitle.

**§ 10-207. Notice of agency action.**

(a) *In general.*- An agency shall give reasonable notice of the agency's action.

(b) *Contents of notice.*- The notice shall:

(1) state concisely and simply:

(i) the facts that are asserted; or

(ii) if the facts cannot be stated in detail when the notice is given, the issues that are involved;

(2) state the pertinent statutory and regulatory sections under which the agency is taking its action;

(3) state the sanction proposed or the potential penalty, if any, as a result of the agency's action;

(4) unless a hearing is automatically scheduled, state that the recipient of notice of an agency's action may have an opportunity to request a hearing, including:

(i) what, if anything, a person must do to receive a hearing; and

(ii) all relevant time requirements; and

(5) state the direct consequences, sanction, potential penalty, if any, or remedy of the recipient's failure to exercise in a timely manner the opportunity for a hearing or to appear for a scheduled hearing.

(c) *Consolidation of notices.*- The notice of agency action under this section may be consolidated with the notice of hearing required under § 10-208 of this subtitle.

(d) *Publication in Register.*- For purposes of this section, publication in the Maryland Register does not constitute reasonable notice to a party.

**§ 10-208. Notice of hearing.**

(a) *In general.*- An agency or the Office shall give all parties in a contested case reasonable written notice of the hearing.

(b) *Contents of notice.*- The notice shall state:

(1) the date, time, place, and nature of the hearing;

(2) the right to call witnesses and submit documents or other evidence under § 10-213(f) of this subtitle;

(3) any applicable right to request subpoenas for witnesses and evidence and specify the costs, if any, associated with such a request;

(4) that a copy of the hearing procedure is available on request and specify the costs associated with such a request;

(5) any right or restriction pertaining to representation;

(6) that failure to appear for the scheduled hearing may result in an adverse action against the party; and

(7) that, unless otherwise prohibited by law, the parties may agree to the evidence and waive their right to appear at the hearing.

(c) *Consolidation of notices.*- The notice of hearing may be consolidated with the notice of agency action required under § 10-207 of this subtitle.

(d) *Publication in Register.*- For purposes of this subtitle, publication in the Maryland Register does not constitute reasonable notice to a party.

**§ 10-209. Notice mailed to address of licensee.**

(a) *In general.*- Where a licensing statute provides for service other than by regular mail, notice under this subtitle may be sent by regular mail to the address of record of a person holding a license issued by the agency if:

(1) the person is required by law to advise the agency of the address; and

(2) the agency has been unsuccessful in giving notice in the manner otherwise provided by the licensing statute.

(b) *Hearing.*- Upon a showing that the person neither knew nor had reasonable opportunity to know of the fact of service, a person served by regular mail under subsection (a) of this section shall be granted a hearing.

(c) *Reasonable opportunity to know of service.*- A person holding a license shall be deemed to have had a reasonable opportunity to know of the fact of service if:

(1) the person is required by law to notify the agency of a change of address within a specified period of time;

(2) the person failed to notify the agency in accordance with the law;

(3) the agency or the Office mailed the notice to the address of record; and

(4) the agency did not have actual notice of the change of address prior to service.

**§ 10-210. Dispositions.**

Unless otherwise precluded by law, an agency or the Office may dispose of a contested case by:

(1) stipulation;

(2) settlement;

(3) consent order;

(4) default;

(5) withdrawal;

(6) summary disposition; or

(7) dismissal.

**§ 10-211. Hearings conducted by electronic means.**

(a) *Permitted.*- In accordance with subsection (b) of this section, a hearing may be conducted by telephone, video conferencing, or other electronic means.

(b) *Objections.*-

(1) For good cause, a party may object to the holding of a hearing by telephone, video conferencing, or other electronic means.

(2) If a party establishes good cause in opposition to the holding of a hearing by telephone or other similar audio electronic means, the hearing shall be held in person or by video conferencing or other similar audiovisual electronic means.

(3) If a party establishes good cause in opposition to the holding of a hearing by video conferencing or other similar audiovisual electronic means, the hearing shall be conducted in person.

**§ 10-212. Open hearings.**

(a) *In general.*- Except as otherwise provided by law, a contested case hearing conducted by the Office shall be open to the public.

(b) *Subtitle 5 not applicable.*- Hearings conducted by the Office are not subject to Subtitle 5 of this title.

**§ 10-212.1. Interpreters.**

(a) *In general.*-

(1) In a contested case, a party or witness may apply to the agency for the appointment of a qualified interpreter to assist that party or witness, if the party or witness is deaf or, because of a hearing impediment, cannot readily understand or communicate the spoken English language.

(2) On application of the party or witness the agency shall appoint a qualified interpreter.

(3) In selecting a qualified interpreter for appointment, the agency may consult the directory of interpreters for manual communication or oral interpretation to assist deaf persons that is maintained by the courts of the State.

(b) *Compensation.*-

(1) An interpreter appointed under this section shall be allowed the compensation that the agency considers reasonable.

(2) Subject to paragraph (3) of this subsection, the compensation shall be paid by the agency.

(3) If the agency has the authority to tax for services and expenses as a part of the costs of a case, the agency may tax the amount paid to an interpreter as a part of these services and expenses in accordance with the federal Americans with Disabilities Act.

**§ 10-213. Evidence.**

(a) *In general.*-

(1) Each party in a contested case shall offer all of the evidence that the party wishes to have made part of the record.

(2) If the agency has any evidence that the agency wishes to use in adjudicating the contested case, the agency shall make the evidence part of the record.

(b) *Probative evidence.*- The presiding officer may admit probative evidence that reasonable and prudent individuals commonly accept in the conduct of their affairs and give probative effect to that evidence.

(c) *Hearsay.*- Evidence may not be excluded solely on the basis that it is hearsay.

(d) *Exclusions.*- The presiding officer may exclude evidence that is:

(1) incompetent;

(2) irrelevant;

(3) immaterial; or

(4) unduly repetitious.

(e) *Rules of privilege.*- The presiding officer shall apply a privilege that law recognizes.

(f) *Scope of evidence.*- On a genuine issue in a contested case, each party is entitled to:

(1) call witnesses;

(2) offer evidence, including rebuttal evidence;

(3) cross-examine any witness that another party or the agency calls; and

(4) present summation and argument.

(g) *Documentary evidence.*- The presiding officer may receive documentary evidence:

(1) in the form of copies or excerpts; or

(2) by incorporation by reference.

(h) *Official notice of facts.*-

(1) The agency or the Office may take official notice of a fact that is:

(i) judicially noticeable; or

(ii) general, technical, or scientific and within the specialized knowledge of the agency.

(2) Before taking official notice of a fact, the presiding officer:

(i) before or during the hearing, by reference in a preliminary report, or otherwise, shall notify each party; and

(ii) shall give each party an opportunity to contest the fact.

(i) *Evaluation.*- The agency or the Office may use its experience, technical competence, and specialized knowledge in the evaluation of evidence.

**§ 10-214. Consideration of other evidence.**

(a) *Findings based on evidence of record.*- Findings of fact must be based exclusively on the evidence of record in the contested case proceeding and on matters officially noticed in that proceeding.

(b) *Regulations, rulings, etc., binding.*- In a contested case, the Office is bound by any agency regulation, declaratory ruling, prior adjudication, or other settled, preexisting policy, to the same extent as the agency is or would have been bound if it were hearing the case.

**§ 10-215. Transcription of proceedings.**

All or part of proceedings in a contested case shall be transcribed if any party:

(1) requests the transcription; and

(2) pays any required costs.

**§ 10-216. Exceptions.**

(a) *Notice of proposed decision; consideration of exceptions.*-

(1) In the case of a single decision maker, if the final decision maker in a contested case has not personally presided over the hearing, the final decision may not be made until each party is given notice of the proposed decision in accordance with § 10-220 of this subtitle and an opportunity to:

(i) file exceptions with the agency to the proposed decision; and

(ii) present argument to the final decision maker that the proposed decision should be affirmed, reversed, or remanded.

(2) In the case of a decision-making body, if a majority of the officials who are to make a final decision in a contested case have not personally presided over the hearing, the officials may not make the final decision until each party is given notice of the proposed decision in accordance with § 10-220 of this subtitle and an opportunity to:

(i) file exceptions to the proposed decision with the agency; and

(ii) present argument to a majority of the officials who are to make the final decision.

(3) If a party files exceptions or presents argument under paragraph (1) or (2) of this subsection, the official or officials who are to make the final decision shall:

(i) personally consider each part of the record that a party cites in its exceptions or arguments before making a final decision; and

(ii) except as otherwise provided by law or by agreement of the parties, make the final decision within 90 days after the exceptions are filed or the argument is presented, whichever is later.

(b) *Changes to proposed decision.*- The final decision shall identify any changes, modifications, or amendments to the proposed decision and the reasons for the changes, modifications, or amendments.

**§ 10-217. Proof.**

The standard of proof in a contested case shall be the preponderance of evidence unless the standard of clear and convincing evidence is imposed on the agency by regulation, statute, or constitution.

**§ 10-218. Contents of record.**

The presiding officer hearing a contested case shall make a record that includes:

(1) all motions and pleadings;

(2) all documentary evidence that the agency or Office receives;

(3) a statement of each fact of which the agency or Office has taken official notice;

(4) any staff memorandum submitted to an individual who is involved in the decision making process of the contested case by an official or employee of the agency who is not authorized to participate in the decision making process;

(5) each question;

(6) each offer of proof;

(7) each objection and the ruling on the objection;

(8) each finding of fact or conclusion of law proposed by:

(i) a party; or

(ii) the presiding officer;

(9) each exception to a finding or conclusion proposed by a presiding officer; and

(10) each intermediate proposed and final ruling by or for the agency, including each report or opinion issued in connection with the ruling.

**§ 10-219. Ex parte communications.**

(a) *Restrictions.*-

(1) Except as provided in paragraph (2) of this subsection, a presiding officer may not communicate ex parte directly or indirectly regarding the merits of any issue in the case, while the case is pending, with:

(i) any party to the case or the party's representative or attorney; or

(ii) any person who presided at a previous stage of the case.

(2) An agency head, board, or commission presiding over a contested case may communicate with members of an advisory staff of, or any counsel for, the agency, board, or commission who otherwise does not participate in the contested case.

(b) *Communications prior to hearing.*- If, before hearing a contested case, a person receives an ex parte communication of a type that would violate subsection (a) of this section if received while conducting a hearing, the person, promptly after commencing the hearing, shall disclose the communication in the manner prescribed in subsection (c) of this section.

(c) *Disclosure.*- An individual who is involved in the decision making process and who is personally aware of an ex parte communication shall:

(1) give notice to all parties;

(2) include in the record of the contested case:

(i) each written communication received;

(ii) a memorandum that states the substance of each oral communication received;

(iii) each written response to a communication; and

(iv) a memorandum that states the substance of each oral response to the communication; and

(3) send to each party a copy of each communication, memorandum, and response.

(d) *Rebuttal.*- A party may rebut an ex parte communication if the party requests the opportunity to rebut within 10 days after notice of the communication.

(e) *Remedial action.*-

(1) To eliminate the effect of an ex parte communication that is made in violation of this section, the presiding officer or, if the presiding officer is a multimember body, the individual board or commission member, may:

(i) withdraw from the proceeding; or

(ii) terminate the proceeding without prejudice.

(2) An order to terminate the proceeding without prejudice shall state the last date by which a party may reinstitute the proceeding.

**§ 10-220. Proposed decisions and orders.**

(a) *Preparation.*- If the Office conducts a hearing under this subtitle, the Office shall prepare proposed findings of fact, conclusions of law, or orders in accordance with the agency's delegation under § 10-205 of this subtitle.

(b) *Submission.*- The Office shall send its proposed findings, conclusions, or orders:

(1) to the parties and the agency directly; or

(2) if the agency's delegation under § 10-205 of this subtitle requires, to the agency for distribution by the agency to the parties.

(c) *Review and issuance.*-

(1) Within 60 days after receipt of the Office's proposed findings, conclusions, or order under subsection (b) (2) of this section, the agency shall:

(i) review the Office's proposed findings, conclusions, or order;

(ii) issue the proposed decision, which may include the Office's proposed findings, conclusions, or order with or without modification; and

(iii) send the proposed decision and a copy of the Office's proposed findings, conclusions, or order to the parties.

(2) The time limit specified in paragraph (1) of this subsection may be extended by the agency head, board, or commission with written notice to the parties.

(d) *Form and contents.*- A proposed decision or order, including proposed decisions or orders issued for contested case hearings subject to this subtitle but not conducted by the Office, shall:

(1) be in writing or stated on the record;

(2) contain separate findings of fact and conclusions of law;

(3) include an explanation of procedures and time limits for filing exceptions; and

(4) if the Office conducted the hearing and the agency's proposed decision includes any changes, modifications, or amendments to the Office's proposed findings, conclusions, or orders, contain an explanation of the reasons for each change, modification, or amendment.

**§ 10-221. Final decisions and orders.**

(a) *Form.*- A final decision or order in a contested case that is adverse to a party shall be in writing or stated on the record.

(b) *Contents.*-

(1) A final decision or order in a contested case, including a remand of a proposed decision, shall contain separate statements of:

(i) the findings of fact;

(ii) the conclusions of law; and

(iii) the order.

(2) A written statement of appeal rights shall be included with the decision.

(3) If the findings of fact are stated in statutory language, the final decision shall state concisely and explicitly the facts that support the findings.

(4) If, in accordance with regulations, a party submitted proposed findings of fact, the final decision shall state a ruling on each proposed finding.

(c) *Distribution.*- The final decision maker promptly shall deliver or mail a copy of the final decision or order to:

(1) each party; or

(2) the party's attorney of record.

**§ 10-222. Judicial review.**

(a) *Review of final decision.-*

(1) Except as provided in subsection (b) of this section, a party who is aggrieved by the final decision in a contested case is entitled to judicial review of the decision as provided in this section.

(2) An agency, including an agency that has delegated a contested case to the Office, is entitled to judicial review of a decision as provided in this section if the agency was a party before the agency or the Office.

(b) *Review of interlocutory order.-* Where the presiding officer has final decision-making authority, a person in a contested case who is aggrieved by an interlocutory order is entitled to judicial review if:

(1) the party would qualify under this section for judicial review of any related final decision;

(2) the interlocutory order:

(i) determines rights and liabilities; and

(ii) has immediate legal consequences; and

(3) postponement of judicial review would result in irreparable harm.

(c) *Jurisdiction and venue.-* Unless otherwise required by statute, a petition for judicial review shall be filed with the circuit court for the county where any party resides or has a principal place of business.

(d) *Parties.-*

(1) The court may permit any other interested person to intervene in a proceeding under this section.

(2) If the agency has delegated to the Office the authority to issue the final administrative decision pursuant to § 10-205(a)(3) of this subtitle, and there are 2 or more other parties with adverse interests remaining in the case, the agency may decline to participate in the judicial review. An agency that declines to participate shall inform the court in its initial response.

(e) *Stay of enforcement.-*

(1) The filing of a petition for judicial review does not automatically stay the enforcement of the final decision.

(2) Except as otherwise provided by law, the final decision maker may grant or the reviewing court may order a stay of the enforcement of the final decision on terms that the final decision maker or court considers proper.

(f) *Additional evidence before agency.-*

(1) Judicial review of disputed issues of fact shall be confined to the record for judicial review supplemented by additional evidence taken pursuant to this section.

(2) The court may order the presiding officer to take additional evidence on terms that the court considers proper if:

(i) before the hearing date in court, a party applies for leave to offer additional evidence; and

(ii) the court is satisfied that:

1. the evidence is material; and

2. there were good reasons for the failure to offer the evidence in the proceeding before the presiding officer.

(3) On the basis of the additional evidence, the final decision maker may modify the findings and decision.

(4) The final decision maker shall file with the reviewing court, as part of the record:

(i) the additional evidence; and

(ii) any modifications of the findings or decision.

(g) *Proceeding.*-

(1) The court shall conduct a proceeding under this section without a jury.

(2) A party may offer testimony on alleged irregularities in procedure before the presiding officer that do not appear on the record.

(3) On request, the court shall:

(i) hear oral argument; and

(ii) receive written briefs.

(h) *Decision.*- In a proceeding under this section, the court may:

(1) remand the case for further proceedings;

(2) affirm the final decision; or

(3) reverse or modify the decision if any substantial right of the petitioner may have been prejudiced because a finding, conclusion, or decision:

(i) is unconstitutional;

(ii) exceeds the statutory authority or jurisdiction of the final decision maker;

(iii) results from an unlawful procedure;

(iv) is affected by any other error of law;

(v) is unsupported by competent, material, and substantial evidence in light of the entire record as submitted; or

(vi) is arbitrary or capricious.

**§ 10-222.1. Administrative orders.**

(a) *Enforcement.*- A party to a contested case may timely seek civil enforcement of an administrative order by filing a petition for civil enforcement in an appropriate circuit court.

(b) *Jurisdiction and venue.*- Unless otherwise required by statute, a party shall file a petition for civil enforcement of an administrative order in the circuit court for the county where any party resides or has a principal place of business.

(c) *Parties - Defendants.*- In an action seeking civil enforcement of an administrative order, a party shall name, as a defendant, each alleged violator against whom the party seeks to obtain civil enforcement.

(d) *Parties - Plaintiffs.*- A party may file an action for civil enforcement of an administrative order if another party is in violation of the administrative order.

(e) *Remedies.*- A party in an action for civil enforcement of an administrative order may request, and a court may grant, one or more of the following forms of relief:

(1) declaratory relief;

(2) temporary or permanent injunctive relief;

(3) a writ of mandamus; or

(4) any other civil remedy provided by law.

**§ 10-223. Appeals to Court of Special Appeals.**

(a) *Scope of section.*- This section does not apply to:

(1) a case that arises under Title 16 of the Transportation Article unless a right to appeal to the Court of Special Appeals is specifically provided; or

(2) a final judgment on actions of the Inmate Grievance Office.

(b) *Right of appeal.*-

(1) A party who is aggrieved by a final judgment of a circuit court under this subtitle may appeal to the Court of Special Appeals in the manner that law provides for appeal of civil cases.

(2) An agency that was a party in the circuit court may appeal under paragraph (1) of this subsection.

**§ 10-224. Litigation expenses for small businesses and nonprofit organizations.**

(a) *Definitions.*-

(1) In this section the following words have the meanings indicated.

(2) "Business" means a trade, professional activity, or other business that is conducted for profit.

(3) "Nonprofit organization" means an organization that is exempt or eligible for exemption from taxation under § 501 (c) (3) of the Internal Revenue Code.

(b) *Scope of section.*- This section applies only to:

(1) an agency operating statewide;

(2) a business that, on the date when the contested case or civil action is initiated:

(i) is independently owned and operated; and

(ii) has less than 50 employees, including, if a corporation owns 50% or more of the stock of the business, each employee of the corporation; and

(3) a nonprofit organization.

(c) *Reimbursement authorized.*- Subject to the limitations in this section, an agency or court may award to a business or nonprofit organization reimbursement for expenses that the business or nonprofit organization reasonably incurs in connection with a contested case or civil action that:

(1) is initiated against the business or nonprofit organization by an agency as part of an administrative or regulatory function;

(2) is initiated without substantial justification or in bad faith; and

(3) does not result in:

(i) an adjudication, stipulation, or acceptance of liability of the business or nonprofit organization;

(ii) a determination of noncompliance, violation, infringement, deficiency, or breach on the part of the business or nonprofit organization; or

(iii) a settlement agreement under which the business or nonprofit organization agrees to take corrective action or to pay a monetary sum.

(d) *Claim required in contested case.*-

(1) To qualify for an award under this section when the agency has initiated a contested case, the business or nonprofit organization must make a claim to the agency before taking any appeal.

(2) The agency shall act on the claim.

(e) *Amount.*-

(1) An award under this section may include:

(i) the expenses incurred in the contested case;

(ii) court costs;

(iii) counsel fees; and

(iv) the fees of necessary witnesses.

(2) An award under this section may not exceed $10,000.

(3) The court may reduce or deny an award to the extent that the conduct of the business or nonprofit organization during the proceedings unreasonably delayed the resolution of the matter in controversy.

(f) *Source of award.*- An award under this section shall be paid as provided in the State budget.

(g) *Appeals.*-

(1) If the agency denies an award under this section, the business or nonprofit organization may appeal, as provided in this subtitle.

(2) An agency may appeal an award that a court makes under this section.

**§ 10-225. Suspension of provisions.**

(a) *In general.*- Upon a finding by the Governor that there is an imminent threat within a time certain of a loss or denial of federal funds to the State because of the operation of any section of this subtitle or of Title 9, Subtitle 16 of this article, the Governor by executive order may suspend the applicability of part or all of this subtitle or of Title 9, Subtitle 16 of this article to a specific class of contested cases.

(b) *Duration.*- A suspension under this section is effective only so long as, and to the extent, necessary to avoid a denial or loss of federal funds to the State.

(c) *Contents of order.*- The executive order shall explain the basis for the Governor's finding and state the period of time during which the suspension is to be effective.

(d) *Termination.*- The Governor shall declare the termination of a suspension when it is no longer necessary to prevent the loss or denial of federal funds.

(e) *Publication of order.*- An executive order issued under this section shall be:

(1) presented to the Legislative Policy Committee; and

(2) published in the Maryland Register pursuant to § 7-206 (a) (2) (viii) of this article.

**§ 10-226. Licenses - Special provisions.**

(a) *Definitions.*-

(1) In this section the following words have the meanings indicated.

(2) "License" means all or any part of permission that:

(i) is required by law to be obtained from a unit;

(ii) is not required only for revenue purposes; and

(iii) is in any form, including:

1. an approval;

2. a certificate;

3. a charter;

4. a permit; or

5. a registration.

(3) "Unit" means an officer or unit that is authorized by law to:

(i) adopt regulations subject to Subtitle 1 of this title; or

(ii) adjudicate contested cases under this subtitle.

(b) *Renewal and expiration.*- If, at least 2 calendar weeks before a license expires, the licensee makes sufficient application for renewal of the license, the license does not expire until:

(1) the unit takes final action on the application; and

(2) either:

(i) the time for seeking judicial review of the action expires; or

(ii) any judicial stay of the unit's final action expires.

(c) *Revocation of suspension.*-

(1) Except as provided in paragraph (2) of this subsection, a unit may not revoke or suspend a license unless the unit first gives the licensee:

(i) written notice of the facts that warrant suspension or revocation; and

(ii) an opportunity to be heard.

(2) A unit may order summarily the suspension of a license if the unit:

(i) finds that the public health, safety, or welfare imperatively requires emergency action; and

(ii) promptly gives the licensee:

1. written notice of the suspension, the finding, and the reasons that support the finding; and

2. an opportunity to be heard.

# Appendix III

Annotated Code of Maryland
State Government
Title 10. Government Procedures
Subtitle 3. Administrative Procedure Act- Declaratory Rulings
§ 10-301 to § 10-305

**§ 10-301. "Unit" defined.**

In this subtitle, "unit" means an officer or unit that is authorized by law to:

(1) adopt regulations subject to Subtitle 1 of this title; or

(2) adjudicate contested cases subject to Subtitle 2 of this title.

**§ 10-302. Scope of subtitle.**

(a) *General exclusions.*- This subtitle does not apply to:

(1) the Governor;

(2) the Department of Assessments and Taxation;

(3) the Board of Appeals of the Department of Labor, Licensing, and Regulation;

(4) the Insurance Administration;

(5) the Injured Workers' Insurance Fund;

(6) the Maryland Parole Commission of the Department of Public Safety and Correctional Services;

(7) the Public Service Commission;

(8) the Maryland Tax Court; or

(9) the State Workers' Compensation Commission.

(b) *Maryland Automobile Insurance Fund.*- If the Insurance Commissioner states in writing that, as to a particular matter, the Maryland Automobile Insurance Fund need not comply with this subtitle, this subtitle does not apply to the Fund with respect to that matter.

**§ 10-303. Political subdivisions and instrumentalities.**

A political subdivision of the State or an instrumentality of a political subdivision is entitled, to the same extent as other legal entities, to be an interested person, party, or petitioner in a matter under this subtitle, including an appeal.

**§ 10-304. Petition for ruling.**

(a) *Authorized.*- An interested person may submit to a unit a petition for a declaratory ruling with respect to the manner in which the unit would apply a regulation or order of the unit or a statute that the unit enforces to a person or property on the facts set forth in the petition.

(b) *Regulations.*- Each unit shall adopt regulations that set:

(1) the form for a petition under this section; and

(2) procedures for the submission, consideration, and disposition of the petition.

**§ 10-305. Ruling.**

(a) *Authorized.*- A unit may issue a declaratory ruling.

(b) *Effect.*- A declaratory ruling binds the unit and the petitioner on the facts set forth in the petition.

(c) *Appeal.*- A declaratory ruling under this section is subject to review in a circuit court in the manner that Subtitle 2 of this title provides for the review of a contested case.

# Appendix IV

Annotated Code of Maryland
State Government
Title 9. Miscellaneous Executive Agencies
Subtitle 2. Office of Administrative Hearings
§9-1601 to §9-1607.2

**§9-1601. Applicability.**

(a) *Exceptions.*- This subtitle does not apply to:

(1) the Governor;

(2) any unit of the Judicial Branch;

(3) any unit of the Legislative Branch;

(4) the Comptroller of the Treasury;

(5) the inmate adjustment hearing officers;

(6) the Public Service Commission;

(7) the State Workers' Compensation Commission;

(8) the Parole Commission;

(9) the Health Services Cost Review Commission;

(10) the Maryland Health Care Commission; and

(11) unemployment insurance benefit determinations and employer obligation determinations in the Department of Labor, Licensing, and Regulation, and appeals from those determinations.

(b) *In general.*- Except as provided in subsection (a) of this section, this subtitle shall apply to each agency that employs or engages one or more hearing officers to adjudicate contested cases unless the agency has been exempted by the Governor under subsection (c) of this section.

(c) *Temporary exemptions.*- Until July 1, 1994, the Governor may temporarily exempt an agency from this subtitle.

**§9-1602. Establishment.**

The Office of Administrative Hearings is created as an independent unit in the Executive Branch of State government.

**§9-1603. Chief Administrative Law Judge - In general.**

(a) *Appointment.*- The Office is headed by a Chief Administrative Law Judge appointed by the Governor with the advice and consent of the Senate.

(b) *Term; other employment.*- The Chief Administrative Law Judge shall:

(1) be appointed for a term of 6 years;

(2) devote full time to the duties of the Office; and

(3) be eligible for reappointment.

(c) *Salary; qualifications; powers and duties generally.*- The Chief Administrative Law Judge shall:

(1) receive the salary provided in the State budget;

(2) be admitted to practice law in the State; and

(3) have the powers and duties specified in this subtitle.

(d) *Staff.*- The Chief Administrative Law Judge may employ a staff in accordance with the State budget.

**§9-1604. Chief Administrative Law Judge - Powers and duties.**

(a) *Duties generally.*- The Chief Administrative Law Judge shall:

(1) supervise the Office of Administrative Hearings;

(2) establish qualifications for administrative law judges;

(3) appoint and remove administrative law judges in accordance with §9-1605 of this subtitle;

(4) assign administrative law judges to conduct hearings in contested cases;

(5) if necessary, establish classifications for case assignment on the basis of subject matter, expertise, and case complexity;

(6) establish and implement standard and specialized training programs and provide materials for administrative law judges;

(7) provide and coordinate continuing education programs and services for administrative law judges, including research, technical assistance, technical and professional publications, compiling and disseminating information, and advise of changes in the law relative to their duties;

(8) develop model rules of procedure and other guidelines for administrative hearings;

(9) develop a code of professional responsibility for administrative law judges; and

(10) monitor the quality of State administrative hearings.

(b) *Powers generally; fees.*-

(1) The Chief Administrative Law Judge may:

(i) serve as an administrative law judge in a contested case;

(ii) furnish administrative law judges on a contractual basis to other governmental entities;

(iii) accept and expend funds, grants, and gifts and accept services from any public or private source;

(iv) enter into agreements and contracts with any public or private agencies or educational institutions;

(v) adopt regulations to implement this subtitle; and

(vi) assess fees to cover administrative expenses as follows:

1. to file an appeal, a fee not exceeding:

A. $125 for an appeal of a driver's license suspension or revocation related to a violation of the Maryland Vehicle Law; and

B. $50 for all other types of appeals; and

2. to process a subpoena, a fee not exceeding $5.

(2) Fees charged under paragraph (1) of this subsection for administrative expenses may not be charged to:

(i) State agencies; or

(ii) petitioners who are determined by the Office of Administrative Hearings to be unable to pay the fees.

(3) A fee charged under paragraph (1) of this subsection for filing an appeal shall be refunded to a party who initiates the appeal if the party receives a favorable decision from the administrative law judge.

(c) *Reports.*-

(1) The Chief Administrative Law Judge shall submit an annual report on the activities of the Office to the Governor and, subject to § 2-1246 of this article, to the General Assembly.

(2) This report may be prepared in conjunction with the annual report required under § 9-1610 of this subtitle.

(d) *Meetings and conferences with advisory council.*- The Chief Administrative Law Judge shall meet and confer regularly with the Advisory Council on Administrative Hearings.

**§ 9-1605. Administrative law judges.**

(a) *In general.*- An administrative law judge:

(1) shall be a special appointment in the State Personnel Management System;

(2) may be removed, suspended, or demoted by the Chief Administrative Law Judge for cause, after notice and an opportunity to be heard;

(3) shall receive the compensation provided in the State budget; and

(4) may not perform duties inconsistent with the duties and responsibilities of an administrative law judge.

(b) *Restrictions.*- An administrative law judge may not be responsible to or subject to the supervision or direction of an officer, employee, or agent engaged in the performance of investigative, prosecuting, or advisory functions for an agency.

(c) *Powers generally.*- In any contested case conducted by an administrative law judge, the administrative law judge may:

(1) authorize the issuance of subpoenas for witnesses;

(2) administer oaths;

(3) examine an individual under oath; and

(4) compel the production of documents or other tangible things.

(d) *Refusal to comply with order; to show cause.*-

(1) Without good cause, a person may not refuse an order by any administrative law judge to:

(i) appear for a hearing;

(ii) testify under oath; or

(iii) produce any relevant evidence, including documents or other tangible things.

(2) (i) An administrative law judge may apply, upon affidavit, to any judge of a circuit court for an order, returnable in not less than 2 nor more than 5 days, to show cause why a person should not be committed to jail for refusal to comply with an order issued under paragraph (1) of this subsection.

(ii) On the return of an order issued under subparagraph (i) of this paragraph, if the judge hearing the matter determines that the person is guilty of refusal to comply with the order of the administrative law judge, the judge may commit the offender to jail as in cases of civil contempt.

**§9-1606. Cooperation of State government units; audits; selection of judges.**

(a) *Cooperation of State government units.*- All units of State government shall cooperate with the Chief Administrative Law Judge in the discharge of his duties.

(b) *Audits.*- The Office shall be subject to audit and examination by the Office of Legislative Audits of the Department of Legislative Services under §2-1220 of this article.

(c) *Selection of judges.*- Except as provided in this subtitle or in regulations adopted under this subtitle, an agency may not select or reject a particular administrative law judge for a particular proceeding.

**§9-1607. Designation of administrative law judges.**

If the Office is unable to assign an administrative law judge in response to an agency request, the Chief Administrative Law Judge shall designate in writing an individual to serve as an administrative law judge in a proceeding before the agency if:

(1) the individual meets the qualifications for an administrative law judge established by the Office under §9-1604 (a) (2) of this subtitle; and

(2) the agency that employs the individual consents to the assignment.

**§9-1607.1. Representation by person not licensed to practice law.**

(a) *Conditions.*- An individual who is not licensed to practice law in this State may represent a party in a proceeding before the Office if:

(1) authorized by law;

(2) the individual is representing:

(i) a recipient of or applicant for benefits that are:

1. based on the recipient's or applicant's income and resources; and

2. provided by the Department of Human Resources or the Department of Health and Mental Hygiene;

(ii) a resident of a facility at a proceeding conducted under §19-344(q)(4) or §19-345.1 of the Health - General Article;

(iii) a health care facility, as defined in §10-101 of the Health - General Article, at a proceeding under the provisions of §10-632 or §10-708 of the Health - General Article or §3-121 of the Criminal Procedure Article; or

(iv) a grievant at a proceeding conducted pursuant to Title 10, Subtitle 2 of the Correctional Services Article concerning a grievance submitted to the Inmate Grievance Office, provided the representation is not otherwise restricted for reasons of security or expense pursuant to regulations, rules, directives, or policies adopted by the Division of Correction or Patuxent Institution;

(3) the individual is a designee of a corporation while appearing on its behalf in an administrative proceeding held under § 27-613 of the Insurance Article;

(4) the individual is an officer of a corporation, an employee designated by an officer of a corporation, a general partner in a business operated as a partnership or an employee designated by a general partner, or an employee designated by the owner of a business operated as a sole proprietorship while the officer, partner, or employee is appearing on behalf of the corporation, partnership, or business in an administrative hearing held under:

(i) § 8-312 of the Business Regulation Article (Home Improvement Commission);

(ii) Title 5 of the Labor and Employment Article (Occupational Safety and Health); or

(iii) regulations adopted pursuant to § 14-303 of the State Finance and Procurement Article, concerning the decertification of a minority business enterprise to conduct business with the Department of Transportation;

(5) in the case of an insurer, the individual is a designee of the insurer who:

(i) is employed by the insurer in claims, underwriting, or as otherwise provided by the Commissioner; and

(ii) has been given the authority by the insurer to resolve all issues involved in the proceeding; or

(6) the individual is representing a unit of State government, at the direction of the unit of State government.

(b) *Business entities.*-

(1) An employee designated by a business entity under subsection (a)(3) or (4) of this section:

(i) shall provide the Office a power of attorney sworn to by the employer that certifies that the designated employee is an authorized agent of the business entity and may bind the business entity on matters pending before the Office; and

(ii) may not be a disbarred or suspended lawyer in any state.

(2) A business entity may not contract, hire, or employ another business entity, other than an attorney, to provide appearance services under subsection (a)(3) or (4) of this section.

(3) An employee designated by a business entity under subsection (a)(4) of this section may not be assigned on a full-time basis to appear in administrative hearings before the Office on behalf of the business entity.

(c) *Right to represent self.*- This section may not be interpreted to limit the right of an individual to appear on the individual's own behalf.

**§ 9-1607.2. Applicability of procedural regulations.**

(a) *In general.*- Subject to subsection (b) of this section, regulations adopted in accordance with § 10-206(a)(1) of this article shall apply to a proceeding before the Office, regardless of whether the proceeding is subject to Title 10, Subtitle 2 of this article (Administrative Procedure Act - Contested Cases).

(b) *Conflict.*- Unless a federal or State law or regulation requires that a federal or State procedure shall be observed, the regulations specified in subsection (a) of this section shall take precedence in the event of a conflict.

# Appendix V

COMAR
Title 28. Office of Administrative Hearings
Subtitle 02. Rules of Procedure
Chapter 01. Rules of Procedure
§ 28.02.01.01 to § 28.02.01.27

**§ 28.02.01.01 Scope.**

A. Applicability. This chapter applies to all hearings before the Office of Administrative Hearings.

B. This chapter shall be construed to ensure the fair and expeditious determination of every action.

C. Subject to § D of this regulation, this chapter supplements the procedures required by law.

D. Unless federal or State law requires that a federal or State procedure shall be observed, this chapter takes precedence in the event of conflict.

**§ 28.02.01.02 Definitions.**

A. In this chapter, the following terms have the meanings indicated.

B. Terms Defined.

(1) "Administrative law judge" or "judge" means an individual appointed by the Chief Administrative Law Judge under State Government Article, § 9-1604, Annotated Code of Maryland, or designated by the Chief Administrative Law Judge under State Government Article, § 9-1607, Annotated Code of Maryland.

(2) "Agency" means:

(a) Any unit of government whose action gives rise to a contested case hearing under State Government Article, Title 10, Subtitle 2, Annotated Code of Maryland; or

(b) Any other unit of government or private entity having a proceeding before the Office of Administrative Hearings to which the Chief Administrative Law Judge may assign a judge pursuant to State Government Article, § 9-1604(b), Annotated Code of Maryland.

(3) "Authorized representative" means an attorney or, when permitted by applicable law, another individual.

(4) Docket Entry.

(a) "Docket entry" means the filing of a pleading by a party, a request for a hearing date, or the scheduling of a proceeding.

(b) "Docket entry" does not include the entry or withdrawal of appearance of counsel, case status reports, or other inquiries.

(5) "Filed" means, unless otherwise indicated in this chapter, the earlier of when the document is postmarked or received at the Office and, when required, served on the other parties to a proceeding or an administrative law judge.

(6) "Final decision maker" means the person or entity authorized by law or delegation to render the final decision in a contested case or other proceeding before the Office.

(7) "Initial pleading" means a notice of agency action, an appeal of an agency action, or any other request for a hearing by a person.

(8) "Law" means State and federal constitutions, statutes, regulations, and relevant case law.

(9) "Office" means the Office of Administrative Hearings.

(10) "Party" means a person or agency named or permitted to participate in a case before the Office.

(11) "Person" means an individual, representative, corporation, or other entity, including a public or nonprofit corporation, or an agency or instrumentality of federal, State, or local government.

(12) "Proposed decision" means the document issued by an administrative law judge in accordance with law or an agency's delegation, when final decision-making authority has not been vested in the Office, and includes recommended decisions and proposed orders.

**§ 28.01.01.03 Transmittal of Request for Hearing.**

A. Initiation. A hearing may be initiated:

(1) On transmittal forms provided by the Office and accompanied by copies of all pertinent documents;

(2) On forms provided by the agency; or

(3) In any other manner permitted by law.

B. A hearing request shall include and be accompanied by the following:

(1) The name of the person requesting the hearing;

(2) The mailing address of the person requesting the hearing;

(3) The notice of agency action or the name of the person or agency against whom the hearing request has been filed; and

(4) Any documents, fees set forth in COMAR, or other information required by law.

C. Dismissal. A case may be dismissed if an initial pleading is received without an item required by § B of this regulation.

D. Unless a case is dismissed pursuant to § C of this regulation, a hearing request received without an item required by § B of this regulation may be returned to the person requesting the hearing for resubmission with all of the required items. Return of the initial pleading under this section does not extend the time within which the initial pleading is required to be filed.

**§ 28.02.01.04 Initial Pleading; Commencement of Case; Computation of Time.**

A. Unless otherwise provided for by law, the Office acquires jurisdiction over a matter when an initial pleading is filed with the Office by:

(1) An agency, pursuant to law or delegation of authority; or

(2) A person when directed by an agency pursuant to law or a delegation of authority.

B. Timeliness. An initial pleading is timely when it is filed:

(1) Within the time period specified by relevant law; or

(2) If no time period is specified, within 30 days of the date of the notice of contested action.

C. Computation of Time.

(1) In computing any period of time, the day of the act, event, or default, after which the designated period of time begins to run, is not to be included.

(2) The last day of the period so computed is to be included unless:

(a) It is a Sunday or a legal holiday, in which event, the period runs until the end of the next day which is not a Sunday or a holiday; or

(b) The act to be done is the filing of some paper at the Office on the last day of the period and the Office is not open, or is closed for part of the day, in which event, the period runs until the end of the next day which is not a Sunday, Saturday, legal holiday, or a day on which the Office is not open the entire day during ordinary business hours.

(3) When the period of time is more than 7 days, intermediate Sundays and holidays shall be considered as other days.

(4) When the period of time is 7 days or less, intermediate Sundays and holidays may not be counted in computing the period of time.

D. A hearing request is considered filed on the earlier of the date of the request, along with any fees, documents, or other information required by law, is postmarked or received by the:

(1) Office, if required to be filed with the Office; or

(2) Agency, if required to be filed with the Agency.

**§ 28.02.01.05 Notice of Hearing.**

A. Reasonable written notice of the hearing shall be provided to the parties.

B. A hearing notice provided by the Office shall contain:

(1) The date, time, place, and nature of the hearing;

(2) A statement of the right to present witnesses and documents, or other evidence, and the right to cross-examine any witness that another party calls under State Government Article, § 10-213(f), Annotated Code of Maryland, if applicable;

(3) A statement of the right to request subpoenas for witnesses and evidence, and specifying the costs, if any, associated with the request;

(4) A statement that a copy of the hearing procedures is available on request, and specifying the costs, if any, associated with the request;

(5) A statement of any rights, restrictions, or requirements pertaining to representation;

(6) A statement that failure to appear for the scheduled hearing may result in an adverse action against that party; and

(7) A statement that, unless otherwise prohibited by law, the parties may agree to the evidence and may waive their right to appear at the hearing.

C. Method of Giving Notice.

(1) The Office shall give any notice required by this regulation by U.S. mail, or other method of personal or courier delivery, to the person at the address on record with the Office.

(2) If notice is given by U.S. mail, the notice is effective at the end of the 5th day after its deposit in the mail.

(3) Proof that notice has been given may be made by the dated file copy in the case file.

**§ 28.02.01.06 Expedited Hearings.**

A. A motion for an expedited hearing may be filed by any party. The motion shall set forth the reasons for expediting the hearing.

B. Any response to the motion shall be filed within 10 days of the date the motion is filed.

C. All parties shall be notified promptly of the decision on the motion. If the motion is granted, the Office shall schedule the hearing as soon as practical.

D. Unless the parties agree to a longer period, or a shorter period is required by law, the judge shall render the proposed or final decision within 30 days after the close of the record.

**§ 28.02.01.07 Venue.**

Hearings shall be conducted at the site designated by the Office in accordance with applicable law.

**§ 28.02.01.08 Appearance of Parties at Hearing; Representation.**

A. Unless prohibited by law, a party may represent himself or herself.

B. A party may be represented by an attorney authorized to practice law in Maryland or, when authorized by law, appear through a representative who is not an attorney.

C. Power of Attorney.

(1) An employee of a business entity who is representing that business entity in accordance with State Government Article, § 9-1607.1, Annotated Code of Maryland, shall provide the Office with a power of attorney.

(2) The Office shall accept any properly executed power of attorney meeting the requirements of State Government Article, § 9-1607.1, Annotated Code of Maryland.

(3) The Office may provide a form for a power of attorney.

(4) A power of attorney required by this regulation may be:

(a) Kept on file with the Office;

(b) Provided to the judge at the outset of a hearing in which the power of attorney is required; or

(c) In the discretion of the judge, provided to the judge at any time before the close of the record.

D. A party's representative shall enter the representative's appearance with the Office.

E. A party's representative of record shall be served with all notices, pleadings, and other correspondence.

**§ 28.02.01.09 Appointment of Interpreter; Request for Accommodations.**

A. Upon request of a party or witness who cannot hear, speak, or understand the spoken or written English language, the Office shall provide a qualified interpreter during the hearing.

B. An interpreter shall take an oath or affirmation that the interpreter will accurately interpret the proceedings.

C. If a party or witness requests a reasonable accommodation required by the Americans with Disabilities Act, the Office shall provide the accommodation.

**§ 28.02.01.10 Service.**

A. A copy of any pleading, motion, response, correspondence, or other paper filed in any proceeding shall be served promptly on all other parties to the proceeding by the party making the filing.

B. Unless otherwise required by law, services of pleadings, correspondence, and all other documents shall be made by personal delivery, by U.S. mail, or by other form of personal or courier delivery.

C. Proof of Service.

(1) Every pleading, motion response, correspondence, or other paper filed with the Office shall contain or be accompanied by a certificate of service.

(2) The certificate of service shall be signed and shall contain the:

(a) Date of service;

(b) Manner of service;

(c) Name of each person served; and

(d) Address at which each person was served.

**§ 28.02.01.11 Powers and Duties of Judges.**

A. A judge shall:

(1) Conduct a full, fair, and impartial hearing;

(2) Take action to avoid unnecessary delay in the disposition of the proceedings; and

(3) Maintain order.

B. A judge has the power to regulate the course of the hearing and the conduct of the parties and authorized representatives, including the power to:

(1) Administer oaths and affirmations;

(2) Issue subpoenas for witnesses and the production of evidence;

(3) Rule upon offers of proof and receive relevant and material evidence;

(4) Consider and rule upon motions in accordance with this chapter;

(5) Examine witnesses and call witnesses as necessary to ensure a full and complete record;

(6) Limit unduly repetitious testimony and reasonably limit the time for presentations;

(7) Grant a continuance or postponement;

(8) Modify or waive, reasonably and for good cause, any time periods established by this chapter;

(9) Request parties to submit legal memoranda, proposed findings of fact, and proposed conclusions of law;

(10) Make proposed or final decisions and take any other appropriate action authorized by law;

(11) Issue orders as are necessary to secure procedural simplicity and administrative fairness and to eliminate unjustifiable expense and delay;

(12) Conduct the hearing in a manner suited to ascertain the facts and safeguard the rights of the parties to the hearing; and

(13) Impose appropriate sanctions for failure to abide by this chapter or any lawful order of the judge.

C. Disqualification; Substitution of Judges.

(1) Conditions.

(a) A judge shall withdraw from participation in any proceeding in which personal bias or other reasons render the judge unable to provide an impartial hearing and decision, or when an appearance of impropriety may reasonably be inferred from the facts.

(b) For purposes of this section, personal bias shall be presumed under circumstances set forth in the Code of Judicial Conduct for Administrative Law Judges at the Maryland Office of Administrative Hearings.

(2) Motion for Disqualification. A party shall move promptly for disqualification of a judge upon discovering facts that establish grounds for disqualification.

(3) Substitution of Judges.

(a) If, for any reason, a judge is unable to continue presiding over a pending hearing, or issue a proposed or final decision after the conclusion of the hearing, to the extent that it is allowed by law, another judge may be assigned to conclude the hearing process and render a proposed or final decision.

(b) The substituted judge may use the existing record and conduct further proceedings as are necessary and proper.

**§ 28.02.01.12 Motions.**

A. Unless otherwise provided by this chapter, this regulation pertains to all motions filed with the Office.

B. In General.

(1) An application to the Office for an order shall be by motion that, unless made during a hearing, shall be made in writing, and shall set forth the relief or order sought.

(2) A written motion and response to a motion shall state their respective grounds and a party shall attach any relevant documents as exhibits.

(3) An answer to a written motion shall be filed on the earlier of:

(a) 15 days after the date the motion was filed; or

(b) The date of the hearing.

(4) Upon notice to all parties, the judge may schedule a conference to consider a written motion.

(5) The judge may issue a written decision on a motion or state the decision on the record.

(6) If a ruling on a motion is not stated on the record, the ruling shall be included in the judge's proposed or final decision.

(7) The filing or pendency of a motion does not alter or extend any time limit otherwise established by this chapter.

C. Motion to Dismiss. Upon motion, the judge may issue a proposed or final decision dismissing an initial pleading which fails to state a claim for which relief may be granted.

D. Motion for Summary Decision.

(1) Any party may file a motion for summary decision on all or part of an action, at any time, on the ground that there is no genuine dispute as to any material fact and that the party is entitled to judgment as a matter of law. Motions for summary decision shall be supported by affidavits.

(2) The response to a motion for summary decision shall identify the material facts that are disputed.

(3) An affidavit supporting or opposing a motion for summary decision shall be made upon personal knowledge, shall set forth the facts that would be admissible in evidence, and shall show affirmatively that the affiant is competent to testify to the matters stated in the affidavit.

(4) The judge may issue a proposed or final decision in favor of or against the moving party if the motion and response show that there is no genuine dispute as to any material fact and that the party in whose favor judgment is entered is entitled to judgment as a matter of law.

E. Motion for Judgment.

(1) A party may move for judgment on any or all of the issues in any action at the close of the evidence offered by an opposing party. The moving party shall state all reasons why the motion should be granted. No objection to the motion for judgment shall be necessary. A party does not waive the right to make the motion by introducing evidence during the presentation of any opposing party's case.

(2) When a party moves for judgment at the close of the evidence offered by an opposing party, the judge may:

(a) Proceed to determine the facts and to render judgment against an opposing party; or

(b) Decline to render judgment until the close of all evidence.

(3) A party who moves for judgment at the close of the evidence offered by an opposing party may offer evidence if the motion is not granted, without having reserved the right to do so and to the same extent as if the motion had not been made. In so doing, the party withdraws the motion.

**§ 28.02.01.13 Discovery.**

A. By written request filed not later than 30 days before the scheduled hearing, a party may require any other party to produce within 15 days, for inspection or copying, any file, memorandum, correspondence, document, object, or tangible item, including electronically stored information, that is:

(1) Relevant to the subject matter of the case; and

(2) Not privileged.

B. Unless provided by law or by agreement of the parties, no other discovery procedure may be required.

C. On motion by the parties or on the judge's own initiative, the judge may enter an order establishing reasonable limits on the scope of discovery and/or prohibiting specific discovery.

D. The parties may enter into binding agreements concerning the inadvertent production and handling of privileged materials.

E. A party who has filed a timely discovery request under this regulation but who has not received a reply may, after providing reasonable notice to the opposing party, file a motion seeking to compel a response and/or a motion for sanctions.

F. Copies.

(1) Copies of requested documents and records shall be made at the expense of the party making the request.

(2) The charge for copies of requested documents and records may be waived by the custodian of the documents in accordance with State Government Article, § 10-611 et seq., Annotated Code of Maryland, or other applicable law.

**§ 28.02.01.14 Subpoenas.**

A. Issuance of Subpoenas. On request of a party, or at the direction of a judge, the Office may issue subpoenas requiring the attendance and testimony of witnesses and the production at the hearing of any tangible items in the possession or under the control of the witness.

B. Requests.

(1) A request for a subpoena shall be made, in writing, to the Office.

(2) To the extent practicable, subpoena requests shall be filed at least 10 days before the hearing.

(3) A request for a subpoena shall specify the:

(a) Name and full address of the person to be subpoenaed; and

(b) Name, full address, and telephone number of the party requesting the subpoena.

(4) A subpoena that requests the production of tangible items, books, papers, or other documents shall describe those items with particularity.

(5) A subpoena that requests the production of medical records shall be made in accordance with Health-General Article, § 4-306, Annotated Code of Maryland.

C. Delivery of Subpoenas.

(1) Subpoenas may be served:

(a) By personal delivery by an individual 18 years old or older who is not a party to the proceeding;

(b) By certified mail to the person at the address specified in the subpoena request; or

(c) If served by the Office, by U.S. Mail, or other personal or courier delivery.

(2) Unless the subpoena request specifies otherwise, the subpoena shall be mailed by the Office as provided in § C(1) of this regulation.

(3) The subpoena may not be enforced pursuant to State Government Article, § 9-1605(d)(2), Annotated Code of Maryland, absent proof of service by certified mail or personal delivery.

(4) Costs of certified mailing or personal delivery of subpoenas are the responsibility of the person requesting service.

(5) Proof of service of subpoenas by certified mail or personal delivery is the responsibility of the person requesting the subpoenas.

(6) The party requesting the subpoena is responsible for notifying the person subpoenaed if the hearing is cancelled or postponed. Subpoenas shall remain in effect until the conclusion of the hearing.

D. Return of service shall be made as follows:

(1) When service is by certified mail, by the filing of the original return receipt; and

(2) When service is by personal delivery, by the filing of an affidavit, signed by the person who made service, containing:

(a) The name of the person served;

(b) The date on which the person was served;

(c) The particular place of service; and

(d) A statement that the affiant is 18 years old or older and not a party to the proceeding.

E. Objections to Subpoenas. A person may object to a subpoena by filing with the Office a motion to quash or for other relief.

F. Enforcement of Subpoenas. If a person fails to comply with a properly served subpoena, at the request of an administrative law judge, the Office may apply to the appropriate circuit court for an order to show cause why the person should not be committed to jail for refusal to comply with a subpoena.

**§ 28.02.01.15 Intervention.**

A. Upon motion filed not later than 15 days before the earlier of the prehearing conference or the hearing date, a person may be permitted to intervene in an action when the person:

(1) Has an unconditional right to intervene as a matter of law; or

(2) Claims an interest relating to the subject matter of the hearing that is:

(a) Adversely affected; and

(b) Not adequately represented by existing parties.

B. The motion shall state the grounds for the motion, accompanied by a statement setting forth the claim or defense for which intervention is sought.

C. Order of Intervention.

(1) The judge shall consider whether the intervention will unduly delay or prejudice the adjudication of the rights of the original parties.

(2) As soon as practicable, the judge shall issue an order denying or allowing intervention.

(3) In an order allowing intervention, the judge may place conditions upon the intervenor's participation in the proceedings.

D. Appeal.

(1) If the judge is not the final decision maker, the denial of a motion to intervene may be appealed to the final decision maker in accordance with the agency's regulations.

(2) When the judge is the final decision maker, a party or other affected person may seek review of the denial of a motion to intervene in accordance with law.

(3) In the discretion of the judge, a request for further review of the denial of a motion to intervene may stay the proceedings.

**§ 28.02.01.16 Postponements.**

A. Except as provided in § D of this regulation, a request for postponement shall be made in writing and filed not less than 5 days before the scheduled hearing.

B. Documentation of the reasons for the postponement shall be required from the party making the request.

C. A request for postponement shall be granted only if the party requesting the postponement establishes good cause for the postponement.

D. Emergency Request for Postponement.

(1) For purposes of this section, "emergency" means a sudden, unforeseen occurrence requiring immediate attention which arises within 5 days of the hearing.

(2) In an emergency, a request for postponement may be made by telephone.

E. When practicable, all parties to a proceeding shall be contacted before a ruling on a postponement request is made.

**§ 28.02.01.17 Prehearing Conferences.**

A. When appropriate, the judge may hold a prehearing conference to resolve matters preliminary to the hearing.

B. The judge may require the parties to submit information before the prehearing conference.

C. A prehearing conference may be convened to address the following matters:

(1) Issuance of subpoenas;

(2) Factual and legal issues;

(3) Stipulations;

(4) Requests for official notice;

(5) Identification and exchange of documentary evidence;

(6) Admissibility of evidence;

(7) Identification and qualification of witnesses;

(8) Motions;

(9) Discovery disputes;

(10) Order of presentation;

(11) Scheduling;

(12) Alternative dispute resolution; and

(13) Any other matters that will promote the orderly and prompt conduct of the hearing.

D. Conduct.

(1) Except as otherwise indicated in this chapter, at the discretion of the judge, all or part of a prehearing conference may be recorded.

(2) Prehearing conferences may be conducted via the telephone or videoconference.

E. Prehearing Orders.

(1) Unless otherwise stated in this chapter, when a prehearing conference has been held, a prehearing order shall be issued by the judge.

(2) The prehearing order shall set forth the actions taken or to be taken with regard to any matter addressed at the prehearing conference.

(3) If a prehearing conference is not held, the judge may issue a prehearing order to regulate the conduct of the proceedings.

(4) The prehearing order shall be a part of the case record.

**§ 28.02.01.18 Alternative Dispute Resolution.**

A. For purposes of this regulation, "alternative dispute resolution" means the process of resolving matters pending before the Office through a settlement conference, neutral case evaluation, neutral fact finding, mediation, other nonadversarial dispute resolution process, or combination of those processes.

B. If all parties agree, an alternative dispute resolution proceeding may be scheduled by the Office.

C. An individual who presides at an alternative dispute resolution proceeding may not be the judge at the prehearing conference, hearing on the merits, or other state of the proceedings.

D. Confidentiality of Alternative Dispute Resolution Proceedings.

(1) Alternative dispute resolution proceedings are confidential and are closed to the public.

(2) Discussions in an alternative dispute resolution proceeding may not be made a part of the case record in any subsequent proceeding.

(3) Alternative dispute resolution proceedings may not be recorded electronically or in any other manner.

(4) A judge or other individual who conducts an alternative dispute resolution proceeding may not be called to testify, participate in discovery, or otherwise provide information in any subsequent proceeding related to the alternative dispute resolution proceeding.

**§ 28.02.01.19 Proceedings Open to the Public.**

A. Unless prohibited by law, all proceedings before the Office are open to the public.

B. Unless otherwise provided by law, documents, notices, and records in the possession of the Office as a result of a contested case proceeding may be inspected and copied by any person as provided in State Government Article, § 10-611 et seq., Annotated Code of Maryland, and regulations adopted by the Office under that Act.

C. The judge may:

(1) Remove individuals whose conduct impedes the orderly progress of the hearing; and

(2) Restrict attendance because of the physical limitations of the hearing room.

D. Audio recording equipment, cameras, or other electronic or photographic equipment shall be excluded from the hearing room when required by law or if the judge determines that the use of this equipment may impede the orderly progress of the hearing or otherwise interfere with the hearing process.

**§ 28.02.01.20 Conduct of Hearings.**

A. In General.

(1) On a genuine issue in a contested case, each party is entitled to call witnesses, offer evidence, cross-examine any witness who testifies, and make opening and closing statements.

(2) A hearing shall be called to order by the judge. The judge shall explain briefly the purpose of the hearing and state the order of presentation of the evidence. The judge may allow the parties to present preliminary matters.

(3) Witnesses shall be sworn or put under affirmation to tell the truth.

B. Telephone Hearings.

(1) The judge may conduct all or part of a hearing by telephone or other similar audio-electronic means, provided each party has an opportunity to participate in and hear the entire proceeding.

(2) If a party establishes good cause in opposition to the holding of a hearing by telephone or other similar audio electronic means, the hearing shall be held in person or by video conferencing or other similar audiovisual electronic means.

(3) All substantive and procedural rights apply to telephone hearings, subject only to the limitations of the physical arrangement.

(4) Documentary Evidence. For a telephone hearing, documentary evidence to be offered shall be mailed or delivered by the proponent to all parties and the Office at least 5 days before the hearing.

C. Video Hearings.

(1) The judge may conduct all or part of a hearing by video or other similar audiovisual electronic means if each party in the hearing has an opportunity to participate in, hear, and see the entire proceeding.

(2) If a party establishes good cause in opposition to the holding of a hearing by video or other similar audiovisual electronic means, the hearing shall be held in person.

(3) All substantive and procedural rights apply to video hearings, subject only to the limitations of the physical arrangement.

(4) Documentary Evidence. For a video hearing not involving the Inmate Grievance Office, documentary evidence to be offered shall be mailed or delivered by the proponent to all parties and the Office at least 5 days before the hearing.

D. Waivers.

(1) Waiver of Right to Appear at a Hearing.

(a) A party may waive the right to appear personally at a hearing unless prohibited by law.

(b) A waiver shall be in writing and filed with the Office.

(c) A party may withdraw a waiver by written notice filed not later than 5 days before the scheduled hearing.

(d) When a party has filed a waiver permitted by law, the failure of a party to appear personally or by representative may not result in a finding of default. The hearing shall be held and the matter decided in the absence of the party.

(2) Waiver of Hearing. A hearing before a judge is not necessary if all parties agree to the admission of the evidence and waive their rights to appear.

**§28.02.01.21 Evidence.**

A. Evidence shall be admitted in accordance with State Government Article, § 10-213, Annotated Code of Maryland, and other pertinent law.

B. The judge may admit evidence that reasonable and prudent individuals commonly accept in the conduct of their affairs, and give probative effect to that evidence.

C. Evidence may not be excluded solely on the basis that it is hearsay.

D. Exclusion of Witnesses.

(1) Upon request by a party, the judge shall exclude witnesses other than parties from the hearing room, except when testifying.

(2) A party, representative, witness, or spectator may not disclose to a witness excluded under this section the nature, substance, or purpose of testimony, exhibits, or other evidence introduced during that witness's absence.

(3) A party that is not an individual may designate an employee or officer as its representative to remain in the hearing room, even though the employee or officer may be a witness.

(4) An expert witness who is to render an opinion based on testimony given at the hearing may remain during the testimony.

(5) The judge may exclude the testimony of a witness who receives information in violation of this section, or take other appropriate action.

E. Prefiled Testimony.

(1) In the discretion of the judge, testimony may be received in written form.

(2) The testimony shall be filed and served on all parties not later than 10 days before the hearing.

F. Official Notice.

(1) At the request of a party or on the judge's own motion, a judge may take official notice of a fact that is:

(a) Judicially noticeable; or

(b) General, technical, or scientific and within the specialized knowledge of the agency.

(2) Before taking official notice of a fact, the judge shall:

(a) Notify each party before or during the hearing; and

(b) Give each party an opportunity to contest the fact.

G. Stipulations.

(1) The parties may, in accordance with law, agree to any substantive or procedural matter.

(2) A stipulation may be filed in writing or entered on the record at the hearing.

(3) The judge may require additional development of stipulated matters.

H. Affidavits. A judge may admit an affidavit as evidence.

**§ 28.02.01.22 The Record.**

A. The Office shall prepare an official case record of each hearing.

B. The record shall include:

(1) All pleadings, motions, responses, correspondence, memoranda, including proposed findings of fact and conclusions of law, and requests filed by the parties;

(2) All hearing notices;

(3) All documentary and other tangible evidence received or considered;

(4) A statement of each fact officially noticed;

(5) All stipulations;

(6) All offers of proof and objections;

(7) All rulings, orders, and decisions, proposed or final;

(8) Matters placed on the record in connection with ex parte communication;

(9) The recording of the hearing, and any prehearing proceeding, and any transcript of the recording prepared by a court reporting service; and

(10) Any other item required by law.

C. All exhibits marked for identification, whether or not offered in evidence and, if offered, whether or not admitted, shall be retained for purposes of judicial review.

**§ 28.02.01.23 Failure to Attend or Participate in a Hearing, Conference, or Other** Proceeding; Default.

A. If, after receiving proper notice, a party fails to attend or participate in a prehearing conference, hearing, or other state of a proceeding, the judge may proceed in that party's absence or may, in accordance with the hearing authority delegated by the agency, issue a final or proposed default order against the defaulting party.

B. Final Default Orders.

(1) Unless otherwise provided by law, a party may move to vacate a final order of default within 30 days after the date of the order. The motion shall state the reasons for the failure to attend or participate in the proceeding.

(2) If the judge finds that there is good cause for the party's failure to attend or participate in the proceeding, the judge shall vacate the order and set the case in for further proceedings as appropriate.

(3) If a motion is not filed under § B(1) of this regulation, or is filed and denied, the final default order is effective.

C. Proposed Default Orders. A proposed default order is reviewable in accordance with the delegating agency's regulations governing review of proposed decisions.

**§ 28.02.01.24 Dismissal for Lack of Prosecution.**

A. Unless otherwise required by law, a case pending before the Office may not be placed on inactive status.

B. At the expiration of 6 months from the last docket entry, a case is subject to dismissal, on request of a party or on a judge's own initiative, for lack of prosecution.

C. If dismissal is initiated by a judge or requested by a party, the judge shall send notice to all parties that a final or proposed dismissal for lack of prosecution will be entered after the expiration of 30 days from the date of the notice unless a motion is filed under § D of this regulation.

D. On motion filed within 30 days after the date of the notice, the judge, for good cause shown, may defer issuance of the final or proposed order of dismissal for the period and on the terms the judge considers proper.

E. Issuance of Order.

(1) If a motion is not filed under § D of this regulation within 30 days or if a motion is filed and denied, the judge shall issue an order or proposed order of dismissal within 30 days after the time for filing the motion has expired.

(2) If a motion is filed and good cause is shown for deferral of the dismissal, the judge shall issue an order deferring dismissal and specifying the period and the terms of the deferral.

**§ 28.02.01.25 Final Decision or Proposed Decision.**

A. A judge shall issue a final decision or proposed decision in accordance with the agency's delegation and pertinent law.

B. Proposed Decision.

(1) If the judge is not the final decision maker, the judge shall submit the proposed decision to the final decision maker with a copy to each party, unless otherwise provided by law or the agency's delegation.

(2) When permitted by law, an adversely affected party may file exceptions to the proposed decision in accordance with the delegating agency's regulations or as otherwise provided by law.

C. Final Decision. Except as otherwise provided by law, when the judge is the final decision maker, the decision is the final decision for purposes of judicial review.

**§ 28.02.01.26 Cases Remanded to the Office.**

A. A case remanded to the Office by a court or agency for further proceedings is considered filed with the Office when the court's or agency's order is received by the Office.

B. Unless the remand order specifies otherwise, the Office shall promptly schedule further proceedings as necessary and issue a decision in accordance with State Government Article, § 10-205(e), Annotated Code of Maryland.

**§ 28.02.01.27 Revision.**

A. A final decision may be revised only by the judge who rendered the decision for which revision is requested.

B. On motion of any party filed at any time, the judge may exercise revisory power and control over a final decision in the event of fraud, mistake, or irregularity.

C. Clerical mistakes in final decisions, orders, or other parts of the record may be corrected by the judge at any time on the judge's own initiative, or on motion of any party after such notice, if any, the judge orders.

D. A request for revision does not automatically stay the action or toll the time for filing an appeal.

E. Proposed decisions may not be revised by the judge.

# Appendix VI

Maryland Rules
Title 7. Appellate and Other Judicial Review in Circuit Court
Chapter 200. Judicial Review of Administrative Agency Decisions
Rule 7-201 to Rule 7-211

**Rule 7-201. General Provisions.**

**(a) Applicability.** The rules in this Chapter govern actions for judicial review of (1) an order or action of an administrative agency, where judicial review is authorized by statute, and (2) a final determination of the trustees of the Client Protection Fund of the Bar of Maryland.

**(b) Definition.** As used in this Chapter, "administrative agency" means any agency, board, department, district, commission, authority, commissioner, official, the Maryland Tax Court, or other unit of the State or of a political subdivision of the State and the Client Protection Fund of the Bar of Maryland.

**Rule 7-202. Method of Securing Review.**

**(a) By Petition.** A person seeking judicial review under this chapter shall file a petition for judicial review in a circuit court authorized to provide the review.

**(b) Caption.** The Petition shall be captioned as follows:

| | | |
|---|---|---|
| IN THE CIRCUIT COURT FOR ______________ | ) | |
| | ) | |
| PETITION OF ____________________________ | ) | |
| [name and address] | ) | |
| | ) | |
| FOR JUDICIAL REVIEW OF THE | ) | CIVIL ACTION |
| DECISION OF THE | ) | |
| ________________________________________ | ) | No.________ |
| [name and address of administrative | ) | |
| agency that made the decision] | ) | |
| | ) | |
| IN THE CASE OF __________________________ | ) | |
| [caption of any processing, | ) | |
| including agency case number] | ) | |

**(c) Contents of Petition.** The petition shall request judicial review, identify the order or action of which review is sought, and state whether the petitioner was a party to the agency proceeding. If the petitioner was not a party, the petition shall state the basis of the petitioner's standing to seek judicial review. No other allegations are necessary. If judicial review of a decision of the Workers' Compensation Commission is sought, the petitioner shall attach to the petition a certificate that copies of the petition were served pursuant to subsection (d)(2) of this Rule.

**(d) Copies; Filing; Mailing.**

(1) *Notice to Agency.* Upon filing the petition, the petitioner shall deliver to the clerk a copy of the petition for the agency whose decision is sought to be reviewed. The clerk shall promptly mail a copy of the petition to the agency, informing the agency of the date the petition was filed and the civil action number assigned to the action for judicial review.

(2) *Service by Petitioner in Workers' Compensation Cases.* Upon filing a petition for judicial review of a decision of the Workers' Compensation Commission, the petitioner shall serve a copy of the petition by first class mail on the Commission and each other party of record in the proceeding before the Commission.

(3) *By Agency to Parties.* Unless otherwise ordered by the court, the agency, upon receiving the copy of the petition from the clerk, shall give written notice promptly by ordinary mail to all parties to the agency proceeding that:

(A) a petition for judicial review has been filed, the date of the filing, the name of the court, and the civil action number; and

(B) a party wishing to oppose the petition must file a response within 30 days after the date the agency's notice was mailed unless the court shortens or extends the time.

**(e) Certificate of Compliance.** Within five days after mailing, the agency shall file with the clerk a certificate of compliance with section (d) of this Rule, showing the date the agency's notice was mailed and the names and addresses of the persons to whom it was mailed. Failure to file the certificate of compliance does not affect the validity of the agency's notice.

**Rule 7-203. Time For Filing Action.**

**(a) Generally.** Except as otherwise provided in this Rule or by statute, a petition for judicial review shall be filed within 30 days after the latest of:

(1) the date of the order or action of which review is sought;

(2) the date the administrative agency sent notice of the order or action to the petitioner, if notice was required by law to be sent to the petitioner; or

(3) the date the petitioner received notice of the agency's order or action, if notice was required by law to be received by the petitioner.

**(b) Petition by Other Party.** If one party files a timely petition, any other person may file a petition within ten days after the date the agency mailed notice of the filing of the first petition, or within the period set forth in section (a), whichever is later.

**Rule 7-204. Response to Petition.**

**(a) Who May File; Contents.** Any person, including the agency, who is entitled by law to be a party and who wishes to participate as a party shall file a response to the petition. The response shall state the intent to participate in the action for judicial review. No other allegations are necessary.

**(b) Preliminary Motion.** A person may file with the response a preliminary motion addressed to standing, venue, timeliness of filing, or any other matter that would defeat a petitioner's right to judicial review. Except for venue, failure to file a preliminary motion does not constitute waiver of an issue. A preliminary motion shall be served upon the petitioner and the agency.

**(c) Time for Filing Response; Service.** A response shall be filed within 30 days after the date the agency mails notice of the filing of the petition unless the court shortens or extends the time. The response need be served only on the petitioner, and shall be served in the manner prescribed by Rule 1-321.

**Rule 7-205. Stays.**

The filing of a petition does not stay the order or action of the administrative agency. Upon motion and after hearing, the court may grant a stay, unless prohibited by law, upon the conditions as to bond or otherwise that the court considers proper.

**Rule 7-206. Record.**

**(a) Contents; Expense of Transcript.** The record shall include the transcript of testimony and all exhibits and other papers filed in the agency proceeding, except those papers the parties agree or the court directs may be omitted by written stipulation or order included in the record. If the testimony has been recorded but not transcribed before the filing of the petition for judicial review, the first petitioner, if required by the agency and unless otherwise ordered by the court or provided by law, shall pay the expense of transcription, which shall be taxed as costs and may be apportioned as provided in Rule 2-603. A petitioner who pays the cost of transcription shall file with the agency a certification of costs, and the agency shall include the certification in the record.

**(b) Statement in Lieu of Record.** If the parties agree that the questions presented by the action for judicial review can be determined without an examination of the entire record, they may sign and, upon approval by the agency, file a statement showing how the questions arose and were decided and setting forth only those facts or allegations that are essential to a decision of the questions. The parties are strongly encouraged to agree to such a statement. The statement, any exhibits to it, the agency's order of which review is sought, and any opinion of the agency shall constitute the record in the action for judicial review.

**(c) Time for Transmitting.** Except as otherwise provided by this Rule, the agency shall transmit to the clerk of the circuit court the original or a certified copy of the record of its proceedings within 60 days after the agency receives the first petition for judicial review.

**(d) Shortening or Extending the Time.** Upon motion by the agency or any party, the court may shorten or extend the time for transmittal of the record. The court may extend the time for no more than an additional 60 days. The action shall be dismissed if the record has not been transmitted within the time prescribed unless the court finds that the inability to transmit the record was caused by the act or omission of the agency, a stenographer, or a person other than the moving party.

**(e) Duty of Clerk.** Upon the filing of the record, the clerk shall notify the parties of the date that the record was filed.

**Rule 7-207. Memoranda.**

**(a) Generally.** Within 30 days after the clerk sends notice of the filing of the record, a petitioner shall file a memorandum setting forth a concise statement of the questions presented for review, a statement of facts material to those questions, and argument on each question, including citations of authority and references to pages of the record and exhibits relied on. Within 30 days after service of the memorandum, any person who has filed a response, including the agency when entitled by law to be a party to the action, may file an answering memorandum in similar form. The petitioner may file a reply memorandum within 15 days after service of an answering memorandum. Except with the permission of the court, a memorandum shall not exceed 35 pages. In an action involving more than one petitioner or responding party, any petitioner or responding party may adopt by reference any part of the memorandum of another.

**(b) When Not Required.** Memoranda are not required in an action for judicial review of a decision of the Workers' Compensation Commission where the review is de novo.

**(c) Modification of Time Requirements.** The time for filing a memorandum may be shortened or extended by (1) stipulation of the parties filed with the clerk so long as the first memorandum and any answering memorandum are filed at least 30 days, and any reply memorandum is filed at least ten days, before the scheduled hearing, or (2) order of the court entered pursuant to Rule 1-204.

**(d) Sanctions for Late Filing of Memoranda.** If a petitioner fails to file a memorandum within the time prescribed by this Rule, the court may dismiss the action if it finds that the failure to file or the late filing caused prejudice to the moving party. A person who has filed a response but who fails to file an answering memorandum within the time prescribed by this Rule may not present argument except with the permission of the court.

**Rule 7-208. Hearing.**

**(a) Generally.** Unless a hearing is waived in writing by the parties, the court shall hold a hearing.

**(b) Scheduling.** Upon the filing of the record pursuant to Rule 7-206, a date shall be set for the hearing on the merits. Unless otherwise ordered by the court or required by law, the hearing shall be no earlier than 90 days from the date the record was filed.

**(c) Additional Evidence.** Additional evidence in support of or against the agency's decision is not allowed unless permitted by law.

**Rule 7-209. Disposition.**

Unless otherwise provided by law, the court may dismiss the action for judicial review or may affirm, reverse, or modify the agency's order or action, remand the action to the agency for further proceedings, or an appropriate combination of the above.

**Rule 7-210. Return of Agency Record.**

After the time for seeking appellate review has expired, if no appellate review has been sought, the clerk shall return the record of the agency proceeding to the agency. If appellate review has been sought, the clerk, unless otherwise ordered by the appellate court, shall return the record of the agency proceedings to the agency upon the conclusion of the appellate review.

**Rule 7-211. Request For Impleader of the Subsequent Injury Fund.**

**(a) Generally.** If a party files a request for impleader of the Subsequent Injury Fund more than 60 days before trial, the court shall grant the request. If a party files a request for impleader within the 60-day period before trial, the court shall determine whether there is good cause to grant the request.

**(b) Order Granting Request for Impleader.** If the court grants a request for impleader, the court shall suspend further proceedings and remand the case to the Workers' Compensation Commission.

(c) **Information To Be Provided to the Subsequent Injury Fund.** Within 10 days after the date of an order granting a request for impleader, the impleading party shall provide to the Subsequent Injury Fund and all other parties:

(1) a copy of the original claim, any amendments, each issue previously filed, and any award or order entered by the Commission on the claim;

(2) identification, by claim number if available, of prior awards or settlements to the claimant for permanent disability made or approved by the Commission, by a comparable commission of another state as defined in Code, Labor and Employment Article, § 1-101;

(3) all relevant medical evidence relied on to implead the Subsequent Injury Fund; and

(4) a certification that a copy of the request for impleader and all required information and documents have been mailed to the Subsequent Injury Fund and all other parties.

# Appendix VII

Maryland Rules
Title 7. Appellate and Other Judicial Review in Circuit Court
Chapter 400. Administrative Mandamus
Rule 7-401 to Rule 7-403

**Rule 7-401. General Provisions.**

(a) **Applicability.** The rules in this Chapter govern actions for judicial review of a quasi-judicial order or action of an administrative agency where review is not expressly authorized by law.

(b) **Definition.** As used in this Chapter, "administrative agency" means any agency, board, department, district, commission, authority, Commissioner, official, or other unit of the State or of a political subdivision of the State.

**Rule 7-402. Procedures.**

(a) **Complaint and Response.** An action for a writ of administrative mandamus is commenced by the filing of a complaint, the form, contents, and timing of which shall comply with Rules 7-202 and 7-203. A response to the filing of the complaint shall comply with the provisions of Rule 7-204.

(b) **Stay.** The filing of the complaint does not stay the order or action of the administrative agency. The court may grant a stay in accordance with the provisions of Rule 7-205.

(c) **Discovery.** The court may permit discovery, in accordance with the provisions of Title 2, Chapter 400, that the court finds to be appropriate, but only in cases where the party challenging the agency action makes a strong showing of the existence of fraud or extreme circumstances that occurred outside the scope of the administrative record, and a remand to the agency is not a viable alternative.

(d) **Record.** If a record exists, the record shall be filed in accordance with the provisions of Rule 7-206. If no record exists, the agency shall provide (1) a verified response that fully sets forth the grounds for its decision and (2) any written materials supporting the decision. The court may remand the matter to the agency for further supplementation of materials supporting the decision.

(e) **Memoranda.** Memoranda shall be filed in accordance with the provisions of Rule 7-207.

(f) **Hearing.** The court may hold a hearing. If a hearing is held, additional evidence in support of or against the agency's decision is not allowed unless permitted by law

**Rule 7-403. Disposition.**

The court may issue an order denying the writ of mandamus, or may issue the writ (1) remanding the case for further proceedings, or (2) reversing or modifying the decision if any substantial right of the plaintiff may have been prejudiced because a finding, conclusion, or decision of the agency:

(A) is unconstitutional,

(B) exceeds the statutory authority or jurisdiction of the agency,

(C) results from an unlawful procedure,

(D) is affected by any error of law,

(E) is unsupported by competent, material, and substantial evidence in light of the entire record as submitted,

(F) is arbitrary or capricious, or

(G) is an abuse of its discretion.

# Table of Cases

# About the Author

Arnold Rochvarg is a professor at the University of Baltimore School of Law where he has taught since 1979. Among the subjects he teaches are Federal Administrative Law and Maryland Administrative Law. He has published extensively on various Administrative Law topics, and is frequently cited in court opinions. He is a regular presenter at continuing legal education programs for attorneys and judges. He has served as a consultant to government agencies and private law firms on cases involving Administrative Law. He is also the author of *Watergate Victory: Mardian's Appeal* which presents Professor Rochvarg's perspective on the Watergate case against Robert Mardian on whose defense team Rochvarg served. Professor Rochvarg was in private practice in Washington, D.C. before becoming a law professor. He is a graduate of the University of Pennsylvania and the George Washington University Law School. He resides in Howard County with his wife Ria and two daughters, Courtney and Molly.

# Index